D1397063

The Official VCP5 Certification Guide

VMware Press is the official publisher of VMware books and training materials, which provide guidance on the critical topics facing today's technology professionals and students. Enterprises, as well as small- and medium-sized organizations, adopt virtualization as a more agile way of scaling IT to meet business needs. VMware Press provides proven, technically accurate information that will help them meet their goals for customizing, building, and maintaining their virtual environment.

With books, certification and study guides, video training, and learning tools produced by world-class architects and IT experts, VMware Press helps IT professionals master a diverse range of topics on virtualization and cloud computing and is the official source of reference materials for preparing for the VMware Certified Professional Examination.

VMware Press is also pleased to have localization partners that can publish its products into more than forty-two languages, including, but not limited to, Chinese (Simplified), Chinese (Traditional), French, German, Greek, Hindi, Japanese, Korean, Polish, Russian, and Spanish..

For more information about VMware Press please visit
http://www.vmware.com/go/vmwarepress

The Official VCP5 Certification Guide

Bill Ferguson

vmware® PRESS

Upper Saddle River, NJ • Boston • Indianapolis • San Francisco
New York • Toronto • Montreal • London • Munich • Paris • Madrid
Cape Town • Sydney • Tokyo • Singapore • Mexico City

The Official VCP5 Certification Guide

Warning and Disclaimer

Corporate and Government Sales

VMware Press offers excellent discounts on this book when ordered in quantity for bulk purchases or special sales, which may include electronic versions and/or custom covers and content particular to your business, training goals, marketing focus, and branding interests. For more information, please contact U.S. Corporate and Government Sales, (800) 382-3419, corpsales@pearsontechgroup.com. For sales outside the United States, please contact International Sales, international@pearsoned.com.

ISBN-13: 978-0-7897-4931-4

ISBN-10: 0-7897-4931-9

Text printed in the United States at Courier in Westford, Massachusettes.

First Printing, August 2012

VMware Press Program Manager
Erik Ullanderson

Associate Publisher
David Dusthimer

Acquisitions Editor
Joan Murray

Senior Development Editor
Christopher Cleveland

Managing Editor
Sandra Schroeder

Project Editor
Mandie Frank

Copy Editor
Keith Cline

Proofreader
Leslie Joseph

Book Designer
Gary Adair

Compositor
Mark Shirar

Editorial Assistant
Vanessa Evans

Cover Designer
Alan Clements

Contents at a Glance

Table of Contents

About the Author

Bill Ferguson, VCI5, VCP5, CCSI, and MCT has been in the computer industry for more than 20 years. Originally in technical sales and IT consulting with Sprint, he made his transition to Certified Technical Trainer in 1997 with ExecuTrain. He now runs his own company, Parallel Connections, as an independent contractor and consultant based in Birmingham, Alabama, working worldwide for most of the national training companies and some regional training companies. In addition, he has written and produced many technical training videos and books. Bill's aspiration is as follows: "My job is to understand the material so well that I can make it easier for others to learn than it was for me to learn. Toward that end, I strive to provide an effective learning environment whether in person, in print, or online."

Dedication

To my wife, who didn't want me to take on this challenge at first because of the tremendous amount of time that it takes to complete a book of this type; yet she still became my prime source of encouragement and support when I decided to do it anyway. I love you, Wilma, and I couldn't have done this without you. Thanks!

Acknowledgments

First I want to thank Joan Murray for giving me the opportunity to write this important book. I am very glad that our paths crossed at vmWorld. I also want to thank John Davidson and Gabrie van Zenten for their "spot on" technical editing of the book. Because of them, I learned a few things myself while writing this book. In addition, the flow and consistency of the book is due to Chris Cleveland, who kept me on target with his skilled developmental editing. I would also like to give a special thanks to Joshua Andrews at VMware, whose first-hand knowledge of the latest products and features in vSphere provided me with the most up-to-date information possible. His review of this book makes it a true collaboration of VMware and Pearson/VMware Press. It takes a lot of people to create a book, and I am sure that I do not know all the names of the people who were involved in this one, but thank you.

Finally, I want to acknowledge the encouragement and prayers of my family and friends and the students in my technical classes and Sunday school classes. In Him, all things are possible!

About the Reviewers

John A. Davidson, VCI, VCP 3 4 5, VCAP-DCA 4, MCT, MCSE, CCSI, CCNA, A+, Network+, has been in the computer industry for more than 20 years. With a career that has included roles in technical sales, sales management, system administration, and network engineering, John made his transition to being a Certified Technical Trainer in 1998, and has worked with many leading training organizations. Today, John serves as the VMware Course Director for Global Knowledge-USA for datacenter and desktop courses. As a lead instructor, John spends his time mentoring new instructors, students, and colleagues, and serves as subject matter expert to design, develop, and implement VMware solutions to support Global Knowledge-USA's training environment.

Gabrie van Zanten is a virtualization specialist working for Open Line in the Netherlands. As a consultant, he designs and implements virtual infrastructures for customers. Besides being a consultant, Gabrie runs one of the top ten ranked blogs on VMware at http://www.GabesVirtualWorld.com. He writes about VMware and helps his readers get in-depth understanding on how VMware products work. His blogging activities, the presentations he gives and the effort he puts in helping members of the VMware community have earned him the VMware vExpert award in 2009, 2010, and 2011.

We Want to Hear from You!

As the reader of this book, *you* are our most important critic and commentator. We value your opinion and want to know what we're doing right, what we could do better, what areas you'd like to see us publish in, and any other words of wisdom you're willing to pass our way.

As an associate publisher for Pearson, I welcome your comments. You can email or write me directly to let me know what you did or didn't like about this book—as well as what we can do to make our books better.

Please note that I cannot help you with technical problems related to the topic of this book. We do have a User Services group, however, where I will forward specific technical questions related to the book.

When you write, please be sure to include this book's title and author as well as your name, email address, and phone number. I will carefully review your comments and share them with the author and editors who worked on the book.

Email: VMwarePress@vmware.com

Mail: David Dusthimer
        Associate Publisher
        Pearson
        800 East 96th Street
        Indianapolis, IN 46240 USA

Reader Services

Visit our website and register this book at Pearsonitcertification.com/register for convenient access to any updates, downloads, or errata that might be available for this book.

Introduction

Welcome to my VCP5 study guide. I'm excited about sharing this information with you to help you prepare to take and pass the VCP510 test. I've been a technical trainer/consultant for more than 15 years, and I've taught thousands of students. Since I teach many of my VMware classes online now, I sometimes tell people that "I teach people I can't see to use computers that don't exist in a physical sense." This book is just an extension of that theme.

Because the test blueprint on VMware's website *http://vmware.com/certification* is your best guide for success on the test, I decided to write this book as directly to the blueprint as possible. This means that we will "jump" into topics that might seem to be out of place if this is your first look at virtualization. This leads me to my first assumption, which is that this is not your first look at virtualization. The reason I can assume this is that you are preparing to take a test that is of a highly technical nature, so it should seem reasonable to assume that you have had prior knowledge and experience with VMware products either in the workplace or in technical classes like that ones that I teach. It is with this assumption that I can follow the blueprint as it is written; but I will take into account areas where I feel there is a need to "backfill" information so that you can fully understand the topic that I am discussing.

My second assumption is that you have access to a vSphere 5 environment or can build yourself a system on which you can practice what we will discuss so that you will retain it better. We all learn in different ways, but I've found that many in the IT world learn by "doing" even more than by "hearing." Since this is the case, and since it fits well with the blueprint, there will be many times throughout this book when I walk you through the steps. Therefore, it would be best for you to have a system with at least vCenter 5.0 and a couple of vSphere 5.0 hosts installed that you can use to follow along. You could even do this using Workstation 8 and all virtual machines.

As to what you need to learn and remember, my third assumption is that you don't want to know everything there is to know about "all things VMware"—just what is important in your situation and what might be on the test. Based on that assumption, I will try my best not to "throw in" a lot of additional material that makes you wonder whether you need to know it as well. I will not repeat "this would be good to know for the test" throughout this book because that would get monotonous; however, if it is in this book you can assume that it is "fair game" for the VCP510 test.

Finally, my last assumption is that you don't really care how much I know, but what you really care about is whether I can help you learn what you need to know. Toward that end, I will use examples, stories, and analogies to help you understand highly technical topics in a more "comfortable" manner than you may have experienced before in a technical book. The way I see it "My job is to know this material so well that I can make it easier for you to learn than it was for me to learn." So, if we are all in agreement, let's get started!

Who Should Read This Book

The VCP5 certification was listed on http://www.techrepublic.com/ as one of the top 10 certifications to have in 2012. If you are currently working with VMware vSphere virtual datacenters, it could be a valuable certification for you. If you are considering your options in the IT world, you will not go wrong if you learn about virtualization now. In either case, this book will help you obtain the knowledge and the skills toward becoming a VCP5.

Goals and Methods

My number one goal of this book is a simple one: to help you pass the VCP510 Certification test and obtain the status of VMware Certified Professional for vSphere 5 (VCP5).

To aid you in gaining the knowledge and understanding of key vSphere topics, I use the following methods:

- **Opening topics list:** This list defines the topics to be covered in the chapter. Each chapter is a part of the exam blueprint and the chapters and topics are written in blueprint order.

- **Do I Know This Already? quizzes:** At the beginning of each chapter is a quiz. The quizzes, and answers/explanations (found in Appendix A), are meant to gauge your knowledge of the subjects. If the answers to the questions do not come readily to you, be sure to read the entire chapter.

- **Key topics:** The key topics indicate important figures, tables, and lists of information that you should know for the exam. They are interspersed throughout the chapter and are listed in table format at the end of the chapter.

- **Review questions:** All chapters conclude with a set of review questions to help you assess whether you have learned the key material in the chapter.

- **Exam-type questions:** Exam questions are included with the printed and digital editions of this book. They are written to be as close to the type of questions that appear on the VCP510 exam.

How to Use This Book

Although you could read this book cover to cover, I designed it to be flexible enough to allow you to easily move between chapters and sections of chapters to work on the areas that you feel are the most important for you. If you intend to read all the chapters, the order in the book is an excellent sequence to follow.

The core chapters, Chapters 1 through 7, cover the following topics:

- **Chapter 1, "Planning, Installing, Configuring, and Upgrading vCenter Server and VMware ESXi":** This chapter focuses on installing, upgrading, and securing all of the key components in your vSphere. I discuss ESXi hosts, vCenter, datastores, and network components.

- **Chapter 2, "Planning and Configuring vSphere Networking":** This chapter focuses completely on networking components in vSphere. I cover both vSphere standard switch and vSphere distributed switch concepts.

- **Chapter 3, "Planning and Configuring vSphere Storage":**This chapter focuses on storage of virtual datacenters and virtual machines. I discuss configuring and managing all forms of storage, including Fibre Channel, iSCSI, and network-attached storage.

- **Chapter 4, "Deploying and Administering Virtual Machine and vApps":** This chapter focuses on creating, configuring, and managing virtual machines and vApps. I cover many other topics, including cloning, troubleshooting, and exporting virtual machines and vApps.

- **Chapter 5, "Establishing and Maintaining Service Levels":** This chapter focuses on keeping your vSphere running smoothly and recovering quickly from any failure. I cover many topics, including services that improve overall utilization and recoverability.

- **Chapter 6, "Performing Basic Troubleshooting":** This chapter focuses on understanding the key components of your vSphere and how they work together. You will learn how to spot a problem and make the necessary corrections. I cover troubleshooting your ESXi hosts, network, storage, and key services.

- **Chapter 7, "Monitoring vSphere Implementation and Managing vCenter Server Alarms":** This chapter focuses on the "core four" resources in any computer system: CPU, memory, disk, and network. I cover guidelines for monitoring each of the core four. By knowing how to monitor your resources and knowing what you should expect to see, you will be able to spot any metrics that seem to "out of place" and take the necessary action.

- Finally, **Chapter 8, "What Do I Do Now?"** is a very small chapter to give you some additional direction and encouragement to schedule, take, and pass the VCP510 test.

Note As I will state again in Chapter 8, I highly recommend that you schedule the test now and then study. Go to Pearson/Virtual University Enterprises (http://vue. com) on the Web and find a testing center close to you. The cost of the exam at the time of this writing is $225. If you "put your money down" and "set the date," you will focus more and study better.

Certification Exam and This Preparation Guide

I wrote this book directly to the VCP510 Exam Blueprint. Each chapter of this book is a section of the blueprint, with all of its objectives in the same order as the blueprint. This way, you can easily identify your strengths and work on your weaknesses. Table I-1 lists the VCP510 Exam Blueprint objectives and the chapter of this book that covers them.

Table I-1 VCP5 Exam Topics and Chapter References

Exam Section/Objective	Chapter Where Covered
Section 1: Plan, Install, Configure, and Upgrade vCenter Server and VMware ESXi	
Objective 1.1 – Install and Configure vCenter Server	Chapter 1
Objective 1.2 – Install and Configure VMware ESXi	Chapter 1
Objective 1.3 – Plan and Perform Upgrades of vCenter Server and VMware ESXi	Chapter 1
Objective 1.4 – Secure vCenter Server and ESXi	Chapter 1
Objective 1.5 – Identify vSphere Architecture and Solutions	Chapter 1
Section 2 – Plan and Configure vSphere Networking	
Objective 2.1 – Configure vNetwork Standard Switches	Chapter 2
Objective 2.2 – Configure vNetwork Distributed Switches	Chapter 2
Objective 2.3 – Configure vSS and vDS Policies	Chapter 2
Section 3 – Plan and Configure vSphere Storage	
Objective 3.1 – Configure Shared Storage for vSphere	Chapter 3
Objective 3.2 – Configure the Storage Virtual Appliance for vSphere	Chapter 3
Objective 3.3 – Create and Configure VMFS and NFS Datastores	Chapter 3

Exam Section/Objective	Chapter Where Covered
Section 4 – Deploy and Administer Virtual Machines and vApps	
Objective 4.1 – Create and Deploy Virtual Machines	Chapter 4
Objective 4.2 – Create and Deploy vApps	Chapter 4
Objective 4.3 – Manage Virtual Machine Clones and Templates	Chapter 4
Objective 4.4 – Administer Virtual Machines and vApps	Chapter 4
Section 5 – Establish and Maintain Service Levels	
Objective 5.1 – Create and Configure VMware Clusters	Chapter 5
Objective 5.2 – Plan and Implement VMware Fault Tolerance	Chapter 5
Objective 5.3 – Create and Administer Resource Pools	Chapter 5
Objective 5.4 – Migrate Virtual Machines	Chapter 5
Objective 5.5 – Backup and Restore Virtual Machines	Chapter 5
Objective 5.6 – Patch and Update ESXi and Virtual Machines	Chapter 5
Section 6 – Perform Basic Troubleshooting	
Objective 6.1 – Perform Basic Troubleshooting for ESXi Hosts	Chapter 6
Objective 6.2 – Perform Basic vSphere Network Troubleshooting	Chapter 6
Objective 6.3 – Perform Basic vSphere Storage Troubleshooting	Chapter 6
Objective 6.4 – Perform Basic Troubleshooting for HA/DRS Clusters and vMotion/Storage vMotion	Chapter 6
Section 7 – Monitor a vSphere Implementation and Manage vCenter Server Alarms	
Objective 7.1 – Monitor ESXi, vCenter Server and Virtual Machines	Chapter 7
Objective 7.2 – Create and Administer vCenter Server Alarms	Chapter 7

Book Content Updates

Because VMware occasionally updates exam topics without notice, VMware Press
might post additional preparatory content on the web page associated with this book
at http://www.pearsonitcertification.com/title/9780789749314. It is a good idea to
check the website a couple of weeks before taking your exam, to review any updated
content that might be posted online. We also recommend that you periodically
check back to this page on the Pearson IT Certification website to view any errata
or supporting book files that may be available.

Pearson IT Certification Practice Test Engine and Questions on the DVD

The DVD in the back of the book includes the Pearson IT Certification Practice Test engine—software that displays and grades a set of exam-realistic multiple-choice questions. Using the Pearson IT Certification Practice Test engine, you can either study by going through the questions in Study Mode or take a simulated exam that mimics real exam conditions.

The installation process requires two major steps: installing the software, and then activating the exam. The DVD in the back of this book has a recent copy of the Pearson IT Certification Practice Test engine. The practice exam—the database of exam questions—is not on the DVD.

Note The cardboard DVD case in the back of this book includes the DVD and a piece of paper. The paper lists the activation code for the practice exam associated with this book. *Do not lose the activation code*. On the opposite side of the paper from the activation code is a unique, one-time-use coupon code for the purchase of the Premium Edition eBook and Practice Test.

Install the Software from the DVD

The Pearson IT Certification Practice Test is a Windows-only desktop application. You can run it on a Mac using a Windows virtual machine, but it was built specifically for the PC platform. The minimum system requirements are as follows:

- Windows XP (SP3), Windows Vista (SP2), or Windows 7
- Microsoft .NET Framework 4.0 Client
- Microsoft SQL Server Compact 4.0
- Pentium class 1GHz processor (or equivalent)
- 512 MB RAM
- 650 MB disc space plus 50 MB for each downloaded practice exam

The software installation process is pretty routine as compared with other software installation processes. If you have already installed the Pearson IT Certification Practice Test software from another Pearson product, there is no need for you to reinstall the software. Just launch the software on your desktop and proceed to activate the practice exam from this book by using the activation code included in the DVD sleeve.

The following steps outline the installation process:

Step 1. Insert the DVD into your PC.

Step 2. The software that automatically runs is the Pearson software to access and use all DVD-based features, including the exam engine and the DVD-only appendixes. From the main menu, click the **Install the Exam Engine** option.

Step 3. Respond to window prompts as with any typical software installation process.

The installation process gives you the option to activate your exam with the activation code supplied on the paper in the DVD sleeve. This process requires that you establish a Pearson website login. You need this login to activate the exam, so please do register when prompted. If you already have a Pearson website login, there is no need to register again. Just use your existing login.

Activate and Download the Practice Exam

After installing the exam engine, you should then activate the exam associated with this book (if you did not do so during the installation process) as follows:

Step 1. Start the Pearson IT Certification Practice Test software from the Windows **Start** menu or from your desktop shortcut icon.

Step 2. To activate and download the exam associated with this book, from the My Products or Tools tab, click the **Activate** button.

Step 3. At the next screen, enter the activation key from paper inside the cardboard DVD holder in the back of the book. Once entered, click the **Activate** button.

Step 4. The activation process downloads the practice exam. Click **Next**, and then click **Finish.**

When the activation process completes, the My Products tab should list your new exam. If you do not see the exam, make sure you have opened the My Products tab on the menu. At this point, the software and practice exam are ready to use. Simply select the exam and click the **Open Exam** button.

To update a particular exam you have already activated and downloaded, open the Tools tab and click the **Update Products** button. Updating your exams will ensure you have the latest changes and updates to the exam data.

If you want to check for updates to the Pearson Cert Practice Test exam engine software, open the Tools tab and click the **Update Application** button. This will ensure you are running the latest version of the software engine.

Activating Other Exams

The exam software installation process, and the registration process, only has to happen once. Then, for each new exam, only a few steps are required. For instance, if you buy another new Pearson IT Certification Cert Guide or VMware Press Official Cert Guide, extract the activation code from the DVD sleeve in the back of that book; you do not even need the DVD at this point. From there, all you have to do is start the exam engine (if not still up and running), and perform Steps 2 through 4 from the previous list.

Premium Edition

In addition to the free practice exam provided on the DVD, you can purchase two additional exams with expanded functionality directly from Pearson IT Certification. The Premium Edition eBook and Practice Test for this title contains an additional full practice exam and an eBook (in both PDF and ePub format). In addition, the Premium Edition title also has remediation for each question to the specific part of the eBook that relates to that question.

If you have purchased the print version of this title, you can purchase the Premium Edition at a deep discount. A coupon code in the DVD sleeve contains a one-time-use code and instructions for where you can purchase the Premium Edition.

To view the Premium Edition product page, go to:
http://www.pearsonitcertification.com/title/9780132965712

This chapter covers the following subjects:

- Installing and Configuring vCenter Server
- Installing and Configuring VMware ESXi
- Planning and Performing Upgrades of vCenter Server and VMware ESXi
- Securing vCenter Server and ESXi
- Identifying vSphere Architecture and Solutions

CHAPTER 1

Planning, Installing, Configuring, and Upgrading vCenter Server and VMware ESXi

Your vCenter Server and ESXi hosts offer a tremendous number of features and utilities, but to get the most from them you will need to install of them properly. In this chapter, I will focus on the proper installation of these important components. You will learn the methods that you should use to secure your system during and after installation. In addition, I will cover your options with regard to your new system, including creating an internal cloud and/or connecting to public clouds. Whether you are considering installing from scratch or upgrading, you will benefit from the information contained in this chapter.

"Do I Know This Already?" Quiz

The "Do I Know This Already?" quiz allows you to assess whether you should read this entire chapter or simply jump to the "Exam Preparation Tasks" section for review. If you are in doubt, read the entire chapter. Table 1-1 outlines the major headings in this chapter and the corresponding "Do I Know This Already?" quiz questions. You can find the answers in Appendix A, "Answers to the 'Do I Know This Already?' Quizzes and Chapter Review Questions."

Table 1-1 "Do I Know This Already?" Foundation Topics Section-to-Question Mapping

Foundations Topics Section	Questions Covered in This Section
Installing and Configuring vCenter Server	1, 2
Installing and Configuring VMware ESXi	3, 4
Planning and Performing Upgrades of vCenter Server and VMware ESXi	5, 6
Securing vCenter Server and ESXi	7, 8
Identifying vSphere Architecture and Solutions	9, 10

1. Which of following features are supported on Enterprise Plus but not on Enterprise? (Choose two.)

   a. vMotion

   b. Storage DRS

   c. Distributed switch

   d. HA

2. Which of the following are *not* advantages of using the vCenter appliance? (Choose two.)

   a. Simplified deployment

   b. Support for IPv6

   c. Lower TCO

   d. Linked Mode

3. Which of the following are *not* recommended media to use when installing ESXi interactively? (Choose two.)

   a. CD/DVD

   b. USB

   c. Network share

   d. Floppy disk

4. Which of the following stores and provides images and host profiles to ESXi host during Auto Deploy?

   a. Auto Deploy Rules Engine

   b. Auto Deploy Server

   c. Image Builder

   d. Answer File

5. How much memory is required as a bare minimum for an ESXi 5.0 host?

   a. 2GB

   b. 3GB

   c. 4GB

   d. 6GB

6. How many CPU cores minimum are required for an ESXi 5.0 host?

   a. 2

   b. 1

   c. 4

   d. 8

7. Which of the following is *not* a system role in vCenter 5.0?

   a. No Access

   b. Read Only

   c. Read

   d. Administrator

8. Which of the following is *not* a network security policy in vCenter 5.0?

   a. Promiscuous Mode

   b. MAC address changes

   c. Forged transmits

   d. IP address changes

9. VMware vSphere by itself is an example of what type of cloud?

   a. Public

   b. Private

   c. Hybrid

   d. VMware vSphere is not a cloud.

10. Which of the following best describes the four main resources used by computers in the vSphere architecture?

   a. CPU, vRAM, RAM, disk

   b. CPU, RAM, disk, network

   c. CPU, shares, network, RAM

   d. Network, bandwidth, storage, CPU

Foundation Topics

Installing and Configuring vCenter Server

This section focuses on the steps involved in the proper installation and configuration of vCenter Server. I will discuss your options with regard to licensing and editions and the various methods and steps that you can use to deploy vCenter Server in your organization.

Identifying Available vSphere and vCenter Server Editions

Your new vCenter Server will be the centralized command, control, and communication for your vSphere environment. Because the needs of organizations vary widely, VMware provides multiple options of vSphere, which are called *editions*. Each edition offers a defined variety of options that you can use to manage your virtual machines (VMs) and your hosts (the physical computers on which the VMs reside). When you finish reading this book, you will have a much better idea of which features would be most valuable to your organization, and you will understand all of the features as they relate to the questions on the test. For now, I will provide a brief explanation of each feature available in vSphere. Table 1-2 lists the most common editions and the features it makes available. If you understand all of this completely already, you might be more ready for the test than you think! If not, keep reading, and I will keep filling in the details.

Table 1-2   vSphere 5.0 Editions

vSphere 5.0 Editions	Standard	Enterprise	Enterprise Plus
Product Components			
Processor entitlement	Per 1 CPU	Per 1 CPU	Per 1 CPU
vRAM entitlement	32GB	64GB	96GB
vCPU entitlement	8-way	8-way	32-way
SUSE Linux Enterprise Server for VMware	X	X	X
Thin provisioning	X	X	X
Update Manager	X	X	X
Data recovery	X	X	X
High availability	X	X	X
vMotion	X	X	X
Storage APIs for data protection	X	X	X

vSphere 5.0 Editions	Standard	Enterprise	Enterprise Plus
Virtual serial port concentrator		X	X
Hot add		X	X
vSheild zones		X	X
Fault tolerance		X	X
Storage APIs for array integration		X	X
Storage APIs for multipathing		X	X
Storage vMotion		X	X
DRS and DPM		X	X
Storage I/O control			X
Network I/O control			X
Distributed switch			X
Host profiles			X
Auto Deploy			X
Storage DRS			X
Profile-driven storage			X

A brief description of each product component follows:

- **Processor entitlement:** The number of physical processors for which each license is required.

- **vRAM entitlement:** vRAM is the amount of virtual memory configured to a VM. This number indicates the amount of vRAM that each license adds to the available pool. The more vRAM you have, the more or larger VMs you can support.

- **vCPU entitlement:** The number of virtual CPUs that can be allocated to each VM using virtual symmetric multiprocessing (SMP).

- **SUSE Linux Enterprise Server for VMware:** Qualified purchases of VMware vSphere entitle free use of Enterprise Linux as a guest OS.

- **vCenter Server:** Indicates the levels of vCenter that are compatible with this edition.

- **Thin provisioning:** A dynamic storage system that reduces storage needs and expands to meet the demand of the VM with no performance degradation.

- **Update Manager:** An optional server application and database utility, which is controlled by a plug-in and which reduces the time spent on patching and upgrading host and VMs.

- **Data recovery:** An agentless disk-based backup system that provides deduplication at the destination and is designed for small to medium-size organizations.

- **High availability:** Provides for the automatic restart of VMs if they are on a host that fails; minimizes server downtime.

- **vMotion:** Allows the migration of a VM from one physical host to another without disrupting the user. This eliminates the need to have server downtime that is due to planned hardware downtime.

- **Storage APIs for data protection:** Allows for scalable backup without disrupting the users by leveraging supported third-party backup software.

- **Virtual serial port concentrator:** Redirects serial ports of VMs so that management traffic is only on the management network, providing a more secure way to manage VMs remotely.

- **Hot add:** Allows the addition of CPUs and memory when needed without disruption or downtime.

- **vShield zones:** Allows the configuration and maintenance of multiple security zones within software among shared hosts.

- **Fault tolerance:** Provides continuous availability for VMs with zero data loss in the event of server failures.

- **Storage APIs for array integration:** Improves performance and scalability by leveraging efficient array-based operations.

- **Storage vMotion:** Avoids application downtime for planned storage maintenance by allowing the migration of the VM files across storage arrays while the VMs are running.

- **DRS and DPM:** Automatically balances VM loads across hosts, optimizing efficiency and power management.

- **Storage I/O control:** Continuously monitors I/O load of storage volumes and dynamically allocates available I/O resources based on administrator settings for specific business needs.

- **Network I/O control:** Prioritizes network access by continuously monitoring I/O load over the network and dynamically allocating available I/O resources to administrator specified flows to support business needs.

- **Distributed switch:** Centralizes provisioning, administration, and monitoring of your virtual network using cluster-level aggregation of resources.

- **Host profiles:** Simplifies host deployment and compliance using baselines to automate the configuration of multiple hosts.

- **Auto Deploy:** Allows for deployment of multiple vSphere hosts in minutes by streaming the installation directly into RAM.

- **Storage DRS:** Provides for more effective balancing of VMs using automated load balancing across datastores in datastore clusters.

- **Profile-driven storage:** Allows for the prioritization of storage options and reduces the steps in the selection of VM storage and ensures that VMs are placed on the right type of storage for each VM.

NOTE   These are the main editions of vSphere and the best general information for the exam. You can research these further at http://www.vmware.com/products/vsphere/buy/editions_comparison.html. In addition, there are different flavors of vCenter, including Essentials, Foundation, and Standard. Finally, there are different flavors of ESXi, including Regional Office, vDesktop, Essentials, Essentials Plus, Standard, Enterprise, and Enterprise Plus. Each of these options is referred to as a *kit*, an *edition*, or a *licensing model*. The purpose of having so many options is to be able to provide a company with the features that they need while not "breaking the bank" with features that they will probably never use. You can obtain more information about all of your options from your VMware representative.

Deploying the vCenter Appliance

Prior to vSphere 5.0, you had to run vCenter on a Windows machine. Your only choice was whether to run it on a physical machine or a virtual machine (VM). Now, you can use a vCenter appliance and thereby save the expense of having another Windows Server license. The vCenter appliance is a prepackaged 64-bit application running on SUSE Linux Enterprise Server 11. It includes an IBM DB2 embedded database for evaluation or for running fewer than 5 ESXi hosts and fewer than 50 VMs. It also provides support for Oracle and IBM DB2 databases.

You configure the vCenter appliance through a web-based interface. There is also support for the vSphere Web Client application. You can configure the appliance to authenticate to the local computer, an Active Directory (AD) domain, or to Network Information Services (NIS).

The benefits of using a vCenter appliance include the following:

- Simplified Deployment and Configuration through a web-based interface

- Lower total cost of ownership by eliminating the Windows operating system dependency and licensing costs

- No change in the user experience when connecting to vCenter Server with the vSphere Client

Before you think that the vCenter appliance provides all of the same functionality as the Windows-based vCenter Server, you should know that three things are not supported. Some of these might not be that important to you anyway, but you should certainly know them for the test.

The three features that are not supported in the vCenter appliance are as follows:

- vCenter Linked Mode

- Microsoft SQL Server

- IPv6

You can obtain the vCenter appliance from the VMware website http://www. vmware.com/download. It comes in the form of three files: an open virtualization format (OVF) file; and two virtual disk (.vmdk) files, one for system and other for data. After you have placed all three of these files in the same folder, you can connect to it, as shown in Figure 1-1, and deploy the template from there. The following are specific steps to deploy to vCenter appliance.

 Activity 1-1 Deploying the VCA from an OVF template

1. Log on to your vSphere Client.

2. From the File menu, choose **File, Deploy OVF Template**.

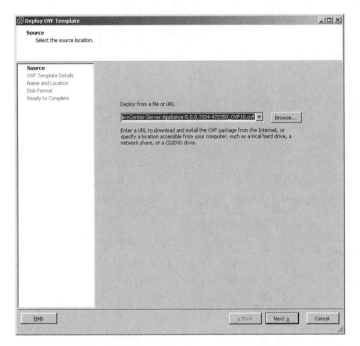

Figure 1-1   Deploying the VCA from an OVF Template

3. Click **Browse** and locate the template in by its file or URL, and then click **Next** and follow the wizard to install of the appliance. This will set a default password for the root account. The default password is vmware. For convenience, select **Power On After Deploying**. You select a datastore during the installation. You should be sure that the datastore is large enough for the appliance (at least 100GB). As you can see from Figure 1-2, the installation without any additional support modules takes about 82GB of thick-provisioned space. (Chapter 4, "Deploying and Administering Virtual Machine and vApps," covers thick and thin provisioning in more detail.)

Figure 1-2   OVF Template Details

4.   When the appliance boots, open the console and configure the network set-
     tings and time zone. You should configure the IP address, subnet mask, default
     gateway, the hostname of the appliance, and the addresses of any proxy servers
     or DNS servers that you want to use, as shown in Figure 1-3. These can also
     be configured through the browser, but you might need to add some network-
     ing information so that you can get to the browser in the first place.

Figure 1-3   VCA Console

5. Next, configure the time zone where the appliance resides. The appliance will default to synchronizing its "absolute time" with the ESXi host on which it is running.

6. When the network configuration is complete, you can access the appliance using your browser. (Internet Explorer and Mozilla Firefox browsers are supported.) Open your browser and type **https://**_appliancename or ipaddress_**:5480**. For example, if your appliance were at 192.168.1.132 (as in Figure 1-3), you would type **https://192.168.1.132:5480**.

7. Log on to the appliance using the root account and the default password, as shown in Figure 1-4.

Figure 1-4   VCA Browser Logon

8. Click **Accept EULA** to accept the end-user license agreement.

9. Select your database, as shown in Figure 1-5. You can select to use the embedded database or you can configure the appliance to connect to and use your Oracle database. (Microsoft SQL databases are not supported with the vCenter Appliance.)

10. Select **Test Settings** to ensure that your settings are configured properly or **Save Settings** to ensure they are retained.

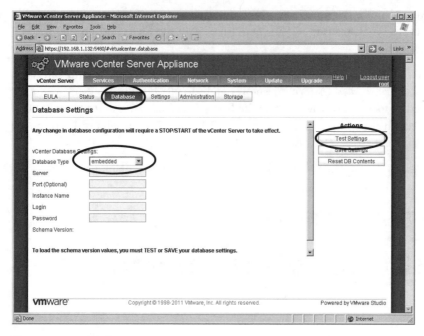

Figure 1-5   VCA Configuration Steps

Installing vCenter Server into a Virtual Machine

When I teach VMware vSphere classes in person, I always ask the students whether they think the vCenter Server should be a VM or a physical machine and why? Many people assume that the vCenter Server is such an important component to the virtual environment that it should be a physical machine. In other words, they do not want to have a situation in which they need to have a vCenter machine to fix the virtual environment that is down, but the machine that they need is also a VM and therefore is also down; a "catch 22" type of situation. In reality, because of vSphere features that I will discuss later (such as high availability [HA]), it is acceptable to install the vCenter Server as a VM. So, now that you know that it can be done, let's talk about how you do it.

The vCenter Server installation software can be found on the vSphere Installation Manager, which also allows you to install of the vSphere Client and other server components. Before you begin a vCenter installation, you should make sure that the machine that you are using meets the basic hardware and software requirements.

The basic requirements for vCenter Server are as follows:

- **Number of CPUs: 2**

- **Processor:** 2.0GHz or higher Intel or AMD processor

- **Memory:** 4GB minimum

- **Disk Storage:** 4GB minimum

- **Operating System:** 64-bit (See the vSphere Compatiblity Matrixes in the vSphere Installation and Setup Guide as noted.)

NOTE   These are the basic requirements without which the installation will fail. For more detailed information about vCenter requirements, consult the *vSphere Installation and Setup Guide* at http://www.pubs.vmware.com.

When you know that your system meets all of the requirements, you are ready to begin the installation. The installation of vCenter is actually straightforward and quite simple. Activity 1-2 outlines the specific steps to install of the vCenter on a virtual machine or on a physical machine.

Activity 1-2 Installing vCenter

1. Locate and open the VMware vCenter Installer. After you have acquired the latest VMware-VIMSetup-all 5.0.0 file, you double-click it to open it.

2. Double-click the autorun.exe file (not the folder) to start the installer.

3. Once the installer is up, ensure that vCenter is selected (it will be selected by default), and then click Install. Figure 1-6 shows the vSphere Installation Manager.

Figure 1-6   vSphere Installation Manager

4. Continue through the wizard and answer the questions based on your own organization. Configuration options include the following:

- Username and organization

- License key or choose Evaluation Mode

- Database information (default local or connection information for remote)

- SYSTEM account information (SYSTEM account or user-specified account)

- Destination folder for software

- Standalone or Linked Mode group

- Ports (Default ports can be used, or you can specify for your organization.)

- JVM memory for vCenter Server Web service

- Ephemeral port configuration (Select if your vCenter will manage hosts that power on more than 2000 VMs simultaneously.)

After you have finished the installation, you should be able to view the new services that are now installed on the vCenter machine, as shown in Figure 1-7.

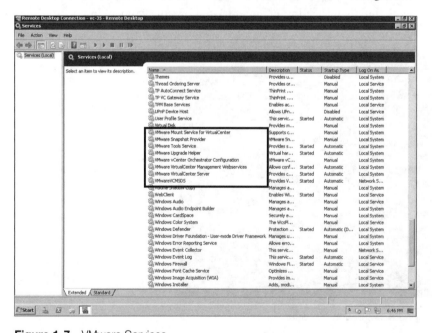

Figure 1-7   VMware Services

It is important that these services are started in order for you to log on to and use your vCenter Server. The list that follows describes services that should now be started and their general purpose:

- **VMware vCenter Orchestrator Configuration:** Controls a workflow engine that can help administrators automate many existing manual tasks.

- **VMware VirtualCenter Management Webservices:** Configuration for vCenter web management.

- **VMware VirtualCenter Server:** The main service for vCenter Server at the core of management of VMs and ESXi hosts. If this service not started, you cannot log on to the vCenter Server.

- **VMware VCMSDS:** Provides vCenter Server Lightweight Directory Access Protocol (LDAP) directory services.

- **VMware Tools:** Because this vCenter is a VM, you should have VMware tools installed on it.

> **NOTE**   If you cannot log on to your vCenter Server with your vSphere Client, always check that the VMware VirtualCenter Server service has started.

Sizing the vCenter Server Database

Before installing your vCenter, you want to know the specific database that you will use. This means that you will really need to have created the database ahead of time; which in turn means that you need to know the size of the database that you will need. The vCenter Server has a tool that you can use to calculate the size of the database; however, you cannot use that tool unless you already have a vCenter installed. This might be the case if you installed one with a SQL Express database for demo; but if you do not have an installation, what do you use? There are database-sizing spreadsheets that you can use for Microsoft SQL and Oracle database sizing. These are available at http://www.vmware.com/support/pubs. This might be a guess on your part as to how many hosts, VMs, clusters, and so on, but it's better than a complete "shot in the dark."

Installing Additional vCenter Server Components

The vSphere Installation Manager is a very flexible tool. You can use it to install vCenter Server, vSphere Client, and other additional vCenter Server components. To install of the additional components, just click that component and select **In-**

stall. The following are two additional components that you can install and their general purpose:

- **VMware vSphere Update Manager:** A utility installed as a plug-in that reduces time patching VMs and hosts.

- **VMware vSphere Web Client:** A web-based management tool that you can use to manage VMs in your vCenter.

NOTE   The vSphere Installation Manager also provides for the installation of support tools and utilities such as the VMware ESXi Dump Collector, VMware Syslog Collector, VMware Auto Deploy, VMware vSphere Authentication Proxy, and vCenter Host Agent Pre-Upgrade Checker; some of which I will discuss later in this chapter.

Installing/Removing vSphere Client Plug-Ins

You install and enable components such as vSphere Update Manager through a two-step process. First, you install of the software on the vCenter Server with the vSphere Installation Manager, and then you download and install the plug-in associated with that software. The software installed on the vCenter Server makes the new component available, but the graphical user interface (GUI) is not changed on the vSphere Client until after you have downloaded and installed the plug-in.

Activity 1-3 outlines the specific steps that you should use to download and install the plug-in.

Activity 1-3 Downloading and Installing a Plug-in

1. Log on to your vCenter Server.

2. On the File menu, locate and click **Plug-Ins**.

3. Click **Manage Plug-Ins**.

4. In the list of available plug-ins, locate the plug-in associated with the software that you have installed. Figure 1-8 shows the Plug-In Manager.

5. Click **Download and Install** (blue link).

To remove a plug-in, you must locate the component installation in Add or Remove Programs within the Control Panel. You can then remove the plug-in by selecting and uninstalling the component.

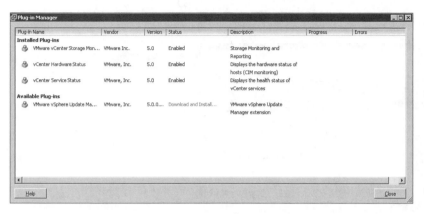

Figure 1-8   vSphere Client Plug-Ins

Enabling/Disabling vSphere Client Plug-Ins

When you first download and install a plug-in, it should be enabled by default. Later, if you want to disable the plug-in, you can right-click it and select **Disable**. You might do this if you are troubleshooting an issue and you want to make sure that the tool is not causing the issue. To enable or disable a plug-in, just right-click the associated plug-in and make your selection.

Licensing vCenter Server

VMware provides a 60-day trial license on which all features are enabled so you can determine what you really need for your organization. After the 60-day trial has expired, you must obtain a license for the level of services and features that you require. Failure to do so will mean that you will be severely limited in your options, including adding hosts to a vCenter and even powering on VMs. To apply a license that you have obtained, follow the steps outlined in Activity 1-4.

Activity 1-4 Applying a License to vCenter

1. Log on to vCenter Server.

2. Click **Home**, and then select **Licensing** within the icons under Administration.

3. Click **Manage vSphere Licenses** in the upper-right corner, as shown in Figure 1-9.

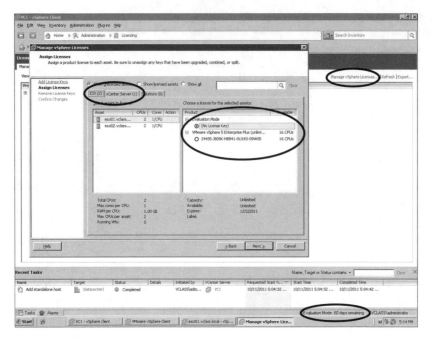

Figure 1-9   Licensing a vCenter Server

4. Enter the licenses in Enter New vSphere License Keys box (one per line).

5. Enter an optional label below, such as Production Licenses.

6. Click **Next** and review the details of your new license keys.

7. Click **Next** and verify that the **Show Unlicensed Assets** radio button is selected.

8. On the left side of Assign Licenses dialog box, select the asset, and on right select the key. Note that keys are "smart" and already "know" what type they are.

9. Repeat the process to assign licenses to the vCenter Server and the hosts. (Pay close attention the tabs.)

10. Click **Next** and verify that all licenses have been assigned.

11. Click **Next** and read the Confirm Changes dialog box to ensure that you have assigned the proper keys to the proper assets.

12. Click **Finish**.

NOTE Don't get too excited about those apparently free license keys; they expired long before this book was published.

Determining Availability Requirements for vCenter Server in a Given vSphere Implementation

As I mentioned previously, your vCenter is the centralized command, control, and communication for your vSphere environment. So what happens if it fails and is not available? You might at first think that it would be a great catastrophic event that would cause all of the VMs to stop functioning and break all of the network connections at once.

This is not the case at all. In fact, a loss of the vCenter has an effect only on your ability as an administrator to control the system from the vCenter. You can still log on to individual ESXi hosts and configure them. In addition, all of the networking remains intact, and the VMs function almost normally. However, Distributed Resource Scheduler (DRS), which provides the capability to automatically migrate VMs to balance the load will be disabled because the vCenter does those calculations and controls those moves. (Chapter 5, "Establishing and Maintaining Service Levels," covers DRS in more detail.) The capability to restart the VMs on a host that fails (HA) will, however, be intact and in fact will restart your VM-based vCenter just as well as any other VM. Chapter 5 covers HA in greater detail.

So, the main question is, "How long can you continue operations without your vCenter?" If your answer is "at least a few minutes," then you might only need to make sure that HA is installed and functional in your host clusters. However, if you do not think that you ever want to lose vCenter, you need a much more complete and sophisticated product from VMware called vCenter Heartbeat, which provides redundancy and 100% fault tolerance for all aspects of your vCenter Server system. You can obtain more information about vCenter Heartbeat at http://www.vmware. com/support/pubs/heartbeat_pubs.html.

NOTE Loss of vCenter also means loss of performance statistics for the duration of the outage. This might be important if you want to utilize these statistics to demonstrate your ability to honor published service level agreements (SLAs).

Determining Use Cases for vSphere Client and Web Client

In most cases, you want to connect to your vCenter using the vSphere Client software. The vSphere Client is the most commonly used graphical user interface GUI. A connection to the vCenter with vSphere Client enables you to manage all aspects of your vSphere environment, including VMs, hosts, datastores, and networks. It should be your "tool of choice" for most configuration needs.

The vSphere Installation Manager package also includes another GUI, known as the VMware vSphere Web Client. It is a browser based, extensible, and platform-independent version of the vSphere Client that is based on Adobe Flex. It includes only a subset of features from the Windows-based vSphere Client. In fact, it is really only useful for displaying your vSphere inventory and configuring and deploying VMs. If you need to configure your hosts, datastores, or network components, you must use the Windows-based vSphere Client instead.

Installing and Configuring VMware ESXi

I can still remember the many configuration steps involved with the installation of earlier versions of ESX. There were so many things to consider and so many places that you could make a mistake that VMware actually made a little video for you to watch to make it easier to know when to make each decision and how.

Well, ESX is not offered in vSphere 5.0, only ESXi. One of the benefits of using ESXi rather than ESX is that the installation is much more straightforward. I tell my students that it is more like installing a new switch than it is like installing a new router or server (much less configuration). Now there is even a way to stream the installation directly into memory and not onto a disk at all. Configuration is also simplified. and there are fewer configuration aspects to consider.

In this section, I will discuss different ways to install and configure ESXi quickly and efficiently. You will learn how to perform an interactive installation, use Auto Deploy, configure Network Time Protocol (NTP), configure Domain Name System (DNS) routing, enable and configure hyperthreading, enable and size the memory compression cache, and license the ESXi host.

Performing an Interactive Installation of ESXi

To install ESXi for vSphere 5.0, access the installer software. There is no GUI installer for ESXi, so the text-based installer is used for new installations and for upgrades. You can obtain the text-based installer from the CD/DVD installation software for ESXi, or you can download the software ISO and burn a CD or DVD. To access the ISO file, connect to http://www.vmware.com/download. You can also load the installation software to a USB flash drive.

After you have obtained the software, proceed with the pre-installation checks. You should /consider the following:

- Verify that the server hardware clock is set to UTC (BIOS setting).

- Verify that a keyboard and monitor are attached to the machine on which you are installing ESXi, or use a remote management application.

- Consider disconnecting network storage, such as fiber-optic cables and network cables to iSCSI arrays. This will save time on the installation because there will be fewer drives for the installation software to examine for you as a potential candidate for installation.

> **NOTE**   Also, if you intend to install the software locally, disconnect network and fiber-optic cables to avoid accidentally overwriting important data. I tell my students that this type of mistake is referred to as an RGE or "resumé-generating event."

With the pre-installation checks done, you are ready to proceed with the installation of the ESXi software as outlined in Activity 1-5.

Activity 1-5 Performing an Interactive Installation of ESXi

1. Set the BIOS on the machine to boot from CD-ROM or USB device, depending on your earlier choice.

2. Insert the ESXi installer into the CD/DVD drive or connect the USB flash drive.

3. On the Select a Disk page, select the drive on which to install ESXi and press **Enter**. Caution: If you choose a disk that contains data, a Confirm Disk Selection page appears. You get one chance, so make sure that you do not perform an RGE.

4. Select the keyboard type for the host.

5. Enter the root password for the host. (You can leave this blank and fill it in on the first boot. If you do not choose a root password on the first boot, you will see a warning associated with the hosts on the vSphere Client.)

6. Press **F11** to start the installation.

7. After the installation is complete, remove the CD/DVD or USB flash drive.

8. Press **Enter** to reboot the host. You should see a screen with the IP address of the system, as shown in Figure 1-10.

9. Finally, reset the boot device to be the drive on which you installed ESXi.

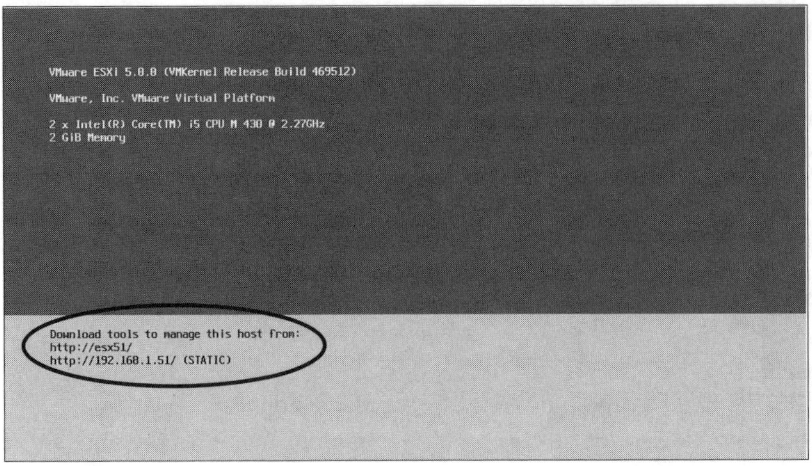

```
VMware ESXi 5.0.0 (VMKernel Release Build 469512)

VMware, Inc. VMware Virtual Platform

2 x Intel(R) Core(TM) i5 CPU M 430 @ 2.27GHz
2 GiB Memory




Download tools to manage this host from:
http://esx51/
http://192.168.1.51/ (STATIC)
```

Figure 1-10   An ESXi Installation

NOTE   Performing an interactive installation in which you answer all of the prompts is only recommended for small implementations of five or fewer hosts. We have much more efficient methods if you have more hosts.

Deploying an ESXi Host Using Auto Deploy

Auto Deploy is a new installation method for vSphere 5.0 ESXi hosts that speeds the installation by leveraging a pre-boot execution environment (PXE) infrastructure and host profiles. The software to run the host is not stored on the host itself, but instead, a specialized Auto Deploy server manages the information for each host. I will not go into detail about the configuration of Auto Deploy itself because this topic is specifically about deploying a host with Auto Deploy, but Figure 1-11 shows the architecture of Auto Deploy.

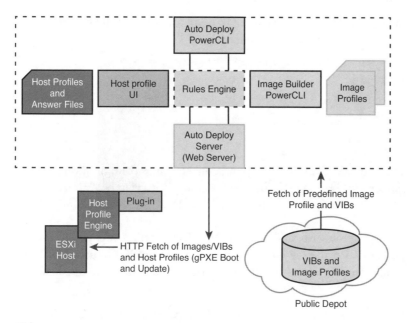

Figure 1-11   Auto Deploy Architecture

The following is a brief description of the most important components:

- **Auto Deploy server:** Stores and provides images and host profiles to ESXi hosts. This is the main component of the Auto Deploy architecture.

- **Auto Deploy rules engine:** Tells the Auto Deploy server which images and which profiles to serve to which hosts. You use Auto Deploy PowerCLI to define the rules that the engine uses.

- **Image profiles:** VMware Infrastructure Bundles (VIBs) made by VMware and its partners. These enable you to define standard and custom installation of ESXi hosts. These are generally stored in public software depots.

- **Host profiles:** Templates that further define the ESXi host's configuration, such as network and storage settings. These can be created from one host and used by many hosts.

- **Answer files:** These files store information that the user provides during the boot process. Only one answer file exists for each host.

Now that you know all of the "players," you need a brief understanding of deploying a host. First, you write rules using vSphere PowerCLI and add them to a ruleset. These rules define the image profiles and host profiles to be used and the hosts on which they can be used. After you have done this, you can turn on the host to provision it. Example rules include the following:

```
add-esxsoftwaredepot <path_to_the_ESXi_offline_image>
get-esximageprofile
new-deployrule -name rule-imageprofile -item <image_profile_name>
-allhosts
```

> **NOTE**   The complete details of an Auto Deploy setup and rules configuration are available at the vSphere 5.0 Documentation Center at http://www.pubs.vmware.com.

Based on the rules that you write and add, the Auto Deploy rules engine tells the Auto Deploy server to provide the image profiles and host profiles to provision the hosts. Any information that you add on the first installation is stored in the answer file.

The answer file is of great importance because when the ESXi is shut down the whole process starts over because no information was kept on the server itself, except for what was running in RAM, which is gone. On the reboot, though, the ESXi host is already known by the rules engine, and the saved information from the last boot as well as the answer file can be used (which saves time).

Configuring NTP on an ESXi Host

As you may know, it's important for computers on a network to agree on what time it is, and ESXi is no exception. In addition, it's important to have the correct time set on a system so that logs and reports reflect the correct time; otherwise you won't know whether it was taken during your peak time or off peak time. Because your ESXi host is a server in your network, it should agree on the time with the other servers in your network. You should therefore configure the Network Time Protocol (NTP) settings on the host to obtain their time from a trusted time source. What you use as a trusted time source will vary based on your organization's decision. Also, keep in mind that ESXi uses coordinated universal time (UTC) and therefore does not have the need or capability for time zone configuration.

Activity 1-6 outlines how to configure NTP on your ESXi host in your vCenter.

Activity 1-6 Configuring NTP on a Host in vCenter

1. Log on to your vSphere Client.

2. Select **Home**, **Hosts and Clusters**, and then click your host.

3. Open the Configuration tab.

4. Under the Software section, click **Time Configuration**.

5. Select **Enable NTP** and click **Next**.

6. Open the Options tab and enter the IP address or hostname of your time server.

7. Select **Update the NTP Server Settings** and click **OK**.

8. Verify that the Time service is running.

Configuring DNS and Routing on an ESXi Host

Just as with other servers, your ESXi host needs to know how to contact the other components of your network. You should configure the address of a DNS server that your ESXi host can you use when needed. Likewise, you should configure a default gateway to be used by the VMkernel management port. (I will discuss your networking options in much greater detail in Chapter 2, "Planning and Configuring vSphere Networking.")

Follow the steps in Activity 1-7 to configure the DNS and routing options on your host.

Activity 1-7 Configuring DNS and Routing Options

1. Log on to your vSphere Client.

2. Select **Home**, **Hosts and Clusters**, and then click your host.

3. Open the Configuration tab.

4. In the Software section, choose **DNS and Routing**.

5. Configure the DNS and Default Gateway tabs.

6. Click **OK** to close and apply.

Enabling/Configuring/Disabling Hyperthreading

Hyperthreading is a technique used by processor manufacturers to split the brain of the processor. Although it is not as effective as having more cores, it does provide enhanced performance on some applications. Most Intel Xeon and AMD Opteron processors support hyperthreading, so they enable it in the BIOS of the server. If it is supported by the manufacturer, but not enabled in the BIOS, you can enable it by changing the BIOS settings. You should look for either Logical Processor or Enable Hyperthreading in the BIOS settings.

After hyperthreading is enabled in the BIOS, it is enabled by default on the ESXi host. If you want to disable it, do the following:

1. Log on to the host or vCenter using the vSphere Client. (It is a best practice to use the vCenter to manage hosts after they are part of a vCenter inventory.)

2. Select the host and then open its Configuration tab.

3. Select **Processors** and click **Properties**, as shown in Figure 1-12. (In this case, hyperthreading is not available, but it would be the same link.)

4. Uncheck the **Enabled** check box.

5. Restart the host to make the changes effective. (You may want to vMotion any running servers first.)

Figure 1-12 Enabling/Disabling Hyperthreading on a Host

Of course, to enable hyperthreading again, you just go back through the process and check the **Enable** box to enable and then restart.

Enabling/Sizing/Disabling Memory Compression Cache

Memory compression cache is a method that the VMkernel uses to make the most out of physical RAM when it is getting low and therefore in contention. Chapter 5 covers resources in greater detail. Memory compression is enabled by default and set to a default size of 10% of the VM memory. It is recommended that you leave the settings at the default, which will be best for most organizations. If you choose to disable memory compression cache, you can do so by following the steps outlined in Activity 1-8.

Activity 1-8 Advanced Memory Configuration

1. Log on to your vCenter Server through your vSphere Client.

2. Select your ESXi host and click its Configuration tab.

3. Under Software, select **Advanced Settings**.

4. In the left pane, select **Mem** and locate Mem.MemZipEnable, as shown in Figure 1-13.

5. Enter **0** to disable this function.

6. Click **OK**. (Of course you can enter 1 later on to enable it again.)

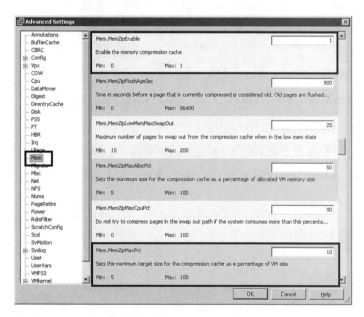

Figure 1-13   Memory Configurations

If you choose to change the size of memory compression cache, follow these steps:

1. Log on to your vCenter Server through your vSphere Client.

2. Select your ESXi host and open its Configuration tab.

3. Under Software, select **Advanced Settings**.

4. In the left pane, select **Mem** and locate Mem.MemZipMaxPct, as shown in Figure 1-13.

5. Enter a % of VM memory between 5 and 100.

6. Click **OK**.

Licensing an ESXi Host

As with vCenter, you have 60 days to use your host without a license, and then you must license the host. You should obtain a key and then add the key by logging on to the ESXi host or the vCenter to which you have added the ESXi host.

To add a key and license the host, follow the steps outlined in Activity 1-9.

Activity 1-9 Adding a License Key to a Host

1. Log on to your vCenter Server or ESXi host with the vSphere Client.

2. Click **Home**, and then select **Licensing** within the icons under Administration.

3. Click **Manage vSphere Licenses** in upper-right corner.

4. Enter the licenses in Enter New vSphere License Keys box (one per line).

5. Enter an optional label below, such as Production Licenses.

6. Verify that the radio button is selected for **Show Unlicensed Assets**.

7. Select the appropriate tab for the license that you want to add (ESX, vCenter Server, Solutions).

8. On the right side, move the radio button from the Evaluation License to the license key that you have entered.

9. Click **Next**.

10. On the left side of Assign Licenses dialog box, select the asset, and on right select the key. Note that keys are "smart" and already "know" what type they are.

11. Repeat the process to assign licenses to all of the hosts. (Pay close attention the tabs.)

12. Click **Next** and verify that all licenses have been assigned.

13. Click **Next** and read the Confirm Changes dialog box to ensure that you have assigned the proper keys to the proper assets.

14. Click **Finish**.

Planning and Performing Upgrades of vCenter Server and VMware ESXi

Until now, I have discussed new installations of vCenter 5.0 and ESXi 5.0; but what if you already have an installation of an earlier vCenter or ESXi product? This section covers the steps involved in planning and performing an upgrade to an existing vCenter and ESXi host. This includes identifying the upgrade requirements and listing the steps to upgrade the vSphere distributed switch, datastores, VMware tools, and VM hardware. This section focuses on performing these updates using the vCenter Update Manager wherever possible. You also learn when an in-place upgrade is appropriate and when you should consider a new installation.

Identifying Upgrade Requirements for ESXi Hosts

As discussed later in this section, you want to use VMware Update Manager (VUM) whenever possible to upgrade your ESXi hosts. This ensures the most "seamless" upgrade and protects your data and server functionality. If you choose to upgrade hosts individually without using VUM, run the Host Agent Pre-Upgrade Checker found on the vSphere Installation Manager. You can upgrade hosts that are ESX4.x /ESXi4.x or later.

I will discuss your options for upgrade later in this section, but for now you just need to make sure the host that you are considering using meets at least the minimum requirements to become an ESXi 5.0 host. To run ESXi 5.0, your host must meet the following criteria:

- **Processor:** 64-bit CPU. Most AMD Opteron and Intel Xeon are supported. (For a complete list, check http://www.vmware.com/resources/compatibility.)

- **Memory:** 2GB minimum (3GB minimum recommended)

- **One or more Ethernet controllers:** 1Gbps and 10Gbps are supported. For best performance, use separate controllers for the management network and the VM networks.

- **Disk storage:** A SCSI adapter, Fibre Channel adapter, converged network adapter, iSCSI adapter, or internal RAID controller.

- **Disk:** A SCSI disk, Fibre Channel LUN, iSCSI disk, or RAID LUN with un-partitioned space: SATA, SCSI, SAS.

> **NOTE** These are the basics without which the upgrade installation will fail. For more details and enhanced performance recommendations, consult the *vSphere Upgrade Guide* at http://pubs.vmware.com.

Identifying Steps Required to Upgrade a vSphere Implementation

The order of the steps involved in the upgrade of a vSphere implementation is every bit as important and the steps themselves. Some steps are irreversible, so doing those at the right time is extremely important. It is highly recommended that you use the VUM software whenever possible to upgrade hosts and VMs. Before you can use the VUM software, you must upgrade the vCenter installation on which it resides. Activity 1-10 outlines the order in which you should upgrade your vSphere implementation.

Activity 1-10 Upgrading vSphere

1. **Upgrade your vCenter Server:** Ensure that your vCenter Server system meets the basic requirements for vCenter 5.0, and then back up your vCenter Server configuration and your inventory database.

   - Must be Virtual Center 2.5 Upgrade 6 or later or vCenter 4.x

   - Number of CPUs: Two 64-bit CPUs or one 64-bit dual core

   - Processor: 2.0GHz or higher Intel or AMD

   - Memory: 4GB RAM minimum

   - Disk storage 4GB minimum

   - Networking: Gigabit connection recommended

   - 64-bit OS (See http://www.pubs.vmware.com, *vSphere Compatibility Matrixes*)

   You can find complete details about backing up your database on Windows and Linux at the following website: http://www.pubs.vmware.com, *vSphere Upgrade Guide*. After the backup is complete, you can upgrade your vCenter by installing the new vCenter over the old one. The installation is almost identical to a new installation of vCenter Server, except for a screen that indicates that a vCenter is detected and asks you whether you want to install over it.

2. **Upgrade your VUM:** Just as with the vCenter Server, you can upgrade your VUM software by installing the new software over the old. You can find the VUM software on the vSphere Installation Manager. You should also download and install the new plug-in for VUM by accessing **Plug-Ins**, **Manage Plug-ins** from the File menu at the top of vCenter Server and then selecting the new VUM plug-in.

3. **Upgrade your ESXi hosts:** Whenever possible, use VUM to update your ESXi hosts (as discussed in more detail later in this section).

4. **Upgrade your VMs:** Whenever possible, use VUM to upgrade the VMware Tools and virtual hardware of your VMs. You must first upgrade VMware Tools, and after that is done you can upgrade the virtual hardware. You will learn about each of these steps in greater detail later in this section.

Upgrading a vSphere Distributed Switch

vSphere distributed switches, first called *vNetwork distributed switches*, were new in vSphere 4.0. Since then, they have been enhanced in vSphere 4.1 and now again in vSphere 5.0. In Chapter 2 I will discuss the architecture of the vSphere distributed switch and the benefits of using them in more detail. For now, you should know that it is possible to upgrade a vSphere distributed switch after upgrading vCenter and ESXi simply by selecting **Upgrade** on the Summary tab, as shown in Figure 1-14.

The reason that you might want to upgrade the switch is to take advantage of new features that the next level offers. However, make sure that all of the ESX/ESXi hosts that you plan on adding to the switch have been upgraded to at least the same level as the switch. Chapter 2 covers the features available on the newest vSphere distributed switch.

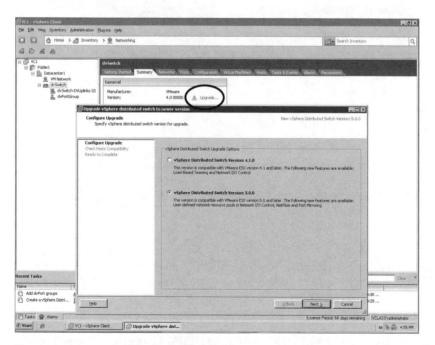

Figure 1-14   Upgrading a vSphere Distributed Switch

Upgrading from VMFS3 to VMFS5

As I will discuss in Chapter 3, "Planning and Configuring vSphere Storage," storage is very different in vSphere 5.0 than it was in earlier versions of vSphere, or at least it can be. When you upgrade your hosts using VUM, your VMFS3 datastores will not automatically upgrade to VMFS5, but you can upgrade them "manually" after the host upgrade is complete. You should perform the steps outlined in Activity 1-11 to upgrade a VMFS3 datastore to a VMFS5 datastore.

Activity 1-11 Upgrading VMFS3 datastores to VMFS5

1. Log on to your vCenter Server through your vSphere Client.

2. Go to the Datastores view and select the VMFS3 datastore that you want to upgrade.

3. Open the Configuration tab, and then select **Upgrade to VMFS-5** at the top of the Datastore Details dialog box, as shown in Figure 1-15.

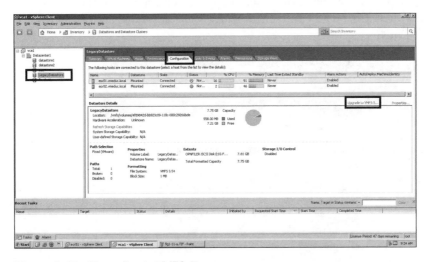

Figure 1-15   Upgrading to VMFS-5

4. Watch the Recent Tasks pane to ensure that the upgrade is successful.

Upgrading VMware Tools

It is possible to upgrade the VMware Tools for each VM by opening a console and selecting **VM**, **Guest**, **Install/Upgrade VMware Tools**, but that would be the hard way. You should upgrade your VMware tools on multiple machines by using the power of VUM. As I mentioned before, you should not upgrade your VMs until after you have successfully upgraded your vCenter, VUM, and ESXi hosts. After that is done, however, you can use VUM to select the VMs that you want to upgrade, and you can upgrade multiple VMs simultaneously. To upgrade your VMware Tools using VUM, follow the procedure outlined in Activity 1-12.

Activity 1-12 Upgrading VMware Tools and Virtual Machine Hardware

1. Select the folder where the VMs reside. If necessary, group the VMs into folders in VMs and Templates view so that you can stay organized.

2. Open the Update Manager tab, as shown in Figure 1-16. This tab should be available once the Update Manager software is installed and the plug-in is enabled.

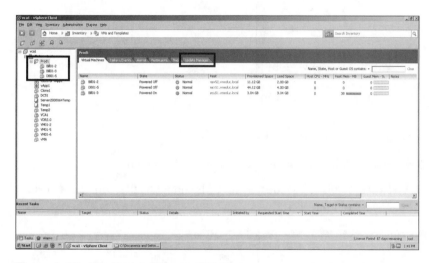

Figure 1-16   The Update Manager Tab

3. Click the **Attach** link on the right of the screen.

4. Check the **VMware Tools Upgrade to Match Host (Predefined)** check box and make sure all others are deselected, as shown in Figure 1-17.

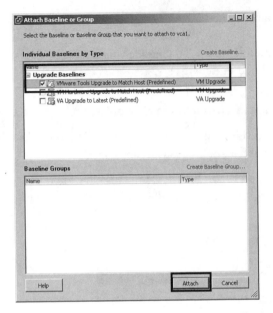

Figure 1-17   Selecting to Upgrade VMware Tools

5. Click **Attach** and verify that the baseline is attached to you VMs.

6. Click the **Scan** link in the upper-right corner of the screen.

7. Select **VMware Tools Upgrades**. Your VMs should be 0% compliant at this point, as shown in Figure 1-18.

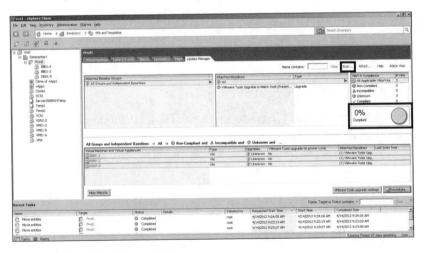

Figure 1-18   Initial Scan of VMs

8. Click **Remediate** and select **VMware Tools Upgrade to Match Host (Pre-defined)**, as shown in Figure 1-19.

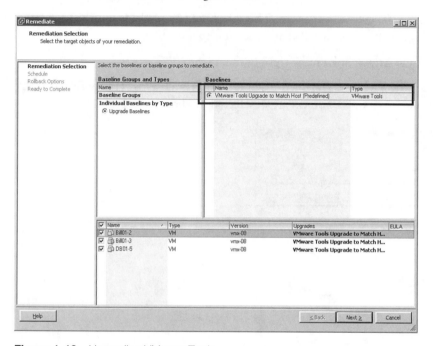

Figure 1-19   Upgrading VMware Tools

9. Verify that VMs that you want to upgrade are selected and click **Next**.

10. Type a name for task and click **Next**. Then, on the Rollback Options page, you can elect to take a snapshot of a VM before remediation (just in case). This is probably not necessary or recommended just to upgrade VMware Tools. Click **Next**.

11. Click **Finish** and watch for the completion of the upgrade in the Recent Tasks pane.

Upgrading Virtual Machine Hardware

After, and only after, you have successfully upgraded your VMware Tools you can begin the process of upgrading the VM virtual hardware to Version 8. As discussed in greater detail in Chapter 4, "Deploying and Administering Virtual Machine and vApps," Version 8 hardware expands the capacity and capabilities of your VMs far beyond that of earlier versions. Even though the steps are almost the same, they are listed here and are also part of Activity 1-12:

12. Select the folder where the VMs reside. If necessary, group the VMs into fold-
    ers in VMs and Templates view so that you can stay organized.

13. Open the Update Manager tab. This tab should be available once the Update
    Manager software is installed and the plug-in is enabled.

14. Click the **Attach** link on the right of the screen.

15. Check the **VMware Hardware Upgrade to Match Host (Predefined)** check
    box and make sure all others are deselected, as shown in Figure 1-20.

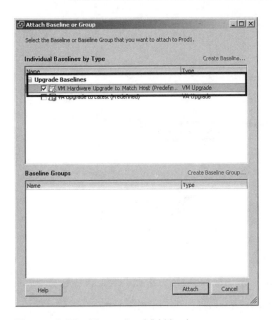

Figure 1-20   Upgrading VM Hardware

16. Click **Attach** and verify that the baseline is attached to your VMs.

17. Click the **Scan** link in the upper-right corner of the screen.

18. Select **VMware Hardware Upgrades**. Your VMs should be 0% compliant at
    this point.

19. Click **Remediate** and select **VMware Hardware Upgrade to Match Host
    (Predefined)**.

20. Verify that VMs that you want to upgrade are selected and click **Next**.

21. On the Rollback Options page, you can elect to take a snapshot of a VM
    before remediation (just in case). This is probably not necessary or recom-
    mended just to upgrade VMware Tools.

22. Click **Finish** and watch for the completion of the upgrade in the Recent Tasks pane.

Upgrading an ESXi Host using vCenter Update Manager

After you have upgraded your vCenter and your VUM, you can use VUM to upgrade your hosts. (This should be done before upgrading your VMs, but I am just covering the exam objectives in order.) Upgrading the host requires that it be placed into Maintenance Mode, so you should ensure that your VMs are either powered down or migrated to another host before you begin the process. If you are upgrading several hosts at the same time, it is possible to further automate the process using DRS and vMotion. Chapter 5 covers DRS and vMotion in detail; for now, let's focus on what is involved in upgrading a single host.

First, ensure that your host meets all of the hardware qualifications to be an ESXi 5.0 host, as outlined earlier in this section. Next, ensure that you have the software image for the new host installation. You may obtain it from the http://www.vmware.com/download or from your VMware representative. After you have the required hardware and the required software, follow the steps outlined in Activity 1-13.

Activity 1-13 Upgrading an ESXi Host

1. Log on to your vCenter Server through your vSphere Client.

2. Select your vCenter Server object in the inventory and open the Update Manager tab.

3. In the upper-right corner, click the **Admin View** link, as shown in Figure 1-21.

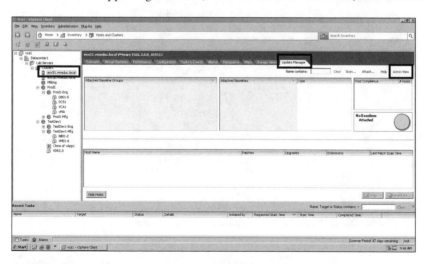

Figure 1-21   The Admin View Link in Update Manager

4. Open the ESXi Images tab and click the Import ESXi images link, as shown in Figure 1-22.

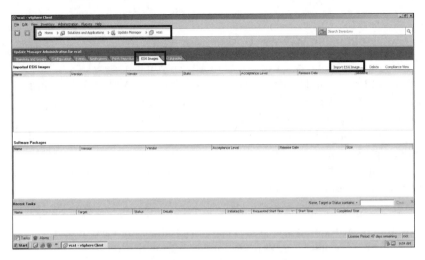

Figure 1-22   BIOS chips and CMOS batteries on typical motherboards

5. On the Select ESXi image page, click **Browse**.

6. Browse to locate your image. It can be on CD/DVD, USB or a shared drive, as shown in Figure 1-23.

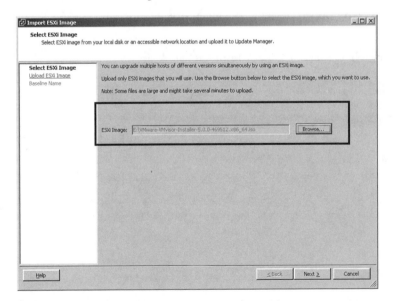

Figure 1-23   Locating and ESXi Image

7. Select the ESXi 5.0 ISO image and click **Open**.

8. Click **Next** and monitor the progress of the image upload, as shown in Figure 1-24.

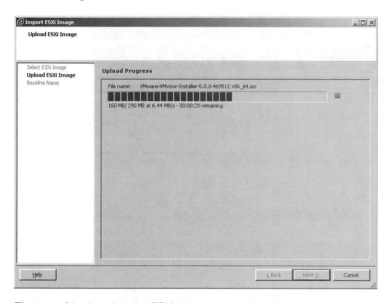

Figure 1-24   Loading the ESXi Image

9. After the upload is complete, click **Next** and give your image a name of your choice, as shown in Figure 1-25.

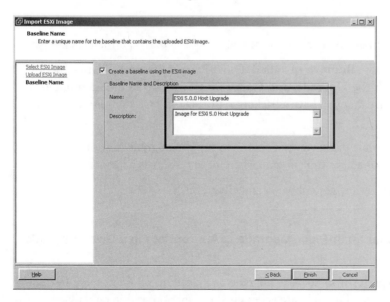

Figure 1-25   Naming the Image

10. Click **Finish**.

11. Open the Baselines and Groups tab, verify that the image has been added, and click the **Compliance View** link, as shown in Figure 1-26.

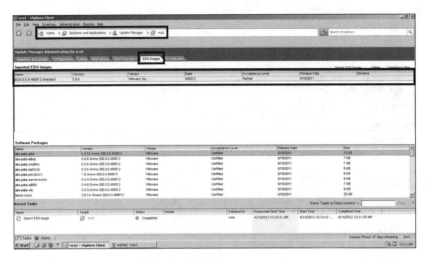

Figure 1-26   Verifying ESXi Image Installation

12. Open the Update Manager tab and click the **Attach** link.

13. Verify that a new entry for your ESXi host appears in the All Groups and Independent Baseline panel.

14. Click **Remediate**.

15. Select your image baseline (if it is not already selected), and then click **Next**.

16. You can choose **Remove Installed Third Party-Software That Is Incompatible with the Upgrade, and Continue With The Remediation**, but you should ensure that you have a backup of the host in case anything were to go wrong.

17. On the Schedule page, you can choose to run the upgrade now or you can schedule it for a later time or date when more resources will be available.

18. Click **Next**, review your choices, and **click** Finish.

Determining Whether an In-Place Upgrade Is Appropriate in a Given Upgrade Scenario

The decision to perform an in-place upgrade or a clean install on new hardware is completely up to you. The software is designed to function well in either case.

Besides, it's not like there are a lot of other applications on those hosts that might not run after the upgrade; it's all very much proprietary to VMware.

That said, you might be influenced by how well your current hardware meets or exceeds the minimum requirements for the new ESXi hosts and possibly vCenter (should you choose a physical server for vCenter). If the hardware does not meet the requirements outlined, your decision is made; you must do a new install on new hardware. If the hardware barely meets the requirements, especially in RAM and processor, you might want to consider new hardware. If your hardware well exceeds the minimum requirements, there is no reason not to upgrade in place and no disadvantage in doing so. Of course, it's always a great idea to have more RAM! To help decide what else might be possible if you had more resources, consult the section on ESXi enhanced performance at http://www.pubs.vmware.com, *vSphere Upgrade Guide*.

Securing vCenter Server and ESXi

In today's security-conscious world, you need every advantage you can get to keep your datacenter secure from malicious attack or even just errant configuration. Both vCenter and ESXi have inherent security features, but you must know how to apply these features to ensure that your virtual datacenter remains as secure as possible. In this section, I will cover the many security features contained in vCenter and ESXi and the best practices for applying them.

In particular, I will identify the common privileges and roles in vCenter and describe how permissions are applied and inherited using these roles. You will also learn about the configuration and administration of the ESXi firewall and how to enable and disable services in the firewall. In addition, you will learn how to enable Lockdown Mode so that an attacker cannot gain access through hacking tools using the root account.

What if I were to tell you that there are network security policy settings for virtual switches that provide a level of security that is not available in the physical world? In this section, I will show you how to configure network security settings that will enhance your security both from external attack as well as from internal attack. Then, I will put it all together and discuss how all of this can be viewed, sorted, exported, cloned, and so on. Finally, I will walk you through a scenario in which we will determine the appropriate set of privileges for the common tasks of managing VMs.

Identifying Common vCenter Server Privileges and Roles

vCenter permissions are very different from Active Directory permissions. Active Directory permissions (as you may know) are based on discretionary access control (DAC) and are for authentication, whereas vCenter permissions are based on role-based access control (RBAC) and are for authorization based on a previous authentication. In other words, vCenter permissions can "piggyback" on Active Directory permissions. In fact, permissions in vCenter are a created by pairing a user or group (usually from Active Directory) with a role in vCenter that is assigned specific privileges. These roles start off simple but the resulting permissions can change depending on where they are applied in your vCenter hierarchy. First, I will discuss general information about the roles, then I will discuss how inheritance affects the roles, and finally I wiil apply them in scenarios so that you can see and understand how the roles work.

There are three different types of roles in vCenter:

- System
- Sample
- Custom

Each of these types has a purpose and there can be multiple roles in each type. The sections that follow provide a brief description of each type of role.

System Roles

System roles are in the vCenter default installation and cannot be changed. There are three system roles, as follows:

- **No Access:** A user or group who is assigned the No Access role to an object cannot see that object when logged on to vCenter. No Access means that it is not even "in their world."

- **Read Only:** A user or group who is assigned the Read Only role can see the objects in the vCenter inventory, but cannot manage the objects. In other words, when the user (usually an administrator) right-clicks the object, the options will be dimmed (grayed out) for that user.

- **Administrator:** A user or group who is assigned the Administrator role for an object has all privileges for that object. When the user right-clicks the object, all options are available.

Sounds simple so far, doesn't it? Well, it is simple on the surface, but it can get a little more complex when applied. Now let's talk about the second type of role, sample roles.

Sample Roles

Sample roles are also in the default vCenter installation. They are "suggestions" from years of best practice as to what privileges would be appropriate for a certain type of administrative role. You can change these sample roles, but I do not recommend it.

Instead, you can simply clone (copy) the role and give it new name, and then you will have both options. (I discuss cloning roles later in this section.) It is not necessary that you know all of the privileges that are associated with each sample role, just know that they were chosen from experience and best practice. The following are sample roles that are included with a default installation of vCenter Server:

- Virtual machine power user
- Virtual machine user
- Resource pool administrator
- VMware consolidated backup user
- Datastore consumer
- Network consumer

Custom Roles

Of course, there might be many other role configurations that you want to create for your environment. When you create additional roles in vCenter, these are referred to as *custom* roles. Custom roles that you create can and should have only the specific privileges that are required to perform the tasks associated with that role. You will learn how to create custom roles later in this section.

Describing How Permissions are Applied and Inherited in vCenter Server

To create permissions, you choose a user or group, pair it to a role, and then apply the user/role pairing to an object in your vCenter inventory. You should apply the user/role pairing to the highest object in the vCenter inventory to which the permission will apply, and then allow the permissions to propagate to child objects. This enables you to manage from the top down, which is much easier and much more organized, as illustrated in greater detail later in this section.

Common rules that apply in other types of permissions, such as "most restrictive wins," might not apply in vCenter permissions. One rule that applies all of the time in vCenter permissions is that the most specific and most directly applied permission wins. In other words, a permission that is applied directly to an object supersedes a permission that has been inherited for the same object. Also, a permission that is applied to a user supersedes that which the user has inherited by being in a group.

Later in this section, you will learn how you set the user/role pairing and the propagation that enables inheritance. For now, it is important that you understand the affect of any settings that you might choose to apply. The following are examples to help you understand the affect of permissions inheritance.

Example 1: Permissions That Apply Directly to an Object Supersede Those That Are Inherited

John has the Administrator role for Datacenter1, and the user/role pairing is applied at Datacenter1 and propagated to all objects within the datacenter, as shown in Figure 1-27. However, John has also been assigned the No Access role at VM2. If John is the one logged on, is the picture even correct? Hopefully, you said "No," because the No Access role applied to John for VM2 would actually prevent him from seeing it at all. As for all of the other components of the inventory, John would have all privileges.

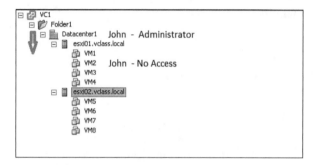

Figure 1-27   Direct Supersedes Inherited

Example 2: If a User Is a Member of More Multiple Groups, the User Is Assigned the Union of the Privileges for Each Group

This example, shown in Figure 1-28, involves John and two co-workers, Kim and Dave. John is a member of two AD global groups, which we will just call GroupA and GroupB. GroupA's user/role pairing allows users to power VMs on. GroupB allows users to take snapshots of VMs. The user/role pairing is applied to Datacenter1 and propagated to the entire inventory.

Because John is a member of both groups, he is allowed to power on VMs and take snapshots. Kim, who is a member of only GroupA, can power on VMs but cannot take snapshots. Dave, who is a member of only GroupB, can take snapshots but cannot power on VMs.

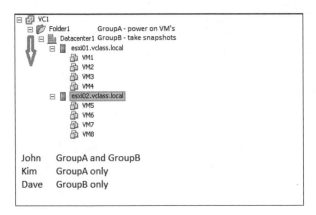

Figure 1-28 Union of Privileges

Example 3: User/Role Pairings Applied Directly to an Object Supersede User/Role Pairings That Are Inherited

This example, shown in Figure 1-29, involves John and two co-workers, Kim and Dave. John is a member of two AD global groups, which we will just call GroupA and GroupB. GroupA is assigned the Administrator role and the user/role pairing is applied to Datacenter1 and propagated throughout the inventory. GroupB is assigned the Read Only role for VM4. John is member of both GroupA and GroupB. Kim is a member of only GroupA. Dave is a member of only GroupB.

Because John is a member of both GroupA and GroupB, he will have administrative privileges for the entire Datacenter1, with the exception of VM4. For VM4, John will have Read Only permissions. Kim, however, will have administrative privileges for entire Datacenter1 without exception because she is not a member of GroupB. Dave can see VM4, but he cannot manage it. Dave also cannot see the rest of Datacenter1.

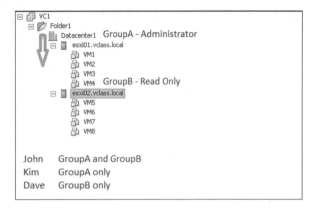

Figure 1-29   Direct Permissions on Groups Supersede Inherited

Example 4: Permissions That Are Applied Directly to a User Supersede Permissions That Are Inherited Through Group Membership

This example, shown in Figure 1-30, only involves John. In this example, John is a member of GroupA and GroupB. GroupA is user/role paired to a custom role that allows the powering on of VMs. GroupB is user/role paired to a custom role that allows snapshots to be taken on VMs. John's user account is also user/role paired to a role that gives Read Only permissions. All are assigned to Datacenter1 and propagated.

The user/role pairing associated directly with John's account supersedes the user/role pairings associated to GroupA and GroupB because they are inherited. The result will be that John will have a nice "picture" of Datacenter1 when he logs on, but he will not be able to manage any of it. If he right-clicks any object, all options will be grayed out.

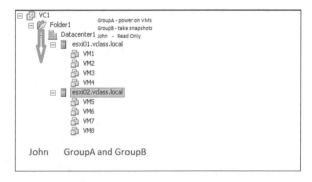

Figure 1-30   User Permissions Supersede Group Permissions

I hope these examples have helped you to see how your settings can affect what a user sees and what the user can do. Later in this section, I will cover how to create, clone, and edit, vCenter Server roles.

Configuring and Administering the ESXi Firewall

In general, firewalls are used to keep things in or keep things out of your network. The ESXi firewall is no exception. It a is service-oriented stateless firewall that you can customize for your needs. This means that you can configure the ESXi firewall to allow or block services and ports. In addition, beginning with ESXi 5.0, you can also configure the firewall to only allow specified IP addresses or specified ranges of addresses to connect to your ESXi server.

By default, the ESXi firewall is configured to block all incoming and outgoing traffic except for the default services of Secure Shell (SSH), Domain Name System (DNS), Dynamic Host Configuration Protocol (DHCP) client, and Simple Network Management Protocol (SNMP) server. You can manage the firewall through the vSphere Client to enable other services that you want to be able to use. You should only allow services that you will actually use, because each new service creates a new potential vulnerability. In addition, the ESXi 5.0 firewall is extensible; in other words, you can add new rules for new services using XML files and the ESXCLI.

To configure your ESXi firewall, follow the steps outlined in Activity 1-14.

Activity 1-14 Configuring an ESXi Firewall

1. Log on to your vCenter using the vSphere Client.

2. In Hosts and Clusters view, click your host.

3. Open the Configuration tab and choose **Security Profile** under Software.

4. Click the **Properties** link next to Services to enable and disable specific services and daemons. You can click options to set whether a service starts automatically, starts and stops with the host, or must be started manually.

5. Click **OK** to save any changes.

6. Click the **Properties** link next to Firewall. You will see the services that are enabled indicated by a checked box, as shown in Figure 1-31. You can enable additional services by checking more boxes, but you should only enable what you really plan to use.

7. By default, connections are allowed from all source addresses. If you want to add a filter that only allows a specified IP address or a specified network to connect, click **Firewall** and enter the IP address or networks that you will allow.

> **NOTE** These precise scripts used to add new services to the firewall are not part of this study, but you can obtain more information about them at http://www.vmware. com, *vSphere 5.0 Operations Guide*.

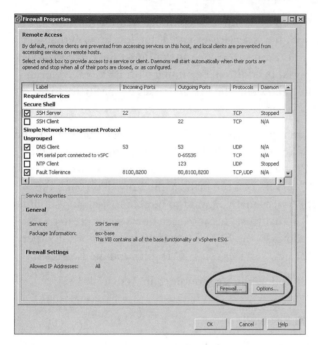

Figure 1-31 Firewall Configuration

Enabling Lockdown Mode

Lockdown Mode increases the security of your ESXi host. When you enable Lockdown Mode, only the vpxuser can access the host remotely. In addition, the root account can only access the Direct Console User Interface (DCUI) of a host if it has a local connection. Because the vpxuser exists on the vCenter, this means that all connections to the ESXi host with anything but the DCUI or the vCenter Server will be blocked. External management tools such as the vCLI, vMA, and vSphere PowerCLI are blocked from direct access to the host but can leverage the vCenter to manage and maintain the hosts. For those who can access the host, all of the same services are available as if it were not in Lockdown Mode.

You can enable Lockdown Mode when you install the ESXi host, or you can also enable or disable Lockdown Mode of a specific host through the vSphere Client. To enable Lockdown Mode on a host, do the following:

1. Log on to your vCenter using the vSphere Client.

2. In Hosts and Clusters view, click your host.

3. Open the Configuration tab and choose **Security Profile** under Software.

4. Scroll down past the firewall settings and click **Edit** next to Lockdown Mode, as shown in Figure 1-32.

5. Check the **Enable Lockdown Mode** check box and click **OK**.

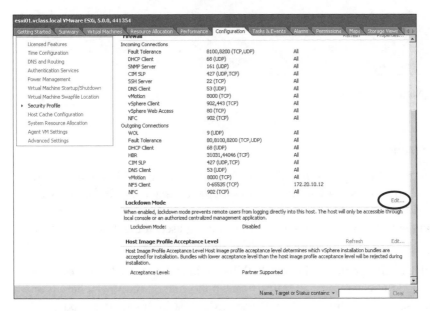

Figure 1-32 Lockdown Mode

Configuring Network Security Policies

You can configure network security policies on standard switches and on port groups for both standard and distributed switches. Network security policies allow you to apply security settings that are only available because of the virtualization layer and are not available in the physical world.

You can configure three network security policies:

- Promiscuous Mode

- MAC Address Changes

- Forged Transmits

I will now cover these in detail. Figure 1-33 shows the default settings for these network security policies.

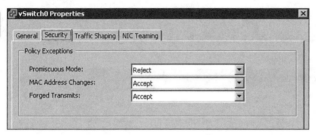

Figure 1-33 Network Security Policies

Promiscuous Mode

In normal (non-Promiscuous) mode, a network interface card (NIC) examines traffic to see whether a destination MAC address matches its address. If the destination MAC address of the traffic does match its address, the NIC further processes the traffic and sends the data up the stack to the awaiting user. If the destination MAC address is different from its address, the NIC simply discards the traffic.

It is possible to change the setting on the NIC (or in this case vNIC) to Promiscuous Mode and thereby receive all traffic to an application on the VM. There is a "good guy" scenario to this as well as a "bad guy" scenario. If you (the good guy) want to run an intrusion detection system (IDS) on the VM, you want to allow all traffic to come into the vNIC and be passed up the stack to the IDS. However, if a rogue administrator within your organization wants to run a protocol analyzer from the VM, you want to stop the attacker from receiving all traffic.

The bottom line is that, because the Promiscuous Mode setting on the virtual switches and port groups defaults to Reject, only the traffic that is actually destined to the vNICs on the VMs is passed through, regardless of the setting in the operating system of the VM itself. In other words, all traffic that is not destined for the VMs on the switch or port group is discarded. The rogue VM administrator cannot change this setting because he does not control the switch. Because you do control the switch, however, you can set up another special port group for your IDS in which you allow Promiscuous Mode. This is a "best of both worlds scenario, and it is only available because of the virtualization layer. Chapter 2 covers port groups in much greater detail.

MAC Address Changes

When you create a VMware virtual machine, it is automatically assigned a MAC address. The MAC address that it is assigned will very likely begin with 00-0C-29 or 00-50-56. These are the two vendor IDs that VMware uses most commonly. (Of course, the MAC address also has six more characters.) If a rogue administrator wants to change that MAC address as part of an attack, he changes the last six characters to something that cannot be tracked back to him. This is commonly done by hackers to "hide their tracks."

Now, here's the catch: If he were to do that and you had your MAC Address Changes set to Reject, the VMkernel would not allow traffic to flow to the new effective MAC address. In other words, the VMkernel would know that the new effective MAC address was different from the initial address and would not allow it to be used. Pretty cool, isn't it?

Forged Transmits

The other thing that an attacker might want to do is make traffic appear to be coming from a different source MAC address. In this case, the attacker uses software to create packets that have a bogus (forged) source. If the attacker tries this, and you have your Forged Transmits set to Reject, the switch checks to see whether the MAC addresses on the packets are truly MAC addresses that are assigned to the VMs. Because they are not, the switch discards the traffic and does not allow it to leave the virtual switch.

NOTE   You might have noticed that the default settings for MAC Address Changes and Forged Transmits are both Accept. This is because, if you are using VMware Converter to convert a physical machine to a virtual machine (P2V) or you are using Microsoft Cluster Server Network Load Balancing (NLB) in Unicast Mode, these settings must remain at "accept." Otherwise, you can consider changing them to Reject. The main point is that these are additional security options that are not available in most physical environments.

Viewing/Sorting/Exporting User and Group Lists

One of the nice things about vSphere is that so many types of things are recognized as objects that you can control. In fact, VMs, hosts, datacenters, datastores, folders, and much more are all objects. One of the advantages to this is that objects can be assigned permissions. When you click any object in the console pane (left side) of your vCenter Server, the Permissions tab for that object appears on the right side. If you open that tab, you can view the permissions assignments for that object, as shown in Figure 1-34. You can use the column names to sort the report in alphabetic order for User/Group, Role, or Defined In, whichever helps you see it best. If you want to export the list to a report, you can export it to a web page (HTML format), XLS, CSV, or XML format.

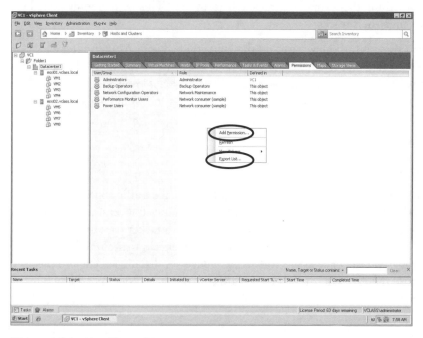

Figure 1-34 User/Group Lists

Adding/Modifying/Removing Permissions for Users and Groups on vCenter Inventory Objects

To add permission, you can right-click the object in the console pane or you can right-click in the blank area below the permissions that are already there and you can assign additional permissions. Then you can select a user or group from those that are in your system or populated by centralized authentication, such as Active Directory, and pair it to a role. The last decision is whether to allow the user/role pairing to propagate down from the object to which you will assign it. As a best practice, you should assign the permissions at the highest point in the hierarchy and let the propagation work for you rather than against you. In this case, I am pairing the Backup Operators global group from the VCLASS domain with the Backup Operators assigned role in my vCenter inventory, as shown in Figure 1-35.

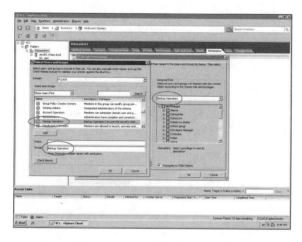

Figure 1-35 User/Role Pairing

It's also easy to modify or remove permission using the same tool. The main thing to keep in mind is that you must be on the object to which the permissions are applied to remove the permissions assignment. If you are looking at permissions where they are not actually assigned, there will be a blue hot-link to help you quickly get to the object where they are assigned. For example, the permissions for Administrator in Figure 1-34 are actually assigned at the root (VC1). If you are reading this in color, you will notice a blue link for VC1.

Creating/Cloning/Editing vCenter Server Roles

As I mentioned previously, roles are sets of privileges that allow users to perform tasks. They are grouped into three categories, system, sample, and custom. Earlier, you learned the difference between these roles; now you will learn how you can create, clone, and edit roles.

Creating Roles

When you create a role, you should only assign the necessary privileges for that role. In other words, you should think through what privileges a person would need to perform the tasks that would be expected from that role. For example, a person who is going to create VMs needs the privileges to assign a network, datastore, resource pool, on so on. A role that is created with these privileges might be named Virtual Machine Creator and would give the user only the necessary permissions to create VMs and only the permissions to create them the way that you want them created. To create a new role in vCenter, follow these steps outlined in Activity 1-15.

Activity 1-15 Creating a Role in vCenter

1. Log on to your vCenter Server using your vSphere Client.

2. Click **Home**, and then, under Administration, select **Roles**.

3. Above the list of roles, click **Add Role**, as shown in Figure 1-36.

4. Give the role a name and then select the specific privileges for the role. (As you can see, there are many to choose from in the list.)

5. When you finish selecting privileges, click **OK**.

6. You can then assign the role to a user and log on to test the role.

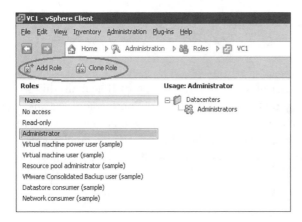

Figure 1-36   Viewing, Adding, Cloning Roles

Cloning Roles

There sure were a lot privileges to choose from, weren't there? How can you possibly know what will work well for what you have in mind? Well, the good news is that you don't have to start out "from scratch" because you have the sample roles.

Suppose, for instance, that you want to create a role that has to do with managing resource pools. (I will discuss resource pools in detail in Chapter 5.) Now, let's say that you examine the privileges associated with the sample role Resource Pool Administrator and find them to be close to what you want, but not exactly. Have no fear, simply clone the role and give it a new name; then make your changes so as to create the role you need. To clone a role in vCenter, follow the steps outlined in Activity 1-16.

Activity 1-16 Cloning a Role in vCenter

1. Log on to vCenter with your vSphere Client.

2. Click **Home**, and then, under Administration, select **Roles**, as shown in Figure 1-37.

Figure 1-37   The Roles Pane Icon

3. Right-click the role that you want to clone and select **Clone**, as shown in Figure 1-38.

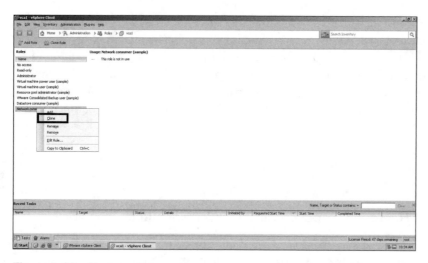

Figure 1-38 Cloning a Role

4. In the window shown in Figure 1-39, type a new name for the role.

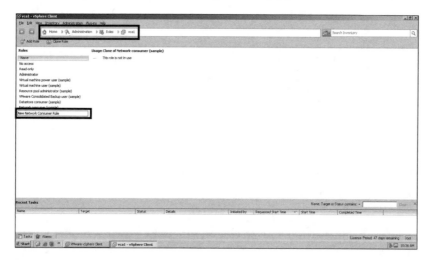

Figure 1-39 Renaming a Cloned Role

5. You can now edit the role to create the exact permission that you need.

Editing Roles

After you have cloned a role, you will likely want to edit the privileges for that role. Also, from time to time you may want to edit the roles that you have put into place in your vCenter. When you edit a role, you should give only the necessary permissions to perform the tasks that will be expected of a user paired with that role. To edit a role, do the following:

1. Log on to vCenter with your vSphere Client.

2. Click **Home**, and then, under Administration, select **Roles**.

3. Right click the role that you want to edit and then select **Edit Role**, as shown in Figure 1-40.

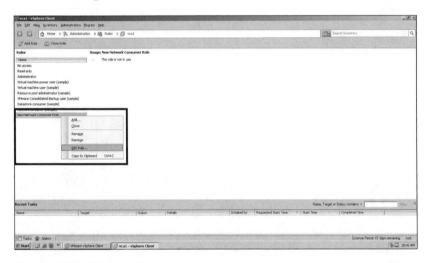

Figure 1-40   Editing a Role

4. You can change the privileges as needed for all categories of the Role. When you have finished editing the role, click **OK** to close and save, as shown in Figure 1-41.

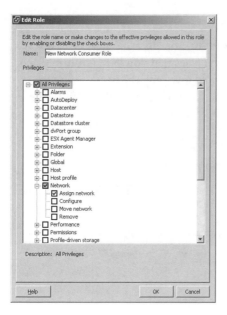

Figure 1-41   Editing Role Privileges

NOTE   A particularly astute reader might be wondering why we didn't just edit the sample role. Although this certainly can be done, it is not a best practice. If you edit the sample role, and then find out later that it was actually better than your new role, then how will you know how to get back to the sample? There will be many things that we will discuss as being technically possible but not recommended. I tell my students that if they don't believe that something could be technically possible but still a bad idea, they should watch the movie *Jurassic Park* one more time!

Adding an ESXi Host to a Directory Service

As you know, most of the time you will manage a host through the vCenter after the host has been added. Sometimes, however, you might want to log on to the host directly to do something that you cannot do through vCenter. This might include collecting logs, configuring backups, or just using the host logon as a "back door" when there is an issue with vCenter.

Because the only account that is defined by default on the host is the "root" user, it might seem that you would have to be assigned root permissions or that a special account might have to be created on every host. Well, this used to be the case, but not anymore. You can now configure the ESXi host to join a domain so that your account can be authenticated against your centralized directory system (AD or NIS). That means that you can use your AD administrative credentials (for example) to logon directly to a host that has been joined to the domain. Don't worry, though; you can still use those special accounts on each host if you need to, because this can be used in addition to or in place of the old model. To join a host to a centralized authentication service, follow the steps outlined in Activity 1-17.

Activity 1-17 Joining an ESXi Hosts in Centralized Authentication

1. Log on to vCenter with your vSphere Client.

2. Click **Home**, and then, under Inventory, select **Hosts and Clusters**.

3. Select the ESXi host, and then open its Configuration tab.

4. Under Software, select **Authentication Services**, and then click the **Properties** link in the upper right, as shown in Figure 1-42.

5. Select **Active Directory** or **NIS** and enter the domain.

6. If you are using a proxy server (optional), enter the information for the proxy.

7. Click **Join Domain** and enter your administrative credentials for the domain and click **Join Domain** again and then **OK**. (Don't worry that the grayed out still indicates "local" before you click OK. If you click Properties again, you should see that is has changed to the centralized service.)

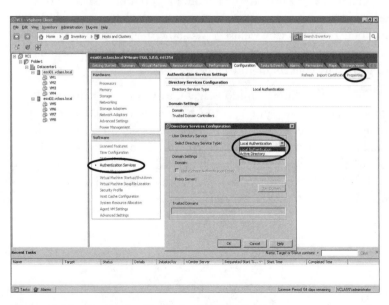

Figure 1-42 Configuring Centralized Authentication

Applying Permissions to ESXi Hosts Using Host Profiles

I will cover host profiles in detail in Chapter 5. Suffice it to say for now that host profiles enable you to take a baseline from a reference host on which you have configured everything just the way you want it. Then, if you want to make more hosts just like that one, you can apply the baseline to a target host and change its configuration to match the reference host. This, of course, includes any permissions that were assigned directly to the host. Prior to the capability of adding the host to the domain, this would have been considered a time-saver; now, it is not quite as important, but it can certainly "piggyback" on configuration changes that are more important to you.

Determining the Appropriate Set of Privileges for Common Tasks in vCenter Server

As noted previously, the main thing about the appropriate set of privileges is that they are the bare-minimum privileges to get the job done. Otherwise, you might as well just give everyone the Administrator role and hope for the best. You will know best what privileges a user needs to perform the task at hand in your organization. The nice thing is that the permissions are very granular and therefore you can assign only what is specifically required. As mentioned previously, you can also start with the Sample roles, clone, and go from there.

Identifying vSphere Architecture and Solutions

This topic wraps us all of the way back to the beginning of our discussion in this chapter. In fact, if we were not following the blueprint "to the letter," I might have put this first. This topic relates to why we use VMs and virtual datacenters in the first place. In addition, it points to where it is all going and what vSphere will have to do with the ever-growing concept of "the cloud."

In particular, I will discuss the vSphere editions again, paying most attention not to what you get with a certain license, but rather to what you do not get if you don't take the next step up from there. You also learn best practices in the structure of your datacenter and the components from which you can choose. Finally, I will do my best to identify what a cloud is and how it is all related to vSphere. Through it all, you might be able to determine the most appropriate vSphere edition for you and your organization.

Identifying Available vSphere Editions and Features

How should you decide which level of vSphere is right for your organization? Take a look back at Table 1-2; you will notice that the license with the least features is Standard. Although this might be fine for a small organization, many features are not supported on Standard but are supported on the next step up, Enterprise. In my opinion, some of these features might also be helpful to an organization of any size (for example, Storage vMotion, DRS, and fault tolerance). If you are considering Enterprise versus Enterprise Plus, I might point out that you get host profiles and distributed virtual switches only with Enterprise Plus. We discuss each of these technologies in detail later, but the point is that this is just my opinion. You should make your decision based on what your organization needs, as you continue to learn more about each feature. In other words, keep reading for now and make the important decisions later.

Explaining ESXi and vCenter Server Architectures

Architecture is defined as a style of construction. I think that is a very good way to look at ESXi and vCenter architectures, as well, because styles are individual and change over time. In other words, the most powerful thing about your architecture is that is can be customized to meet your needs and changed over time as needed.

That said, every ESXi and vCenter architecture has some common elements. Using vCenter allows you to aggregate (pull together) the resources from multiple ESXi hosts and then distribute them to the VMs of your choice. You are the "puppeteer" behind the scenes who controls all of the CPU, RAM, disk, and network resources that the VMs "see." With full virtualization, the operating systems of the VMs are not even aware of what is actually going on. You present the resources to them in a way that they can understand them and work with them, and you can prioritize between specific VMs or groups of VMs.

In addition, you use many fewer physical computers because each physical host can now run multiple VMs. Of course, if you are going to put "all of your eggs in one basket," you had best have some services and features to provide for availability, security, and scalability. To address this concern, VMware provides features that we discuss later such as vMotion, Storage vMotion, HA, DRS, fault tolerance, and so on, and continues to add features as needs arise. Again, it's a little early in the book to discuss what might be best for you, but you can rest assured that I will discuss each one of these features in detail and in order. Figure 1-43 shows the vSphere Architecture.

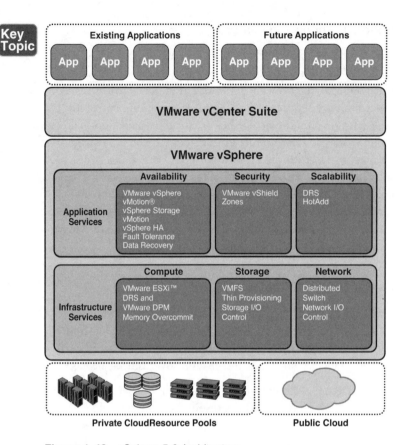

Figure 1-43   vSphere 5.0 Architecture

Explaining Private/Public/Hybrid Cloud Concepts

I think if you were to ask 5 people what a *cloud* is you would get 10 different responses. To explain this in simple terms, let me use the analogy of an electric socket in your home. When you plug anything into an electric socket, you expect to get power, and you expect that device to run, because that's the way it was designed. You would be surprised if it did not run based on the power that was there or if it ran in some erratic way. You would just expect to plug it in and use it.

Now let's relate our analogy to computers and devices of the present day and of the future. The kids who are growing up today, and texting their friends about every peanut butter and jelly sandwich they eat, just expect this stuff to work. They don't care where the resources are coming from or how they are actually working to their benefit. Some of the computing resources might come from their device, and others might come from their service provider; they don't have to know the details.

In other words, a cloud is not so much a product as it is a service, as shown in Figure 1-44. It's a service that provides the resources necessary to accomplish the task for the user who has plugged into it with the appropriate device. The appropriate device could be could be a user's desktop or server, an iPhone, iPad, Android device, or even something yet to be invented. The point is that the user who connects with the appropriate device will expect that the resources to accomplish the task will be provided by the cloud, no matter how much CPU, RAM, storage, network, content, or monitoring is needed.

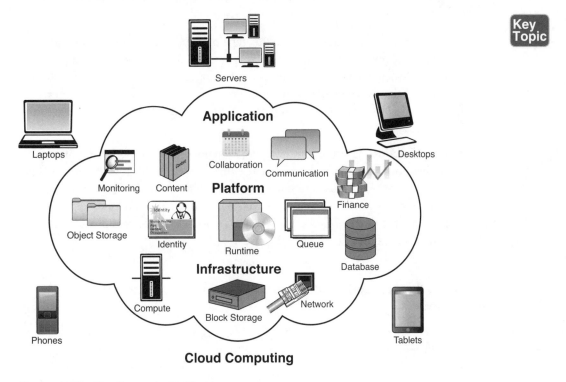

Figure 1-44   The Concept of a Cloud

So that is the general concept of a cloud, but you should also know that there are three main types of clouds that you can use in your organization or for your organization, as follows:

- **Private clouds:** In a private cloud, all of the resources such as CPU, RAM, disk, and networking are aggregated (pulled together) and then can be distributed to multiple entities for their individual needs. This can be done while maintaining full control and ownership of the resources and prioritizing where necessary. Does this familiar? That's right; vSphere is a perfect example of a private cloud. In fact, a virtualized environment like vSphere is absolutely essential for any type of cloud.

- **Public clouds:** As you may have guessed, public clouds are created by companies that then make those resources available to the general public. This means that the end user can obtain a service without having to invest the time and money to set up the infrastructure that would normally be required for the service. The tradeoff is that an organization does not have as tight a control or ownership of the resources or of the prioritization of those resources for specific services.

  Still, some organizations choose this type of cloud because it is faster and easier to implement. Companies such as Azure and Amazon provide compute capacity associated with web application development. Many others offer storage capacity that is accessible from anywhere that you have access to the Internet. These are just a couple of examples of public clouds; there are many, many more.

- **Hybrid clouds:** As you might imagine, in many organizations a combination of these two concepts is used in an attempt to provide the best of both worlds. The private cloud is used to enhance security and control of resources that require it; meanwhile, a public cloud is used to save time and money on new projects that fit that mold. In this way, a hybrid cloud concept gives the organization the best of both virtual worlds.

Determining the Appropriate vSphere Edition Based on Customer Requirements

So now let's say that you are consulting with someone else and they want to know which edition is best for them. Suppose that money is tight and they just want to choose the right edition for their needs. How could they know what they might end up needing even before they have begun? The answer, they can't... and VMware knows it! That's why VMware allows them (and you) to have all of the features and benefits for 60 days to evaluate and decide what you think will be most important for your organization. If you think about it, that's a good amount of time to make a determination. How many other things do you get to "try on" for 60 days?

Summary

The main topics covered in this chapter are the following:

- I began this chapter by discussing the installation of vCenter Server and the ESXi host. I then turned to the deployment of the vCenter appliance and of the vCenter Server as a VM, including sizing the database.

- You also learned about securing vCenter Server and ESXi, including the ESXi firewall, network security policies, user group lists, and server roles.

- Finally I discussed vCenter architecture and its role in the clouds of today and tomorrow.

Exam Preparation Tasks

Review All of the Key Topics

Review the most important topics from inside the chapter, noted with the Key Topic icon in the outer margin of the page. Table 1-3 lists these key topics and the page numbers where each is found.

Table 1-3 Key Topics for Chapter 1

Key Topic Element	Description	Page Number
Table 1-2	vSphere 5.0 Editions	6
Activity 1-1	Deploying the VCA from an OVF Template	10
Bullet List	Requirements for vCenter	14
Activity 1-2	Installing vCenter	15
Activity 1-3	Downloading and Installing a Plug-In	18
Activity 1-4	Applying a License to vCenter	19
Activity 1-5	Performing an Interactive Installation of ESXi	23
Bullet List	Most Important Components of Auto Deploy	25
Activity 1-6	Configuring NTP on a Host in vCenter	26
Activity 1-7	Configuring DNS and Routing Options	27
Activity 1-8	Advanced Memory Configuration	29
Activity 1-9	Adding a License Key to a Host	30
Bullet List	Minimum Requirements for ESXi Host	31
Activity 1-10	Upgrading vSphere	32
Activity 1-11	Upgrading VMFS3 Datastores to VMFS5	34
Activity 1-12	Upgrading VMware Tools and Virtual Machine Hardware	35
Activity 1-13	Upgrading an ESXi Host	39
Bullet List	System Roles	44
Activity 1-14	Configuring and ESXi Firewall	49
Figure 1-33	Network Security Policies	52
Activity 1-15	Creating a Role in vCenter	56
Activity 1-16	Cloning an Role in vCenter	57

Key Topic Element	Description	Page Number
Activity 1-17	Joining an ESXi Host to Centralized Authentication	61
Figure 1-43	vSphere Architecture	64
Figure 1-44	The Concept of a Cloud	65

Review Questions

The answers to these review questions are in Appendix A.

1. Which of the following features are supported with Enterprise Plus but not with Enterprise? (Choose two.)

    a. Storage I/O control

    b. Distributed switch

    c. DRS

    d. Hot add

2. Which of the following is *not* a basic requirement for CPU for vCenter Server 5.0?

    a. 64-bit

    b. Two CPUs or dual-core

    c. 2.0GHz higher

    d. Hyperthreading enabled

3. Which of the following is *not* one of the minimum requirements for an ESXi 5.0 host?

    a. 64-bit CPU

    b. 4GB RAM

    c. One or more Ethernet controllers

    d. Unpartitioned space

4. Which of the following is the correct order to upgrade your vSphere installation?

   a. VUM, vCenter, hosts, VMs

   b. vCenter, hosts, VMs, VUM

   c. VUM, hosts, VMs, vCenter

   d. vCenter, VUM, Hosts, VMs

5. Which of the following is *not* a system role in vCenter?

   a. No Access

   b. Virtual Machine User

   c. Administrator

   d. Read Only

6. Which of the following is *not* a sample role in vCenter?

   a. Virtual machine power user

   b. Administrator

   c. Virtual machine user

   d. Datastore consumer

7. Which of following are true about vCenter permissions? (Choose two.)

   a. Permissions that are applied to a user take precedence over those applied to a group in which the user is a member.

   b. Permissions that are applied to a group take precedence over those that are applied to a user.

   c. Permissions that are applied to multiple groups result in only the least privilege for the user.

   d. Permissions that are applied to multiple groups result in the user receiving the union of the privileges.

8. Which of the following tools enable you to manage a host that is in Lockdown Mode? (Choose two.)

   a. DCUI

   b. PowerCLI

   c. vMA

   d. vCenter

9. Which of the following is a network security policy that is set by default to Reject?

   a. Forged Transmits

   b. Promiscuous Mode

   c. MAC Address Changes

   d. NIC Teaming

10. Which type of cloud offers the most control of resources and the prioritization of those resources?

   a. Public

   b. Private

   c. Hybrid

   d. No cloud offers control of resources.

This chapter covers the following subjects:

- Configuring vSphere Standard Switches
- Configuring vSphere Distributed Switches
- Configuring vSS and vDS Policies

CHAPTER 2

Planning and Configuring vSphere Networking

In our discussion on vSphere networking, I will address many topics such as vSphere standard switches (vSS), vSphere distributed switches (vDS), port groups, and the properties for all of these. It's easy to get overwhelmed in all the terminology, especially when most of the components are not something that you can see or hold in your hand. To keep from becoming overwhelmed with the technology, I want you to focus on two primary questions. The first question is, "What type of connections can I create and what do they do?" The second is, "Where does the 'virtual world' meet the 'physical world,' and how is that point of reference defined?" If you just focus on these two questions, I believe that the rest of the picture will come to your mind.

That said, this section covers configuring vSSs, configuring vDSs, and configuring vSS and vDS policies. In each section, I will explain why these should be configured, and then I will discuss how you can configure them. In addition, I will walk you through the steps to configure each of these settings.

"Do I Know This Already?" Quiz

The "Do I Know This Already?" quiz allows you to assess whether you should read this entire chapter or simply jump to the "Exam Preparation Tasks" section for review. If you are in doubt, read the entire chapter. Table 2-1 outlines the major headings in this chapter and the corresponding "Do I Know This Already?" quiz questions. You can find the answers in Appendix A, "Answers to the 'Do I Know This Already?' Quizzes and Chapter Review Questions."

Table 2-1 "Do I Know This Already?" Section-to-Question Mapping

Foundations Topics Section	Questions Covered in This Section
Configuring vSphere Standard Switches	1–3
Configuring vSphere Distributed Switches	4–6
Configuring vSS and vDS Policies	7–10

1. Which of following will result if you choose **Add Networking** on the Networking link of your ESXi host?

   a. You can add a new VMkernel port to an existing switch.

   b. You can add a new VM port to an existing switch.

   c. You will be creating a new vSS.

   d. You can add a new vmnic to an existing switch.

2. Which of the following is *not* a common use of a VMkernel port?

   a. IP storage

   b. Storage vMotion

   c. vMotion

   d. Management

3. Which of the following is true about switch and port group policies on a vSS?

   a. Switch settings override port group settings.

   b. You cannot configure port group settings different from switch settings.

   c. There are no switch settings on a vSS.

   d. Port group settings override switch settings for the VMs on the port group.

4. What is the maximum number of hosts that can be connected to a single vDS?

   a. 32

   b. 1000

   c. 350

   d. 100

5. Which of the following is the minimum license requirement to create a vDS?

   a. Enterprise Plus

   b. Enterprise

   c. Advanced

   d. Essentials

6. Which view should you be in to add a host to an existing vDS?

   a. Hosts and Clusters

   b. Networking

   c. vSphere

   d. VMs and Templates

7. Which of the following is *not* a common policy for vSS switch and port groups?

   a. Traffic shaping

   b. NIC teaming

   c. Permissions

   d. Security

8. Which of the following is true about vDS policies?

   a. Policies set at the port group level override those are the port level.

   b. Policies cannot be set at the port level.

   c. Policies are always set at the port level.

   d. Policies set at the port level override policies set at the port group level.

9. Which of the following is *not* a load-balancing option in vSphere?

   a. Route based on the originating virtual port ID

   b. Beacon probing

   c. Route based on source MAC hash

   d. Route based on IP hash

10. Which of the following is *not* a type of private VLAN?

    a. Isolated

    b. Trunking

    c. Promiscuous

    d. Community

Foundation Topics

Configuring vSphere Standard Switches

A vSphere standard switch (vSS) is a logical construct within one ESXi host that connects virtual machines (VMs) to other VMs on the same switch. In addition, using connections called uplinks, it can connect VMs to other virtual or physical machines on other ESX/ESXi hosts, other vSSs in the same host, or anywhere in the physical environment. In this section I will discuss vSS capabilities and how to create and delete them. In addition, I will cover adding, configuring, and removing vmnics; configuring VMkernel ports and services; adding and removing port groups; and determining use cases for a vSS.

Identifying vSphere Standard Switch (vSS) Capabilities

A vSS models a simple Layer 2 switch that provides networking for the VMs connected to it. It can direct traffic between VMs on the switch as well as link them to external networks. Figure 2-1 shows a diagram of a vSS. I'm sorry that I don't have a photograph, but remember that they only exist in a software state. Note that there are actually two VMkernel ports on the vSS in this ESXi host. One is for management (management network), and the other is for other purposes that I will describe later in this section).

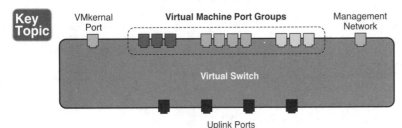

Figure 2-1　A Diagram of a vSphere Standard Switch

As I mentioned earlier, a vSS models an Ethernet Layer 2 switch on which a virtual machine network interface card (vNIC) can connect to its port and thereby be connected to other machines on the same switch; or off of the switch by way of an uplink to the physical world. Each uplink adapter also uses a port on a vSS. As I said before, one of the main questions to ask yourself is, "What type of connections can I create?" So, now I will discuss connections on vSSs.

You can create two main types of connections that you can create on vSSs; VMkernel ports and VM ports. The difference between these two types of connections is dramatic. It is important to understand how each type of connection is used.

VMkernel ports are used to connect the VMkernel to services that it controls. There is only one VMkernel on an ESXi host (also called the hypervisor), but there can be many VMkernel ports. In fact, it is best practice to use a separate VMkernel port for each type of VMkernel service. There are four main types of VMkernel services that require the use of a VMkernel port, as follows:

- **IP storage:** iSCSI or networked-attached storage (NAS). (Chapter 3, "Planning and Configuring vSphere Storage," covers these in more detail.)

- **vMotion:** A VMkernel port is required and a separate network is highly recommended. (Chapter 5, "Establishing and Maintaining Service Levels," covers vMotion in more detail.)

- **Management:** Because ESXi does not have a service console, or service console ports, management is performed through a specially configured VMkernel port.

- **Fault-tolerant logging:** A feature in vSphere that allows a high degree of hardware fault tolerance for the VMs involved, but also requires a separate and distinct VMkernel port. (Chapter 5 covers fault-tolerant logging in greater detail.)

VM port groups, however, are only used to connect VMs to the virtual switches. They are primarily a Layer 2 connection that does not require any configuration other than a label to identify a port group, such as Production. A VLAN can be configured for a port group, but that is optional as well. You can have multiple VM port groups on a single switch and use them to establish different polices, such as security, traffic shaping, and NIC teaming for various types of VMs. You will learn more about these in the section "Configuring vSS and vDS Policies," later in this chapter.

Creating / Deleting a vSphere Standard Switch

The first question that you might want to ask yourself is, "Do I really need a new vSS?" The answer to this question might not be as straightforward as you think. You do not necessarily need a new vSS for every new port or group of ports, because you can also just add components to the vSS that you already have. In fact, you might make better use of your resources by adding to a vSS that you already have, instead of creating a new one. Later in this chapter, in the section "Adding/Editing/Removing Port Groups on a vNetwork Standard Switch," I will discuss the power of using port groups and policies. In this section, I will discuss how to create a new vSS and how to delete a vSS that you no longer require.

If you decide to create a new vSS, you should select **Add Networking** from the Networking link and follow the wizard from there. The main thing to remember is that when you select Add Networking you are always creating a new vSS, not just adding networking components to an existing vSS. For example, if you want to create a new vSS for a VMkernel port used for vMotion, follow the steps outlined in Activity 2-1.

Activity 2-1 Creating a New vSphere Standard Switch

1. Log on to your vSphere Client.

2. Select **Home** and then **Hosts and Clusters**.

3. Select the ESX host on which you want to create the new vSS and then open the Configuration tab.

4. Click the **Networking** link under Hardware.

5. In the upper-right corner, click the **Add Networking** link, as shown in Figure 2-2.

Figure 2-2   The Add Networking Link on a vSS

6. On the Connection Type of the Add Network Wizard, select **VMkernel** and click **Next**, as shown in Figure 2-3.

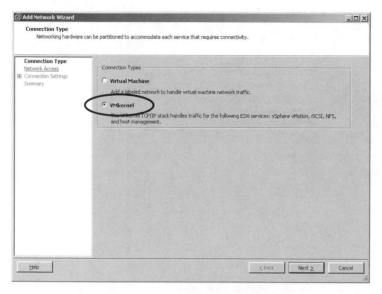

Figure 2-3   Selecting the VMkernel Connection Type

7. In VMkernel - Network Access, select the vmnic that you will use for the VM-kernel port and click **Next**, as shown in Figure 2-4.

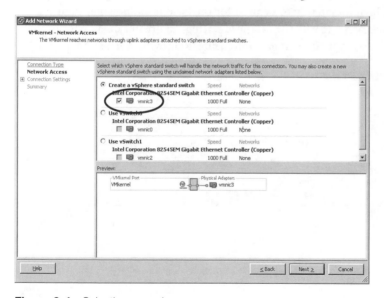

Figure 2-4   Selecting a vmnic

8. In VMkernel - Connection Settings, enter the Network Label and optionally the VLAN, as shown in Figure 2-5. (The Network Label should generally indicate the purpose of the switch or port group. In this case, you might use vMotion, and then enable it for vMotion.) Click **Next**.

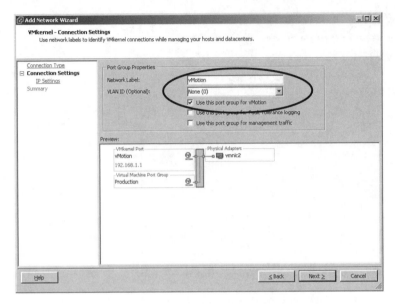

Figure 2-5 Selecting the VMkernel Connection Type

9. In VMkernel - IP Connection Settings, enter the IP address, subnet mask, and VMkernel Default Gateway to be used for the switch, as shown in Figure 2-6, and then click **Next**. (I will discuss these settings in greater detail later in this chapter in the section "Creating/Configuring/Removing Virtual Adapters.")

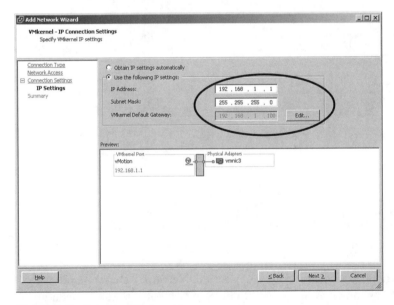

Figure 2-6 Entering IP Information

10. In Ready to Complete, review your configuration settings and click **Finish**.

Deleting a vSphere Standard Switch

There might come a time when you no longer require a vSS that you have in your inventory. This might be because you have chosen to upgrade to a vSphere distributed switch (vDS) or because you are changing the networking on each of the hosts to provide consistency across the hosts, which is a very good idea. In this case, follow the steps outlined in Activity 2-2.

Activity 2-2 Deleting a vSphere Standard Switch

1. Log on to your vSphere Client.

2. Select **Home** and then **Hosts and Clusters**.

3. Select the ESX host on which you want to delete the vSS, and then open the Configuration tab.

4. Click the **Networking** link under Hardware.

5. Click the **Remove** link next to the switch that you want to remove and then confirm your selection by clicking **Yes**, as shown in Figure 2-7. (There is a Remove link for each switch, so take care to select the right one.)

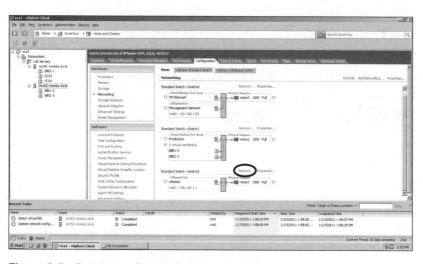

Figure 2-7   Deleting a vSphere Standard Switch

Adding / Configuring / Removing vmnics on a vSphere Standard Switch

As I mentioned earlier, you might not want to create a new switch every time you need a new connection. In fact, you will make better use of your resources by adding to a current switch and thereby leveraging NIC teaming. In this section, I will discuss how to add new vmnics to a switch that you already have. In addition, I will discuss configuring vmnics and VMkernel ports on switches, including changing the IP address, VLAN, and so on. Finally, you will learn how to remove a vmnic from a switch if you no longer require it.

To add a new vmnic to an existing switch, you should *not* click Add Networking! As you might remember, clicking Add Networking takes you into a wizard that adds a new switch, not just into the networking properties of a switch you already have. So if you don't click Add Networking, what do you do? Well, if you think about it, what you really want to do is edit the configuration of a switch. For example, if you want to add a new vmnic to an existing switch to be used for vMotion, follow the steps outlined in Activity 2-3.

Activity 2-3 Adding a vmnic to a switch

1. Log on to your vSphere Client.
2. Select **Home** and then **Hosts and Clusters**.
3. Select the ESX host on which you want to edit the vSS.
4. Click the **Networking** link under Hardware.
5. Click the **Properties** link next to the switch that you want to edit, as shown in Figure 2-8.

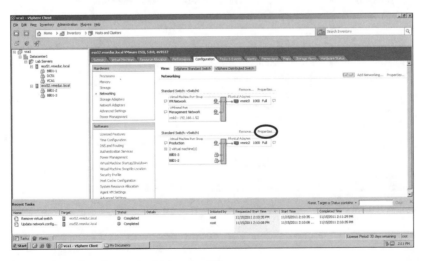

Figure 2-8   The Properties Link on a vSS

6. On the Properties dialog box for the switch, click **Add**, as shown in Figure 2-9.

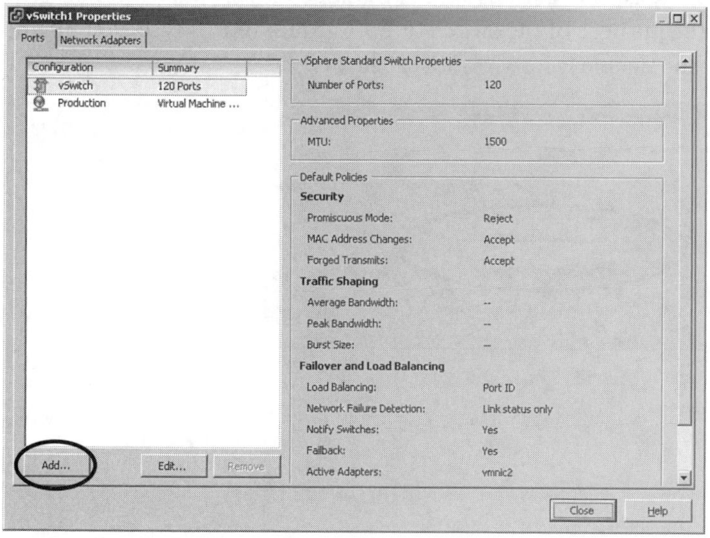

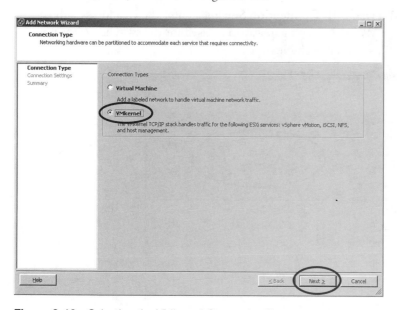

Figure 2-9   Adding a vmnic to a Switch

7. On the Connection Type of the Add Network Wizard, select **VMkernel** and click **Next**, as shown in Figure 2-10.

Figure 2-10   Selecting the VMkernel Connection Type

8. From **VMkernel > Connection Settings**, enter the Network Label and optionally the VLAN, as shown in Figure 2-11. (The Network Label should generally indicate the purpose of the switch or port group. In this case, you might
   use "vMotion" and enable it for vMotion.) Click Next.

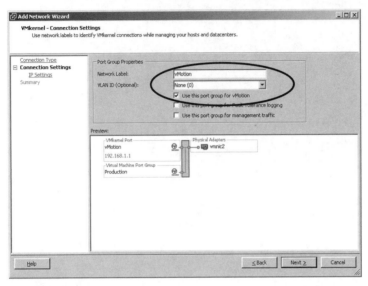

Figure 2-11   Entering a Network Label

9. From **VMkernel > IP Connection Settings**, enter the IP address, subnet
   mask, and VMkernel default gateway to be used for the switch, as shown in
   Figure 2-12, and then click **Next**.

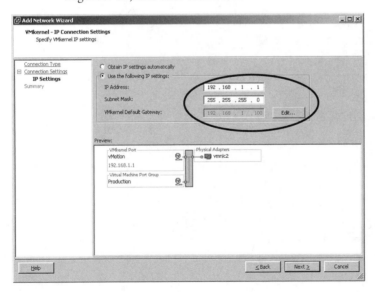

Figure 2-12   Entering IP Information

10. In Ready to Complete, review your configuration settings and click **Finish**.

NOTE   As you might have noticed, after you select Add and Edit, the rest of the steps are very much the same whether you are creating a new switch for the port or just adding a port to an existing switch. This is not just a coincidence in this case, it is always true.

You will sometimes need to change the settings of a vmnic that you have already configured for a vSS. For example, you might want to edit the physical configuration such as the speed and duplex settings to match those of a physical switch to which your ESXi host is connected. To edit the physical configuration of the vmnic, follow the steps outlined in Activity 2-4.

Activity 2-4 Configuring the physical aspects of a vmnic

1. Log on to your vSphere Client.

2. Select **Home** and then **Hosts and Clusters**.

3. Select the ESXi host on which you want to edit the vSS.

4. Click the **Networking** link under Hardware.

5. Click the **Properties** link next to the switch that you want to edit, as shown in Figure 2-13.

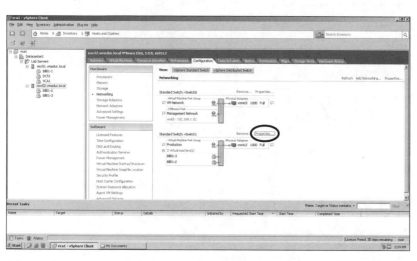

Figure 2-13   The Properties Link

6. On the Properties dialog box for the switch, open the Network Adapters tab and select the vmnic that you want to configure, as shown in Figure 2-14.

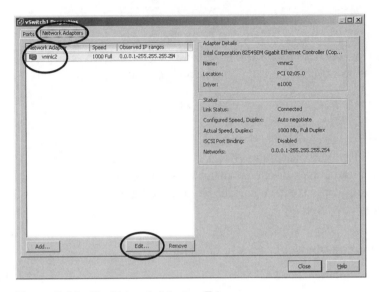

Figure 2-14   The Network Adapters Tab

7. Click **Edit**, and then select the speed and duplex that matches the physical switch to which the ESXi host is connected, as shown in Figure 2-15, and click **OK**.

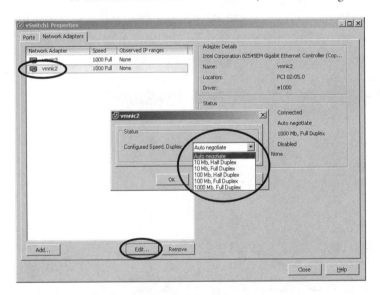

Figure 2-15   Configuring Physical Aspects of a vmnic

8. Click **Close** to exit the Properties dialog box.

NOTE Auto Negotiate is the default, but is not always considered a best practice when more than one vendor is involved. This is because the result will often be less than the desired setting (such as 100Mb Half Duplex). If you use Auto Negotiate, verify that the resulting setting is what you expected.

There might come a time when you need to remove a vmnic from a switch. This might happen if you are changing network settings to provide consistency or if you intend to use the vmnic on a new switch. If you need to remove a vmnic from a vSS, follow the steps outlined in Activity 2-5.

Activity 2-5 Removing a vmnic from a vSphere Standard Switch

1. Log on to your vSphere Client.
2. Select **Home** and then **Hosts and Clusters**.
3. Select the ESX host on which you want to remove the vmnic.
4. Click the **Networking** link under Hardware.
5. Click the **Properties** link next to the switch that contains the vmnic that you want to remove.
6. On the Properties dialog box for the switch, open the Network Adapters tab, select the vmnic that you want to remove, select **Remove**, and confirm your selection by clicking **Yes**, as shown in Figure 2-16.

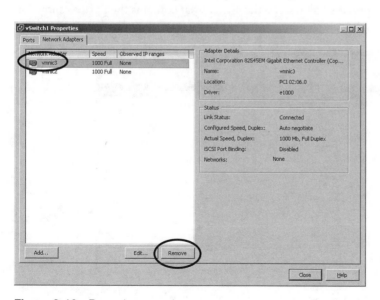

Figure 2-16   Removing a vmnic

Configuring VMkernel Ports for Network Services

As I mentioned earlier, there are only four reasons that you would create a VM-kernel port: management, IP storage, fault-tolerant logging, and vMotion. I will discuss each of these in much greater detail in the chapters that follow, but for now you should understand that they all share the same configuration requirements for network services (namely, an IP address and subnet mask). In addition, you should know that all VMkernel ports will share the same default gateway. You might also want to configure a VLAN, and you will want to enable the port with the services for which it was created (such as vMotion, management, or fault-tolerant logging).

To configure a VMkernel port with network service configuration, you should configure the IP settings of the port group to which is it assigned. I will discuss port group configuration in much greater detail later in this chapter. For now, if you want to configure the IP settings of a VMkernel port, follow the steps outlined in Activity 2-6.

Activity 2-6 Configuring a VMkernel port for Network Services

1. Log on to your vSphere Client.

2. Select **Home** and then **Hosts and Clusters**.

3. Select the ESX host on which you want to configure the VMkernel port.

4. Click the **Networking** link under Hardware.

5. Click the **Properties** link next to the switch that contains the port, as shown in Figure 2-17.

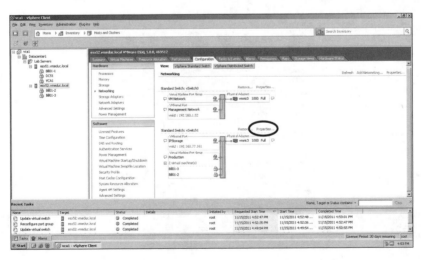

Figure 2-17   Properties Link for vSS

6. On the Properties dialog box for the switch, on the Ports tab, select the port group to which the VMkernel port is assigned and click **Edit**, as shown in Figure 2-18.

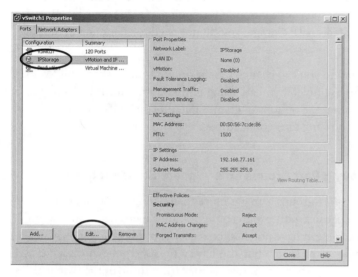

Figure 2-18   Editing a Port Group

7. Open the IP Settings tab, and enter the IP information for your network, as shown in Figure 2-19, and click **OK**.

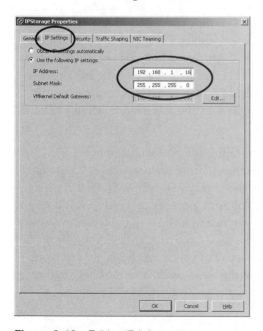

Figure 2-19   Editing IP Information

8. If you want to configure a VLAN for the port group, open the General tab and enter the VLAN information directly under the Network Label.

9. On the General tab, you can also enable the vmnic for the specific services for which it was created, such as vMotion, FT Logging, or Management. If the port was only created for IP storage, you do not need to check any of the Enabled boxes.

10. Finally, if appropriate you can change the maximum transmission unit (MTU) for the vmnic (for example, if you are using jumbo frames for iSCSI storage). (Chapter 3 covers storage options in greater detail.) Click **OK** to close the Properties dialog box and save your settings.

Adding / Editing / Removing Port Groups on a vSphere Standard Switch

The main reason to use port groups is to get more than one function out of each switch. This is possible because port group configuration supersedes switch configuration. Because of this, you can have policies for security, traffic shaping, NIC teaming, and so on that apply to the switch but also have a separate policy for each that applies to any port group on which the settings differ from those of the switch. This tremendously improves your flexibility and gives you options such as those security options discussed in Chapter 1, "Planning, Installing, Configuring, and Upgrading vCenter Server and VMware ESXi." In this section, I will discuss adding, editing, and removing port groups on a vSS.

Suppose you decide to add a new group of VMs on which you will test software and monitor performance. Furthermore, suppose you decide that you will not create a new switch but that you will instead add the VMs to a switch that you already have in your inventory. However, suppose the VMs that are already on the switch are not for testing and development but are actually in production. Chances are good that you do not want to "mix them in" with the new testing VMs, but how can you keep them separate without creating a new vSS?

Well, if you create a new port group and assign a different vmnic to it, you can manage the new testing VMs completely separate from the production VMs, even though they are both on the same vSS. In this case, you might want to label your existing port group Production and label your new port group Test-Dev. It does not matter what label you use, but it is a best practice to relate it to the function of the port group, which is generally related to the function of the VMs that will be on it. Also, you should strive for consistency across all of your ESXi hosts in a small organization or at least across all of the hosts in the same cluster in a medium-sized or large organization. (Chapter 5 covers clusters in greater detail.)

So, what was the purpose of all of that labeling? Well, after you have done that, you will have a set of five tabs on the Properties link of the port group that only apply to that port group. You can make important changes to port group policies such as security, traffic shaping, and NIC teaming that will override any settings on the vSS properties tabs. I will discuss the details of these port group policies later in this chapter in "Configuring vSS and vDS Policies." For now, if you want to add a new VM port group to an existing vSS, follow the steps outlined in Activity 2-7.

Activity 2-7 Adding a Port Group to a vSphere Standard Switch

1. Log on to your vSphere Client.

2. Select **Home** and then **Hosts and Clusters**.

3. Select the ESX host on which you want to add the port group.

4. Click the **Networking** link under Hardware.

5. Click the **Properties** link next to the switch on which you want to add the port group.

6. On the Ports tab, click **Add**, and then choose **Virtual Machine**, as shown in Figure 2-20. Click **Next**.

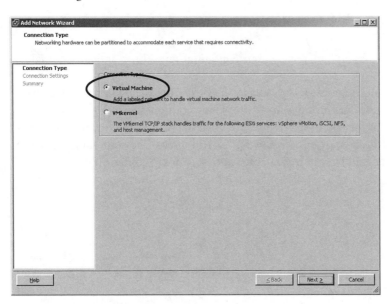

Figure 2-20   Adding a Virtual Machine Port Group

7. From **Virtual Machines > Connection Settings**, enter the label that you want to use (such as Test-Dev) and the VLAN if you are using a VLAN, as shown in Figure 2-21. Click **Next**.

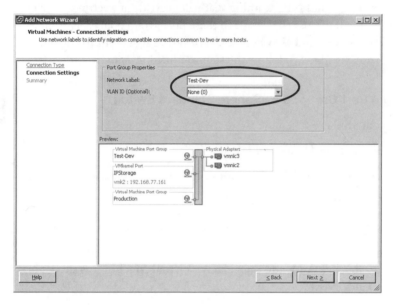

Figure 2-21   Entering and Network Label

8. On Ready to Complete, review your configuration settings and click **Finish**.

Your new port group should now appear in the Properties dialog box under Configuration. This new port group is now completely configurable and will have its own set of five tabs for you to configure. Just click the port group under Configuration and select **Edit**, as shown in Figure 2-22. I will discuss the configuration of port group policies in detail later in this chapter in the section "Configuring vSS and vDS Policies."

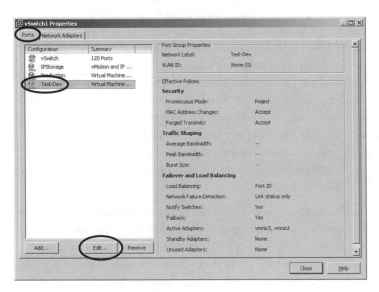

Figure 2-22   Port Group Configuration

Finally, you might want to remove a port group that you no longer need. This might happen because you are reorganizing your network or because you are no longer using the VMs to which the port group was associated. To remove the port group, click the port group, select **Remove**, and confirm your selection by clicking **Yes**, as shown in Figure 2-23.

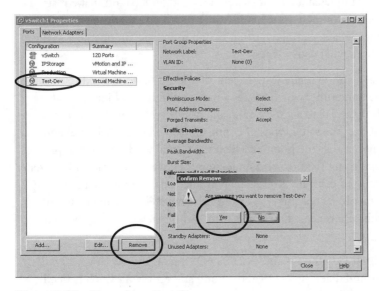

Figure 2-23   Removing a Port Group

Determining Use Cases for a vSphere Standard Switch

Now that I have discussed how you would create and manage a vSS, let's talk about why you would want one in the first place. In other words, what would cause you to use a vSS instead of a vDS? One very practical reason might be that you do not have the appropriate license to use a vDS. As I previously discussed in Chapter 1, in the section, "Installing and Configuring vCenter Server," creating a vDS requires an Enterprise Plus license. Another reason might be that you have a small to medium-size organization and therefore the settings on a vSS are sufficient for your needs. Your organization can have many hosts and those hosts can communicate to each other using vSSs.

The main point to consider is how you can keep the networking that is inside of each ESXi host consistent with the networking that is inside the other hosts, or at least all the hosts in the same cluster. If possible, you should have the same number of vSSs in each of your hosts and the same port groups on each of them as well (at least the ones that are in the same clusters). In fact, the consistent spelling of the port group names is even important. In addition, to leverage the power of port groups, you should have as few vSSs on each host as possible while still maintaining consistency across the hosts. If you balance these two factors in your organization as much as possible, you will be on the right track.

Configuring vSphere Distributed Switches

Now that you understand what a virtual switch does and understand that consistency of configuration is a key component, what if I were to tell you that there is a way to guarantee consistency by associating a virtual switch to more than one host at the same time? Well, that's what a vDS does.

A vDS is the same as a vSS in many ways except that it can be connected to more than one host at the same time, which makes a radical difference. I know what you're thinking, "Is it similar to a vSS or radically different?" Well, in a word, "Yes." It's similar in that it uses the same types of connections (namely, VMkernel and VMs). It's also similar in that the point at which the virtual world meets the physical world is an important thing to know and understand. However, it's radically different because it is managed centrally in the vCenter and can be connected to multiple hosts at the same time. In fact, a single vDS can be connected to as many as 350 hosts. Because of this difference, vDSs come with a whole new set of terms to understand.

In this section, I will discuss the capabilities of a vDS versus those of a vSS. I will also discuss creating and deleting a vDS and adding and removing ESXi hosts. In addition, I will cover adding, configuring, and removing dvPort groups, dvUplinks (new terms in vDSs). A vDS also has virtual adapters just like a vSS, except that they can be connected to more than one host. I will discuss creating, configuring, migrating, and removing virtual adapters. I will also cover migrating VMs to and from a vDS. In addition, you will learn how to determine a use case for a vSphere distributed switch.

Identifying vSphere Distributed Switch Capabilities

If I were you, what I would want to know is what vDSs can do that vSSs cannot do. In other words, "Why should I consider using one instead of the other?" In fact, there is quite a large list of features that are specific to a vDS, but to really understand them you need to see what they both can do and then what only the vDS can do. Table 2-2 illustrates the features that are common between vSSs and vDSs and then those that are unique to vDSs.

Table 2-2   vSS Capabilities Versus vDS Capabilities

	vSS	vDS
Layer 2 switch	X	X
VLAN segmentation	X	X
802.1Q tagging	X	X
NIC teaming	X	X
Outbound traffic shaping	X	X
Inbound traffic shaping		X
VM network port block		X
Private VLANs		X
Load-based teaming		X
Datacenter-level management		X
Network vMotion		X
vSphere switch APIs		X
Per-port policy settings		X
Port state monitoring		X
Link Layer Discovery Protocol (LLDP)		X
User-defined network I/O control		X
NetFlow		X
Port mirroring		X

The following is a brief description of each of the features available on a vDS that are not available on a vSS.

- **Inbound traffic shaping:** A port group setting that can throttle the aggregate bandwidth inbound to the switch. This might be useful for a port group containing VMs that are being used a web servers.

- **VM network port block:** Specific ports can be configured as "blocked" for a specified VMs use. This might be helpful for troubleshooting or for advanced configurations.

- **Private VLANs:** This is a vSphere implementation of a VLAN standard that is available on the latest physical switches. With regard to vSphere, private virtual local-area networks (PVLANs) can be created in the vSphere that are only used in the vSphere and not on your external network. In essence, a PVLAN is a VLAN within a VLAN. In addition, the PVLANs in your vSphere can be kept from seeing each other. Later in this chapter, the section "Configuring vSS and vDS Policies" covers PVLANs in greater depth.

- **Load-based teaming:** You can configure network load balancing in a much more intelligent fashion than with vSSs, by enabling the system to recognize the current load on each link before making frame forwarding decisions. This could be useful if the loads that are on each link vary considerably over time.

- **Datacenter-level management:** A vDS is managed from the vCenter as a single switch from the control plane, even though many hosts are connected to each other at the I/O plane. This provides a centralized control mechanism and guarantees consistency of configuration.

- **Network vMotion:** Because a port group that is on a vDS is actually connected to multiple hosts, a VM can migrate from one host to another without changing ports. The positive effect of this is that the attributes assigned to the port group (such as security, traffic shaping, and NIC teaming) will migrate as well.

- **vSphere switch APIs:** Third-party switches have been and are being created that can be installed in the control plane. On switches such as the Cisco Nexus 1000v, the true essence of the switch is installed into the vCenter as a virtual appliance (VA).

- **Per-port policy settings:** Most of the configuration on a vDS is at the port group level, but it can be overridden at the individual port level. This allows you tremendous flexibility with regard to port settings such as security, traffic shaping, and so on.

- **Port state monitoring:** Each port on vDS can be managed and monitored independently of all other ports. This means that you can quickly identify an issue that relates to a specific port.

- **Link Layer Discovery Protocol:** Similar to Cisco Discovery Protocol (CDP), Link Layer Discovery Protocol (LLDP) enables vDSs to discover other devices such as switches and routers that are directly connected to them. The advantage of LLDP is that it is an open protocol which is not proprietary to Cisco.

- **User-defined network I/O control:** You can set up a quality of service (QoS) (of a sort), but instead of defining traffic paths by protocols, you can define the traffic paths by types of VMware traffic. In earlier versions of vDSs, you could define traffic as vMotion, Management, and others, but now you can define your own categories. This adds to flexibility in network control and design.

- **NetFlow:** You can use the standard for traffic monitoring, NetFlow, to monitor, analyze, and log traffic flows in your vSphere. This enables you to easily monitor virtual network flows with the same tools that you use to monitor traffic flows in the physical network. Your vDS can forward NetFlow information to a monitoring machine in your external network.

- **Port mirroring:** Most commonly used with intrusion detection systems (IDSs) and intrusion prevention systems (IPSs), port mirroring provides for a copy of a packet to be sent to a monitoring station so that traffic flows can be monitored without the IPS/IDS skewing the data. Port mirroring is new to vSphere 5.0 vDSs.

NOTE   As you might remember, one of the main goals with vSSs was consistency of networking between hosts that are in the same clusters. Likewise, one of the main benefits of vDSs is that they "force" this consistency, because multiple hosts are connected to the same virtual switch.

Creating/Deleting a vSphere Distributed Switch

The first thing to consider if you want to create a vDS is your license level, because they can be created only with an Enterprise Plus license. Oh, I suppose you could create them with the 60-day evaluation license, but you would then need to purchase an Enterprise Plus license before the evaluation period expires; otherwise, your switch would cease to function. You also need to consider the level of hosts that you have in the datacenter onto which you are adding the switch, because this will have an impact on the version of the switch that you create. That said, to begin to create a new vDS, follow the steps outlined in Activity 2-8.

Activity 2-8 Creating an New vSphere Distributed Switch

1. Log on to your vSphere Client.

2. Select **Home** and then **Networking**.

3. Right-click your datacenter and then select **New vSphere Distributed Switch**, as shown in Figure 2-24.

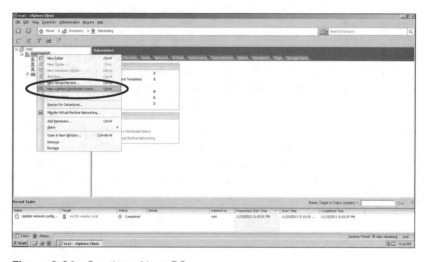

Figure 2-24   Creating a New vDS

4. On Select vDS Version, choose the level of switch that fits your datacenter based on the hosts that you have in it. For example, if all of your hosts are ESXi 5.0, you can use a Version 5.0.0 switch. However, if you have hosts that are older than ESXi 5.0, you want to choose the version corresponding to the earliest version in your datacenter. This will, of course, affect the list of features that you will have on your switch, as shown in Figure 2-25. Click **Next**.

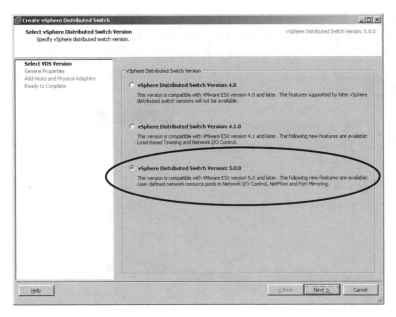

Figure 2-25   vDS Versions

5. On General Properties, type a name for your new switch that implies what it does and select the maximum number of uplinks that you will want to use per host for this switch, as shown in Figure 2-26. Click **Next**.

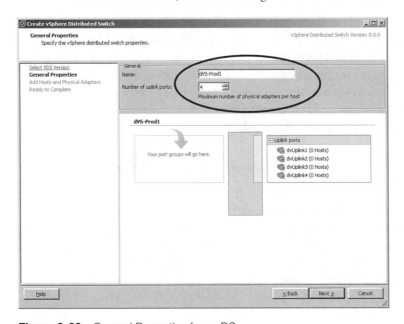

Figure 2-26   General Properties for a vDS

6. From Add Hosts and Physical Adapters, select the hosts that you want to add and the vmnic that you will connect to on each host, as shown in Figure 2-27. (I am selecting just one host for now.) Click **Next**.

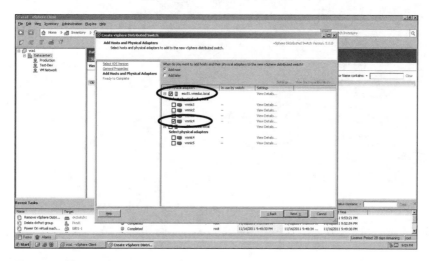

Figure 2-27   Adding Hosts while Creating a vDS

7. On Ready to Complete, review your configuration settings and click **Finish**.

Deleting a vDS

You might assume that deleting a vDS would just be a matter of right-clicking it and selecting to remove it. This is almost true. However, you first need to remove the hosts and the port groups from the vDS. Then you can right-click it and select to remove it. In the next two sections, I will discuss (among other topics) removing hosts and port groups from a vDS. Once you know how to do that, deleting the vDS is as simple as right-clicking and selecting **Remove**.

Adding/Removing ESXi Hosts from a vSphere Distributed Switch

As you observed earlier, you can add hosts to a vDS when you create the switch in the first place, but you certainly do not have to recreate the switch to change the number of hosts that are connected to it. Instead, you can use the tools provided by the vCenter to make the modifications with relative ease. In the following activities, I will first illustrate how to add a host to an existing vDS, and then I will show you how to remove a host from an existing vDS.

To add a host to an existing vDS, follow the steps outlined in Activity 2-9.

Activity 2-9 Adding a Host to a vSphere Distributed Switch

1. Log on to your vSphere Client.

2. Select **Home** and then **Networking**.

3. Right-click the vDS on which you want to add a host and click **Add Host**, as shown in Figure 2-28.

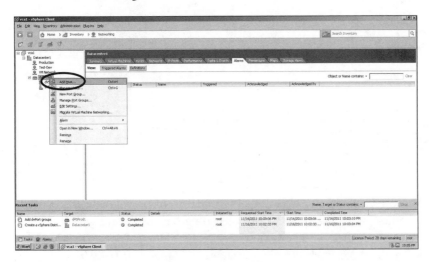

Figure 2-28   Adding Hosts After Creating a vDS

4. From Select Hosts and Physical Adapters, choose the host and the vmnic to which you want to connect, as shown in Figure 2-29. (You can determine the appropriate vmnic by clicking **View Details** and examining the properties of the card and the CDP information associated with it. Take care that you know whether it is in use by another switch.) Click **Next**.

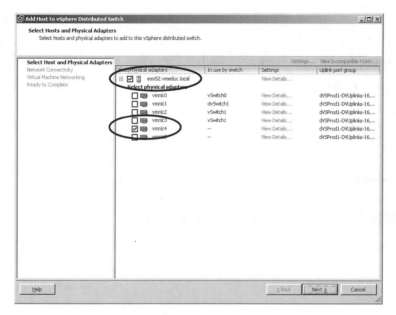

Figure 2-29   Connecting vmnics on a vDS

5. On Network Connectivity, select the port group that will provide network connectivity for the host. If you choose a VMkernel port group that is already associated to a vmnic on another switch, you must migrate the VMkernel port to the vDS or choose another VMkernel port group, as shown in Figure 2-30. Click **Next**.

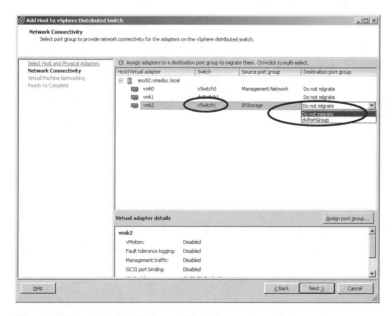

Figure 2-30   Migrating VMkernel Port Groups to a vDS

6. From Virtual Machine Networking, select the VMs on the vSSs of the host that you want to migrate to the vDS and the port group that you want to migrate them to, as shown in Figure 2-31. Click **Next**.

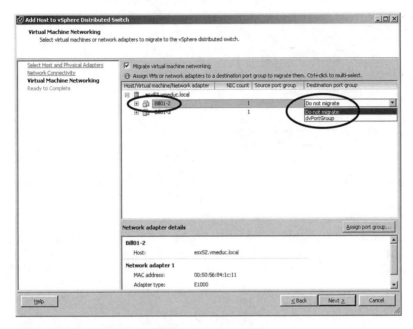

Figure 2-31   Migrating VM Networking to a VDS

7. From Ready to Complete, review your configuration settings and click **Finish**.

To remove a host from an existing vDS, follow the steps outlined in Activity 2-10.

Activity 2-10 Removing a Host from a vSphere Distributed Switch

1. Log on to your vSphere Client.

2. Select **Home** and then **Networking**.

3. Click the vDS on which you want to remove a host and open the Hosts tab.

4. On the Hosts tab, right-click the host that you want to remove from the switch and select **Remove from vSphere Distributed Switch**, as shown in Figure 2-32.

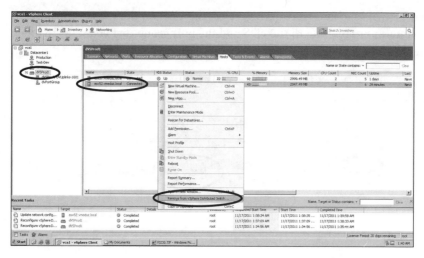

Figure 2-32 Removing a Host from a VDS

5. On the warning screen, confirm your selection by clicking **Yes**. (You should ensure that that there are no VM resources on the switch; otherwise, the removal will fail.)

> **NOTE** It is necessary to remove a host from a vDS before you can remove the host from vCenter.

Adding/Configuring/Removing dvPort Groups

As you might remember, I said earlier that port groups allow you to get more than one set of attributes out of the same switch. This is especially true with vDS port groups. The port groups that you create on a vDS are connected to all of the hosts to which the vDS is connected; hence they are called *dvPort groups*. Because a vDS can be connected to up to 350 hosts, the dvPort groups can become very large and powerful indeed. After you create port groups on a vDS, you can migrate your VMs to the dvPort groups. In the following activities, I will illustrate how to add, configure, and remove dvPort groups on vDSs.

To add a port group to a vDS, follow the steps outlined in Activity 2-11.

Activity 2-11 Adding a Port Group to a vSphere Distributed Switch

1. Log on to your vSphere Client.

2. Select **Home** and then **Networking**.

3. Right-click the vDS on which you want to add the port group and select **New Port Group**, as shown in Figure 2-33.

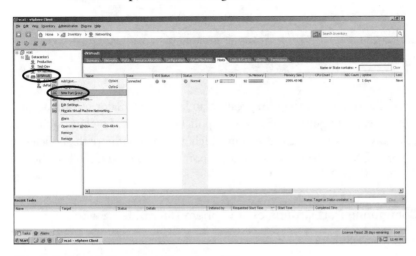

Figure 2-33   Adding a Port Group to a vDS

4. Type a name for your new port group that will help you identify the types of VMs that you will place on that port group, choose the number of ports that will be assigned to this port group (0–8192), and choose the VLAN type (I will discuss VLANs later in this chapter in the section "Configuring VLAN Settings"), as shown in Figure 2-34.

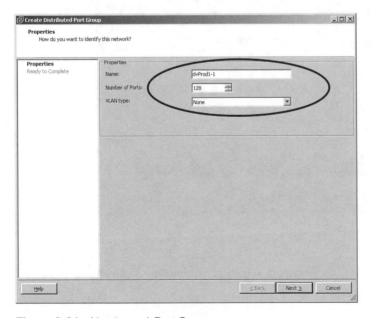

Figure 2-34   Naming a dvPort Group

5. On Ready to Complete, confirm your selections by clicking **Finish**.

NOTE   One port group, named dvPortGroup, is created by default when you create the switch. For your first port group, you could just rename that one.

I will discuss configuring port groups in great detail in the next major section of this chapter, which covers configuring vSS and vDS polices. For now, I will just point out the steps involved in accessing the area in which you can configure the policies of port groups on vDSs. To begin to configure a port group on a vDS, follow the steps outlined in Activity 2-12.

Activity 2-12 Configuring Port Groups on a vSphere Distributed Switch

1. Log on to your vSphere Client.

2. Select **Home** and then **Networking**.

3. Expand on the vDS on which you want to configure the port group, right-click the port group that you want to configure, and select **Edit Settings**, as shown in Figure 2-35.

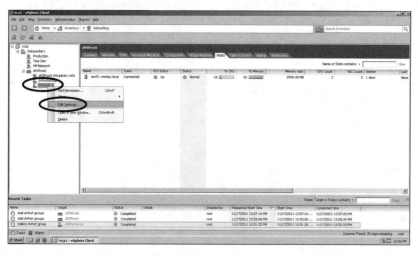

Figure 2-35   Configuring a dvPort Group

4. In the warning box, confirm your selection by choosing **Yes**.

Over time, your networking needs will change, and you might decide to reorganize by removing some port groups. Take care not to "orphan" the VMs by removing the port group while they are still assigned to it. Instead, carefully consider your options and plans, and simply migrate the VMs to another port group as part of your plan. I will discuss your options with regard to migrating VMs later in Chapter 5. For now, I'll just point out how you would go about removing a port group after you have migrated the VMs.

To remove a port group that you no longer are using, follow the steps outlined in Activity 2-13.

Activity 2-13 Removing a Port Group from a vSphere Distributed Switch

1. Log on to your vSphere Client.

2. Select **Home** and then **Networking**.

3. Click the vDS on which you want to remove the port group.

4. Right-click the port that you want to remove and select **Delete**, as shown in Figure 2-36.

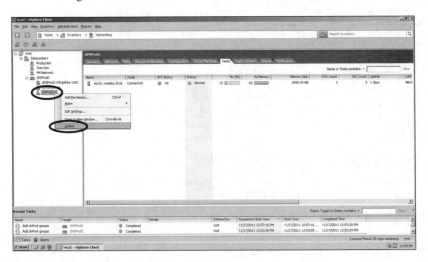

Figure 2-36   Removing a dvPort Group

5. On the warning screen, confirm your selection by clicking **Yes**.

Adding/Removing Uplink Adapters to dvUplink Groups

As shown in Figure 2-37, dvUplink groups connect your vDS to the hidden switches that are contained in your hosts and then from there to the physical world. This allows you to control networking at the control plane on the vDS while the actual input/out (I/O) is still passing from host to host at the I/O plane. Each host keeps its own network configuration in its hidden switch that is created when you add a host to a vDS. This ensures that the network will continue to function even if your vCenter fails or is not available.

I know that's a lot more terminology all of the sudden, but as you might remember, I said that one of the main things to understand was where the virtual meets the physical. Well, you should know that the dvUplink groups are virtual but the uplink adapters are physical. Connecting multiple uplink adapters to a dvUplink group opens up the possibilities of load balancing and fault tolerance, which I discuss in detail later in the section "Configuring Load Balancing and Failover Policies." For now, I will show you how to add and remove uplink adapters.

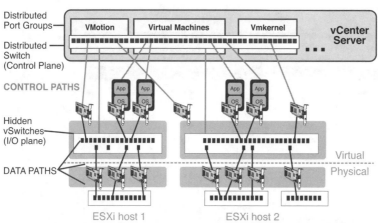

Figure 2-37   Distributed Switch Architecture

To add uplink adapters to a dvUplink group, follow the steps outlined in Activity 2-14.

Activity 2-14 Adding an Uplink Adapter to a dvUplink Group

1. Log on to your vSphere Client.

2. Select Home and then **Hosts and Clusters**.

3. Select the host on which you want to configure an uplink and open the Configuration tab.

4. Choose **Networking**, click the **vSphere Distributed Switch** link, and then click the **Manage Physical Adapters** link, as shown in Figure 2-38.

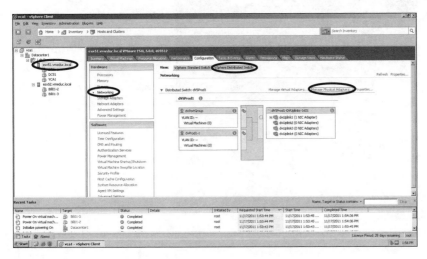

Figure 2-38 Adding an Uplink Adapter to a dvUplink Group

5. From Manage Physical Adapters, choose the uplinks group to which you want to add a physical adapter, and select **<Click to Add NIC>**, as shown in Figure 2-39.

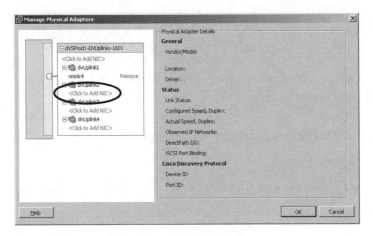

Figure 2-39 Selecting the Physical NIC

6. From Add Physical Adapter, choose the appropriate vmnic based on your network topology, and click **OK**. You can view the status information about the NIC, as shown in Figure 2-40.

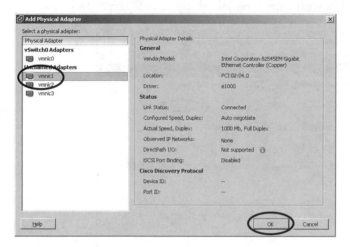

Figure 2-40   Viewing NIC Status

NOTE   If you choose a vmnic that is already assigned, it will be removed from its current assignment. For this reason, take care not to remove the vmnic that is assigned to the management network that you are using to manage the host. This would be like "cutting off the limb that you are sitting on", and would cause you to lose control of the host until you could gain local access and restore the link.

When you reorganize, you might want to remove an uplink from a dvUplink group. Activity 2-15 outlines the process to remove the uplink.

Activity 2-15 Removing an Uplink Adapter from an dvUplink Group

1. Log on to your vSphere Client.

2. Select **Home** and then **Hosts and Clusters**.

3. Select the host on which you want to configure an uplink and open the Configuration tab.

4. Choose **Networking**, click the **vSphere Distributed Switch** link, and then click the **Manage Physical Adapters** link.

5. From the Manage Physical Adapters dialog box, choose the uplinks group to which you want to remove a physical adapter, and select **Remove** next to the uplink that you want to remove, as shown in Figure 2-41.

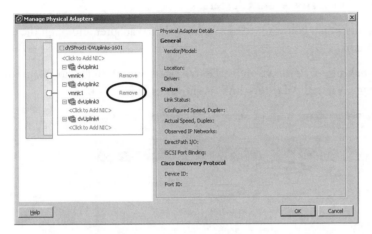

Figure 2-41 Removing an Uplink from a vDS

6. In the warning box, confirm that you want to remove the uplink by clicking **Yes**.

Creating/Configuring/Removing Virtual Adapters

Prior to vSphere 5.0 and ESXi 5.0, virtual adapters on vDSs included service console ports as well as VMkernel ports. In fact, if you are still using ESX hosts in your virtual datacenter, you must take into account that they will require a service console port on either a vSS or a vDS, for the purpose of connecting to and managing the switch from the physical world. Because ESXi 5.0 hosts do not have service consoles, they also do not have service console ports, so with regard to this topic I will limit the discussion of virtual adapters to VMkernel ports. That said, this section covers creating, configuring, and removing virtual adapters.

As you might remember, I discussed the fact that we create VMkernel ports for one of four reasons: IP storage, management, vMotion, or FT logging. There is only one VMkernel on the ESXi host, which is the hypervisor, but there can be many VMkernel ports. To create a new VMkernel port on a vDS, you simply create and configure a virtual adapter.

To create a virtual adapter, follow the steps outlined in Activity 2-16.

Activity 2-16 Creating a Virtual Adapter

1. Log on to your vSphere Client.

2. Select **Home** and then **Hosts and Clusters**.

3. Select the host on which you want to configure a virtual adapter and open the Configuration tab.

4. Choose **Networking,** click the **vSphere Distributed Switch** link, and then click the **Manage Virtual Adapters** link, as shown in Figure 2-42.

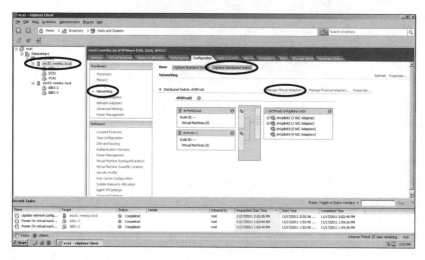

Figure 2-42 The Manage Virtual Adapters Link

5. From Manage Virtual Adapters, click **Add**, as shown in Figure 2-43.

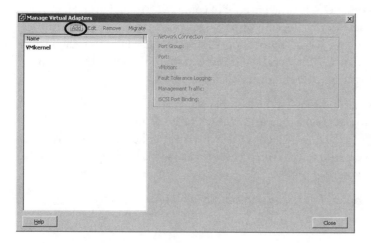

Figure 2-43 Creating a Virtual Adapter

6. From Add Virtual Adapter, choose **New Virtual Adapter** and click **Next**, as shown in Figure 2-44.

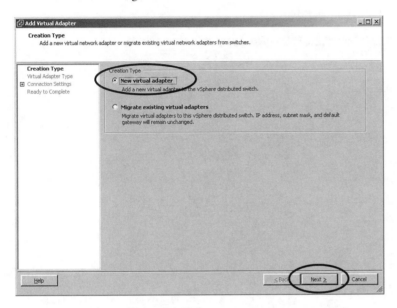

Figure 2-44   Adding a Virtual Adapter

7. Select **VMkernel** (the only selection on ESXi hosts) and click **Next**, as shown in Figure 2-45.

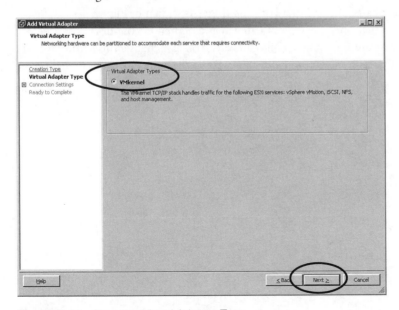

Figure 2-45   Choosing Virtual Adapter Type

8. Select the port group or port to which the VMkernel port will be added and select the box indicating the function of the VMkernel port, as shown in Figure 2-46, and then click **Next**.

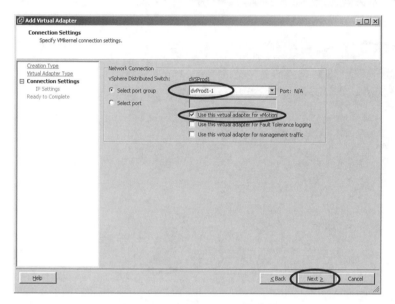

Figure 2-46   Connecting a Virtual Adapter to a vDS

9. Enter the IP address, subnet mask, and default gateway to be used for the VMkernel port; based on your network topology, as shown in Figure 2-47. Click **Next**. Note that once the default gateway is assigned for the first VMkernel port, the rest use the same default gateway. You can change this setting for all VMkernel ports by selecting **Edit**, but most of the time you do not need to change it.

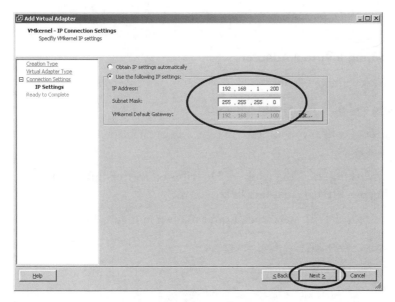

Figure 2-47   Entering IP Information for Virtual Adapter

10. On Ready to Complete, confirm your selections and click **Finish**.

After you have finished configuring it, you can check the setting of your virtual adapter by coming back to Manage Virtual Adapters and clicking the adapter, as shown in Figure 2-48. To make changes to those configuration settings, you can simply elect to edit the properties of the virtual adapter.

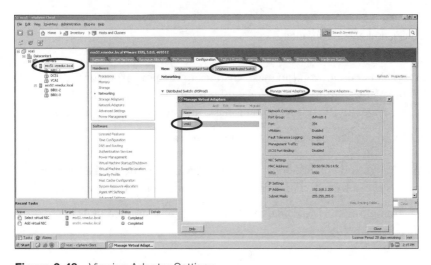

Figure 2-48   Viewing Adapter Settings

To configure a virtual adapter, follow the steps outlined in Activity 2-17.

Activity 2-17 Configuring a Virtual Adapter

1. Log on to your vSphere Client.

2. Select **Home** and then **Hosts and Clusters**.

3. Select the host on which you want to configure a virtual adapter and open the Configuration tab.

4. Choose **Networking**, click the **vSphere Distributed Switch** link, and then click the **Manage Virtual Adapters** link.

5. From Manage Virtual Adapters, click **Edit**, as shown in Figure 2-49.

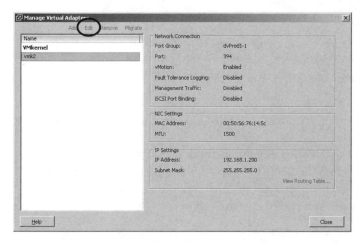

Figure 2-49   Configuring a Virtual Adapter

6. From the General tab, you can make changes to the port group or the port as well as the MTU settings (useful for jumbo frames). On the IP Settings tab, you can change the IP address, subnet mask, and default gateway if necessary.

7. Click **OK** to confirm and save all of your changes.

When things change and you no longer need the service that the VMkernel port was providing, you can free up the vmnic by removing it from the virtual adapter.

To remove a vmnic from a virtual adapter, follow the steps outlined in Activity 2-18.

Activity 2-18 Removing a Virtual Adapter

1. Log on to your vSphere Client.

2. Select **Home** and then **Hosts and Clusters**.

3. Select the host on which you want to remove a virtual adapter and open the Configuration tab.

4. Choose **Networking**, click the **vSphere Distributed Switch** link, and then click the **Manage Virtual Adapters** link.

5. From Manage Virtual Adapters, click the virtual adapter that you want to remove and select **Remove**, as shown in Figure 2-50.

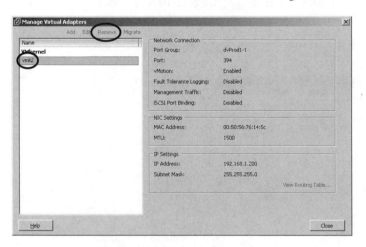

Figure 2-50   Removing a Virtual Adapter

6. In the warning box, confirm your selection by clicking **Yes**.

Migrating Virtual Adapters to/from a vSphere Standard Switch

You do not necessarily have to migrate virtual adapters from your vSSs to your vDSs, but you might want to, especially if your ultimate goal is to do away with the vSS altogether. In that case, make sure that all the VMkernel ports that you have been using on your vSSs are successfully migrated to your vDSs. This section shows how you can use the tools provided by the vCenter to easily migrate VMkernel ports from vSSs to vDSs.

To migrate virtual adapters from a vSS to a vDS, follow the steps outlined in Activity 2-19.

Activity 2-19 Migrating Virtual Adapters from a vSS to a vDS

1. Log on to your vSphere Client.

2. Select **Home** and then **Hosts and Clusters**.

3. Select the host on which you want to migrate a virtual adapter and open the Configuration tab.

4. Choose **Networking**, click the **vSphere Distributed Switch** link, and then click the **Manage Virtual Adapters** link.

5. On Manage Virtual Adapters, click **Add**.

6. On Creation Type, choose **Migrate Existing Virtual Adapters**, as shown in Figure 2-51, and then click **Next**.

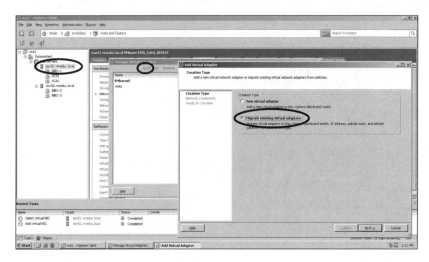

Figure 2-51   Migrating Virtual Adapters

7. Select the virtual adapter that you want to migrate and the port group to which you want to migrate it, as shown in Figure 2-52. Click **Next**.

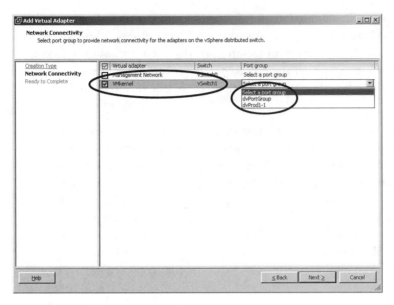

Figure 2-52   Choosing a Port Group

8. From Ready to Complete, review your settings and then confirm by clicking **Finish**.

NOTE   If you have redundant links on both the VMkernel and the VM ports, it is possible to migrate your virtual adapters during production time with no loss of service. If you choose to go down this path, however, take great care as to the order in which you migrate the links so as to ensure users always retain the links that they need.

Migrating Virtual Machines to/from a vSphere Distributed Switch

As I mentioned earlier, the purpose of port groups is to get more than one function from a switch. In other words, port groups give you options on which to connect your VMs. You can configure different policies on port groups that are specific to the VMs that you will connect to them. In this regard, port groups on vDSs are no different from vSSs; they both give you more options for your VMs.

To help you understand the concept of migrating the VMs from a vSS to a vDS, let's pretend for a moment that the switches are physical. You walk into your network closet and you have some switches that have been there for years. They are old and noisy, and they have a limited set of features compared to new switches available today. Well, as luck would have it, you have received some money in the budget to buy a shiny new switch that has lots of features that the old noisy switches do not have. You have racked the switch and powered it up for testing, and you are now ready to start moving the cables that the computers are using from the old switch to the new switch.

In essence, this is the opportunity that you have when you create a new vDS. You can take advantage of all of the new features of vDS, but only after you have actually moved the VMs over to the vDS. You could do this one at time, much like you would be forced to do in the physical world, but there are tools in vSphere that make it much faster and easier to move multiple VMs at the same time. In this section, I will first discuss how you would move an individual VM from a vSS to a vDS or vice versa, and then I will show you how to use the tools provided by vSphere to move multiple VMs at the same time. In both cases, the focus will be on the VM port group, which you might remember is one of the connection types that I said were very important.

To migrate a single VM to/from and vDS, follow the steps outlined in Activity 2-20.

Activity 2-20 Migrating a Single VM to/from a vDS

1. Log on to your vSphere Client.

2. Select **Home** and then **Hosts and Clusters**.

3. Right-click the VM that you want to migrate and select **Edit Settings**, as shown in Figure 2-53.

Figure 2-53 Migrating a VM to/from a vDS

4. Choose the network adapter that you want to migrate and the Network label (port group) to which you want to migrate it and ensure the **Connected** box in the upper-right corner is checked, as shown in Figure 2-54.

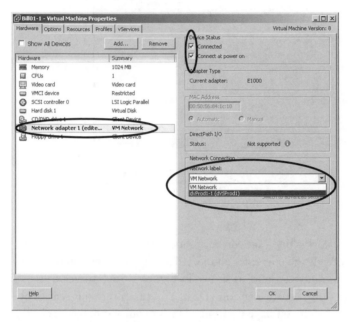

Figure 2-54 Choosing the Port Group

5. Click **OK** to confirm and save your settings.

6. If the port group is on a different IP subnet, it might be necessary to release and renew the IP address of the VM or restart the OS.

If you only have a few VMs to move, this might be an attractive option for you and your organization. However, if you have many VMs to move, you might want a better way that will allow you to move many VMs at once.

To migrate multiple VMs from one port group to another simultaneously, follow the steps outlined in Activity 2-21.

Activity 2-21 Migrating Multiple VMs Using vSphere

1. Log on to your vSphere Client.

2. Select **Home** and then **Networking**.

3. Right-click the vDS to which you want to migrate VMs and choose **Migrate Virtual Machine Networking**, as shown in Figure 2-55.

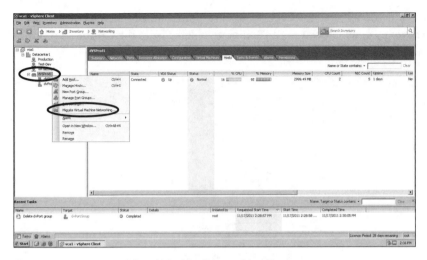

Figure 2-55 Migrate Virtual Machine Networking Tool

4. From Migrate Virtual Machine Networking, choose the source network that indicates where the VMs are currently connected and the destination network to which you want to migrate them, as shown in Figure 2-56. Sources will include port groups on vSSs as well as on vDSs. (You can filter your search by network or even by vDS if you have multiple vDSs in your vSphere.)

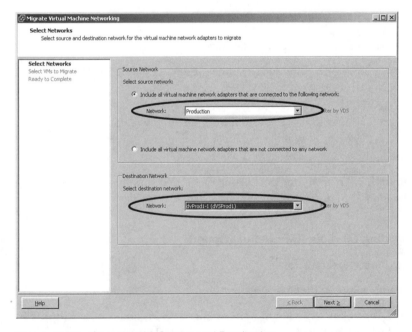

Figure 2-56 Choosing the Source and Destination

5. From Select VMs to Migrate, choose the VMs that you want to migrate from the results of the search, as shown in Figure 2-57. Click **Next**.

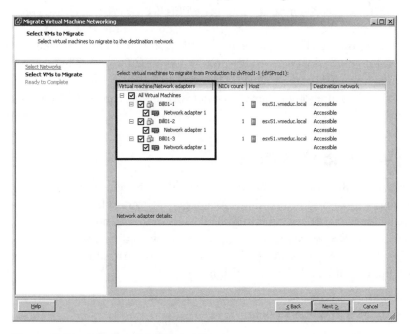

Figure 2-57   Selecting the VMs to Migrate

6. From Ready to Complete, review your settings and then confirm by clicking **Finish**.

Determining Use Cases for a vSphere Distributed Switch

As I mentioned earlier, if you decide that you are going to use a vDS in your vSphere, you first need to obtain an Enterprise Plus license. Of course, the Enterprise Plus license gives you many other features in addition to those that relate to networking, but this section focuses on networking features and ways that they might benefit a medium-sized to large-sized organization.

As outlined in Table 2-2, many features are available only on vDSs. These include features such as inbound traffic shaping, private VLANs, more granular port control for blocking, mirroring, and so on. These features can benefit your organization by giving you greater flexibility, tighter control, and enhanced security in your network. How you use them will likely vary based on what you are currently using in the physical world.

One of the nice things about this decision is that it does not have to be an "all or nothing" one. In other words, you can continue to use vSSs and begin to incorporate vDSs as well, as long as you have an Enterprise Plus license. You can leave your VMkernel ports or even service console ports (on ESX hosts) on the vSSs and use only VM port groups on the vDSs if you so desire. It's really up to you to decide what will be best for your virtual networking now and into the future and how to best use the features that VMware provides. The flexibility is there, and it's your decision as to its implementation in your virtual network and its connection to your physical network.

Configuring vSS and vDS Policies

In previous sections of this chapter, I said that we would discuss many things in greater detail later in the chapter. Well, now we are getting toward the end of this chapter, so we had better start getting into some details. In this section, I will identify common vSS and vDS policies and discuss how you can configure them on your port groups. In addition, I will discuss TCP Segmentation Offload support for VMs, jumbo frames support, and VLAN configuration.

Identifying Common vSS and vDS policies

Policies are configuration settings that enable you to customize your switches and port groups with regard to traffic control, security, and so on. In general, you can set a policy that applies to a larger network object and then "tweak" the policy to establish new settings for a smaller network object within the larger network object. The biggest difference between how this applies to vSSs versus vDSs is the network objects that are used for the large and small configurations.

With regard to vSSs, policies can be set at the switch level or they can be set at the port group level. Policies that are set at the switch level will apply to all of the ports on the switch, unless overridden by policies set the port group level. In other words, policies that are set at the port group level override any policies that are set at the switch level. This allows you to get the "best of both worlds." For example, you could set strong security policies for the switch, but then allow a "weakening" of the security policies on one port group to be used for testing and development.

There are three main polices for vSSs:

- Security
- Traffic shaping
- NIC teaming

Each of these can be set at the switch level and overridden at the port group level if necessary. You can set these polices in the properties of the switch and/or port group.

To identify and configure switch and port group settings, follow the steps outlined in Activity 2-22.

Activity 2-22 Identifying Common vSS Policies

1. Log on to your vSphere Client.

2. Select **Home** and then **Hosts and Clusters**.

3. Ensure that vSphere Standard Switch is selected next to View, and then click the **Properties** link next to the switch with the policies that you want to identify and configure, as shown in Figure 2-58.

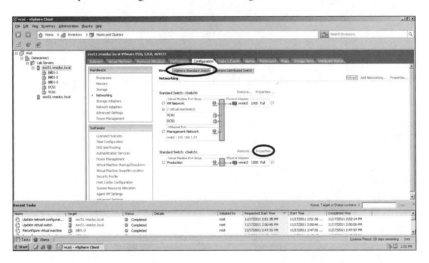

Figure 2-58   Properties Link on vSS

4. Under the Configuration column, click the switch, and then click **Edit**, as shown in Figure 2-59.

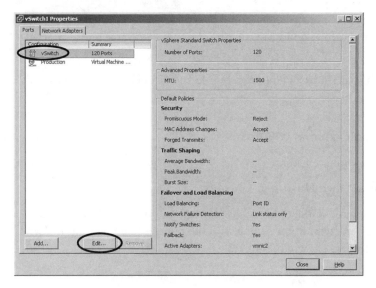

Figure 2-59   Editing vSS Policies

5. Note the tabs for General, Security, Traffic Shaping, and NIC Teaming shown in Figure 2-60.

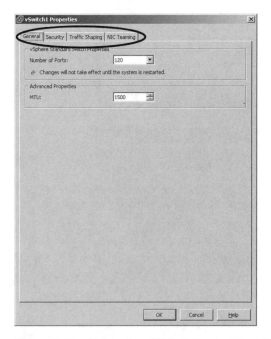

Figure 2-60   Policies for vSS Switches and Port Groups

6. Later in this chapter, in the section "Configuring vSS and vDS policies," we discuss many of these in more detail. For now, just browse the settings, and then click **OK** or **Cancel** when you have finished.

7. Click a port group within the switch and click **Edit**, as shown in Figure 2-61.

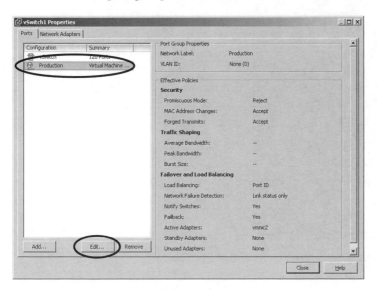

Figure 2-61 Editing Port Group Policies

8. Note the tabs for General, IP Settings (if VMkernel), Security, Traffic Shaping, and NIC Teaming.

9. Open the Security, Traffic Shaping, and NIC Teaming tabs and note the difference, especially the white "override box." This is the setting that will cause the port group to override the switch. Figure 2-62 shows an example for Security.

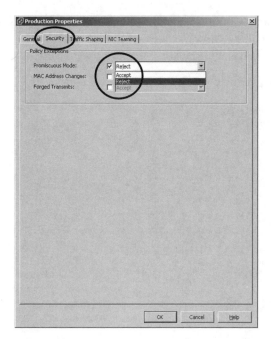

Figure 2-62   Default Security Settings for a vSS and its Port Groups

   10. Click **OK** or **Cancel** when you have finished.

So, now that you've seen the policies available for vSSs, you might wonder how the policies differ for vDSs. As I mentioned earlier, the main difference is between "what overrides what." As you have now seen, in vSSs most the settings are on the switch level with the port group settings occasionally overriding those of the switch. If you think about it, this cannot really apply in a vDS because the vDS could span multiple hosts (up to 350) and be connected to a huge virtual network that would have very different settings in each of its individual segments or locations. For this reason, only a few settings apply to a vDS on the switch level (which I will discuss later in the section "Configuring vSS and vDS Policies"). Instead, most policies are applied at the port group level. Now, before you start thinking that this will give you less flexibility, you should know that these policies can be overridden at the individual port level. In other words, there is even more flexibility in vDSs than there is in vSSs.

Policies that can be set at the port group level on a vDS and be overridden at the port level include Security, Traffic Shaping, VLAN, Teaming and Failover, Resource Allocation, Monitoring, Miscellaneous (port blocking), Advanced (override settings).

To identify these policy settings for a particular port group, follow the steps out-lined in Activity 2-23.

Activity 2-23 Identifying Common vDS Port Group Policies

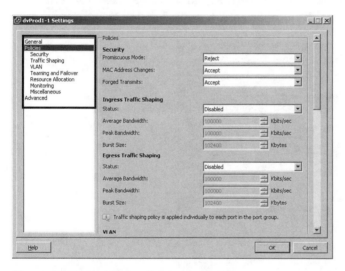

Key Topic

1. Log on to your vSphere Client.

2. Select **Home** and then **Networking**.

3. Right-click the port group that you want to examine and select **Edit Settings**.

4. Note the list of settings under the general category of Policies, as shown in Figure 2-63. Also note that the Policies category is a dialog box that gives an overview of each setting. We discuss many of these settings later in the section "Configuring vSS and vDS policies."

Figure 2-63 Port Group Policies on a vDS

5. View each of the settings noting their features versus those of vSSs and also those settings that exist here that are not on vSSs, such as inbound (Ingress) traffic shaping.

6. When you have finished, click **OK** or **Cancel** to close.

Now you might be wondering how you can override these settings at each port. Well, it's a two-step process. First, you have to configure the port group to allow changes to a particular setting at port level and then you have to locate the port that you want to configure. For example, suppose that you wanted to configure a setting for security on a specific port that will override your security settings for the port group. In that case, follow the steps outlined in Activity 2-24.

Activity 2-24 Overriding vDS Port Group Policies at the Port Level

1. Log on to your vSphere Client.

2. Select **Home** and then **Networking**.

3. Right-click the port group that you want to configure and click **Edit Settings**.

4. Select **Advanced** from the bottom of the list of Policies, ensure that **Allow Override of Port Policies** is selected and click the **Edit Override Settings** link.

5. Note all the settings that you can override, and select **Yes** next to Security Policy, and then click **OK** to confirm, as shown in Figure 2-64.

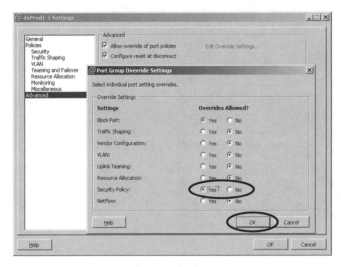

Figure 2-64 Editing Override Settings on a vDS Port Group

6. Later in the section, "Configuring vSS and vDS Policies," we discuss many of these in more detail. For now, just browse the settings, and then click **OK** or **Cancel** when you have finished.

7. Click **OK** to change the port group settings.

8. In the console pane (on the left), click the vDS and then on the Ports tab, right-click the individual port that you want to configure, and click **Edit Settings**, as shown in Figure 2-65.

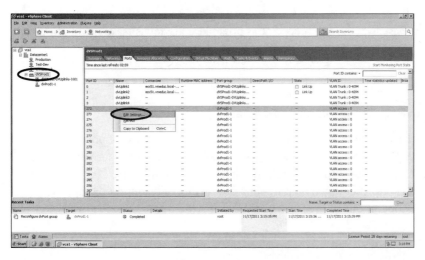

Figure 2-65   Editing Port Settings on a vDS Port Group

9. From Port Settings, select **Security,** and then select **Override** next to the security settings that you want to change for this port only. Change to your desired settings, as shown in Figure 2-66.

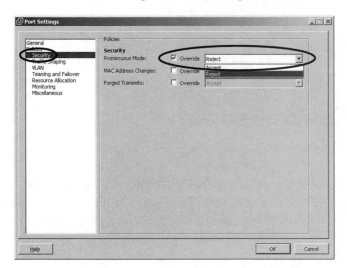

Figure 2-66   Override Settings for Ports on a vDS Port Group

10. Click **OK** to confirm and save your changes.

> **NOTE**   To stay as close the test blueprint as possible, I am focusing my configuration discussion on those topics that are specified on the blueprint.

Configuring dvPort Group Blocking Policies

You might have noticed that I included Miscellaneous in the list of port group policies and specified that it involves port group blocking. That is because that's what it says on the dialog box. Interestingly enough, as shown in Figure 2-67, it also says "Selecting Yes will shut down all ports in a port group. This might disrupt the normal network operations of the hosts or VMs using the ports." Gee, ya think?

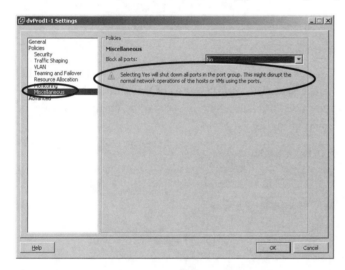

Figure 2-67   Configuring dvPort Group Blocking

Based on this, why would anyone want to select Yes? Well, this isn't your everyday setting. It's more of a "one-off" scenario setting that can come in handy if you know how to use it. Suppose that you do want to isolate all machines on a port group from the network for a period of time while you are making a software change. After the change, you want to connect them all again.

You could remove the vmnics from the port group, but what about any internal links? Also, you could disconnect each of the vNICs on the individual VMs, but what if there are many VMs, and what if you miss one or two of them? With the option of dvPort port group blocking, you can throw a "master switch" that disables networking for all VMs on that port group, no matter where they are connected. Before you throw that switch, though, make sure that you are on the right port group and make sure that the VMs that are on the port group are the ones that you want to isolate!

Configuring Load Balancing and Failover Policies

If you assign more than one vmnic (physical NIC) to a switch or port group, you can configure load balancing and failover policies using the vmnics that you assign. This is the concept of *NIC teaming*, which you should clearly understand is not using more than one vNIC on a VM, but instead using more than one vmnic on a switch or port group. In this section, I discuss configuring load balancing and failover policies, first on vSSs and then on vDSs.

On a vSS, as you might remember, NIC teaming is one of the three policies that you can configure at the switch level or at the port group level. As discussed, any policy setting that you configure at the port group level will override the settings at the switch level. So, now I will discuss the policies that you can configure at the switch level and override at the port group level.

On the NIC Teaming tab of vSS, or a port group on a vSS, you will find a list of policy exceptions, as shown in Figure 2-68. They are called *exceptions* because they each have a default setting, but that setting can be changed if necessary. I will now discuss each of these settings and the options that you have from which to choose.

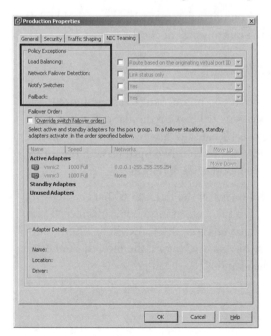

Figure 2-68   Policy Exceptions on dvPort Groups

Load Balancing

There are four load balancing options from which you can choose:

- **Route based on the originating virtual port ID:** The physical NIC is determined by the ID of the virtual port to which the VM is connected. This option has the lowest overhead and is the default option for vSSs and port groups on vSSs.

- **Route based on source MAC hash:** All of each VM's outbound traffic is mapped to specific physical NIC that is based on the MAC address associated with the VM's virtual network interface card (vNIC). This method has relatively low overhead and is compatible with all switches; even those that do not support the 802.3ad protocol.

- **Route based on IP hash:** The physical NIC for each outbound packet is chosen based on a hash of the source and destination addresses contained in the packet. This method has the disadvantage of using more CPU resources; however, it can provide better distribution of traffic across the physical NICs. This method also requires the 802.3ad link aggregation support or Ether-Channel on the switch.

- **Use explicit failover order:** The switch will always choose from its list of active adapters the highest order uplink that is not currently in use.

You should make these choices based on your virtual networking needs and based on how your virtual network connects to your physical network.

Network Failover Detection

As I discussed earlier, one of the reasons that you might want to assign more than one vmnic to a switch or port group is that you will have redundancy so that if one physical NIC fails another one can take over. That said, how will you know whether your redundancy is still intact? The following are your two options with regard to network failure detection and a brief description of each option:

- **Link Status Only:** This option relies solely on the link status that the network adapter provides. In other words, "Do I feel electricity?" or with fiber "Do I see a light?" This option detects cable pulls and physical switch failures, but it does not detect configuration errors that are beyond the directly connected switch. This method has no overhead and is the default.

- **Beacon Probing:** This option listens for link status but also sends out beacon packets from each physical NIC that it expects to be received on the other physical NIC. In this way, physical issues can be detected as well as configuration errors such as improper settings on Spanning Tree Protocol (STP) or VLANs. Also, you should not use Beacon Probing with IP-hash load balancing because the way the beacon traffic is handled does not work well with this option and can cause a "network flapping" error.

Notify Switches

The main job of a physical switch is to learn the MAC addresses of the computers and other devices on the network to which it is connected. If these change, its job is to make the change in its MAC address table. In most cases, you want to notify the physical switch of any changes in your virtual network that affect the MAC address table of the physical switch, but not always. The following are your two simple options with regard to notifying switches:

- **Yes:** If you select this option, the switch is notified whenever a VM's traffic will be routed over a different physical NIC because of a failover event. In most cases, this is the setting that you want to configure because it offers the lowest latency for failover occurrence and for vMotion migrations.

- **No:** If you select this option, the switch will not be notified and will not make the changes to its MAC address table. You should only select this option if you are using Microsoft Network Load Balancing (NLB) in unicast mode because a selection of **Yes** prevents the proper function of Microsoft Network Load Balancing in unicast mode

Failback

On each switch and/or port group, you can assign vmnics (physical NICs) as Active, Standby, or Unused, as shown in Figure 2-69.

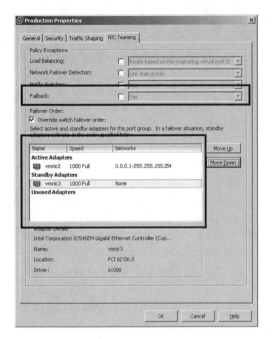

Figure 2-69 Active/Standby NICs and Failback

If a vmnic is listed as Active, it will be used unless it fails. If a vmnic fails, the first vmnic in the Standby list will be used. Now, what if the first vmnic should come back? Then, should you go back to it immediately or should you stay with the vmnic that is currently working fine? The following are your two simple options for Failback settings:

- **Yes:** If you select this option, a failed adapter that has recovered will be returned to Active status immediately after its recovery, thereby replacing the vmnic that is working fine. This might be an advantage if the primary adapter is somehow superior to the secondary one, such as a faster speed or other features. The disadvantage of this option is that a "flapping" connection could cause the system to play "ping pong" with itself, continually changing between adapters.

- **No:** If you select this option and an adapter fails and then recovers, the adapter that took its place when it failed will continue to be used. This "if it ain't broke, don't fix it" approach avoids the "ping pong" of the other option, but might leave the traffic on a slower or less desirable adapter.

On a vDS, many of the settings are reasoned in the same way, but the dialog boxes are a little different. In addition, as I mentioned before, the settings are typically configured at the port group level and can be overridden at the port level. As you might recall from earlier in this chapter, Uplink Teaming is one of the Policy settings that you can edit for port groups, as shown in Figure 2-70.

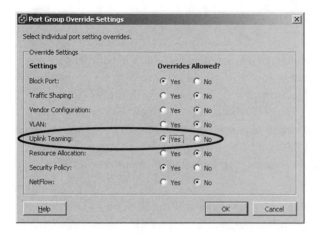

Figure 2-70   Uplink Teaming Override Settings on dvPort Groups

Once you are on the right dialog box, you will notice that the settings are exactly the same, except that they can be overridden at the individual port level, as shown on Figure 2-71.

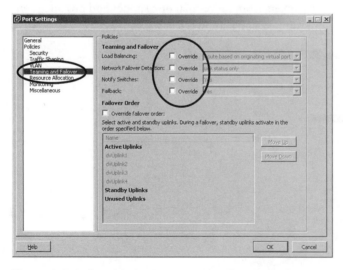

Figure 2-71   Override Settings for Uplink Teaming at Port Level

Configuring VLAN Settings

Virtual local-area networks (VLANs) are commonly used in today's networks to create and manage subnets in networks that contain many switches. They offer a high degree of flexibility and security and are useful for carrying many subnets on one or a few cables using a packet marking method called tagging. vSphere fully supports IEEE 802.1Q tagging.

Because this is not a Cisco discussion, or a Cisco test, you don't need to know all of the details of VLAN configuration, but you should know how to configure your port group properties or individual port properties to work with the VLANs that you already have in your organization. The bottom line is that if you want to bring more subnets in and out of your virtual network than you want to use physical NICs to carry, you will need to use VLANs and 802.1Q tagging. VLANs will also give you the flexibility to use the load balancing and fault tolerance options of which we've spoken, in more creative ways.

I will first discuss the configuration of VLANs on a vSS and then on a vDS. For each type of switch, I will cover your options and the impact of your decisions. In addition, I will discuss the advantages of using a vDS versus a vSS with regard to VLANs.

On vSS port groups, you can configure the VLAN setting on the General tab of the properties for the port group as shown in Figure 2-72. You can do so by typing the VLAN number from your network in the box labeled VLAN ID (Optional). If you have VMs that need to receive packets from more than one subnet and provide their own tagging for more than one subnet, you should select **All** (4095).

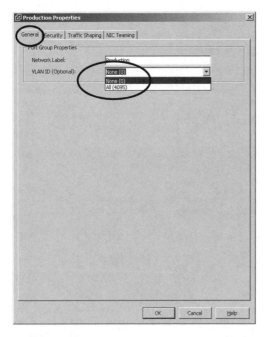

Figure 2-72 VLAN Configuration on a vSS Port Group

> **NOTE** The All (4095) setting configures the port group to receive all VLANs (0–4094). It is only necessary if a VM that is on the port group is actually creating its own tagging and needs to be connected to port groups on other VLANs as well. The All (4095) setting is not necessary to establish a trunk between the vSS and the physical switch; however, the interface on the physical switch should be set to trunk. The All (4095) setting is rarely used.

On vDS port groups, you can configure the VLAN in a much more granular fashion. You might have noticed that the VLAN setting is one of options under Polices. On this setting, you have three options from which to choose: VLAN, VLAN Trunking, and Private VLAN. In this section, I will discuss each of these options briefly and illustrate how you would configure them.

Configuring VLAN Policy Settings on a VDS

If you select VLAN, the screen changes and you are presented with a simple box in which you can input a number, as shown in Figure 2-73. This number should be an actual VLAN number that you are using on your physical network and that you want to incorporate into your virtual network as well, on this port group. Your range of choices is from 1– 4094.

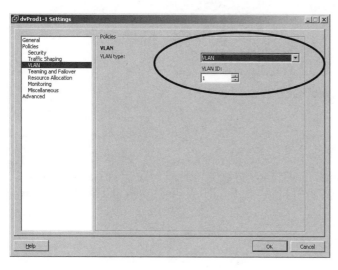

Figure 2-73 VLAN Configuration on a vDS

> **NOTE**   VLAN 1 is often used as a management VLAN for management traffic, including CDP, so it may not be a valid choice in your network.

Configuring VLAN Trunking Policies on a VDS

This option establishes the port group as a trunk that can carry multiple VLANs to VMs that are connected to it. However, rather than having to carry all 4094 VLANs just to have more than one, on vDSs this setting can be pruned to carry only the VLANs or range of VLANs that you specify, as shown in Figure 2-74.

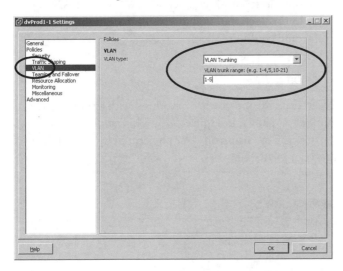

Figure 2-74   VLAN Trunking Configuration on a vDS

Configuring Private VLAN Policy Settings on a vDS

This setting, shown in Figure 2-75, allows you to use a VLAN that you have created on the vDS that can only be used by your vSphere environment and not by your external network.

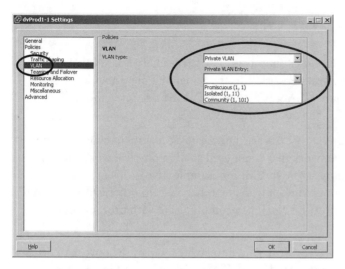

Figure 2-75   BIOS Chips and CMOS Batteries on Typical Motherboards

To create a private VLAN, you in essence further segment a VLAN that you are already receiving into the switch. You must first create these on the vDS, as shown in Figure 2-76.

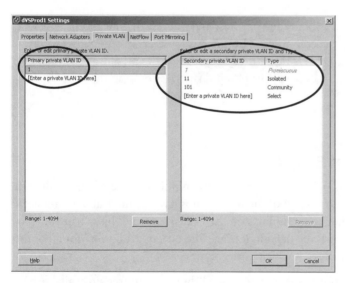

Figure 2-76   Private VLAN Creation on a vDS

There are three types of private VLANs that you can create and use in your vSphere:

- **Promiscuous:** This is named (numbered) by the primary VLAN that you chose from your physical network. It is the remaining piece that is not separated from the primary VLAN. VMs on this VLAN are reachable and can be reached by any VM in the same primary VLAN.

- **Isolated:** This is a private VLAN used to create a separate network for one VM in your virtual network that is not used at all in physical world. It can be used to isolate a highly sensitive VM, for example. If a VM is in an isolated VLAN, it will not communicate with any other VMs in other isolated VLANs or in other community VLANs. It can communicate with promiscuous VLANs.

- **Community:** This a private VLAN used to create a separate network to be shared by more than one VM. This VLAN is also only used in your virtual network and is not used in your physical network. VMs on community VLANs can communicate only to other VMs on the same community or to VMs on a promiscuous VLAN.

> **NOTE**   To use private VLANs between your host and the rest of your physical network, the physical switch connected to your host needs to be private VLAN capable and configured with the VLAN IDs being used by ESXi for the private VLAN functionality. The precise configuration of your physical switch is beyond the scope of this book.

Configuring Traffic Shaping Policies

By default, all of the VMs on a port group have an unlimited share of the bandwidth assigned to that port group, and all of the port groups have an unlimited share of the bandwidth that is provided by the uplinks on the virtual switch. This is true on vSSs and on vDSs. In other words, by default, it is an "all you can eat buffet" for all of the VMs on the switch, regardless of which port group.

When you decide to use traffic shaping, your goal should be to free up available bandwidth by limiting the bandwidth usage on port groups that contain VMs that can function with less bandwidth. This might not be as straightforward as it first seems. You might be thinking that there are some "bandwidth hogs" on your network that you want to traffic shape right away. Well, if those have anything to do with Voice over Internet Protocol (VoIP) or video, you might want to reconsider your options. In fact, you might want to traffic shape port groups that hold VMs that are file and print servers first, because they can take the bandwidth reduction hit, and thereby give the VoIP and video VMs more available bandwidth. That said, traffic shaping should never be done without first studying your virtual network to determine what you want to accomplish and to find out if you have the resources to accomplish it.

Your options for traffic shaping are very different on vSSs versus vDSs. In addition, the tools that you use to configure them are very different as well. In this section, I will first discuss your traffic shaping options on vSSs and then I will examine your additional options on vDSs.

Traffic Shaping Policies for vSphere Standard Switches

On vSSs, all traffic shaping is for outbound traffic only. This is the case regardless of which version vSS you are using. You might have heard that inbound traffic shaping is available in vSphere. This is true, but only with vDS port groups (which I will discuss next). As with other policies, you can configure traffic shaping on a vSS at the switch level and then you can override it at the port group level. After you enable traffic shaping, you can configure three main settings for outbound traffic on vSS switches and port groups, as shown with their default settings (not configured yet) in Figure 2-77.

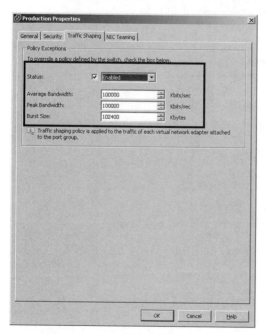

Figure 2-77 Traffic Shaping on vSS

The following is a brief description of each of these settings:

- **Average Bandwidth:** This establishes the number of kilobits per second to allow across a port, averaged over time. It should be an amount based on that which you have observed or monitored in the past.

- **Peak Bandwidth:** This is the maximum aggregate traffic measured in kilobits per second that will be allowed for a port group or switch. It should be an amount that will not hamper the effective use of the VMs connected to the port group or switch.

- **Burst Size:** This is maximum number of bytes to be allowed in a burst. A burst is defined as exceeding the average bandwidth. This setting determines how long the bandwidth can exceed the average as a factor of how far it has exceeded the average. The higher it goes, the less time it can spend there. In other words, this setting is a factor of "bandwidth X time".

Traffic Shaping Policies for vSphere Distributed Switches

On vDSs, traffic shaping can be configured for the port group and overridden if necessary at the individual port level; just as with other policies. The biggest difference from that of vSSs being that it can be configured for both inbound (ingress) and outbound (egress) traffic. You might have noticed that traffic shaping is listed under the policies of a vDS port group and/or individual port, as shown in Figure 2-78.

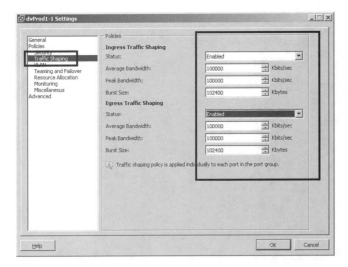

Figure 2-78 Traffic Shaping on vDS Port Groups

You can choose to enable ingress, egress, neither, or both. The other settings are very much the same as those for vSSs. You can use ingress traffic to control the amount of bandwidth that hit a port group in a given period of time. This might be useful for web servers as an additional throttling mechanism.

Enabling TCP Segmentation Offload support for a Virtual Machine

TCP Segmentation Offload (TSO) enhances the networking performance of VMs by allowing the TCP stack to emit very large frames (up to 64KB) even though the maximum transmission unit (MTU) of the interface is much smaller. The network adapter will then separate the large frames into MTU sized frames and prepend an adjusted copy of the original TCP/IP headers. In other words, you can send more data through the network in a given time and the vnic on the VM can "take sips from the fire hose." This is especially useful for VMkernel ports that are being used for iSCSI. TSO is enabled by default for the VMkernel port, but must be enabled on the VM.

As you can imagine, not just any vNIC can handle TSO. In fact, not just any OS can handle it either. If you want to use TSO, you must install an enhanced vmxnet adapter. You can enable TSO support on the VMs that run the following guest OSs:

- Microsoft Windows Server 2003 Enterprise Edition with Service Pack 2 (32 bit and 64 bit)

- Red Hat Enterprise Linux 4 (64 bit)

- Red Hat Enterprise Linux 5 (32 bit and 64 bit)

- SUSE Linux Enterprise Server 10 (32 bit and 64 bit)

To enable replace the existing adapter and enable TSO, follow the steps outlined in Activity 2-25.

Activity 2-25 Enabling TSO on a VM

1. Log on to your vCenter Server through your vSphere Client.

2. Locate the VM that you want to configure.

3. Right-click the VM and click **Edit Settings**.

4. Select the network adapter from the hardware list.

5. Record the network settings and the MAC address that the network adapter is using, as shown in Figure 2-79.

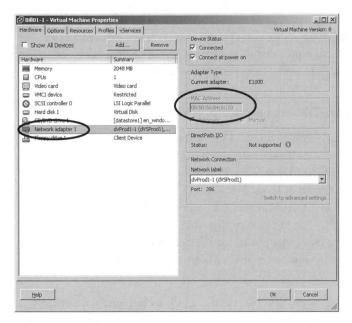

Figure 2-79   Enabling TSO on a VM

6. Click **Remove** to remove the network adapter from the VM.

7. Click **Add**, select **Ethernet Adapter**, and click **Next**.

8. In the Adapter Type group, select **Enhanced vmxnet**.

9. Select the network setting and MAC address that the old network adapter was using and click **Next**.

10. Click **Finish**, and then click **OK**.

11. If the VM is not set to upgrade the VMware tools when powered on, upgrade the VMware tools now; otherwise just restart the VM to upgrade the tools.

NOTE   TSO is enabled by default on a VMkernel interface. If TSO becomes disabled, the only way to enable it if to delete the VMkernel interface and re-create it with TSO enabled.

Enabling Jumbo Frames Support on Appropriate Components

Another way to enhance network performance and reduce CPU load is through the use of jumbo frames. Enabling jumbo frame support on your ESXi host and VMs allows them to send out much larger frames than normal into the network (9000 bytes versus 1518 bytes). If you are going to send the larger frames, the physical network to which are sending them must be enabled for jumbo frames as well. Before you enable jumbo frames on your ESXi host and VMs, check your vendor documentation to ensure that your physical adapter supports them.

You can then enable jumbo frames for the VMkernel interfaces and for the VMs. Of course, the actual steps to enable jumbo frame support for vSSs are different from those for vDSs. This section first covers enabling jumbo frames on vSSs, then on vDSs, and finally on VMs.

Enabling Jumbo Frames for VMkernel Interface on a vSS

To enable jumbo frames on a VMkernel interface, you only need to change the MTU for the interface. On a vSS, you can make this change in the properties of the switch as outlined in the steps in Activity 2-26.

Activity 2-26 Enabling Jumbo Frames for a VMkernel Interface on a vSS

1. Log on to your vCenter Server through your vSphere Client.

2. Click **Home** and then **Hosts and Clusters**.

3. Select the ESXi host that contains the VMkernel port, and open the Configuration tab.

4. Click the **Networking**, link and then click the **Properties** link next to the switch that contains the VMkernel port that you want to configure.

5. On the Ports tab, select the VMkernel interface and click **Edit**.

6. Set the MTU to **9000**, as shown in Figure 2-80, and click **OK** to confirm and save.

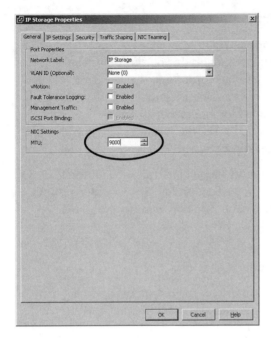

Figure 2-80   Enabling Jumbo Frames on a vSS

Enabling Jumbo Frames on a vDS

You can enable jumbo frames for an entire vDS. Just as with the VMkernel port on the vSS, you must increase the MTU. Activity 2-27 outlines the steps that you should take.

Activity 2-27 Enabling Jumbo Frames on a vDS

1. Log on to your vCenter Server through your vSphere Client.

2. Click **Home** and then **Networking**.

3. Right-click the vDS that you want to configure and click **Edit**.

4. Click **Advanced**, and then set Maximum MTU to **9000**, as shown in Figure 2-81.

5. Click **OK** to confirm your change and save.

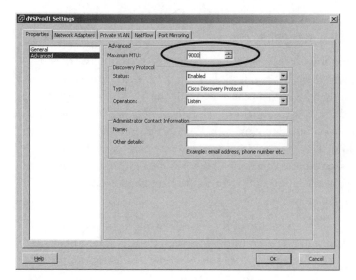

Figure 2-81   Enabling Jumbo Frames on a vDS

Enabling Jumbo Frame Support on Virtual Machines

After you have enabled jumbo frames on your physical network and your virtual switches, configuring the VMs to work with them is simply a matter of installing the proper vnic on the VM and configuring the guest OS to use it. You might think that the best vNIC to use would be the vmxnet3. Actually, there is a known issue with the vmxnet3, so you should choose either the vmxnet2 (enhanced vmxnet) or the e1000 vnic, whichever is best for the OS on the VM. (The precise configuration of the guest OS to use jumbo frames will vary by guest OS and is beyond the scope of this text.)

Determining Appropriate VLAN Configuration for a vSphere Implementation

VLANs can be a very powerful tool if used correctly in your network. You can create and control multiple subnets using the same vmnic, or your group of subnets with a small group or vmnics, and provide for load balancing and fault tolerance as well. Using multiple subnets enhances the flexibility and the security of your network because the subnets can indicate a defined purpose for that part of the network, such as iSCSI storage, vMotion, management, NFS datastores, and so on (all of which are covered in Chapter 3). VLANs provide some security if configured properly, but they can also be susceptible to a VLAN hopping attack whereby a person who has access to one VLAN can gain access to the others on the same cable. This is not a good scenario, especially if one of the other networks is the management network. This can typically be prevented by proper configuration of your physical switches and keeping them up to date with firmware and patches.

Still, an even more defined way to separate the components of your network is by using a new vmnic for each one. This is referred to as *physical separation*. It is considered even more secure than VLANs because it avoids the VLAN hopping attack. It is a best practice to use a separate vmnic for each type of network that you create. For example, you should use a separate vmnic for VM port groups than you do for management VMkernel ports. Also, you should separate vmnics for each type of VMkernel port whenever possible. For example, it would be best to have a different vmnic for each of your VMkernel ports for vMotion, FT logging, iSCSI storage, NFS datastores, and management.

So to recap, you are supposed to make use of the VLANs while at the same time using a separate vmnic for just about everything. How can these two best practices possibly coexist? Figure 2-82 illustrates an example whereby a different vmnic is used as the active adapter for each important service, but at the same time VLANs are used to allow those adapters to be a standby adapter for another service. (In the table, *A* stands for active, *S* for standby, and *U* for unused.)

This is just one scenario on one ESXi host's vSS, but it shows the power of what can be done when you begin to use all of your options. Hopefully, you can take the principles learned from this scenario and apply them to your own virtual network. Examine Figure 2-82 to determine what you like about it and what you want to change. For example, adding another physical switch would definitely be a good practice. What else do you see? Again, this is just one scenario of many. So, see whether you can take what I have discussed and build your own scenarios.

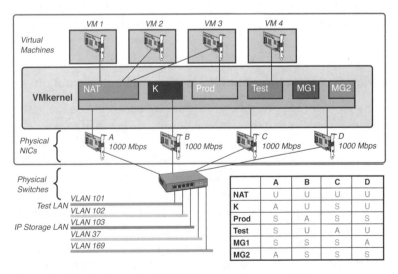

Figure 2-82   An Example of VLAN Configuration on a vSS

Summary

The main topics covered in this chapter are the following:

- I began this chapter by identifying the capabilities of vSSs and the creation, configuration, editing, and removal of vSSs and the port groups they contain.

- I then discussed the creation, configuration, management, and removal of vDSs and the port groups that they contain, including comparing and contrasting their features with those of vSSs.

- Finally, I covered the configuration of port groups on both vSSs and vDSs, including policies such as port group blocking, load balancing, failover, traffic shaping, TCP Segmentation Offload, and jumbo frames.

Exam Preparation Tasks

Review All of the Key Topics

Review the most important topics from inside the chapter, noted with the Key
Topic icon in the outer margin of the page. Table 2-3 lists these key topics and the
page numbers where each is found. Know the main differences between vSSs and
vDSs and the port groups on each. Understand how to create, configure, edit, and
delete these components and policies.

Table 2-3   Key Topics for Chapter 2

Key Topic Element	Description	Page Number
Figure 2-1	A Diagram of a vSphere Standard Switch	76
Bullet List	Uses of VMkernel Ports	77
Activity 2-1	Creating a New vSphere Standard Switch	78
Activity 2-2	Deleting a vSphere Standard Switch	81
Activity 2-3	Adding a vmnic to a Switch	82
Activity 2-4	Configuring the Physical Aspects of a vmnic	85
Activity 2-5	Removing a vmnic from a vSphere Standard Switch	87
Activity 2-6	Configuring a VMkernel Port for Network Services	88
Activity 2-7	Adding a Port Group to a vSphere Standard Switch	91
Table 2-2	vSS Capabilities Versus vDS Capabilities	95
Bullet List	vDS Capabilities	96
Activity 2-8	Creating a New vSphere Distributed Switch	98
Activity 2-9	Adding a Host to a vSphere Distributed Switch	101
Activity 2-10	Removing a Host from a vSphere Distributed Switch	103
Activity 2-11	Adding a Port Group to a vSphere Distributed Switch	104
Activity 2-12	Configuring Port Groups on a vSphere Distributed Switch	106
Activity 2-13	Removing a Port Group from a vSphere Distributed Switch	107
Figure 2-37	Distributed Switch Architecture	108
Activity 2-14	Adding an Uplink Adapter to a dvUplink Group	108

Key Topic Element	Description	Page Number
Activity 2-15	Removing an Uplink Adapter from a dvUplink Group	110
Activity 2-16	Creating a Virtual Adapter	112
Activity 2-17	Configuring a Virtual Adapter	116
Activity 2-18	Removing a Virtual Adapter	117
Activity 2-19	Migrating Virtual Adapters from a vSS to a vDS	118
Activity 2-20	Migrating a Single VM to/from a vDS	120
Activity 2-21	Migrating Multiple VMs Using vSphere	121
List	Three Main Polices for vSSs	124
Activity 2-22	Identifying Common vSS Policies	125
Activity 2-23	Identifying Common vDS Port Group Policies	129
Activity 2-24	Overriding vDS Port Group Policies at the Port Level	130
Bullet List	Settings for Traffic Shaping	144
Activity 2-25	Enabling TSO on a VM	145
Activity 2-26	Enabling Jumbo Frames for a VMkernel Interface on a vSS	147
Activity 2-27	Enabling Jumbo Frames on a vDS	148

Review Questions

The answers to these review questions are in Appendix A.

1. Which of the following is not a valid use for a VMkernel port?

   a. IP storage

   b. vMotion

   c. FT logging

   d. Service console port

2. Which of the following are types of connections on a vSS on an ESXi 5.0 host? (Choose two.)

   a. Service console

   b. VM

   c. Host bus adapter

   d. VMkernel

3. If you configure policies on a specific port group that conflict with polices on the switch, which of the following will result?

   a. The port group policies on the switch always override those on a port group.

   b. The port group policies override the switch policies for the VMs on that port group.

   c. The port group policies override those on the switch and will be applied to all VMs on all port groups.

   d. A configuration error will be indicated.

4. What is the maximum number of hosts that you can connect to a vDS?

   a. 100

   b. 10

   c. 350

   d. 32

5. Which of the following is the correct traffic shaping metric for average bandwidth, peak bandwidth, and burst size, respectively?

   a. Kbps, Kbps, KB

   b. KB, KB, KB

   c. Kbps, Kbps, Kbps

   d. KB, KB, Kbps

6. What should you change to enable TSO on a VMkernel interface on ESXi 5.0?

   a. You must place a check mark in the correct configuration parameter.

   b. TSO is enabled by default on all VMkernel interfaces on ESXi 5.0.

   c. You need more than one vmnic assigned to the port.

   d. You must enable the interface for IP storage as well.

7. Which of the following is a capability of a vDS but not of a vSS?

   a. Outbound traffic shaping

   b. Network vMotion

   c. VLAN segmentation

   d. NIC teaming

8. If you have a vDS network policy configured for a port group and a conflicting network policy configured for a specific port within the port group, which of the following will result?

    a. The port group policy overrides the specific port policy.

    b. A configuration error will be indicated.

    c. The specific port setting overrides the port group setting for the VM on that port.

    d. The specific port setting is applied to all VMs connected to the port group.

9. Which of the following load balancing policies requires 802.3ad or Ether-Channel on the switch?

    a. Route based on IP hash

    b. Route based on MAC hash

    c. Route based on originating virtual port ID

    d. Use explicit failover order

10. To what should you configure the MTU setting on a vSS or vDS to allow for jumbo frames?

    a. 1500

    b. 15000

    c. 150

    d. 9000

11. Which of the following is not a part of the configuration of a VMkernel port?

    a. IP address

    b. Subnet mask

    c. Default gateway

    d. MAC address

12. Which two types of ports can you create on a vSphere 5.0 vSS when you select Add Networking? (Choose two.)

    a. Service console

    b. VM

    c. Host bus adapter

    d. VMkernel

13. Which feature is available with a vDS but not with a vSS?

   a. VLAN segmentation

   b. Network vMotion

   c. 802.1Q tagging

   d. NIC teaming

14. Which of the following is required for VM port group configuration?

   a. IP address

   b. MAC address

   c. Label

   d. Uplink

15. Which of the following is not a requirement when configuring a VMkernel port?

   a. MAC address

   b. IP address

   c. Subnet mask

   d. Default gateway

16. Which of the following tools allows you to migrate multiple VMs from a vSS onto a vDS?

   a. vMotion

   b. The Migrate Virtual Machine Wizard

   c. Storage vMotion

   d. DRS

17. Which of the following is *not* one of the three main policies on a vSS?

   a. Security

   b. IP storage

   c. Traffic shaping

   d. NIC teaming

18. Which of the following best describes NIC teaming?

    a. NIC teaming is using more than one vmnic on a VM.

    b. NIC teaming is using more than one vNIC on a VM.

    c. NIC teaming is using more than one vmnic on a switch or port group.

    d. NIC teaming is connecting more than one virtual switch to the same vmnic.

19. Which of the following load balancing policies is the default for a vSphere vSS?

    a. Route based on originating virtual port ID

    b. Route based on MAC hash

    c. Route based on IP Hash

    d. Use explicit failover order

20. Which VLAN setting should you use on a port group if a VM within it is going to create its own "tagging" and needs to be connected to port groups on other VLANs as well?

    a. 1500

    b. 1111

    c. 1

    d. 4095

This chapter covers the following subjects:

- Configuring Shared Storage for vSphere
- Configuring the Storage Virtual Appliance for vSphere
- Creating and Configuring VMFS and NFS Datastores

CHAPTER 3

Planning and Configuring vSphere Storage

Let's pretend that you are happy with the host on which your virtual machines (VMs) reside and you do not plan on moving them at all. In other words, you live in a world where features such as vMotion, High Availability (HA), Distributed Resource Scheduler (DRS), and Distributed Power Management (DPM) have no value for you. In that case, the best place to keep all of the files that your VMs will need might be only on the local (direct attached) drives of the host.

Of course, you probably do not live in that world, and chances are good that you want to use the aforementioned features. This means that you will have to create and maintain some type of shared storage. This shared storage will in turn provide the redundancy and centralized management that you require. Until vSphere5, that storage would have to be a form of centralized shared storage, such as a storage-area network (SAN) or network-attached storage (NAS). These options can still be used on vSphere5, but you can also elect to use distributed shared storage that actually exists because of replicated local drives on two or three ESXi hosts.

In this chapter, I will discuss the planning and configuring of all types of vSphere storage, including Fibre Channel, Internet Small Computer System Interface (iSCSI), Fiber Channel over Ethernet (FcoE), NAS, and vSphere Storage Appliance (VSA). In addition, you learn how to configure both Virtual Machine File System (VMFS) and NAS datastores. Finally, I will cover "real-world" use cases for various types of storage.

"Do I Know This Already?" Quiz

The "Do I Know This Already?" quiz allows you to assess whether you should read this entire chapter or simply jump to the "Exam Preparation Tasks" section for review. If you are in doubt, read the entire chapter. Table 3-1 outlines the major headings in this chapter and the corresponding "Do I Know This Already?" quiz questions. You can find the answers in Appendix A, "Answers to the 'Do I Know This Already?' Quizzes and Chapter Review Questions."

Table 3-1   Headings and Questions

Foundations Topics Section	Questions Covered in This Section
Configuring Shared Storage for vSphere	1–3
Configuring the Storage Virtual Appliance for vSphere	4–6
Creating and Configuring VMFS and NFS Datastores	7–10

1. Which of following is *not* a type of storage access?

   a. Fibre Channel

   b. Network-attached storage

   c. VMFS

   d. Fibre Channel over Ethernet

2. In the runtime name of VMFS datastore vmhba1:0:2:4, to which storage processor is the datastore connected?

   a. 1

   b. 4

   c. 0

   d. 2

3. Which of the following can prevent a host from seeing LUNs that are on a storage processor to which it is connected?

   a. Zoning

   b. Shares

   c. Permissions

   d. Masking

4. Which of the following cannot be used by the VMs on a VSA cluster?

   a. vMotion

   b. DRS clusters

   c. vSphere HA

   d. NFS

5. How many static IP addresses are required for a VSA with three hosts?

   a. 14

   b. 3

    c. 11

    d. 20

6. What is the maximum tested amount of RAM that be used on a host that is a member of a VSA?

    a. 1TB

    b. 72GB

    c. 32GB

    d. 500GB

7. Which of the following are *not* types of datastores? (Choose two.)

    a. VMFS

    b. Fibre Channel

    c. NFS

    d. iSCSI

8. Which of the following is *not* an advantage of VMFS5?

    a. Support for greater than 2TB storage devices for each extent

    b. Standard 1MB block size with support for 2TB virtual disks

    c. Support for greater than 2TB disk size for RDMs

    d. Fully backward compatible to ESX/ESXi 4.x hosts

9. Which of the following is the result of unmounting an NFS datastore?

    a. All data on the NFS server's share is deleted.

    b. All the metadata on the NFS server's share is deleted.

    c. The datastore is not deleted from the host and the data remains on the NFS server.

    d. The datastore is unmounted from the host, but the data remains on the NFS server.

10. Which of the following is the largest extent that you can have in a VMFS-5 datastore?

    a. 2TB minus 512KB

    b. 4TB

    c. 64TB

    d. 256GB

Foundation Topics

Configuring Shared Storage for vSphere

As I mentioned earlier, there are many reasons that shared storage is often superior to local storage. This is true even outside of a virtual datacenter. Some of the reasons that shared storage is preferable to local storage in vSphere are the following:

- Central repository that is accessible from multiple hosts
- Scalable and recoverable implementations
- Clustering of VMs across physical hosts
- Data replication
- Using VMware vMotion, HA, DRS, and DPM

Because we are all in agreement that shared storage is important to have, let's look at how we configure and manage shared storage in vSphere.

Identifying Storage Adapters and Devices

At its essence, a storage adapter is like a glorified network interface card that is used for storage. In fact, with the help of the VMkernel, a normal supported network interface card can be used for some types of storage. In this section, I will focus on four main types of storage adapters:

- Fibre Channel
- Fibre Channel over Ethernet (FCoE)
- iSCSI
- Network-attached storage (NAS)

For each, I will briefly describe the technology and identify its advantages and disadvantages. Figure 3-1 shows an overview of these storage technologies.

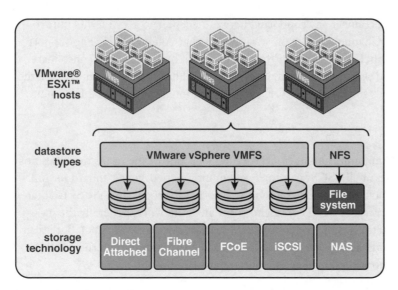

Figure 3-1 Storage Overview

Fibre Channel

You might have noticed that Fibre Channel is generally spelled with an "re" at the end rather than an "er." The "re" is actually referring to the technology that began in the 1980s by a European group and has evolved substantially since then. Generally speaking, Fibre Channel is a technology used primarily for storage-area networking (SAN). In spite of its name, it can use fiber-optic cable or copper cable. Fibre Channel has a lower overhead than TCP/IP and is offered with speeds of 1, 2, 4, 8, 10, and 20Gbps. The main advantages of Fibre Channel are its flexibility and the fact that it does not put a load on the Ethernet network. Its chief disadvantage is cost; Fibre Channel implementations often cost considerably more than other options.

NOTE   vSphere5 supports Fibre Channel connections up to 8Gbps.

FCOE

Fibre Channel over Ethernet (FCoE) is an encapsulation of Fibre Channel frames so they can be sent over Ethernet networks. FCoE allows the Fibre Channel protocol to be used on Ethernet networks of 10Gbps or higher speeds. You can use a specialized type of adapter called a converged network adapter (CNA) or, beginning with vSphere5, you can connect any supported network adapter to a VMkernel port to be used for Fibre Channel. The main advantage is that you do not have to support both a Fibre Channel fabric and an Ethernet network, but instead can consolidate all networking and storage to the Ethernet network. The chief disadvantages are the higher cost of cards suitable for FCOE and the additional traffic on the Ethernet.

iSCSI

Internet Small Computer System Interface (iSCSI) is one of the terms that does not define what it does at all! iSCSI is actually a common networking standard for linking data storage facilities that is based on the Internet Protocol (IP). iSCSI facilitates data transfers by carrying SCSI commands over an IP network, generally the intranets of organizations. It is mostly used on local-area networks (LANs), but it can also be used on wide-area networks (WANs) or even through the Internet with the use of tunneling protocols. vSphere supports up to 10Gbps iSCSI.

NAS

Network-attached storage (NAS) is file-level data storage provided by a computer that is specialized to provide not only the data but also the file system for the data. In some ways, NAS is like a very glorified mapped drive. The similarity is that the data to which you are connecting is seen as a share on the NAS device. The difference is that the device that is storing the data and providing the file system is specially designed for just this purpose and is generally extremely efficient at sharing the files. Protocols that can be used on a NAS include Common Internet File Systems (CIFS) and Network File Systems (NFS). The only one of these that is supported in vSphere is NFS. In fact, the only supported NAS protocol in vSphere is NFS v3 over TCP.

Identifying Storage Naming Conventions

As you can see, you have a great number of technologies from which to choose to build your datastores for your vSphere. Later, in the section "Creating and Configuring VMFS and NFS Datastores," I will discuss much more specifically how you build your datastores and exactly how you use them. For now, let's focus on how you will identify the physical storage locations with which you will create your datastores.

Actually, your naming convention will depend on the technology that you have chosen. If you are using local drives or a SAN technology, such as iSCSI or Fibre channel, you will use a naming convention associated with a vmhba. If you are using NAS, your naming convention will be associated with the share name of the data source. In this section, I will discuss each of these naming conventions as they relate to vSphere.

Storage Naming Conventions for Local and SAN

The naming convention that vSphere uses to identify a physical storage location that resides on a local disk or on a SAN consists of several components. In fact, you can refer to the location a few different ways depending on the question that you are asking and how specific you really need to get. The following are the three most common naming conventions for local and SAN and a brief description of each:

- **Runtime name:** Uses the convention vmhbaN:C:T:L, where

  —*vm* stands for VMkernel.

  —*hba* is host bus adapter.

  —*N* is a number corresponding to the host bus adapter location (starting with 0).

  —*C* is channel and the first connection is always 0 in relation to vSphere. (An adapter that supports multiple connections will have different channel numbers for each connection.)

  —*T* is target, which is a storage adapter on the SAN or local device.

  —*L* is logical unit number (LUN), which is described in more detail in the section "Creating and Configuring VMFS and NFS Datastores."

  A runtime name is created by the host and is only relative to the installed adapters at the time of creation; it might be changed if adapters are added or replaced and the host is restarted.

- **Canonical name:** The Network Address Authority (NAA) ID that is a unique identifier for the LUN. This name is guaranteed to be persistent even if adapters are added or changed and the system is rebooted.

- **SCSI ID:** The unique SCSI identifier that signifies the exact disk or disks that are associated with a LUN.

You can view the storage paths expressed in each of these naming conventions on the Storage View tab, as shown in Figure 3-2.

SCSI ID	Canonical Name	Runtime Name	Lun
010001000020204573785...	t10.9454450000000000000000001000000...	vmhba34:C0:T0:L1	1
020003000060060160eb7...	naa.60060160eb7026007ef7a4b3a50adf11	vmhba0:C0:T1:L3	3
02001900060060160eb7...	naa.60060160eb7026002666a802a60adf11	vmhba0:C0:T1:L25	25
0200030000600805f3001...	naa.600805f30016be8000000000131700d6	vmhba0:C0:T0:L3	3

Figure 3-2 Storage Naming Conventions

To access the Storage Views tab for your host, follow the steps outlined in Activity 3-1.

Activity 3-1 Accessing the Storage Views Tab to View Naming Conventions

1. Log on to your vSphere Client.

2. Select **Home** and then **Hosts and Clusters**.

3. Select the ESX host on which you want to view the storage, and then open the Storage Views tab.

4. Change the view by selecting the drop-down arrow, as shown in Figure 3-3.

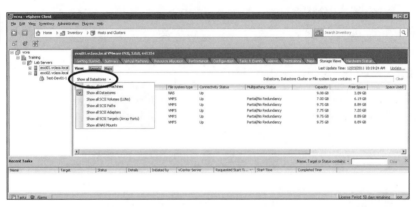

Figure 3-3 Changing Storage Views

As I will discuss later in the section "Identifying VMFS and NFS Datastore Properties," the naming convention of a NFS datastore is simply the name of the target that you create on the NFS Server. This can be an IP address or hostname. Also, you use a folder hierarchy for the share and give it a name on your host as well.

Identifying Hardware/Dependent Hardware/Software iSCSI Initiator Requirements

Suppose that you have decided to go with iSCSI as your storage technology of choice. Well, now you have yet another decision to make. This decision centers on how much work you want the VMkernel to do with regard to iSCSI versus how much you want to pay for your network interface cards that will be used for iSCSI. Figure 3-4 illustrates your choices.

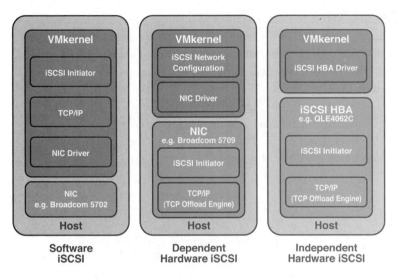

Figure 3-4   iSCSI Initiators

Two processes have to take place to create effective iSCSI storage:

- **Discovery:** The process of the host finding the iSCSI storage and identifying the LUNs that are presented

- **TCP offload:** The process of deferring some of the management aspects of the TCP connection from the host's CPU. The device or service that does this is referred to as the TCP Offload Engine (TOE).

The real question then is whether you want the VMkernel to be associated with discovery and/or with TOE. You have three choices, as follows:

- **Hardware (independent hardware) iSCSI initiator:** In this case, a smarter and more expensive adapter is used that provides for discovery of the LUN as well as TOE. This completely removes the responsibility from the VMkernel and from the processors on the host. VMkernel ports are not required for this type of card. The host has only to supply the card with the drivers and the card does the rest. If you have determined that your VMkernel is overloaded, this is an option that can improve performance.

- **Dependent hardware iSCSI initiator:** In this case, the card provides for the TOE, but the VMkernel must first provide the discovery of the LUN. This takes some of the work off of the VMkernel and the processors on the host, but not all of it. In addition, VMkernel ports are required for this type of card. If possible, they should be on the same subnet as the iSCSI array that contains the data. In addition, if possible, the cards should be dedicated to this service.

- **Software iSCSI initiator:** In this case, the VMkernel is providing for the discovery of the LUNs as well as for the TOE. The disadvantage of this type of initiator is that the VMkernel is doing all of the work. This fact does not necessarily mean that performance will suffer. If the VMkernel is not otherwise overloaded then benchmark tests show this type of initiator to be every bit as fast as the others. In addition, software initiators allow for options such as bidirectional Challenge Handshake Authentication Protocol (CHAP) and per-target CHAP, which I will discuss later in the section "Creating/Renaming/Deleting/Unmounting a VMFS Datastore."

> **NOTE**   As a summary, know the following. For software iSCSI and dependent hardware iSCSI, your ESXi 5.0 hosts will support per-discovery and per-target CHAP. For independent hardware iSCSI, your ESXi 5.0 hosts will support only one set of CHAP credentials per initiator. In other words, with independent hardware iSCSI, you cannot assign different credentials for different targets.

Comparing and Contrasting Array Thin Provisioning and Virtual Disk Thin Provisioning

In a general sense, thin provisioning of disks allows you to over promise what you can possibly deliver. This might not seem to be an advantage when you first think about it, but if you have unrealistic clients, it can be a lifesaver. However, you don't need unrealistic clients to take advantage of what thin provisioning has to offer. If you know that some disks will grow quite a lot while others will not, but you aren't sure which ones will grow the most, then you might be a good candidate for thin provisioning. Finally, if being able to allocate disk space to servers in a method in which they receive just enough and just in time (while constantly monitoring to make sure that you have enough) appeals to you, then you might be a candidate for thin provisioning.

Some administrators really love thin provisioning, others do not. In this section, I will describe two different types of thin provisioning: array and virtual disk. I will compare and contrast these two types. I am not trying to sell you on it or away from it either; I'm just providing information so that you can decide for yourself.

Array Thin Provisioning

As the name implies, array thin provisioning is done in the storage arrays themselves before VMware vSphere is ever connected. It is a strategy used by some organizations to optimize utilization of available storage by purchasing less storage capacity up front and deferring capacity upgrades until they are in line with actual business usage. In this way, they do not have to pay for a lot of disk space that is actually unused.

You can overallocate or oversubscribe the storage by allowing a server to view more storage than has actually been set aside for it. As I mentioned before, this increases flexibility when you don't know which servers will really grow the most, but you are sure that some will grow. Physical storage capacity is dedicated to each server only when data is actually written to the disk. Of course, because you are overpromising what you can actually deliver (if all servers were to want all that was promised them), you should always monitor the arrays and add physical capacity when needed. This might require some downtime for the servers and end users of the data.

Virtual Disk Thin Provisioning

Virtual disk thin provisioning is specified when a VM is created and/or when a disk is added to a VM. It controls how much of the datastore capacity will actually be dedicated to the VM's disk. If you elect to thin provision a VMs disk, the size of the disk will indicate how much of the datastore is dedicated to it, but only the amount that is written to it will be subtracted from the datastore capacity. You should be familiar with the virtual disk thin provisioning terms that follow:

- **Virtual disk allocation:** The size of the disk on the VM as it is told to the guest OS.

- **Available datastore capacity:** The actual amount of storage capacity on the created datastore.

- **Used storage capacity:** The amount of data that has actually been written to the datastore.

As illustrated in Figure 3-5, your three VMs have a total of 140GB of virtual disk allocation on a datastore that has only a 100GB available datastore capacity, but are you out of space? Well, "no," at least not yet; however, you have overpromised what you can deliver. Currently, the used storage capacity is only 80GB, but that is only half of the story. Should the applications on the VMs decided to write to the space that they think they have, they could quickly run out of space. Because of this, you should monitor the situation and be ready to add available datastore capacity if needed. Later, in the section "Extending/Expanding VMFS Datastores," I will discuss your options for adding available datastore capacity without disturbing the end user.

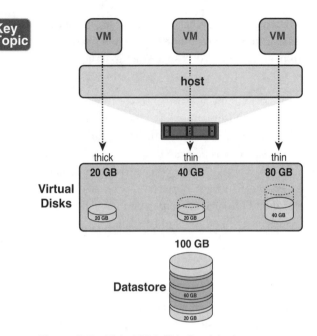

Figure 3-5 Virtual Disk Thin Provisioning

NOTE You are not "stuck" with thin provisioning of a disk (or thick provisioning for that matter) just because you created it that way at first. There are many ways to change a disk from thin to thick or vice versa, including inflating the VMDK file, Enhanced Storage vMotion, and vCenter Converter. I also discuss these options in Chapter 5, "Establishing and Maintaining Service Levels."

NOTE The VMDKs for VMs stored on NFS datastores in vSphere are always thin provisioned. This is just the nature of the protocol.

Describing Zoning and LUN Masking Practices

One of your goals as a virtual datacenter administrator is to configure a method whereby your hosts can see a physical storage area on the SAN and in essence ask it "What LUNs do you have for me today?" Meanwhile, the storage administrator's goal is to make sure that all LUNs are accessed appropriately and that the data on them is protected. These two goals should not be at odds with each other, but instead you and your storage administrator should be working as a team to protect each other. If you were able to access a LUN that you should not actually use, and you accidentally deleted important data, I would call that an RGE (resumé-generating event), and I hope to help you avoid those.

That said, there are a couple of practices used with Fibre Channel SANs that can be employed by the storage administrator to keep you from seeing LUNs that you have no need to see. These are referred to as zoning and masking. Zoning and masking are two very different methods of accomplishing a similar result. I will now briefly discuss each of these practices.

Zoning

As you can see in Figure 3-6, each component (also called a node) of a Fibre Channel fabric is identified uniquely by a 64-bit address that is expressed in hexadecimal, called a World Wide Name (WWN). I will focus on two types of nodes: the storage processor and the Fibre Channel host bus adapter (HBA). The storage administrator can configure zoning on the Fibre Channel switches to control which WWNs can see which other WWNs through the switch fabric, also referred to as *soft zoning*. In addition, the Fibre Channel switch might also employ *hard zoning*, which determines which ports of the switch will be connected to storage processors. The purpose of using both of these methods is to keep you from accidentally accessing storage processors that do not apply to you and thereby accessing volumes that do not apply to you either.

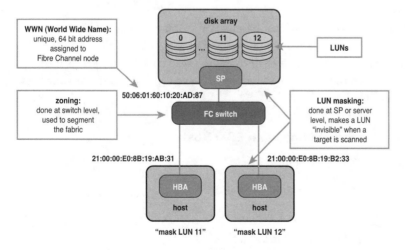

Figure 3-6 Zoning and Masking

Masking

Whereas *zoning* is controlling which HBAs can see which SPs through the switch fabric, *masking* is controlling what the SPs tell the host with regard to the LUNs that they can provide. In other words, you or the storage administrator can configure the SP to "lie" to you about the LUNs to which it is connected. You might configure masking on your host if you notice that you can see a LUN that you know should not be used, but a much better practice is to contact the storage administrator to have the change made on the SP. In fact, masking cannot be done in the GUI of an ESXi 5.0 host, but only on the command line. So, what does that tell you? It should tell you that VMware recommends that the masking be done on the SP through communication with the storage administrator. That way everyone knows about it and it does not cause "troubleshooting opportunities" later on.

Scanning/Rescanning Storage

As I previously discussed, the datastores that you create will be connected to physical storage capacity on a local disk, SAN, or NAS. vSphere offers many alternatives to suit your needs and to allow you to make changes when needed. When you add a new host, that host automatically scans up to 256 Fibre Channel SAN LUNs (0–255). In fact, as I discussed in Chapter 1, "Planning, Installing, Configuring, and Upgrading vCenter Server and VMware ESXi," if you are installing the host locally then you might want to keep the Fibre Channel disconnected until you have the host installed and then connect the Fibre Channel and perform the scan. However, iSCSI storage is automatically scanned whenever you create and configure a new iSCSI storage adapter.

In the interim, if you make a change to the physical storage, you should rescan to make sure that your hosts see the latest physical storage options. This is not done automatically because it takes resources perform the scan so VMware leaves it to your control as to when the scan should be done. To rescan the storage of your host, follow the steps outlined in Activity 3-2.

Activity 3-2 Rescanning the Storage of an ESXi Host

1. Log on to your vSphere Client.

2. Select **Home** and then **Hosts and Clusters**.

3. Select the ESX host on which you want rescan the storage.

4. Click the **Storage** link under Hardware.

5. In the upper-right corner, click the **Rescan All** link, as shown in Figure 3-7.

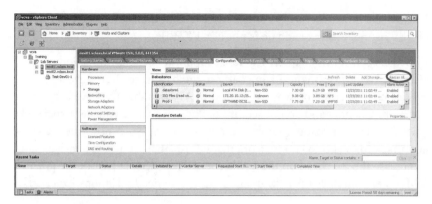

Figure 3-7   The Rescan All Link

6. Choose to **Scan for New Storage Devices** or **Scan for New VMFS Volumes**, as shown in Figure 3-8. If you are actually looking for a newly created volume, you should select to Scan for New VMFS Volumes because it will be must faster than scanning storage adapters for new LUNs and devices. Click **OK**.

Figure 3-8   Scanning for New Storage Devices and Volumes

7. Monitor the Recent Tasks pane and your **Storage** and **Storage Adapters** links for the results of the scan.

Identifying Use Cases for FCOE

FCoE increases the use of an existing physical infrastructure that incorporates both Fibre Channel and Ethernet. It does so by encapsulating Fibre Channel traffic into Ethernet frames and thereby allowing Fibre Channel traffic to flow through the Ethernet network. This reduces the overall number of ports that must exist in the network because the infrastructure is combined instead of duplicated. FCOE then uses the Fibre Channel protocol and does not use TCP/IP.

As I mentioned earlier in this chapter, vSphere5 supports both hardware and software FCoE. If performance is your main goal, use the hardware alternative and special cards called converged network adapter (CNA) cards that preserve the performance of Fibre Channel and do not require the overhead mechanisms associated with TCP/IP. However, if cost is your greatest concern, vSphere5 now offers a software version that allows you to choose from many cards that are less expensive than CNAs but increase the overhead on the VMkernel. They support part of the job and then the VMkernel then does the rest. In either case, you need a 10Gbps Ethernet network.

Creating an NFS Share for Use with vSphere

As I mentioned earlier, a different method of accomplishing the same result (storage options for VMs) can be configured using an NFS share. An NFS share is generally located on a computer that is specialized for creating and sharing files using the NFS protocol. This type of computer is referred to as a NAS device. The overall system and practice of using a NAS device to provide shared files is generally referred to as using an NFS server. An NFS server contains one or more directories that can be shared with your ESXi hosts over a TCP/IP network. Your ESXi host will use one of its VMkernel ports to access the share.

NOTE vSphere5 supports only NFS Version 3 over TCP.

To create an NFS server, you start with a NAS device that you have built on a Windows, Linux, or UNIX box or that you have acquired through a third party. You must configure the share with the appropriate permissions and other attributes (also known as flags) so that your ESXi host can use its VMkernel ports to gain access to the share. The main aspects of your configuration should be as follows:

- A hostname or IP address that will be used as the target of the share. You should take great care to always use the same IP address when connecting multiple host to the datastore. If the NAS device has two IP addresses, even for redundancy, it will be seen as two different datastores and not as one shared datastore.

- The shared folder or hierarchy of folders. This is case sensitive.

- Read-Write permissions for the share, so that you can configure your side for normal permissions or for Read-Only, as needed. You should not use Read-Only if you will be running VMs from this datastore.

- Sync (synchronous) rather than asynchronous for the type of communication. If you are going to run VMs, you need the system to communicate that a task is done when it is actually done, not when it is listed to be done or when it has begun.

- No root_squash. As a security measure, most administrators configure NFS shares with root_squash so that an attack presenting itself as root will not be given privileges. (In fact, it is the default setting.) Because this might keep you from accessing the VM files, you should configure the NFS share with no root_squash.

Connecting to a NAS Device

Once the NFS server is created, connecting to the NAS device is rather simple. You just add a new storage location, but instead of it being another LUN, it is the share that you have created on the NAS. You can then configure the new storage to be normal (Read and Write) or Read-Only. As I mentioned before, you should only use Read-Only if you are configuring the share for ISO files and not to store VM files.

To connect to a NAS device that is being used as an NFS server, follow the steps outlined in Activity 3-3.

Activity 3-3 Connecting to a NAS Device Used as an NFS Server

1. Log on to your vSphere Client.

2. Select **Home** and then **Hosts and Clusters**.

3. Select the ESX host on which you want to add the datastore.

4. Click the **Storage** link under Hardware.

5. In the upper-right corner, click the **Add Storage** link, as shown in Figure 3-9.

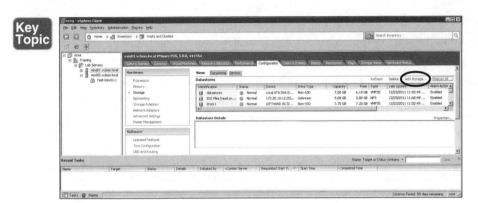

Figure 3-9   The Add Storage Link

6. From Add Storage, select **Network File System**, as shown in Figure 3-10.

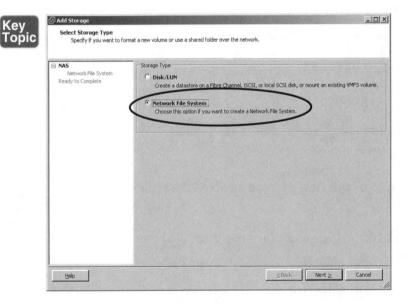

Figure 3-10   Adding an NAS Device

7. Enter the IP address or hostname of the target NAS device, the folder (case sensitive), and the datastore name. Also choose whether to mount NFS Read-Only or not. (You should not mount Read-Only if you intend to use this datastore for VMs.) Click **Next**. (I will go into more detail about this later in this chapter, in the section "Mounting/Unmounting an NFS Datastore.")

8. Monitor the progress of the datastore creation in the Recent Tasks pane. When completed, you should see your new datastore in the **Storage** link.

Enabling/Configuring/Disabling vCenter Server Storage Filters

Whenever you create a VMFS datastore or increase an existing one, vCenter uses set of filters to ensure that you do not corrupt the LUNs that you are already using. There are also filters for raw device mappings (RDMs), which I will discuss later in this chapter.

As a general rule and best practice, you should have only one VMFS per LUN. One of the filters enforces this rule, but there are also a few other filters. Each of these filters is enabled by default on vCenter, but can be disabled if you have a need to break the normal rules. You should only disable these filters if you have other third-party methods that are used to prevent device corruption.

To disable the filters, you must add configuration to the advanced settings of vCenter. More specifically, you will add a key that disables the filter. The following is a list of the keys that that you can add:

- **VMFS Filter:** config.vpxd.filter.vmfsFilter. This filters out devices or LUNs that already contain a VMFS and does not allow them to be presented as a candidate to be used for a new datastore or an extent.

- **RDM Filter:** config.vpxd.filter.rdmFilter. This filters out LUNs that are already referenced by an RDM so that they cannot be used as an RDM for another VM.

- **Same Host and Transport Filter:** config.vpxd.filter.SameHostAndTransports-Filter. This filters out LUNs that are ineligible for use because of host or storage type incompatibility.

- **Host Rescan Filter:** config.vpxd.filter.hostRescanFilter. This automatically rescans and updates datastores after you perform datastore management operations.

Activity 3-4 outlines the steps for disabling a vCenter Server storage filter.

Activity 3-4 Disabling vCenter Server Storage Filters

1. Log on to your vSphere Client.

2. From the File menu at the top left, select **Administration**, and then **vCenter Server Settings**, as shown in Figure 3-11.

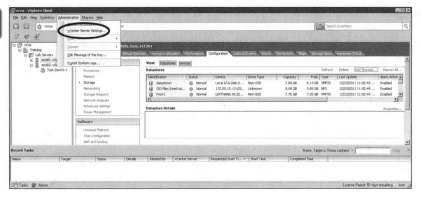

Figure 3-11   vCenter Server Settings

3. Select **Advanced Settings**.

4. In the Key field, type the key that you want to add and then value for the key. For example type **config.vpxd.filter.vmfsFilter** in the Key field and **False** in the Value field, if you want to have more than one VMFS on your LUNs, as shown in Figure 3-12.

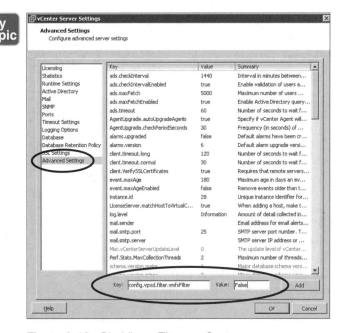

Figure 3-12   Disabling a Filter on vCenter

5. Click **Add**.

6. Click **OK**.

NOTE   Do not turn vCenter storage filters off unless you have another method to prevent LUN corruption.

If you later decide that you want to enable the filter again, simply locate the key and change the value to **True**, as shown in Figure 3-13. You cannot remove a key once it is added, but you can change the value when needed.

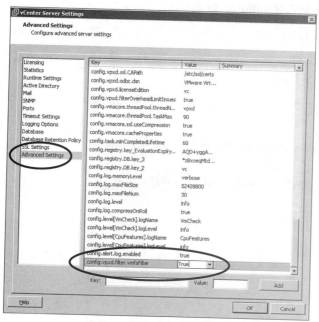

Figure 3-13   Enabling a Disabled Filter on vCenter

Configuring/Editing Hardware/Dependent Hardware Adapters

A dependent hardware iSCSI adapter is a specialized third-party adapter that you have purchased to install into your ESXi host (for example, a Broadcom 5709 NIC). When you install the adapter, it presents two components to the same port: a simple network adapter and an iSCSI engine. Once installed, the iSCSI engine appears on your list of storage adapters. It is enabled by default, but to use it, you must associate it with a VMkernel port and then configure it. You should also follow any third-party documentation associated with the card.

Enabling/Disabling Software iSCSI Initiator Settings

Instead of purchasing expensive cards that perform the discovery or TOE, you can rely on the VMkernel to do both. To configure a software iSCSI initiator, you must add iSCSI software initiator and associate it to a VMkernel port. It is a best practice to use a separate vmnic for each type of IP storage that you use. To enable software iSCSI initiator settings, follow the steps outlined in Activity 3-5.

Activity 3-5 Enabling Software iSCSI Initiator Settings

1. Log on to your vSphere Client.

2. Click **Home**, **Hosts and Clusters**, and select the host on which you want to configure the software iSCSI settings.

3. Click the **Storage Adapters** link, and then click the **Add** link, as shown in Figure 3-14.

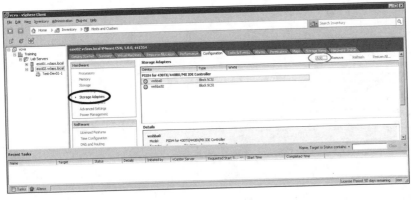

Figure 3-14 Adding Storage Adapters

4. From the Add Storage Adapter dialog box, choose **Add Software iSCSI Adapter**, as shown in Figure 3-15.

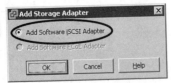

Figure 3-15 Adding a Software iSCSI Adapter

5. In the Software iSCSI Adapter warning box, click **OK**.

6. Monitor Recent Tasks and Storage Adapters until the new adapter is created, and then select the new adapter and click the **Properties** link under Details.

7. From the new adapter's Properties dialog box, open the Dynamic Discovery tab and click **Add**.

8. In the Add Send Target Server dialog box, type the IP address or hostname of the storage process on the iSCSI array, as shown in Figure 3-16. You can leave the port at 3260.

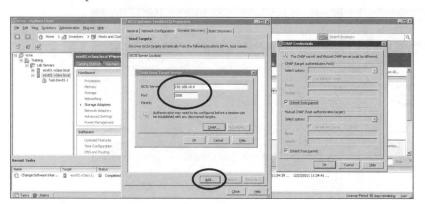

Figure 3-16 Addressing an iSCSI Target

9. If CHAP will be configured, click **CHAP** and enter the secret and mutual CHAP secret (if you are configuring for both). You can also elect to inherit the CHAP from the parent settings, which I discuss later in this chapter.

Configuring iSCSI Port Binding

Another enhancement to vSphere 5 is a user interface (UI) that enables you to specify the network interfaces that iSCSI can use, also called iSCSI port binding. This UI allows you to configure in GUI what could only be configured on the command line in previous versions of ESX/ESXi. It is especially useful when you are setting up multipathing for your storage.

To configure iSCSI port binding, you associate specific VMkernel ports to specific iSCSI adapters. You can associate more than one so that if one should fail then the other can take its place. In this way, you can create a multipath configuration with storage that only presents a single storage portal, such as DELL EqualLogic or HP/Lefthand.

Before you configure dynamic discovery, you should configure iSCSI port binding using the steps outlined in Activity 3-6.

Activity 3-6 Configuring iSCSI Port Binding

1. Log on to your vSphere Client.

2. Click **Home**, **Hosts and Clusters**, and select the host on which you want to configure the software iSCSI port binding.

3. Click the **Storage Adapters** link and then the iSCSI adapters that you want to bind, and then click the **Properties** link under Details, as shown in Figure 3-17.

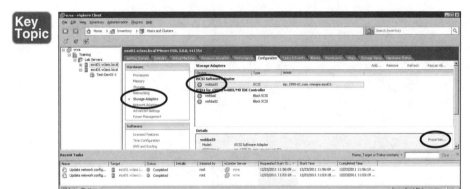

Figure 3-17   Selecting a Storage Adapter

4. Open the Network Configuration tab and click **Add**, as shown in Figure 3-18.

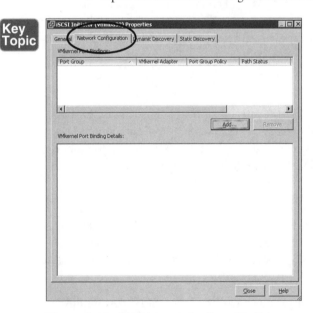

Figure 3-18   The Network Configuration Tab

5. Select the VMkernel port that you want to bind to the iSCSI storage, as shown in Figure 3-19.

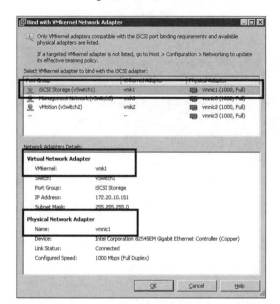

Figure 3-19   Binding a VMkernel Port

6. Open the Dynamic Discovery tab and configure the links as normal. All iSCSI targets should be on the same subnet as their associated VMkernel ports.

Enabling/Configuring/Disabling iSCSI CHAP

To enhance security between hosts and iSCSI arrays, you, or the SAN administrator, might require CHAP authentication at the iSCSI array. If this is configured on the array, the host must be configured properly as well. This includes identifying the target and configuring the secret. With vSphere 5 and software initialization, you can configure separate secrets for each target as well as mutual (bidirectional) authentication. These advancements over the earliest versions of VMware further enhance security of your data.

To enable and configure iSCSI CHAP on your ESXi 5.0 host, follow the steps outlined in Activity 3-7.

Activity 3-7 Enabling and Configuring iSCSI CHAP

1. Log on to your vSphere Client.

2. Click **Home, Hosts and Clusters** and select the host on which you want to configure CHAP.

3. Click the **Storage Adapters** link, right-click your iSCSI software adapter, and click **Properties**, as shown in Figure 3-20.

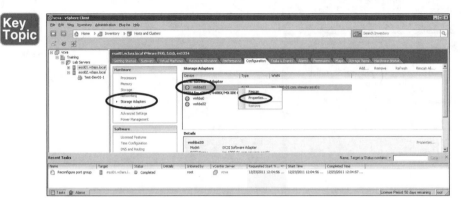

Figure 3-20 Configuring an iSCSI Adapter

4. In the iSCSI Initiator Properties dialog box, click **CHAP**, as shown in Figure 3-21.

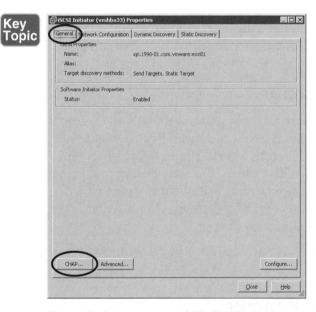

Figure 3-21 Configuring iSCSI CHAP

5. From the CHAP Credentials dialog box, choose the correct option for your iSCSI array and enter the secret that applies.

6. If you are configuring Mutual CHAP, choose the option and enter the secret that applies. The mutual CHAP secret should be different from the CHAP secret, as shown in Figure 3-22.

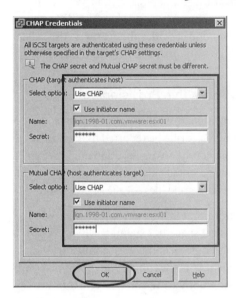

Figure 3-22   Configuring Mutual CHAP

7. Click **OK** and **Close** to save your settings.

NOTE   These settings will now be used for all targets associated to this initiator unless they are overridden by settings on a specific target.

Determining Use Cases for Hardware/Dependent Hardware/Software iSCSI Initiator

As I mentioned previously, the option that you choose with regard to hardware, dependent hardware, or software iSCSI is based on money and on performance. Also, the HBA cards that you already have might factor into your decision. For example, if the cards that you are currently using are compatible for your ESXi host in terms of software-based iSCSI, you might want to monitor the performance of those cards before you purchase additional and more expensive cards.

In general, the more sophisticated the card, the more chance there is to improve performance with that card, but there is no guarantee. In other words, if your VM-kernel is not otherwise overloaded, you might find that the software initialization option will perform just as well as the hardware or dependent hardware options. Also, keep in mind that bidirectional is only available (from VMware) with software initialization and dependent hardware initialization and per-target CHAP is available (from VMware) only with software initialization, so you might be trading options for performance, unless the third-party vendor provides the feature. Also, keep in mind that the bidirectional CHAP is available only with software initialization.

Determining Use Cases for and Configuring Array Thin Provisioning

Whether the array is thick provisioned or thin provisioned, it is hidden from native vSphere. This means that the size of the LUN might actually be reported to the host as much larger than its actual size. As I mentioned previously, an organization might set up storage initially in this way to save money and manage storage in a just-in-time manner. In that case, array thin provisioning could be considered a good idea for the organization.

This also means that you could create a datastore that is logically larger than what you can actually support and not have the physical space to expand it when needed. If you manage many datastores and LUNs, this could become very confusing and unmanageable over time. This is especially true if you are compiling virtual disk thin provisioning right on top of it. This is why using both array and VMDK thin provisioning is never a best practice.

However, with vSphere 5.0, you can now use Storage APIs - Array Integration to allow the host to become aware of the underlying thin-provisioned LUNs in time for you to make changes. You will still have to keep up with what you actually have, but you will have a better tool to use to keep up.

To use Storage APIs - Array Integration, you must have ESXi 5.0 or later hosts that support the T-10 based Storage APIs - Array Integration feature. This feature enables you to use the entire logical size of the LUN for your datastore. First, the storage administrator can set a threshold alarm that reports to the hosts when it is running out of space on the LUN. This is a vendor-specific configuration. When the alarm is triggered on the SAN and sent to your host, your host triggers an alarm for you. You can then contact the storage administrator to request more physical space, or you can use Storage vMotion to move the VM files to another storage location if one is available. In a worst-case scenario, if you run out of space for the VMs, your host will report an out-of-space alarm and will pause the VMs until the problem is resolved.

Configuring the Storage Virtual Appliance for vSphere

Many of the best features of vSphere require shared storage in order to function. Features such as vMotion, DRS, DPM, and HA all require shared storage. In the past, this shared storage had to come from either a SAN or a typical NAS. For some small organizations, these shared storage options have been too expensive, and therefore they were not able to use these important features.

New to vSphere 5.0, you can configure a vSphere Storage Appliance (VSA) that provides shared storage as a distributed, clustered, virtual NAS. In this section, I will first discuss the architecture of this new type of storage and the advantages that it offers. Then, I will discuss configuring and deploying the hosts, the VSA network, and the VSA Manager component. Finally, I will discuss administration of a VSA cluster and determine use cases for deploying one.

Defining the VSA Architecture

The VSA is a VMware virtual appliance that packages SUSE Linux Enterprise Server 11 and storage clustering services. It runs on two or three hosts to abstract the storage resources that are installed on the hosts and thereby create a VSA cluster that is seen by all hosts as an NFS datastore, as shown in Figure 3-23.

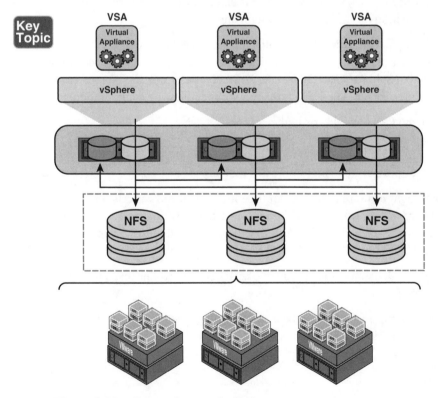

Figure 3-23   vSphere Storage Appliance

The VSA cluster enables the following features:

- Shared datastores for all hosts in the datacenter

- Replica of each shared datastore

- vSphere vMotion and vSphere HA

- Hardware and software failover capabilities

- Replacement of a failed VSA cluster member

- Recovery of an existing VSA cluster

Configuring ESXi Hosts as VSA Hosts

As I mentioned previously, you will choose two or three ESXi 5.0 hosts for your VSA cluster. This is an important choice because if you decide to create a cluster with only two hosts, you cannot add a host later on to the existing cluster. You also cannot remove a host from a VSA cluster after it is created. In addition, these hosts should be new installations and should not contain any VMs.

You should also have vCenter Server 5.0 installed on a separate host that will not be included in the VSA cluster. This can be a physical or a virtual machine(VM). In addition, you should have vSphere Client 5.0 installed on a computer that can be used to connect to the vCenter Server. The ESXi hosts require the following configuration:

- **CPU:** 64-bit x86 CPUs, 2GHz or higher.

- **Memory:** 24GB recommended, 6GB minimum, 72GB maximum tested.

- **NIC:** Two dual-port or four single-port GigE NICs.

- **Hard disks:** Eight or more hard disks of the same model and with the same capacity. All hard disks must be either Serial Advanced Technology Attachment (SATA) or Serial Attached SCSI (SAS). In other words, all must be one or the other; a combination of SATA disks and SAS disks is not supported.

- **RAID:** A redundant array of inexpensive disks (RAID) controller that supports RAID 5, 6, or 10.

- **Networking:** Each ESXi host must be assigned a unique static address that is in the same subnet as the vCenter Server.

- **VLAN:** A physical switch that supports the 802.1Q trunking protocol is highly recommended.

In addition, all hosts must not participate in a vSphere HA cluster. (High availability will be supplied through the VSA cluster instead.) The hosts in the VSA cluster must not have any vSphere standard switches or port groups created besides the default ones that are created during the ESXi installation.

Configuring the Storage Network for the VSA

Your VSA cluster traffic is divided into two categories, front end and back end. In this section, I will briefly describe the types of traffic and their purpose. Also, I will discuss the physical infrastructure that you must provide for this traffic.

The front-end traffic is used primarily for communication. This includes three types of communication, as follows:

- Communication between each VSA cluster member and the VSA Manager

- Communication between ESXi and the NFS datastores

- Communication between the VSA member cluster and the VSA cluster service

The back-end traffic is used for replication, clustering information, and vMotion and Storage vMotion. This traffic can be defined further as follows:

- Replication between an NFS volume and its replica that resides on another host

- Clustering information between all VSA cluster members

- vMotion and Storage vMotion traffic between the hosts

Your physical networking hardware requirements will vary depending on whether you have chosen two hosts or three hosts for your cluster. For a VSA with 2 hosts, you will need 11 static IP addresses that are in the same subnet. If your cluster contains 3 hosts, you will need at a minimum 14 static IP addresses in the same subnet. All addresses must be in same subnet as the vCenter Server.

Deploying/Configuring the VSA Manager

To manage your VSA cluster, you must first download and configure the VSA Manager software for your vCenter Server. This will also include downloading and enabling a plug-in for your vSphere Client that you can use to manage your VSA cluster. You must run the VSA Manager on a 64-bit server that runs vCenter Server 5.0. To deploy the VSA Manager, follow the steps outlined in Activity 3-8.

Activity 3-8 Deploying the VSA Manager

1. Download the VSA Manager installer from the VMware website.

2. On your 64-bit vCenter Server 5.0 machine, locate and click the **VMware-vsamanager-en-version_number-build_number.exe** file.

3. Accept the end-user agreement and click **Next**.

4. Verify that the vCenter Server IP address is that of the local machine and click **Next**. (Caution: Do not modify port configuration.)

5. On the License Information page, type your valid vCenter Server license and click **Next**.

6. On the Ready to Install page, click **Install**. (You can also select to **Show the Windows Installer Log**.) Then, click **Finish**.

7. If the VSA Manager tab does not appear, select **Plug-ins > Manage Plug-Ins** from the File menu and enable the plug-in for VSA Manager. (You might also need to restart the VMware VirtualCenter Management Webservices service at services.msc.)

The specific configuration of your VSA cluster will be dependent on the choices that you make with regard to its design. For example, configuration of a two-host cluster will be very different from that of a three-host cluster. In the next section, I will discuss configuration components as well as administration of VSA clusters.

Administering VSA Storage Resources

In general, you can view and administer three categories of information in your VSA Manager:

- VSA clusters
- VSA datastores
- VSA membership

Each of these categories has a subset of components that give you additional information about your clusters. You can manage all of these from the VSA Manager tab in vCenter, as shown in Figure 3-24. In this section, I will briefly discuss administration of each of these categories.

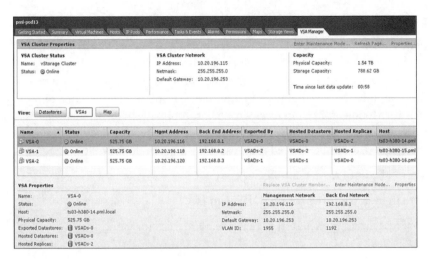

Figure 3-24   VSA Manager

Administering VSA Clusters

On the VSA Manager tab, you can view information such as your cluster name and status. In addition, you can view the IP address of your cluster within the VSA Cluster Network. Finally, you can view the capacity of your cluster, including the physical capacity and the storage capacity after fault tolerant space is considered.

Administering VSA Datastores

If you open the VSA Manager tab and then the **Datastores** view, you can view information about the VSA datastore. This information includes the capacity, network settings, exported volume, and its replica. You can also browse the contents of a VSA datastore by simply right-clicking it and clicking **Browse Datastore** as you would with any other datastore.

Administering VSA Cluster Membership

If you select **Appliances** under the VSA Manager tab, you can view information about all of the members in a VSA cluster and their connections to each other. This includes their status, capacity, addresses, host, and replica host information. In addition, you can click **Map** to see a graphical map of the entire cluster.

Determining Use Case for Deploying the VSA

As I mentioned previously, the VSA is primarily designed to lower IT infrastructure costs while enabling higher level of protection without requiring the purchase of an expensive SAN or even NAS solution. It is intended for an organization that does not currently have another shared storage alternative but that still wants to be able to use features such as vMotion and HA in its environment. It provides a distributed shared storage alternative as opposed to the centralized shared storage provided by a SAN or NAS. The benefits that can be derived from using a VSA include the following:

- Lower total cost of ownership (TCO)

- Storage framework for vMotion, DRS, and HA

- Pools server direct-attached storage to create shared storage

- Supports thin provisioning for efficient use of disk space

- Intuitive VSA Manager, so complex storage array skills and experience are not needed

Determining Appropriate ESXi Host Resources for the VSA

Whether you choose to create a VSA cluster with two hosts or three, the resulting cluster must meet a specific set of criteria. In addition, there are resources to consider when creating a VSA cluster. In this section, I list the criteria that that you should consider when creating a VSA cluster.

- ESXi hosts cannot contain VMs before creating the cluster.

- vCenter must be installed and running before creating a VSA cluster.

- If you run vCenter on a host in a VSA datastore and the datastore goes offline, you might not be able to manage the VSA cluster.

- You must decide on two or three hosts; you cannot extend a two-host VSA to three hosts.

- The VSA cluster will require RAID 5, 6, or 10 disk configuration on each host.

- Consider the number of VMs and take into account HA admission control. (I discuss HA admission control later in Chapter 5.

> **NOTE**   In addition to these recommendations, your VSA storage hosts and network must be configured as I described earlier in this chapter.

Creating and Configuring VMFS and NFS Datastores

With all of the terminology that we throw around with regard to datastores, it's easy to lose focus on the fact that there are really only two types of vSphere datastores: VMFS and NFS. In this section, I will cover the properties and capabilities of each of these two types of datastores. In addition, I will discuss creating, renaming, deleting, mounting, unmounting, and upgrading each of these types of datastores. I will also examine use cases for multiple VMFS and NFS datastores. Then, I will show you how to determine an appropriate path selection policy for your datastores.

Identifying VMFS and NFS Datastore Properties

In general, a datastore is a logical container that connects a host to physical storage while at the same time hiding the specifics of each storage device from the VMs. This provides a uniform model for storing and using VM files. As I mentioned previously, there are only two types of datastores: VMFS and NFS. If you are using a VMFS, the underlying hardware will be either local, Fibre Channel SAN, FCoE, or iSCSI. On the other hand, if you are using an NFS datastore, the underlying hardware will be an NFS server.

In either case, you can examine your datastores to view their properties, such as the device name, drive type, capacity, free space, and other information. You can also view more detailed information about each datastore. To identify your datastore properties, follow the steps outlined in Activity 3-9.

Activity 3-9 Identifying VMFS and NFS Datastore Properties

1. Log on to your vSphere Client.

2. Click **Home**, **Hosts and Clusters**, and select the host on which you want to identify storage.

3. Open the Configuration tab, click the **Storage** link, and then click the **Datastores** view, as shown in Figure 3-25.

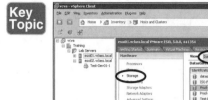
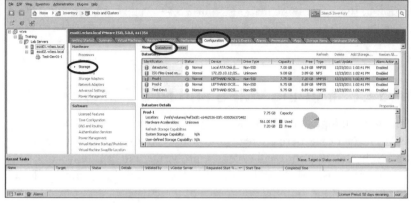

Figure 3-25   The Datastores View

4. In the upper panel under Datastores, view general information about your datastores. You can also modify the view by right-clicking on any column heading and selecting only the properties that you want to view, as shown in Figure 3-26.

Figure 3-26   Modifying the Datastores View

5. Select a specific datastore and view the detailed information about it in the lower panel, including a pie chart indicating its capacity as well as used and available space. You can also identify path selection policy, paths used, formatting (VMFS 3 or 5) and extents.

> **NOTE**   You can also view datastore properties on the Storage Views tab.

Identifying VMFS-5 Capabilities

Whereas ESX/ESXi 3.5 and 4.x hosts can only use a version of VMFS referred to as VMFS-3, ESXi 5.0 hosts can use a new and improved version referred to as VMFS-5. This new version of VMFS has capabilities that exceed the previous version and allow for more efficient use of storage and greater flexibility for the storage administrator and the vSphere administrator. The following is a partial list of the new capabilities of VMFS-5 and the benefit that each new capability provides:

- Support for greater than 2TB storage devices for each VMFS extent. This increases the flexibility for you and the storage administrator when creating and using LUNs. You can create and use up to 64TB extents.

- Standard 1MB file system block size with support of 2TB virtual disks. Previous versions required a larger block size in order to store larger files. This meant that the administrator would have to choose between more efficient file storage or the capability to store larger files. Now you can have both at the same time.

- Support of greater than 2TB disk size for RDMs in physical compatibility mode. You can use physical compatibility RDMs up to 64TB in size.

- Online, in-place upgrade capability. You can upgrade VMFS-3 datastores to VMFS-5 without any disruption to your hosts or VMs.

> **NOTE**   If you are using advanced features such as VAAI, you might want to consider creating new VMFS-5 datastores rather the upgrading the ones you are currently using. This will ensure that block sizes match and that these features can be used successfully.

Creating/Renaming/Deleting/Unmounting a VMFS Datastore

You can use the tools included in vCenter to quickly create, rename, delete, or unmount VMFS datastores. To create a datastore, you should start the wizard, name the datastore, and choose the LUNs to be used for the datastore. You can only use LUNs that do not currently have a VMFS datastore on them. To create a new VMFS datastore, follow the steps outlined in Activity 3-10.

Activity 3-10 Creating a VMFS Datastore

1. Log on to your vSphere Client.

2. Click **Home**, **Hosts and Clusters**, and select the host on which you want to create the datastore.

3. Open the Configuration tab and click the **Storage** link.

4. In the upper right under Datastores, click the **Add Storage** link, as shown in Figure 3-27.

Figure 3-27   The Add Storage Link

5. Select **Disk/LUN**, as shown in Figure 3-28.

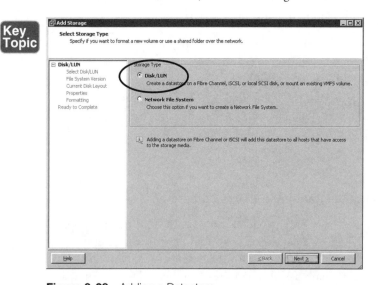

Figure 3-28   Adding a Datastore

6. Choose an available LUN, as shown in Figure 3-29. The only LUNs that will
    be available are those that do not currently have a VMFS. Click **Next**.

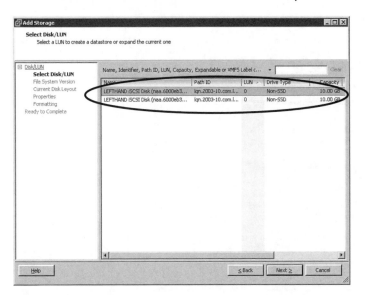

Figure 3-29 Choosing a LUN

7. From File System Version, select **VMFS-5** or **VMFS-3**. You should use
    VMFS-3 if the datastore will be accessed by hosts earlier than ESXi 5.0; other-
    wise, you should choose VMFS-5, as shown in Figure 3-30.

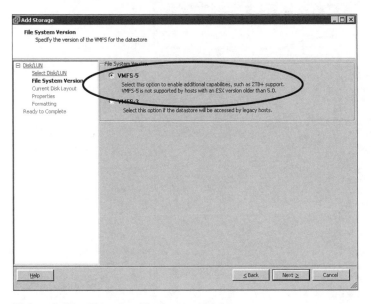

Figure 3-30 Choosing File System Version

8. From Current Disk Layout, review the information, as shown in Figure 3-31, and click **Next**.

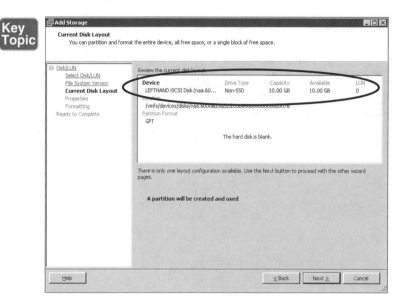

Figure 3-31 Disk Layout Information

9. From Properties, enter a name for your datastore, as shown in Figure 3-32, and click **Next**.

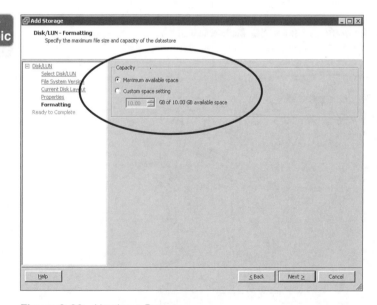

Figure 3-32 Naming a Datastore

10. From Disk/LUN - Formatting, select to use **Maximum Available Space** or to use a **Custom Space Setting**, as shown in Figure 3-33. In most cases, you should choose **Maximum Available Space**.

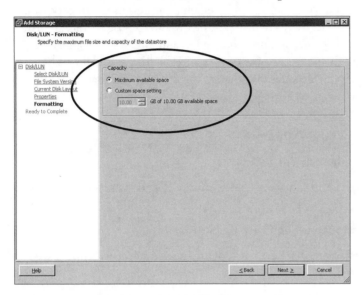

Figure 3-33   Configuring Datastore Capacity

11. From Ready to Complete, review the Disk layout and File system information and ensure that it's what you wanted, and then click **Finish**, as shown in Figure 3-34.

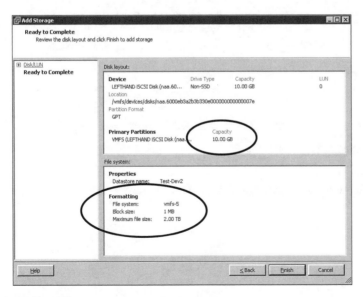

Figure 3-34   The Ready to Complete Page

12. Monitor Recent Tasks pane and your **Storage** link for the creation of your new datastore.

In general, you should name your datastores based on their purpose. In most cases, their purpose should be to store a particular type of VM, an ISO file library, templates, and so on. As we all know, organizational goals and directions change over time, thereby redefining the purposes of your datastores. When this happens, you should consider changing their names. To change the name of your datastore, follow the steps outlined in Activity 3-11.

Activity 3-11 Renaming a VMFS Datastore

1. Log on to your vSphere Client.

2. Click **Home**, **Hosts and Clusters**, and select the host on which you want to rename the datastore.

3. Open the Configuration tab and click the **Storage** link.

4. Right-click the datastore that you want to rename and select **Rename**, as shown in Figure 3-35.

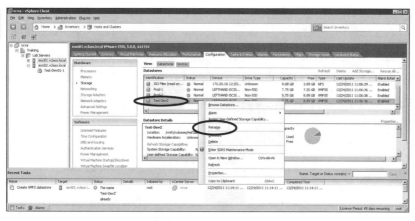

Figure 3-35   Selecting a Datastore to Rename

5. Type the new name for your datastore, as shown in Figure 3-36.

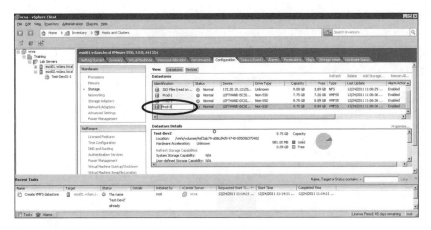

Figure 3-36   Entering the New Name for Your Datastore

6. Ensure that the Identification of the datastore is changed.

If you decide that you no longer need a VMFS datastore, you can choose to delete it. You should be aware that deleting a VMFS datastore is a "permanent" action that deletes all of the metadata on the LUNs in the SAN. In other words, there is no "going back" in any normal sense. Because of this, you should make absolutely sure that there is no data on the datastore that you will need. You can use Storage vMotion to migrate a VMs files, or you can cold migrate VM files to other datastores before deleting the datastore if you need to keep them. You should also move or back up any ISO files that you may need later. (Chapter 5 covers Storage vMotion and cold migration.) That said, to delete a VMFS datastore, follow the steps outlined in Activity 3-12.

Activity 3-12 Deleting a VMFS Datastore

1. Log on to your vSphere Client.

2. Click **Home**, **Hosts and Clusters**, and select the host on which you want to delete the datastore.

3. Open the Configuration tab and click the **Storage** link.

4. Right-click the datastore that you want to delete and select **Delete**, as shown in Figure 3-37.

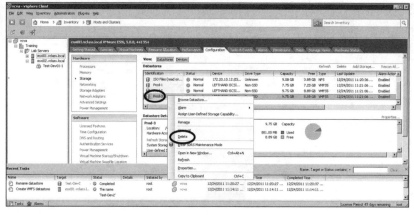

Figure 3-37   Deleting a VMFS Datastore

5. On the Confirmation page, select **Yes**, as shown in Figure 3-38 (but think first).

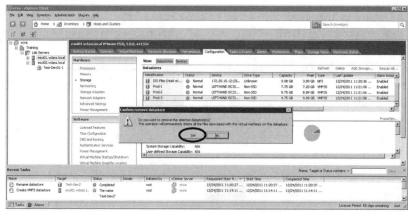

Figure 3-38   Confirming Deletion of VMFS Datastore

6. Monitor the Recent Tasks pane and the **Storage** link to ensure that the datastore is deleted.

NOTE   As a practical note, because only the metadata is deleted, the data could still be recovered in a clean room by opening the hard disks. If you decide to do this, you should immediately discontinue normal use of the disks involved and remove them from the array.

As you can see, deciding to delete a datastore can require a significant amount of thought and work. Sometimes it might be better to just disconnect the datastore from the LUNs but leave the data on the LUNs intact. In earlier versions of vSphere, this was not possible with a VMFS datastore. With vSphere 5.0 and later, it is possible, but a lot of conditions must be met before it is possible. Figure 3-39 shows an attempt to unmount a datastore that does not quite meet the requirements.

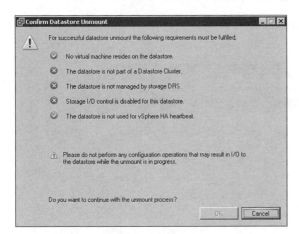

Figure 3-39 A VMFS Datastore that Cannot Be Unmounted

The following is a list of conditions which you must address before unmounting a VMFS datastore:

- No VMs can reside in the datastore.

- The datastore cannot be part of a datastore cluster. (I will discuss datastore clusters in Chapter 5.)

- The datastore cannot be managed by Storage DRS. (I will discuss Storage DRS in Chapter 5.)

- Storage I/O Control must be disabled. (I will discuss storage I/O control in Chapter 5.)

- The datastore cannot be used for vSphere HA Heartbeat. (I will discuss HA Heartbeat in Chapter 5.)

As you can see, this limits the number of your VMFS datastores that can be successfully unmounted. Think about it this way, though. If you had a VMFS datastore that was used exclusively for ISO files, chances are good that you could meet these criteria and unmount the datastore while leaving the ISO files in place on the LUNs for later use, or available to connect to another datastore. To unmount a VMFS datastore, follow the steps outlined in Activity 3-13.

Activity 3-13 Unmounting a VMFS Datastore

1. Log on to your vSphere Client.

2. Click **Home**, **Hosts and Clusters**, and select the host on which you want to unmount the datastore.

3. Open the Configuration tab and click the **Storage** link.

4. Right-click the datastore that you want to unmount and select **Unmount**, as shown in Figure 3-40.

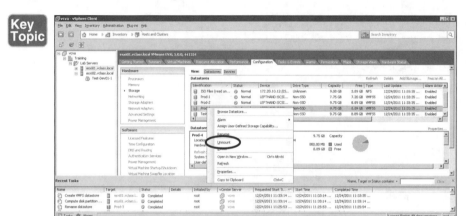

Figure 3-40   Unmounting a VMFS Datastore

5. On the Confirm Datastore Unmount page, verify that your datastore meets all the requirements to be unmounted, and click **OK** to continue, as shown in Figure 3-41.

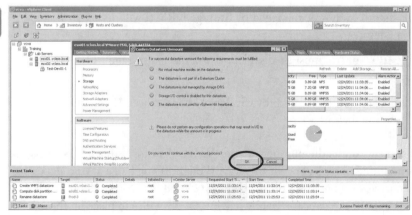

Figure 3-41   Confirming VMFS Datastore Unmount

6. Monitor the Recent Tasks pane and the **Storage** link to ensure that the datastore is unmounted. The datastore will be grayed out and identified as inactive and unmounted. Interestingly, though, its status will be listed as a grayed out Normal, as shown in Figure 3-42. Normal is still displayed (although grayed out) because the default alarm set at the vCenter object level has not been tripped.

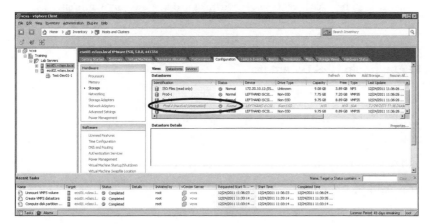

Figure 3-42 An Unmounted VMFS Datastore

NOTE To mount the datastore again, assuming that the data is still on the LUN, you just right-click the datastore and select **Mount**.

Mounting/Unmounting an NFS Datastore

Even though VMFS datastores and NFS datastores can store the same types of files (VMs, templates, and ISO files), they are very different types of file systems. Because of this fact, mounting and unmounting an NFS datastore is very different from mounting and unmounting a VMFS datastore. In this section, I will first discuss mounting an NFS datastore, and then I will discuss unmounting one.

You can liken mounting an NFS datastore to creating a mapped drive. In other words, there is a share in the network; and if you connect to that share with the correct permissions, you can access the data on the share. Based on this analogy, what information would you think that you might need for the connection? You guessed it. You would need the address of the share and the name. In essence, that is exactly what you need to mount an NFS datastore. Of course, the NFS server must first be set up somewhere in the network from which you can access it. After this is done, to mount the NFS datastore to your host, follow the steps outlined in Activity 3-14.

NOTE You might notice that mounting the NFS datastore is just an extension to my earlier discussion of creating an NAS device. This is because these technologies and methods work "hand in hand" with each other with regard to your environment.

Activity 3-14 Mounting an NFS Datastore

1. Log on to your vSphere Client.

2. Click **Home**, **Hosts and Clusters**, and select the host on which you want to mount the NFS datastore.

3. Open the Configuration tab and click the **Storage** link.

4. Click the **Add Storage** link.

5. On Select Storage Type, select **Network File System**, as shown in Figure 3-43, and then click **Next**.

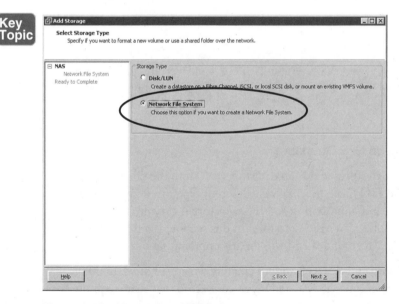

Figure 3-43 Mounting an NFS Datastore

6. On Locate Network File System, enter the IP address (IPv4 or IPv6), or the hostname of the NFS server. Also, enter the folder name (case sensitive) where

the shared files are stored. In addition, if you are mounting ISO files only, you may want to check the **Mount NFS Read Only** check box, but if you are planning on storing VMs in this datastore, you should leave the box unchecked. Finally, enter the datastore name based on the purpose of the datastore, such as **iso_library1**, as shown in Figure 3-44, and then click **Next**.

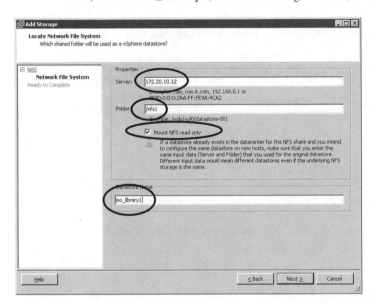

Figure 3-44   Addressing and Naming an NFS Datastore

7. On Network File System, review your settings and click **Finish**.

8. Monitor your Recent Tasks pane and the **Storage** link for the creation of the new NFS datastore.

Just as mounting an NFS datastore can be likened to mapping a drive, unmounting an NFS datastore can be likened to removing a mapped drive. The key point here is that when you remove a mapped drive you only remove your link to the data it contains, but you do not remove the data or the metadata. The same holds true for unmounting an NFS datastore. In other words, unmounting the NFS datastore does delete the datastore from your host, but it does not delete the data contained on the share or even its metadata. To unmount an NFS datastore, follow the steps outlined in Activity 3-15.

Activity 3-15 Unmounting an NFS Datastore

1. Log on to your vSphere Client.

2. Click **Home**, **Hosts and Clusters**, and select the host on which you want to unmount the datastore.

3. Open the Configuration tab and click the **Storage** link.

4. Right-click the datastore that you want to unmount and select **Unmount**, as shown in Figure 3-45.

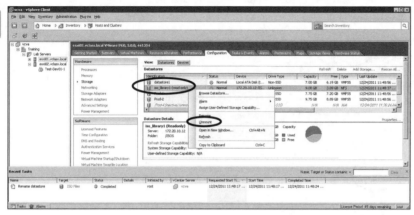

Figure 3-45 Unmounting an NFS Datastore

5. On the Confirmation page, select **Yes** (note the dramatic difference between unmounting NFS versus VMFS), as shown in Figure 3-46.

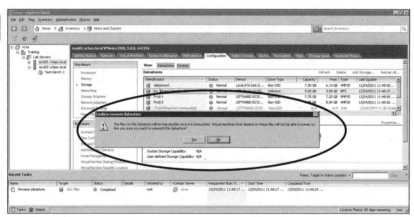

Figure 3-46 Confirming the Unmount of an NFS Datastore

6. Monitor the Recent Tasks pane and the **Storage** link to ensure that the datastore is deleted. The datastore will completely disappear from the list.

Extending/Expanding VMFS Datastores

As your organization continues to grow, so will your need for disk space. In the past, we had to tell users that the system would be offline for a while during the evening hours so that we could increase the storage capacity by adding LUNs or increasing the size of the LUNs that we were using. Have you ever written or received an email with that message or something similar to it?

In our current world, where many organizations run 24/7, this is no longer an acceptable alternative. We now need to be able to expand the physical disk space and then expand the logical disk space right behind it, without having to take any servers offline or affect the user's functionality.

You might think that extending and expanding are just two words that essentially mean the same thing, but you should understand that this is not true with regard to VMFS datastores. In this section, I will discuss extending datastores, and then I discuss expanding datastores, comparing and contrasting the two methods of growing your datastores. You should clearly recognize the differences between these two methods of adding datastore space.

Extending VMFS Datastores

Extending a datastore means adding another LUN to it. In legacy versions of VMware software (prior to vSphere), this was the only option with regard to growing a datastore. Now, you also have the option to expand the datastore (which I will discuss next), but the option to extend might be the right choice depending on the situation. If your storage administrator is using only relatively small LUNs (500GB and less), extending might be your best alternative.

For example, if you have a 10GB datastore and want to grow it to 20GB while maintaining all the data on the datastore, you could ask your storage administrator for another 10GB LUN and then create an extent, which is basically a spanned volume between the two LUNs, thereby increasing your datastore to approximately 20GB. To create an extent on a VMFS datastore, follow the steps outlined in Activity 3-16.

NOTE   I am intentionally using very small LUNs for this training scenario, at least compared to what you might use in a production environment.

Activity 3-16 Extending a VMFS Datastore

1. Log on to your vSphere Client.

2. Click **Home**, **Hosts and Clusters**, and select the host on which you want to extend the datastore.

3. Open the Configuration tab and click the **Storage** link. Click **Rescan All** to ensure that you are seeing everything that is there.

4. Click the datastore that you want to extend, and in the Datastore Details (in the bottom pane) area, click **Properties**.

5. On Volume Properties, note the number of extents and then click **Increase**, as shown in Figure 3-47.

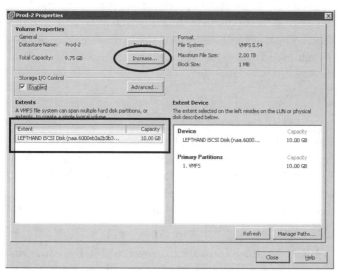

Figure 3-47 Viewing Datastore Extents

6. From Extent Device, choose from the list of available LUNs and click **Next**, as shown in Figure 3-48. (A LUN will only be listed if it does not contain a VMFS.)

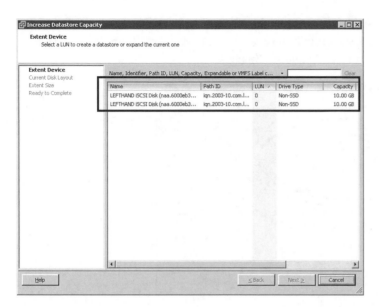

Figure 3-48   Selecting an Extent Device

7. From Current Disk Layout, note the capacity of the datastore and click **Next**, as shown in Figure 3-49.

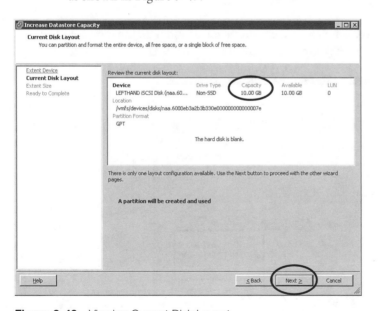

Figure 3-49   Viewing Current Disk Layout

8. From Extent Size, choose either the **Maximum Available Space** or **Custom Space** setting, as shown in Figure 3-50, and click **Next**. (In most cases, you will choose **Maximum Available Space**.)

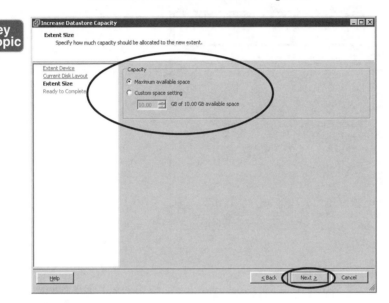

Figure 3-50   Configuring Datastore Capacity

9. From Ready to Complete, review your choices and note the increased size of the datastore and click Finish, as shown in Figure 3-51.

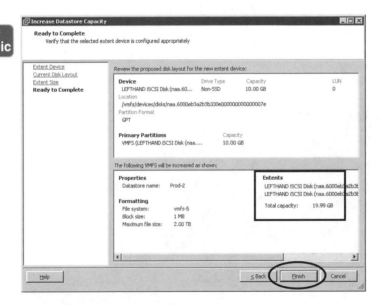

Figure 3-51   The Ready to Complete Page

10. From Volume Properties, note the additional extent and the total capacity of the datastore, as shown in Figure 3-52, and select **Close**.

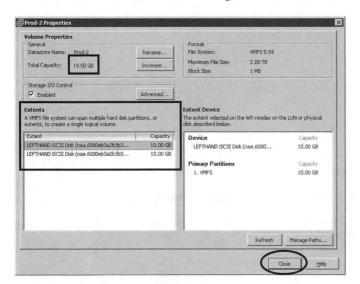

Figure 3-52   The Volume Properties Page

11. On the Storage link, note the new capacity of the datastore and the Free Space in the Datastores and Datastore Details panes.

NOTE   The maximum number of extents that you can have on a datastore is 32.

Expanding VMFS Datastores

Suppose that you do not want to add a LUN to your datastore to increase its size. Suppose instead you just want to ask the storage administrator to increase the size of the LUN that you already have and then you will increase the size of the datastore within the same LUN. In that case, you would not be creating an extent, but instead you would be *expanding* the datastore into the newly expanded LUN.

For example, if you have a 5GB datastore using one LUN and you need a 10GB datastore, you could ask the storage administrator to increase the size of your LUN to 10GB. After this is done, you could increase the size of your datastore within the same LUN. If your storage administrator is willing to increase the LUNs to whatever size you need, this might be your best alternative for increasing the size of the datastore. To expand your datastore after the storage administrator has increased the size of the LUN, follow the steps outlined in Activity 3-17.

Activity 3-17 Expanding a VMFS Datastore

1. Log on to your vSphere Client.

2. Click **Home**, **Hosts and Clusters**, and select the host on which you want to expand the datastore.

3. Open the Configuration tab and click the **Storage** link.

4. Right-click the datastore that you want to expand and click **Properties**, as shown in Figure 3-53. (This is another way to get to datastore properties.)

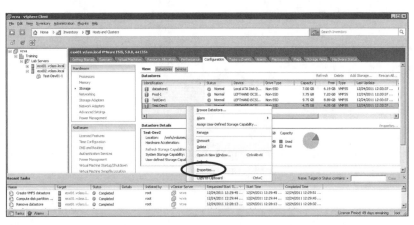

Figure 3-53   Another Way to Access Datastore Properties

5. From Volume Properties, note the size of the datastore and the NAA (Network Address Authority) number (you can adjust the columns or rest your mouse pointer on the extent to see the whole address), and then click **Increase**, as shown in Figure 3-54.

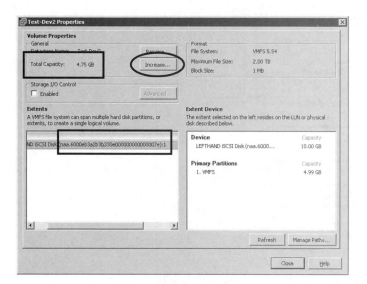

Figure 3-54   Volume Properties and the NAA

> **6.** From Extent Device, choose your current NAA number. Note the explanation
>   at the bottom of the page, as shown in Figure 3-55, and click **Next**.

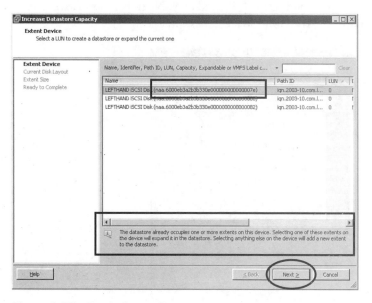

Figure 3-55   Expanding an Extent

> **7.** From Current Disk Layout, note the future capacity of the new datastore and
>   click **Next**, as shown in Figure 3-56.

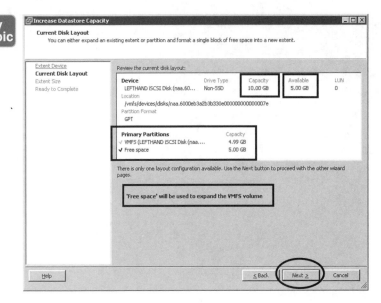

Figure 3-56   A Glimpse of the Future

8. From Extent Size, choose either **Maximum Available Space** or **Custom Space Setting**, as shown in Figure 3-57, and click **Next**. (In most cases, you will choose **Maximum Available Space**, a best practice.)

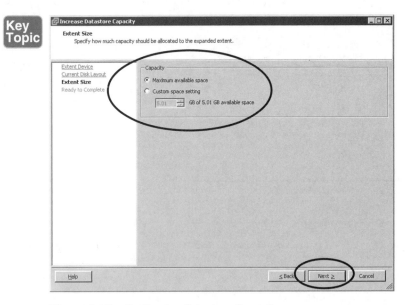

Figure 3-57   Configuring Datastore Capacity

9. From Ready to Complete, review your choices and note the increased capacity of the datastore, and then click **Finish**, as shown in Figure 3-58.

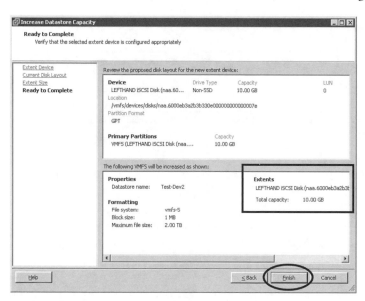

Figure 3-58   The Ready to Complete Page

10. From Volume Properties, note that you still just have one extent but that the total capacity of the datastore is increased, as shown in Figure 3-59, and then click **Close**.

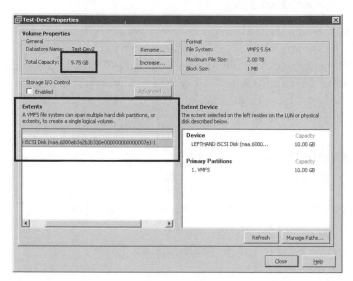

Figure 3-59   Volume Properties of an Expanded Datastore

11. On the **Storage** link, note the new capacity of the datastore and the Free Space in the Datastores and Datastore Details panes, as shown in Figure 3-60.

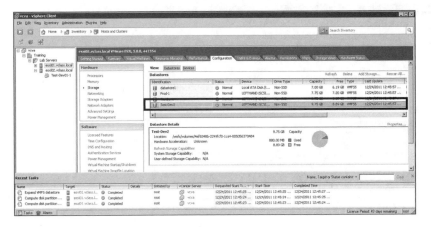

Figure 3-60 The Storage Link for a Host

NOTE A single extent formatted with VMFS-5 can be expanded any number of times, but only to a maximum of 64TB.

Upgrading a VMFS-3 Datastore to VMFS-5

As I mentioned earlier in this chapter, VMFS-5 datastores have advantages over VMFS-3 datastores. When you upgrade your vCenter and your hosts, your datastores are not automatically upgraded. You can upgrade your datastores as long as you are using vCenter 4.0 or later and as long as all of the hosts that need to use the datastores are ESXi 5.0 or later. To upgrade a datastore from VMFS-3 to VMFS-5, follow the steps outlined in Activity 3-18.

Activity 3-18 Upgrading a VMFS Datastore

1. Log on to your vSphere Client.

2. Click **Home**, **Hosts and Clusters**, and select the host on which you want to upgrade the datastore.

3. Open the Configuration tab and click the **Storage** link.

4. Click the datastore that you want to upgrade, note that the type is VMFS-3, and in the Datastore Details (in the bottom pane) click the **Upgrade to VMFS-5** link, as shown in Figure 3-61.

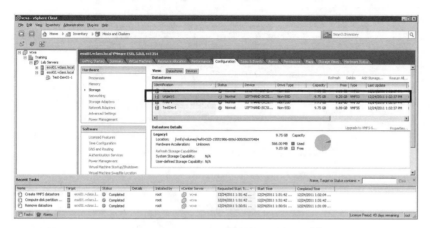

Figure 3-61   Choosing to Upgrade a VMFS-3 Datastore

5. On the warning page, ensure that all of your hosts are ESXi 5.0 or later and click **OK**, as shown in Figure 3-62.

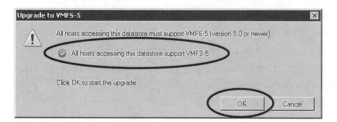

Figure 3-62   Confirmation Page for VMFS Datastore Upgrade

6. Monitor the upgrade in the Recent Tasks pane, and then view the datastore type under Datastores. It should now be listed as VMFS-, as shown in Figure 3-63. (I should probably rename that datastore now, don't you agree?)

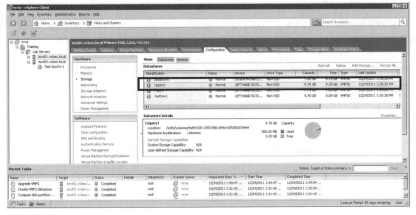

Figure 3-63   A View of a Recently Updated Datastore

Placing a VMFS Datastore in Maintenance Mode

Because I have yet to discuss Storage DRS, it might be premature to discuss datastore Maintenance Mode. Suffice it to say that it is now possible to create storage clusters of datastores that support each other. That said, in the event that you want to take this type of datastore out of service, you could place the datastore in Maintenance Mode. When you place the datastore in Maintenance Mode, the system uses Storage vMotion to move all of the VM files off of the disks associated with the datastore and places them on other disks. I will discuss Storage DRS and Storage vMotion in detail in Chapter 5. If you want to place a datastore that is part of a datastore cluster with at least two datastores, into datastore Maintenance Mode, follow the steps outlined in Activity 3-19.

Activity 3-19 Placing a VMFS Datastore in Maintenance Mode

1. Log on to your vSphere Client.

2. Click **Home, Datastores and Datastore Clusters**.

3. Locate and right-click the datastore that you want to put into Maintenance Mode, and select **Enter SDRS Maintenance Mode**, as shown in Figure 3-64.

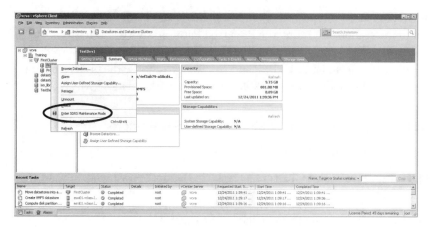

Figure 3-64 Entering SDRS Maintenance Mode

4. View and apply any placement recommendations to remove VM files from the datastore.

5. Monitor your Recent Tasks pane, and then view the datastore again. You should see that the icon is changed to one with "construction site tape" across it, as shown in Figure 3-65. (If you want to exit Maintenance Mode, right-click the datastore and select **Exit SDRS Maintenance Mode**.)

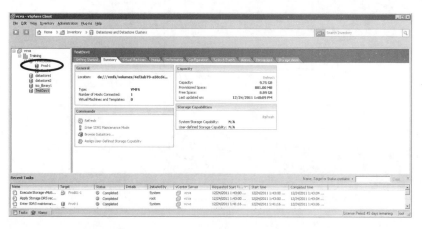

Figure 3-65 A Datastore in SDRS Maintenance Mode

Selecting the Preferred Path for a VMFS Datastore

Generally speaking, you do not have to change the default multipathing settings that your host uses for a specific storage device, the host software is very good at making the right choice. VMware supports three native policies, and I will define all three polices later in the section "Selecting the Preferred Path for a VMFS Datastore." In this section, I will focus on only one path selection policy (PSP), a policy referred to as Fixed. If you have selected a Fixed PSP and you want to choose the preferred path instead of letting VMware do it for you, follow the steps outlined in Activity 3-20.

Activity 3-20 Selecting the Preferred Path for a VMFS Datastore

1. Log on to your vSphere Client.

2. Click **Home**, **Hosts and Clusters**, and select the host on which you want to upgrade the datastore.

3. Open the Configuration tab and click the **Storage** link.

4. Click the datastore that you want to configure and click the **Properties** link in the bottom pane.

5. Choose **Manage Paths**, as shown in Figure 3-66.

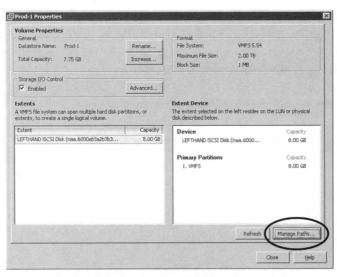

Figure 3-66   Selecting a Preferred Path

6. In Path Selection, choose **Fixed (VMware)**, and then right-click your preferred path and select **Preferred**.

7. Note that the asterisk (*) under the Preferred column denotes the preferred path.

> **NOTE**   This action should only be taken in consultation with your storage vendor or VMware support.

Disabling a Path to a VMFS Datastore

You might wonder why you would want to disable a path to a datastore. Well, what if you wanted to make changes to the underlying components in that path, such as the switches or cables that connect the host to the datastore? In that case, you might want to temporarily disable that path so that the system would not use it or even try to rely on it for fault tolerance. You should make sure that there is another path available, but, as a precaution, the system will not allow you to disable a path if it is the only path to the datastore, as shown in Figure 3-67. To disable a path to VMFS datastore, follow the steps outlined in Activity 3-21.

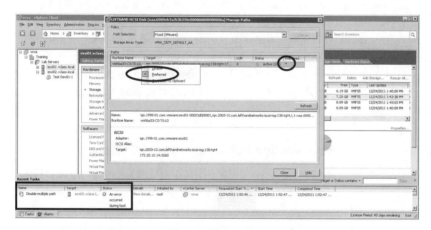

Figure 3-67   An Attempt to Disable the Only Path to a Datastore

Activity 3-21 Disabling a Path to a VMFS Datastore

1. Log on to your vSphere Client.

2. Click **Home**, **Hosts and Clusters**, and select the host on which you want to upgrade the datastore.

3. Open the Configuration tab and click the **Storage** link.

4. Click the datastore that you want to configure and click the **Properties** link in the bottom pane.

5. Choose **Manage Paths**.

6. In Path Selection, choose **Fixed (VMware)**, and then right-click your preferred path and select **Disable**.

Determining Use Cases for Multiple VMFS and NFS Datastores

As I mentioned previously, your datastores are logical containers that are analogous to the file systems within them. In other words, datastores hide the specifics of a storage device and provide a uniform model for storing VMs. As you know, you can also use them for storing ISO images, VM templates, and floppy images. I also mentioned that a good practice is to name your datastores based on what you are using them for, such as Production, Test-Dev, ISO_Library, and so on.

That said, the number of datastores that you need will be based on how diversified you are with regard to their use. In other words, you may want to create different datastores for different types of VMs. This approach will be especially helpful if the underlying disk for the datastores also differs in performance, which is highly likely. In that regard, you can group datastores into folders based on what types of VMs they contain. This makes it possible to assign permissions and alarms at the folder level, thereby reducing administrative effort. In addition, it is now possible to create storage profiles to make sure that your VMs are connecting to the appropriate datastore. I discuss storage profiles in Chapter 4, "Deploying and Administering Virtual Machine and vApps."

Determining Appropriate Path Selection Policy for a VMFS Datastore

As I mentioned earlier, VMware supports three native PSPs. The three native PSPs that VMware supports are Fixed, Most Recently Used, and Round Robin. Of the three, the only one that allows more than one path to be used during the same data transfer is Round Robin. The others are availability polices used for fault tolerance and fail over. The following is a brief description of each of these policies:

- **Fixed:** This is the default used with a SAN that is set to Active/Active. In this case, the preferred path is used whenever available. If the preferred path should fail, another path is used until the preferred path is restored, at which point the data moves back onto the preferred path. The disadvantage of this solution is that a flapping connection could cause the paths to "play ping-pong" with each other, a condition known as *thrashing*.

- **Most Recently Used:** This is the default used with a SAN that is set to Active/Passive. With this policy, a path is chosen and continues to be used so long as it does not fail. If it fails, another path is used, and it continues to be used so long as it does not fail, even if the previous path becomes available again.

- **Round Robin:** This is the only path selection policy that uses more than one path during a data transfer session. Data is divided into multiple paths, and the paths are alternated to send data. Even though data is sent on only one path at a time, this increases the size of "the pipe" and therefore allows more data transfer in the same period of time. If you decide to use Round Robin, the settings should be coordinated and tested between you and the storage administrator.

> **NOTE**   If you have third-party software installed on your host, these options can be expanded by that software.

Summary

The main topics covered in this chapter are as follows:

- I began this chapter by identifying the various types of centralized shared storage supported by vSphere. I discussed the identification, creation, and configuration of each type of storage. Finally, I examined use cases for various types of storage.

- I then discussed another type of shared storage, which is distributed over two or three hosts instead of centralized to a SAN or NAS, the vSphere Storage Appliance (VSA). I covered deploying, configuring, and administering this type of storage solution. Then, I examined use cases for deploying a VSA rather than a SAN or NAS, and the host resources required.

- The discussion then turned to the two types of datastores that are supported by vSphere: VMFS and NFS. I discussed identification, creation, renaming, deleting, and unmounting of each of these types of datastores. In addition, I discussed multipathing and path selection policies. I also examined use case scenarios for multiple VMFS/NFS datastores. Finally, you learned how to determine the appropriate path selection policies for a given VMFS datastore.

Exam Preparation Tasks

Review All of the Key Topics

Review the most important topics from inside the chapter, noted with the Key Topic icon in the outer margin of the page. Table 3-2 lists these key topics and the page numbers where each is found. Know the main differences between vSSs and vDSs and the port groups on each. Understand how to create, configure, edit, and delete these components and policies.

Table 3-2 Key Topics for Chapter 3

Key Topic Element	Description	Page Number
Bullet List	Advantages of Shared Storage	162
Figure 3-1	Storage Overview	163
Note	Fibre Channel Support for vSphere	163
Figure 3-2	Storage Naming Conventions	165
Activity 3-1	Accessing the Storage Views Tab to View Naming Conventions	166
Figure 3-3	Changing Storage Views	166
Figure 3-4	iSCSI Initiators	167
Figure 3-5	Virtual Disk Thin Provisioning	170
Figure 3-6	Zoning and Masking	171
Activity 3-2	Rescanning the Storage of an ESXi Host	172
Figure 3-7	The Rescan All Link	173
Figure 3-8	Scanning for New Storage Devices and Volumes	173
Note	vSphere Supports NFS Version 3 over TCP	174
Bullet List	Configuring an NFS Server	174
Activity 3-3	Connecting to an NAS Device Used as an NFS Server	175
Figure 3-9	The Add Storage Link	176
Figure 3-10	Adding an NAS Device	176
Bullet List	Keys for filters	177
Activity 3-4	Disabling vCenter Server Storage Filters	177
Figure 3-11	vCenter Server Settings	178

Key Topic Element	Description	Page Number
Figure 3-12	Disabling a Filter on vCenter	178
Figure 3-13	Enabling a Disabled Filter on vCenter	179
Activity 3-5	Enabling Software iSCSI Initiator Settings	180
Figure 3-14	Adding Storage Adapters	180
Figure 3-15	Adding a Software iSCSI Adapter	180
Figure 3-16	Addressing an iSCSI Target	181
Activity 3-6	Configuring iSCSI Port Binding	182
Figure 3-17	Selecting a Storage Adapter	182
Figure 3-18	The Network Configuration Tab	182
Figure 3-19	Binding a VMkernel Port	183
Activity 3-7	Enabling and Configuring iSCSI CHAP	183
Figure 3-20	Configuring an iSCSI Adapter	184
Figure 3-21	Configuring iSCSI CHAP	184
Figure 3-22	Configuring Mutual CHAP	185
Note	CHAP Settings	185
Figure 3-23	vSphere Storage Appliance	187
Bullet List	ESXi Host Configuration for VSA	188
Bullet Lists	The Front-End and Back-End Network Traffic on VSA	189
Activity 3-8	Deploying the VSA Manager	189
Figure 3-24	VSA Manager	191
Bullet List	Advantages of VSA	192
Bullet List	Required Hardware on ESXi Hosts for VSA	192
Activity 3-9	Identifying VMFS and NFS Datastore Properties	193
Figure 3-25	The Datastores View	194
Figure 3-26	Modifying the Datastores View	194
Bullet List	Advantages of VMFS-5	195
Activity 3-10	Creating a VMFS Datastore	196
Figure 3-27	The Add Storage Link	196
Figure 3-28	Adding a Datastore	196
Figure 3-29	Choosing a LUN	197

Key Topic Element	Description	Page Number
Figure 3-57	Configuring Datastore Capacity	216
Figure 3-58	The Ready to Complete Page	217
Figure 3-59	Volume Properties of an Expanded Datastore	217
Note	Configuration maximum of VMFS-5 datastores	218
Activity 3-18	Upgrading a VMFS Datastore	218
Figure 3-61	Choosing to Upgrade a VMFS-3 Datastore	219
Figure 3-62	Confirmation page for VMFS Datastore Upgrade	219
Figure 3-63	A View of a Recently Updated Datastore	220
Activity 3-19	Placing a VMFS Datastore in Maintenance Mode	220
Figure 3-64	Entering SDRS Maintenance Mode	221
Figure 3-65	A Datastore in SDRS Maintenance Mode	221
Activity 3-20	Selecting the Preferred Path for a VMFS Datastore	222
Figure 3-66	Selecting a Preferred Path	222
Figure 3-67	An Attempt to Disable the Only Path to a VMFS Datastore	223
Activity 3-21	Disabling a Path to a VMFS Datastore	223
Bullet List	Native Multipathing Policies for vSphere	224

Review Questions

The answers to these review questions are in Appendix A.

1. Which storage adapter type is similar to a mapped drive?

    a. SAN

    b. Fibre Channel

    c. FCoE

    d. NAS

2. Which two types of iSCSI initiator provide for TOE without the use of the VMkernel? (Choose two.)

    a. Software

    b. Independent hardware

    c. Thin provisioned

    d. Dependent hardware

3. Which type of Fibre Channel network segmentation method controls whether one WWN can see another WWN?

   a. LUN masking

   b. Zoning

   c. VLAN

   d. VPN

4. Which permissions should be set on a NAS datastore that will be used to store VM files?

   a. Read

   b. Root

   c. Read-Write

   d. Full Access

5. What does a VSA cluster datastore appear as to a host that uses it?

   a. An NFS datastore

   b. A SAN LUN

   c. The type is configurable in the VSA Manager.

   d. Hosts cannot use a VSA cluster, only VMs.

6. How many hosts can be included in a VSA cluster?

   a. As many as needed

   b. 2 or 3

   c. 32

   d. 256

7. How many static IP addresses will be required at a minimum for a two-host VSA cluster?

   a. 14

   b. 11

   c. 2

   d. 4

8. Which of the following is a feature of VMFS-5 but not of VMFS-3?

   a. Can store VMs, ISOs, and VM templates

   b. Can have up to 32 extents in a datastore

   c. Can support 2TB files with a 1MB block size

   d. Can be expanded online

9. When you unmount a VMFS datastore, which of the following happens to the data and metadata on its LUNs?

   a. The data and metadata are retained but the datastore is inactive and un-available.

   b. The metadata is deleted, but the data could be recovered in a clean room.

   c. The data and metadata are both immediately deleted.

   d. The data are metadata are still available for use.

10. What is the maximum number of times that you can expand a single extent on a VMFS-5 datastore?

   a. 32

   b. You cannot expand a single extent on a VMFS-5 datastore.

   c. You can expand the extent an unlimited number of times, but only to a maximum size of 2TB.

   d. You can expand the extent an unlimited number of times, but only to a maximum size of 64TB.

11. Which of following is *not* considered an advantage of Fibre Channel SAN storage?

   a. Flexible management

   b. Lower overhead

   c. Takes load off Ethernet network

   d. Low cost

12. Which of the following is the only protocol supported for NAS on vSphere 5.0?

   a. CIFS

   b. NFS v3 over UDP

   c. NFS v4

   d. NFS v3 over TCP

13. What is the maximum speed of iSCSI storage connection in vSphere 5.0?

    a. 100Gbps

    b. 10Gbps

    c. 8Gbps

    d. 1Gbps

14. Which additional setting should be configured on an NAS datastore that will be used to store ISOs that you want to protect?

    a. Read

    b. Root

    c. Read-Only

    d. Full Access

15. Which storage filter excludes from consideration LUNs that are ineligible for use because of host or storage type incompatibility?

    a. Same Host and Transport

    b. RDM

    c. VMFS

    d. Host Rescan

16. Which of the following is the default port used by iSCSI for dynamic discovery?

    a. 80

    b. 3260

    c. 20224

    d. 902

17. How many static IP addresses will be required at a minimum for a three-host VSA cluster?

    a. 14

    b. 11

    c. 2

    d. 4

18. Which of the following is a feature of VMFS-5 but not of VMFS-3?

    a. Can store VMs, ISOs, and VM templates

    b. Can have up to 32 extents in a datastore

    c. Can support extents up to 64TB in size

    d. Can be expanded online

19. When you unmount a NFS datastore, which of the following happens to the data and metadata?

    a. The data and metadata are retained but the datastore is unavailable to the host from which it was unmounted.

    b. The metadata is deleted, but the data could be recovered in a clean room.

    c. The data and metadata are both immediately deleted.

    d. The data are metadata are still available for use.

20. What of the following is a best practice when configuring extent size on a VMFS datastore?

    a. Customize each extent for your datastore.

    b. You cannot configure extent size when creating a LUN.

    c. Always set the extent size to 50% of the available space.

    d. Select **Maximum Available Space**.

This chapter covers the following subjects:

- Creating and Deploying Virtual Machines
- Creating and Deploying vApps
- Managing Virtual Machine Clones and Templates
- Administering Virtual Machines and vApps

CHAPTER 4

Deploying and Administering Virtual Machine and vApps

None of the virtual networking or the datastores would be necessary if it weren't for the fact that you want to create and deploy virtual machines (VMs). In other words, everything else that I discuss in the book, besides the VMs themselves, is just a "life support system" for the VMs. In this section, I will discuss creating, deploying, managing and administering VMs. In addition, I will define a relatively new concept that combines multiple VMs, referred to as a *vApp*, and you will learn how you can create, deploy, and manage vApps for your organization.

"Do I Know This Already?" Quiz

The "Do I Know This Already?" quiz allows you to assess whether you should read this entire chapter or simply jump to the "Exam Preparation Tasks" section for review. If you are in doubt, read the entire chapter. Table 4-1 outlines the major headings in this chapter and the corresponding "Do I Know This Already?" quiz questions. You can find the answers in Appendix A, "Answers to the 'Do I Know This Already?' Quizzes and Chapter Review Questions."

Table 4-1 "Do I Know This Already?" Section-to-Question Mapping

Foundations Topics Section	Questions Covered in This Section
Creating and Deploying Virtual Machines	1–4
Creating and Deploying vApps	5, 6
Managing Virtual Machine Clones and Templates	7, 8
Administering Virtual Machines and vApps	9, 10

1. What is the maximum amount of memory that can be assigned to a Version 8 virtual machine?

   a. 2TB

   b. 256GB

   c. 1TB

   d. 64GB

2. Which of the following are *not* supported on a Version 8 virtual machine? (Choose two.)

   a. 12 vnics

   b. 5 serial ports

   c. USB

   d. Hot add memory

3. Which of the following is a virtual machine feature that comes only with VMware Tools?

   a. Hot add hard disk

   b. Connections to virtual switch

   c. More than one datastore

   d. SVGA display

4. Which type of disk provisioning is slowest to create but required for some high-performance applications and databases?

   a. Thin

   b. Thin eager zeroed

   c. Thick eager zeroed

   d. Thick lazy zeroed

5. Which of the following *cannot* be added to a vApp?

   a. Host

   b. VM

   c. Resource Pool

   d. vService

6. When you power off a vApp, which of the following happens?

    a. The vApp powers off but VMs remained powered on.

    b. The VMs in the vApp gracefully shut down based on their shutdown order.

    c. The VMs in the vApp are all powered off immediately.

    d. It is not possible to control the power of a vApp.

7. What is maximum number of registered VMs on vCenter 5?

    a. 10,000

    b. 1000

    c. 15,000

    d. 30,000

8. What is maximum amount of RAM on ESXi5?

    a. 1TB

    b. 4TB

    c. 512GB

    d. 2TB

9. If a VM is created with an available memory of 2GB and no reservation is assigned, how large will its VSWP file be when it is powered on?

    a. 0GB

    b. 2GB

    c. There is not enough information to determine.

    d. It will not have .vswp file when it is powered on.

10. Which of the following files is only a description of the virtual disk on a VM?

    a. -flat.vmdk

    b. .vmdk

    c. .vmx

    d. .vmss

Foundation Topics

Creating and Deploying Virtual Machines

You should understand that a virtual machine (VM) is a computer. In fact, it's every bit as much of computer as is a physical machine. The difference is that the VM exists in a software state rather than a hardware state. The software state of the VM exists on one host or another, but the resources that it uses with regard to networking and storage can be spread across the network. In fact, some of them can be anywhere in the world!

In this section, I will focus on deploying VMs. I will start by identifying the capabilities of VMs based on their virtual hardware versions. In addition, I will discuss specialized software developed to match the hardware and installed OS, called VMware Tools. Also, I will cover methods used to access and use the VM console and the VM storage resources. Finally, I will discuss the many aspects of configuration, installation, modification, and upgrading that you will be required to know to manage your own environment and to pass the exam.

Identifying Capabilities for Virtual Machine Hardware Versions

The VM hardware is the components that make up the VM and allow it to perform computing and communication. It's kind of funny to me that we call it VM hardware because it's really software. This software connects to hardware on the host or somewhere else in the network. It can generally be divided into four categories:

- CPU
- Memory
- Disk
- Network

Although the basic components haven't changed in the past several years, their capabilities have been greatly expanded; thereby expanding the capabilities of the average VM.

Each time a new version of ESX/ESXi has been introduced, it has brought with it a new virtual hardware version for the VMs intended for that type of host. Each new virtual hardware version has increased the capabilities of the VM in many different ways. In this section, I will focus on the last three versions; because any before then would now be considered legacy. As you will see, the changes in just the past three versions have been dramatic.

When vSphere 4.0 was first introduced in 2009, it included a new virtual hardware version called Version 7 hardware. It represented a dramatic improvement over the Version 4 hardware that came with ESX/ESXi 3.5 hosts and vCenter 2.5. Since vSphere 5.0 was introduced, however, its new Version 8 hardware has proven to l far superior to the Version 7 hardware of vSphere 4.x.

As I mentioned before, you can divide VM hardware into four categories: CPU, memory, disk, and network. Each of the categories can have one or more components of VM hardware. The major improvements in these categories generally involve higher configuration maximums or additional support of a new component. Table 4-2 illustrates many aspects of VM hardware and the capabilities of each version.

Table 4-2 Virtual Machine Hardware Versions

	Version 4	**Version 7**	**Version 8**
# of vCPUs for SMP	1, 2, or 4	1–8	1–32[3]
Maximum memory	64GB	256GB	1TB
Video (with VMware Tools)	SVGA	SVGA	SVGA, 3D graphics[1]
Audio	None	None	HD[1]
IDE	1 controller, 4 devices	1 controller, 4 devices	1 controller, 4 devices
Max. parallel ports	3	3	3
Max. serial ports	4	4	4
USB support	None	None	Supported
Floppy drives	1 controller, 2 drives	1 controller, 2 drives	1 controller, 2 drives
Mouse	Supported	Supported	Supported
Keyboard	Supported	Supported	Supported
vNICs	1–4	1–10	1–10
SCSI adapters	1–4 SCSI adapters, 1–15 devices per adapter	1–4 SCSI adapters, 1–15 devices per adapter	1–4 SCSI adapters, 1–15 devices per adapter
Hot add capability	Disk only	Disk, Ethernet controller, SCSI device, memory, CPU[2]	Disk, Ethernet controller, SCSI device, USB, memory, CPU[2]

1 Requires support on the device running the vSphere Client.

2 Requires supported OS and must be first enabled with VM powered down.

3 Supported CPUs is license-level dependent.

Identifying VMware Tools Device Drivers

The operating system (OS) that you install in a VM can have a dramatic effect on how the virtual hardware will be used. When you create a VM, a Typical installation attempts to choose the correct components to complement the OS and version that you are intending to run on the VM. This is only one part of customizing or "tweaking" the installation. The other part is installing the correct device drivers for the virtual hardware after the OS is installed. For this step, VMware provides VMware Tools. These are specialized device drivers that can be installed after the OS is installed. They enhance the performance of the VM in many ways. The following are some of the enhancements that VMware Tools device drivers can provide your VM:

- **SVGA display:** Without VMware Tools, a VM has Video Graphics Array (VGA) graphics (640x480). With VMware Tools, VMs can have Super Video Graphics Array (SVGA) graphics (800x600), and often even better.

- **vmxnet - vmxnet3 vNIC drivers:** With VMware Tools installed, the virtual network interface card (vNIC) driver support is expanded to support most operating systems using specialized drivers created by VMware.

- **Balloon driver for memory management (vmmemctl):** This driver provides for efficient memory allocation between VMs.

- **Sync driver for quiescing I/O:** This driver can be especially important for features such as vMotion and Storage vMotion and for obtaining clean snapshots.

- **Improved mouse support:** Without VMware Tools, the mouse is often slow and not properly responsive to commands. Also, the mouse cannot seamlessly move in and out of a VM console. With VMware Tools, the mouse operates as expected.

- **VM Heartbeat:** This is especially useful for the high-availability (HA) feature called VM monitoring. VMware can detect that the OS has failed and can restart the VM to attempt to correct the problem.

- **Time synchronization:** VMware Tools make it easy to synchronize the VM time with that of the host on which it resides.

- **Ability to shut down the VM:** With VMware Tools installed, you can gracefully shut down the VM guest OS without first logging on.

Identifying Methods to Access and Use Virtual Machine Console

Because the VM exists in the "virtual world," but you exist in the "physical world," you need a door or portal through which you can access and control the VM. The VM console on your vSphere Client provides this portal. To access the VM console, you just right-click a VM and select **Open Console** or click the **Open Console** icon, as shown in Figure 4-1. From the VM console, you can log on to the VM or use the tools at the top of the console to control the VM. These tools enable you to power on, power off, shut down, add ISOs, and so on.

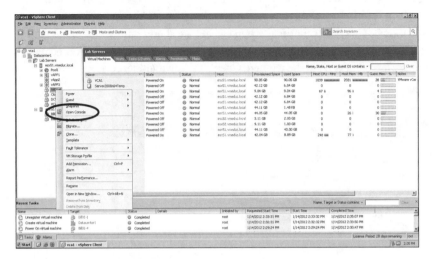

Figure 4-1   Opening a VM Console

Another method of accessing the console of your VM is by opening the Console tab, as shown in Figure 4-2. Although this might be more convenient for some vSphere administrators, it does not offer the File menu options that actually opening a console offers; however, these options can be accessed from other areas as well. Later, in the section "Installing/Upgrading/Updating VMware Tools," I will discuss the function of many of these tools.

Figure 4-2   The VM Console Tab

Identifying Virtual Machine Storage Resources

Your VMs almost always see their storage as local SCSI disks. This is true whether it is actually coming from Fibre Channel (FC), Fibre Channel over Ethernet (FcoE), Internet Small Computer System Interface (iSCSI), network-attached storage (NAS) or direct-attached storage. Even though your VM cannot determine what logical unit number (LUN) is actually providing its storage, you can see what datastore it's on by examining the resources panel on the Summary tab of the VM in the vSphere Client, as shown in Figure 4-3.

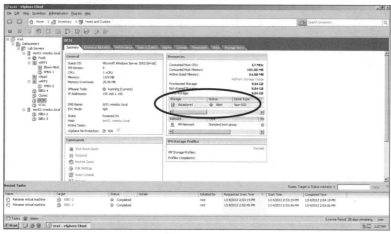

Figure 4-3   Identifying Storage

You can also browse the storage by right-clicking the datastore and then clicking **Browse Datastore**, as shown in Figure 4-4. As you can see, this datastore has a triggered alert, indicated by its Status, which you might want to investigate further.

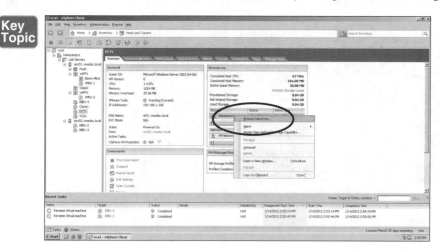

Figure 4-4   Browsing a Datastore

Placing Virtual Machines in Selected ESXi Hosts/Clusters/Resource Pools

When you create a VM, you can decide the most appropriate place in your hierarchy for that VM. For example, you can decide on which host it will initially be created. If that host is a member of a cluster, the VM might not stay on that host all the time, but might instead be migrated to other hosts within the same cluster when you use VMotion or even automatically by the system (using Distributed Resource Scheduler [DRS]). You decide what the options are for each VM when you place it into a specific area of your hierarchy. In addition, there might be groups of VMs to which you want to give more priority with regard to resources and groups that you want to give less priority. Instead of having to manage each VM individually, you can use Resource Pools to manage the VMs as a group. Chapter 5, "Establishing and Maintaining Service Levels," I will discuss each of these concepts in much greater detail. For now, you should just understand that it all starts with building your hierarchy and then placing the VMs into the appropriate place within it.

Configuring and Deploying a Guest OS Into a New Virtual Machine

As part of creating a VM, you can install a guest OS. Note that I said *can* and not *must*. In other words, a VM is a VM even without any guest OS or applications. It is a "box" that is made of software, called virtual hardware, that can support a guest OS. It's very important to understand that distinction.

That said, at the very end of the wizard that you use to create a VM you have an **Edit the Virtual Machine Settings Before Completion** option. If you choose this setting, the Finish button changes to Continue, as shown in Figure 4-5.

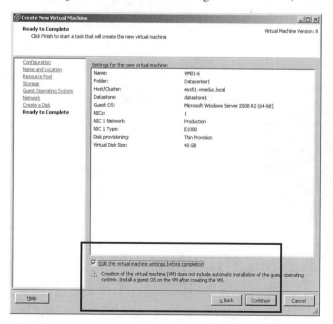

Figure 4-5   Editing Settings During the Creation of a VM

If you click **Continue**, you are taken directly into the VM properties. From there, by using **New CD/DVD (Adding)**, you can add the ISO that loads your guest OS, as shown in Figure 4-6.

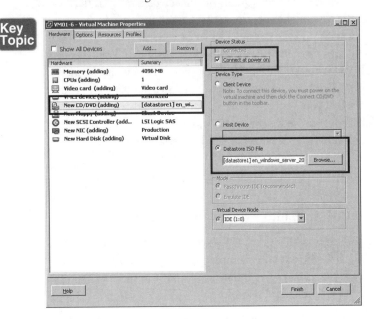

Figure 4-6 Adding the ISO

You should also remember to check the **Connect at Power On** check box. Now when you click **Finish**, and then power on the VM, you should see an installation beginning, as shown in Figure 4-7.

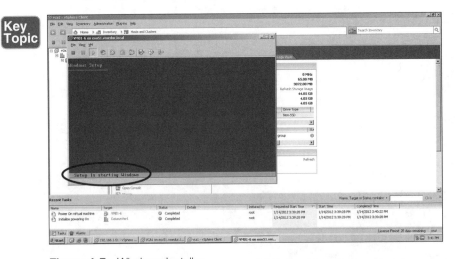

Figure 4-7 Windows Installer

Creating/Converting Thin/Thick Provisioned Virtual Disks

As I have discussed before, thin disks on your VMs can be beneficial because the disk space on your datastore is not actually committed until the VM actually uses the space. As you will remember, the total amount of disk space that is allocated (promised) can far exceed the actual amount of disk space on the datastore and the LUNs to which it is connected. As long as this type of disk management is monitored properly, it can assist an organization by allowing more flexible and efficient use of disk space.

In this section, I am not focusing so much on the concept of thin and thick disks as I am on how they are created. When you create a VM, one of your choices is the type of disk to create for the VM. As shown in Figure 4-8, you can choose between three types of provisioning.

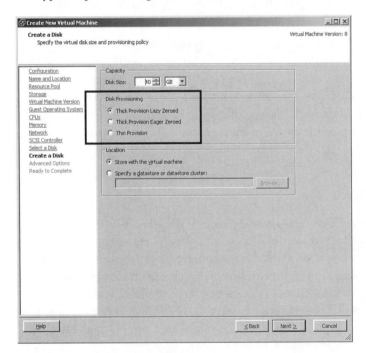

Figure 4-8   Virtual Disk Provisioning

The following list gives a brief description of each type.

- **Thick Provision Lazy Zeroed:** This type of provisioning provides a fully pre-allocated type of storage. In other words, its capacity is removed from the datastore upon creation. It's quick to create compared with Eager Zeroed, but it does not have the same inherent (first use) performance characteristics as Eager Zeroed. This is because the file blocks are actually zeroed out when the disk is written to, and not when it is created. In most cases, this performance difference is marginal.

- **Thick Provision Eager Zeroed:** This type of provisioning provides a fully pre-allocated type of storage that has the highest chance of being contiguous. Its capacity is removed from the datastore when the disk is created. It is slow to create, compared with Lazy Zeroed, because the file blocks are allocated and zeroed out when the disk is created. This provides for much more contiguous blocks of storage, which some high performance applications and databases might require.

- **Thin Provision:** This type of provisioning does not provide fully pre-allocated space or highly likely contiguous blocks. Instead, space is allocated and zeroed out when it is actually used. This type of provisioning is much faster on the initial creation of VMs, but might not be the proper type to use for some applications and databases. This type of storage should also be monitored, because it is quite possible to overpromise in the VMs what the datastore can actually deliver.

Configuring Disk Shares

When you have multiple VMs that access the same VMFS datastore (and therefore the same LUNs), you have a contention for a finite physical resource. If you want to give a high priority to some VMs when there is contention for the bandwidth to the LUNs, and you want give a lower priority to others, you can do so using disk shares. Disk shares are a relative value that the system uses to control disk bandwidth. More specifically, they control I/O operations per second (IOPS) that the virtual disk is allowed to take from the physical resource. The values are Low, Normal, High, or Custom, with a relative value as follows:

- **Low:** 500 shares

- **Normal:** 1000 shares

- **High:** 2000 shares

Actually, shares can be used for more than just disk. You can also use them to control CPU, memory, and even network I/O (which I will discuss in Chapter 5), but in this section I will focus on disk. For example, if one of your VMs has twice as many shares as another, it will win the access to the physical resource (in this case, the LUN) twice as often, thereby improving its performance at the expense of the other VM (when there is contention).

The important parts to understand here are that shares matter only if there is contention for the physical resource and that all the shares compete within the same host. In other words, if one VM needs twice as much of physical resource as another VM, but there is plenty of physical resource available, and then some left over, its shares don't matter. However, if one VM needs twice as much as the other and the resource is scarce, its shares matter because the VM with the higher shares will take twice as much of the resource, even if it causes the VM with the lower shares to perform poorly. In fact, that is the way you want it. That's how you establish high-priority and low-priority VMs.

NOTE   The relative and proportional relation of disk shares on a host is a very important concept. For example, if there are two VMs on your host that each have 1000 shares and both are contending for the disk reads, they will each get one-half of the disk reads. However, if there are four VMs that each have 1000 shares and they are contending for the disk reads, each VM will receive one-quarter of the reads. In other words, it's not the number of shares that a VM has that is the most important, it's the number of shares the VM has in proportion to the total number of shares available.

To change the disk shares applied to a VM, follow the steps outlined in Activity 4-1.

Activity 4-1 Configuring Disk Shares on a VM

1. Log on to your vSphere Client.

2. Select **Home** and then **Hosts and Clusters**.

3. Right-click the VM on which you want to configure disk shares and select **Edit Settings**, as shown in Figure 4-9.

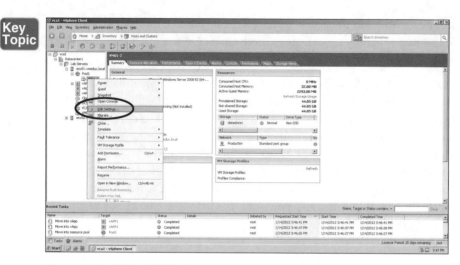

Figure 4-9 Editing VM Settings

4. Open the **Resources** tab and click **Disk**, as shown in Figure 4-10.

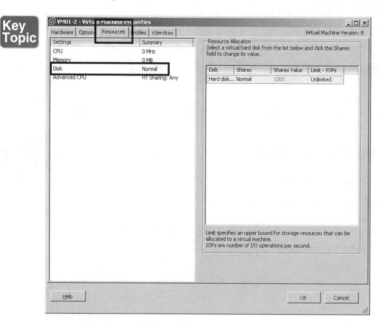

Figure 4-10 Configuring Disk Resources

5. If the VM contains more than one disk, choose the appropriate disk from the Resource Allocation page on the right, and then choose **Low**, **Normal**, **High**, or **Custom**, as shown in Figure 4-11.

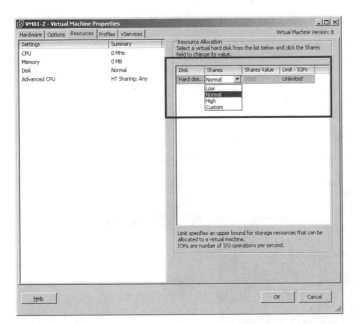

Figure 4-11   Configuring Disk Shares

6. If you have chosen Custom, enter the value that you want to configure in the Shares Value; otherwise, proceed to Step 7.

7. Click **OK**. Note the relative share value changes when you click OK.

Installing/Upgrading/Updating VMware Tools

As I mentioned earlier in this chapter, VMware Tools are the "other part" of the installation after you install the OS. The installers are ISO image files that look like a CD/ROM image to the guest OS. There is a separate ISO file for each type of OS, including Windows, Linux, Solaris, FreeBSD, and NetWare. With few exceptions, you should install VMware Tools immediately after you have completed the initial installation of a VM. Of course, this does not apply if you are using templates or clones, or if you are using Update Manager to update the VMs, but here I am discussing the full installation of a VM with an OS (such as Windows Server 2008 or Windows Server 2003) using the wizard provided by the vSphere Client and the subsequent automatic installation of VMware Tools.

To install or upgrade the VMware Tools, follow the steps outlined in Activity 4-2.

Activity 4-2 Automatic Installation/Upgrade of VMware Tools

1. Log on to your vSphere Client.

2. Select **Home** and then **Hosts and Clusters**.

3. Right-click the VM on which you want to install the VMware Tools and select **Open Console**.

4. At the top of the VM console, select **VM**, then **Guest**, and then **Install/Upgrade VMware Tools**, as shown in Figure 4-12.

Figure 4-12   Install/Upgrade VMware Tools

5. Choose the type of upgrade that you require (in this case, **Automatic Tools Upgrade**) and click **OK**, as shown in Figure 4-13.

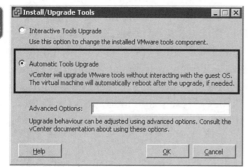

Figure 4-13   Automatic Upgrade of VMware Tools

6. Monitor the Recent Tasks pane to confirm that the VMware Tools upgrade/installation has begun and then is complete.

If this sounds like a lot of work for each machine, there are methods to make it much more automatic. You can configure your VMs to check for and install newer versions of VMware Tools. In this case, the guest OS will check the version of VMware Tools and compare it with the latest. The status bar of the VM will indicate that a new version is available.

Even easier, for Windows and Linux VMs, you can configure the VM to automatically upgrade itself when a new version is available, as shown in Figure 4-14. In that case, the version check will be performed when you power on the VM, but the automatic upgrade will not occur until you power off and restart the VM. This strategy is used to avoid unexpected interruptions on the VM and its network components.

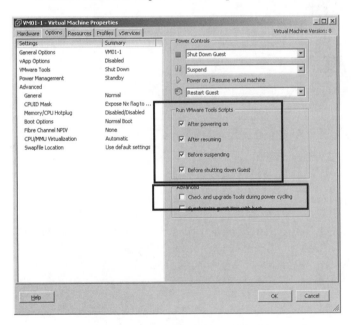

Figure 4-14   Version Checking for VMware Tools

Configuring Virtual Machine Time Synchronization

It's extremely important to have your VMs in time synchronization with each other and with the other components in your network. This is especially important when discussing vSphere because most of the VMs are servers. That said, how you provide that time synchronization is up to you. Some administrators might prefer to use native time synchronization software such as Network Time Protocol (NTP) for

Linux or Win32Time for Microsoft, whereas others might prefer to use the native time synchronization provided by VMware Tools. The most important thing is that you should use only one form of time synchronization. So, if you prefer to use a native method, you should disable VMware Tools time synchronization. To configure VMware Tools time synchronization, right-click the VMware Tools icon in the notification area on the VM, and then select **Time Synchronization Between the Virtual Machine and the ESX Server**, as shown in Figure 4-15.

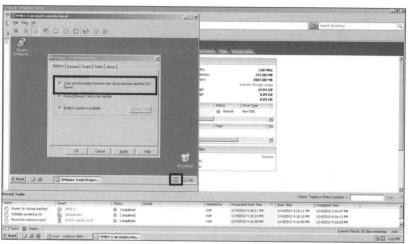

Figure 4-15 Configuring Time Synchronization

NOTE Even if you don't check **Time Synchronization Between the Virtual Machine and the ESX Server**, all VMs will still synchronize their time with that of the host once during their power-on sequence.

Converting a Physical Machine Using VMware Converter

I tell people in my classes that VMware Converter is like the "Swiss army knife from VMware." Think back to the first time that you ever picked up a Swiss army knife. You likely expected to see a blade, since it's a knife, but then you began to see many other tools that you didn't know were there and some that you couldn't even identify. Well, VMware Converter is like that, as well; at first you see it as a tool used to convert physical machines to VMs, but as you continue to "turn it over" you see that there are many other tools. In this section, I will discuss the *blade*, which is VMware's capability to convert a running physical machine to a VM. In the sections that follow this, I will discuss the other tools that it can provide.

As of vSphere 5.0, the integrated version of vCenter Converter is no longer available, but a standalone version is freely available for download. To download the standalone version of Converter, go to http://downloads.vmware.com and search for the "VMware Converter Standalone." After you have downloaded the Converter, you can use it to convert a physical machine to a VM and to do many other conversions as well. For example, to convert a physical machine to a virtual machine using VMware Converter Standalone, follow the steps outlined in Activity 4-3.

Activity 4-3 Converting a Physical Machine to a Virtual Machine Using VMware vCenter Converter Standalone

1. Download and install the vCenter Converter Standalone. This is a simple wizard-driven installation, as shown in Figure 4-16.

Figure 4-16   Installing the vCenter Converter Standalone

2. When you have finished with the installation, you can start the Conversion Wizard by clicking **Convert Machine** in the application window, as shown in Figure 4-17.

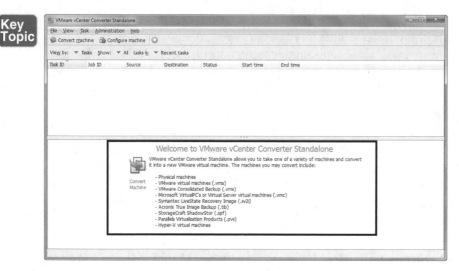

Figure 4-17 Starting the Conversion Wizard

3. Select a source machine to convert and click **Next**, as shown in Figure 4-18.

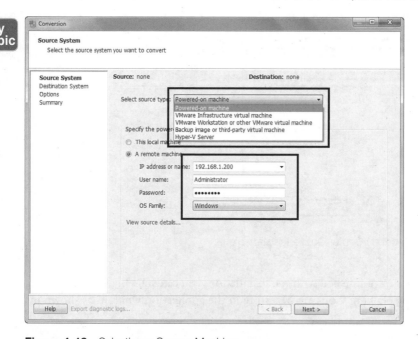

Figure 4-18 Selecting a Source Machine

4. Select a destination for the new VM and click **Next**, as shown in Figure 4-19.

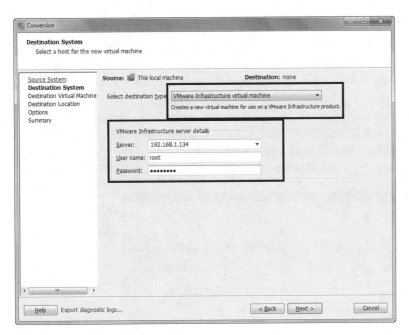

Figure 4-19   Selecting a Destination

5. Depending on the source machine, the Options page provides setup options. Choose the setup options that you need.

6. Review the summary and submit the conversion job. The agent that was used during the conversion should be uninstalled automatically.

Importing a Supported Virtual Machine Source Using VMware Converter

As I mentioned, in addition to converting a physical machine to a VM, you can also use vCenter Converter to convert a VM to a different type of VM. Why would you want to do that? Well, for example, you could convert a VMware Workstation VM to a VMware Infrastructure VM that can be used in a vSphere environment or vice versa. This could be useful if you had been experimenting with one type of VM and then wanted to convert it to the other. This is just one example of what the Converter can do. (You may have also noticed that you can convert Microsoft Hyper-V machines into VMware VMs, as well.) The process for the conversion is the same as outlined earlier, but you just make different choices.

Modifying Virtual Hardware Settings Using VMware Standalone Converter

Suppose that you use VMware Converter to convert a physical machine to a VM, but you don't really want the same hardware configuration on the VM as you had on the physical machine. For example, the physical machine might have two CPUs, but you only want one vCPU on the VM, or the physical machine might have only one NIC, but you want two vnics on the VM. You can make these changes while you are doing the conversion by selecting them in the Options section, as shown in Figure 4-20. As you can see, virtual hardware settings are just some of the many parameter changes you can make in the Options of VMware vCenter Converter Standalone.

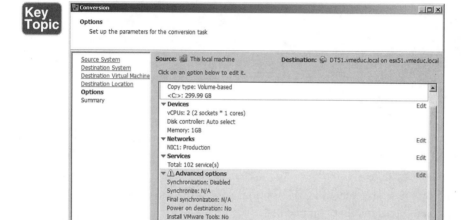

Figure 4-20   Modifying Virtual Hardware Settings

Configuring/Modifying Virtual CPU and Memory Resources According to OS and Application Requirements

As I mentioned before, with full virtualization, the guest OS on your VM has no idea that it is running on a VM. It has not been altered in any way, and it "believes" that it is running on a physical machine and therefore that everything that you "tell it" is a physical resource is actually a physical resource. When you first configure a VM, you should configure the CPU and the memory based on what the application needs to run. In this section, I will first discuss CPU configuration and modification, and then I will discuss memory configuration and modification.

Configuring and Modifying Virtual Machine CPU

When you create the VM and you configure the number of vCPUs, you obtain a maximum of one "core's worth" of processing power for each vCPU that you configure. In other words, if you have a host that has a Quad Core 2.5GHz processor, you will obtain a maximum of 2.5GHz of processing power per vCPU that you create on a VM. The VMkernel actually load balances over multiple cores, but this will be the numeric result.

Generally speaking, you should not create VMs with more than one vCPU unless the application that will be running on them actually requires more than one vCPU or would truly run much faster with more than one. In fact, if you use a Typical installation, the default setting is one vCPU. Most applications these days are single threaded, so a VM that is dedicated to them and has one vCPU with somewhere between 2GHz and 3 GHz of processing power is more than enough. In some cases, with multithreaded high-performance applications (such as SQL, Exchange, or Lotus Notes), you can gain performance advantages by creating VMs with more than one vCPU. In those cases, you should take care as to where you place those VMs, as I will discuss in much more detail in Chapter 5.

In addition, with the right operating system and a little configuration beforehand, you can add vCPUs to a running VM. It might not be as simple as it sounds, because you must have everything just right, but it is possible. To make it possible for you, you must use a supported guest OS, and you must enable **CPU Hot Plug** in the Advanced Hardware settings for the VM with the VM powered down, as shown in Figure 4-21.

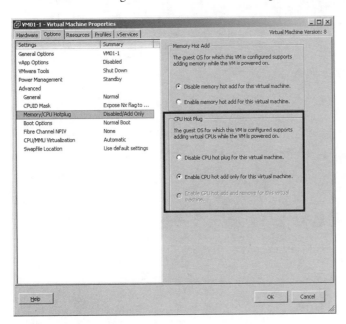

Figure 4-21   Hot Plug CPU

Once this is enabled, with the right OS you can add another vCPU to the VM and have the guest OS recognize it and use it. With some guest OSs, you can add vCPU to the virtual hardware, but the guest OS won't recognize it without a reboot. Is that truly a Hot Plug? I'll let you decide on that point. At the time of this writing, there were 82 guest OSs that supported hot add vCPU for vSphere. You can obtain the latest list at http://www.vmware.com/resources/compatibility.

Configuring and Modifying Virtual Machine Memory

You should also configure the VM with right amount of memory for the application that you will be running on it. The catch here is that if you create a new VM using the Typical settings, you will never see a selection for the amount of memory that you want to configure. This is because VMware will use a default amount of memory based on the OS and the version of the OS that you are installing. If you want to configure a different amount of memory than the default, you will need to create the VM using the Custom settings, as shown in Figure 4-22.

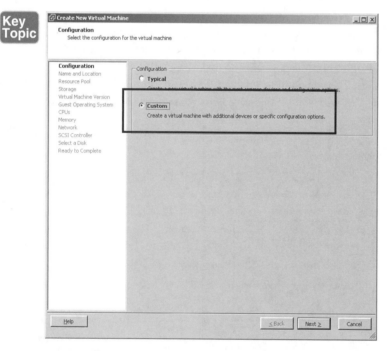

Figure 4-22   Selecting a Custom VM Installation

By selecting **Custom**, you will then be able to choose many more settings, but I will focus here on the memory settings, as shown in Figure 4-23.

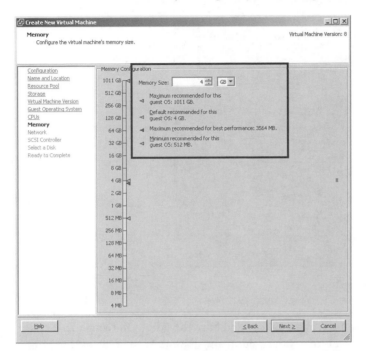

Figure 4-23   Custom Memory Settings for a VM

As you can see, even when you choose **Custom**, the system will still give you guidance as to the default, minimum recommended, and maximum recommended settings. The important thing to remember here is that this is not a guarantee to the OS for a certain amount of physical RAM, but instead it's what you are telling the guest OS that it has in memory. In other words, you could still provide this memory from disk using a swap file, which I will discuss in much greater detail in Chapter 5.

As with CPU, you can hot add memory on a VM as long as the guest OS supports it and as long as you have configured it in advance. You must first enable **Memory Hot Add** in the Advanced Hardware settings for the VM with VM powered down, as shown in Figure 4-24.

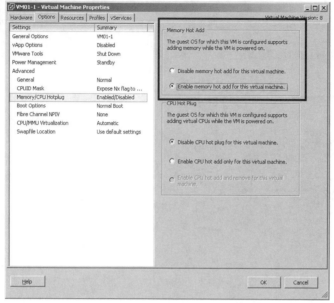

Figure 4-24   Hot Add Memory

Once this is enabled, you can add memory and have the guest OS recognize it and use it. Some guest OSs require a restart, but many do not. At the time of this writing, there were174 guest OSs that supported hot add memory. You can obtain the latest list at http://www.vmware.com/resources/compatibility.

Configuring/Modifying Virtual NIC Adapter and Connecting Virtual Machines to Appropriate Network Resources

When you create a VM with Typical settings, it will have one virtual network interface card (vNIC). For many VMs, this will be enough. However, if you need to have the VM connected to more than one network at the same time, you will need to have more than one vNIC on the VM, and you will need to connect each one to its associated network. This would be true if the VM were also connected to a backup network, a demilitarized zone (DMZ), or if it served as a Network Address Translation (NAT) router, just to name a few examples.

To create a VM with more than one vNIC, you will need to use the Custom settings during the creation of VM. Once you specify that the VM has more than one vNIC, you can then specify which vNIC connects to which port group. To change these settings after you have created the VM, just right-click the VM, select **Edit Settings**, and make the changes you require, as shown in Figure 4-25.

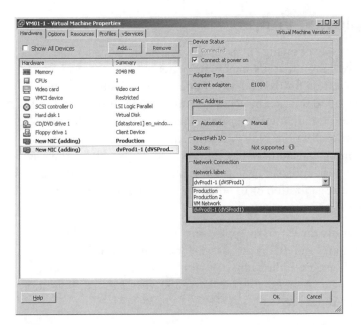

Figure 4-25   Editing Virtual Network Interface Card Settings

Determining Appropriate Datastore Locations for Virtual Machines Based on Application Workloads

In general, a bottleneck caused by the weakest resource will have a negative effect on a VM's performance, even if the other resources are strong. In other words, if you have ample CPU and memory resources for your VMs but they are lacking in disk performance, the overall result could still be a VM that performs poorly. If you are using applications that put a large workload on disk, such as a database server, make sure that your VMs are using the fastest disk available, which means they should be on your fastest datastores.

The catch is that you might not know which datastore is fastest at the time you create the VM. You and your team can name the datastores based on the types of VMs that you plan on placing on them. That would be a great start, but the name couldn't actually guarantee the performance. What you really need is a way to create a storage policy (or profile) that pairs up the right datastore with the right VMs so that you and your team don't make a mistake. In the section "Assigning a Storage Policy to a VM," later in this chapter, you will learn how you can assign a VM to a storage policy (new to vSphere 5.0).

Creating and Deploying vApps

A vApp is not just a fancy way of saying *virtual appliance*, it's really much more. For a long time now, we have known that it's sometimes better to use more than one server to provide an application for the end user. For example, a high-performance database might be provided to the user by actually using an application server and a separate database server, not to mention a separate domain controller. This was true in our networks before virtualization. Now, with virtualization, you can package all three of those servers into one inventory object and use settings to control the way that they communicate to each other. Furthermore, you can export the whole package to other parts of your organization or to other organizations using the Open Virtualization Format (OVF).

In this section, I will identify the various vApp settings that you can use when creating your vApps. In addition, I will discuss creating, cloning, and exporting vApps. More specifically, I will illustrate adding objects to a vApp, configuring IP pools, and suspending a resuming a vApp. Finally, I will examine when a tiered application should be deployed as a vApp.

Identifying vApp Settings

Creating a vApp is rather simple, as I will discuss next, but configuring all the settings on a vApp can be a little more complex. Because the purpose of the vApp is to allow the VMs to communicate more effectively with each other while securing them from other machines, all of your settings should be configured with these goals in mind. There are three tabs for the settings of each vApp. You can access these by right-clicking the vApp and selecting **Edit Settings**. This brings up the Edit vApp Settings dialog box. I will now identify the settings that you can configure on each of these tabs and give a brief description of each setting.

Options

In general, on the Options tab for vApps, you can configure Resources, Properties, IP Allocation Policy, and Advanced settings. Because each of these settings is a subject on its own, I have listed them separately so that I can discuss them in greater depth. You should be able to identify each of these settings. In later chapters, I will discuss modifying some of these types of settings for troubleshooting and fine-tuning your virtual datacenter:

- **Resources:** As shown in Figure 4-26, this setting allows you to fine-tune the CPU and physical memory resources that will be allowed to the vApp and therefore the cumulative amount that the VMs in the vApp can use at any given time. (In Chapter 5, I will discuss much more about these types of resource controls for vApps and VMs.)

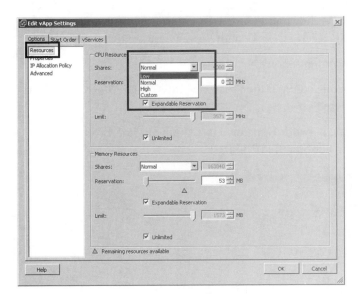

Figure 4-26   Resource Settings for vApps

■ **Properties:** As shown in Figure 4-27, this setting allows you to edit properties that you have defined in Advanced property configuration; which I will discuss later in this section.

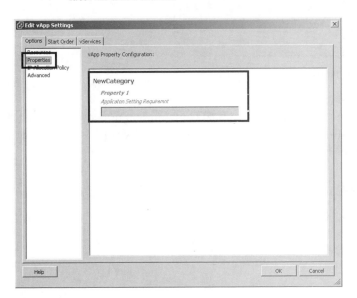

Figure 4-27   Properties Settings for vApps

■ **IP Allocation Policy:** As shown in Figure 4-28, this setting determines how the VMs in the vApp will receive their IP addresses. There are three options:

—Fixed: A manual configuration

—Transient: A dynamic configuration managed by vCenter, which is released when VM is powered off

—DHCP: Allows the network Dynamic Host Configuration Protocol (DHCP) server to allocate the IP address

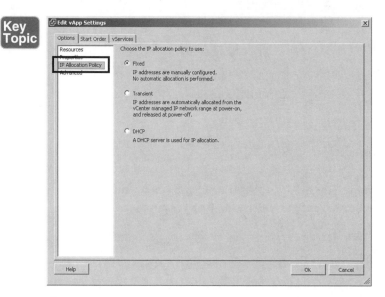

Figure 4-28   Configuring IP Settings for vApps

Using the DHCP setting requires additional configuration not covered here, as shown in Figure 4-29. I discuss configuring IP pools later in this chapter in the "Configuring IP Pools" section.

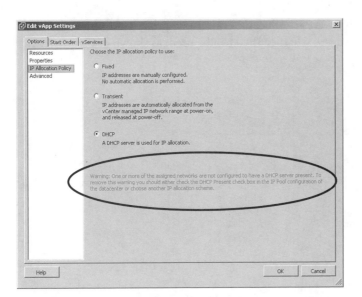

Figure 4-29   Configuring DHCP Settings for vApps

- **Advanced:** As shown in Figure 4-30, this setting allows you to note the Product Name, Version, Vendor, Vendor URL, and so on. There are also Properties settings that are used for the Open Virtualization Format (OVF) that will be created and can then be exported. You can define your own properties for a vApp if the properties that you need are not already defined. This proves especially useful if you plan to use the vApp in other locations as well.

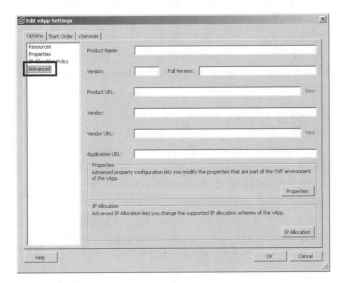

Figure 4-30   Advanced Settings for vApps

Also included in this setting are IP Allocation fine-tuning that determines whether a DHCP server can be used and whether IPv6 can be used, as shown in Figure 4-31.

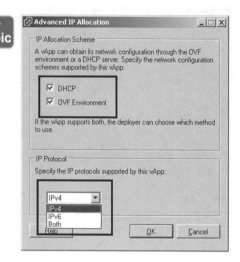

Figure 4-31   Advanced IP Allocation Settings for vApps

Start Order

You might remember my earlier example of a database service being provided to the end user by three different VMs, an application server, a database server, and a domain controller. You might also remember that the VMs in the vApp will all be treated as one inventory object. That means that they will power on "as one" and power off "as one." Now, if you think about that for a moment, you might see a potential issue. What if the database server powers up first and looks for the Active Directory, which is not there yet because the domain controller is lagging behind on its power up? What would happen is the database server would likely register errors that you might have to address later.

To prevent this issue from occurring, you can use the Start Order screen to control the startup of the domain controller and the database server in such a way that the domain controller will always be up and ready with the Active Directory before the database server will be allowed to start. You can do this by placing the VMs into multiple startup groups, as shown in Figure 4-32, and then setting them so that one group must wait on another group. You can configure the number of seconds that a group must wait and/or the detection that VMware Tools are started and ready on the VM. All the VMs in the same group will be started before proceeding to the next group. Also, when you shut down the vApp, the system will use your settings in reverse order.

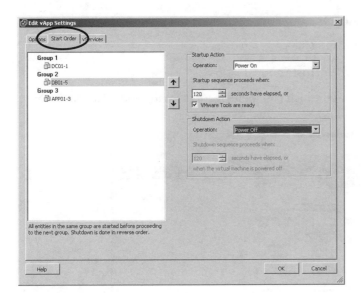

Figure 4-32   Start Order Settings for vApps

vServices

Instead of providing everything that the vApp needs through the virtual hardware of the VMs that it contains, it's possible to provide some of what it needs through a service that it can access through the network, referred to as a *vService*. These vServices are available for vApps as well as for individual VMs. For example, a vService could provide a backup service or a logging service for a vApp or a VM.

The catch is that if you specify a vService in this setting, the VM will be dependent on that service. At the time you specify the service, the system will make a connection to the vendor of the service and bind that service to the VM. After that, the VM will have to be able to connect to that service in order to power on. When you specify vService bindings, you can also encode application-specific information into the OVF package that determines how the VM or vApp interacts with a specific solution. This encoding is beyond the scope of this text.

Creating/Cloning/Exporting a vApp

Creating a vApp is rather simple. To create a new vApp, you just right-click in a place where you can create one, select **New vApp**, give the vApp a name, and populate it by creating new VMs or even dragging existing VMs into it. For example, to create a vApp named vApp-05 just follow the steps outlined in Activity 4-4.

Activity 4-4 Creating a vApp

1. Log on to your vSphere Client.

2. Select **Home** and then **Hosts and Clusters**.

3. Right-click the host on which you want create the vApp and select **New vApp**, as shown in Figure 4-33.

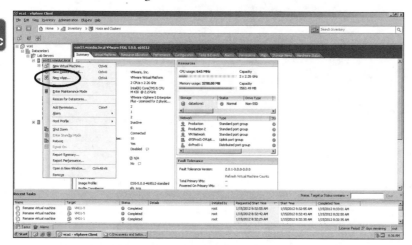

Figure 4-33 Creating a vApp

4. In the New vApp Wizard, type a name for your new vApp (in this case vApp-05), as shown in Figure 4-34.

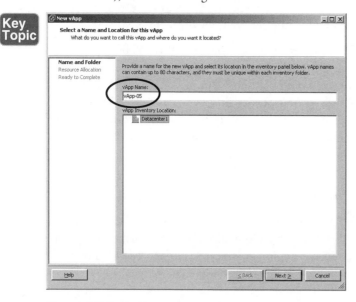

Figure 4-34 Naming a vApp

5. On the Resource Allocation page, leave the defaults for now (but you could make changes, as I discussed earlier), and then click **Next**, as shown in Figure 4-35.

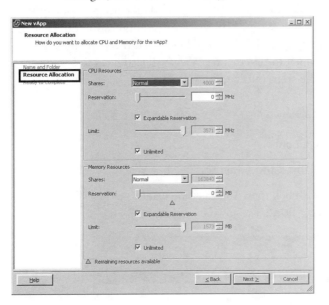

Figure 4-35   The Resource Allocation Page

6. On the Ready to Complete page, review your configured settings and click **Finish**, as shown in Figure 4-36.

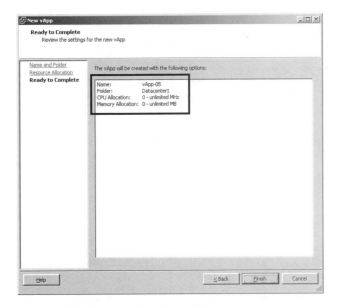

Figure 4-36   The Ready to Complete Page

If you have a vApp that you really like and you would like another one just like it, you can clone the vApp (in other words, make an exact copy of it). You can also use the cloning technique to make an exact copy first and then configure only the changes that you want for your new vApp. This saves you configuration time and improves configuration accuracy as well. You should note that the vApp must be powered off before cloning, which means that the VMs will also need to be powered off. To clone a vApp, follow the steps outlined in Activity 4-5.

Activity 4-5 Cloning a vApp

1. Log on to your vSphere Client.

2. Select **Home** and then **Hosts and Clusters**.

3. In the console pane, right-click the vApp that you want to clone, verify that it is powered off, and select **Clone**, as shown in Figure 4-37.

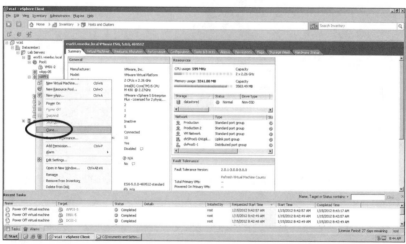

Figure 4-37 Cloning a vApp

4. In the Clone vApp Wizard, select the host for the clone of your vApp, as shown in Figure 4-38, and click **Next**.

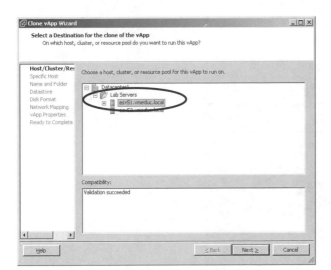

Figure 4-38   Selecting the Host for a vApp

5. On the Name and Location page, type a name for your new cloned vApp (in this case, Clone of vApp1) and the inventory location (Datacenter) and click **Next**, as shown in Figure 4-39.

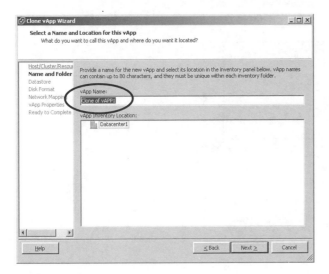

Figure 4-39   The Name and Location Page

6. On the Datastore page, select the datastore where you want to store the vApp, and then click **Next**, as shown in Figure 4-40.

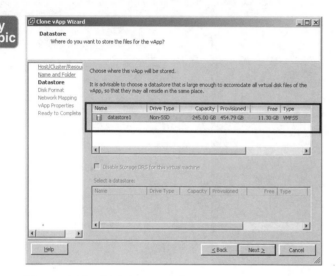

Figure 4-40   Selecting a Datastore for a vApp

> **7.** On the Disk Format page, select the format (same format as source, thin provisioned format, thick format), and then click **Next**, as shown in Figure 4-41.

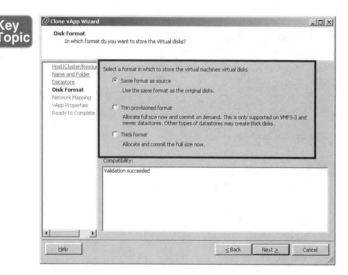

Figure 4-41   The Disk Format Page

> **8.** On the vApp Networks page, select the networks that the vApp will use, and then click **Next**, as shown in Figure 4-42.

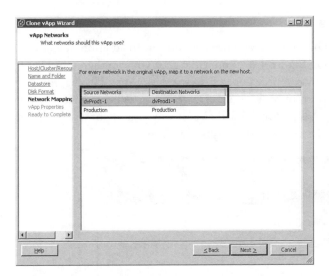

Figure 4-42   The vApp Networks Page

9. On the Ready to Complete page, review your settings, and then click **Finish**, as shown in Figure 4-43. A new vApp will be created with the same settings as the original and the same VMs as members of the vApp.

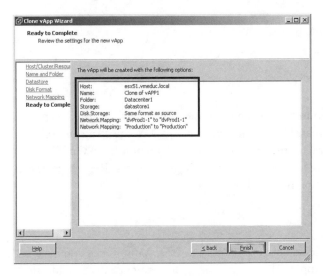

Figure 4-43   The Ready to Complete Page

274   The Official VCP5 Certification Guide

Adding Objects to an Existing vApp

You can add VMs to a vApp by simply dragging them into it. In addition, if you right-click a vApp, as shown in Figure 4-44, you will notice you can then select to add a new virtual machine, new resource pool, or even a new vApp. That's right, you can add a vApp to a vApp! Later, in the section, "Determining When a Tiered Application Should Be Deployed as a vApp," I will discuss why you might want to use a vApp and also when you might want to use a vApp in a vApp.

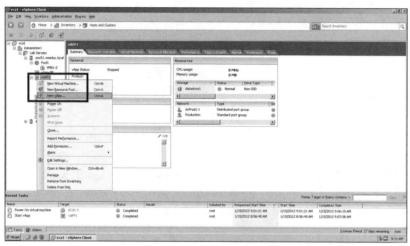

Figure 4-44   Adding Objects to a vApp

Editing vApp Settings

As time goes by and you need to make changes to the vApp's settings, there is no need to re-create the vApp. Instead, you can simply right-click the vApp and select **Edit Settings**. Changing some settings will require that you power off the VM (such as Advanced properties), but there are many settings (such as Resources) that you can configure with the vApp powered on.

Configuring IP Pools

You can use IP pools to provide a network identity to your vApp. Once you have configured an IP pool, the vApp can leverage vCenter to automatically provide an IP configuration to the VMs contained within it. The addresses from a pool will be configured for the VMs when the vApp is set to use Transient IP allocation. You can configure IP pool ranges with IPv4 or IPv6. To configure an IP pool for a vApp, follow the steps outlined in Activity 4-6.

Activity 4-6 Configuring IP Pools

1. Log on to your vSphere Client.

2. Select **Home** and then **Hosts and Clusters**.

3. Select the datacenter on which you want to configure the vApp, open the IP Pools tab, and click the **Add** link, as shown in Figure 4-45.

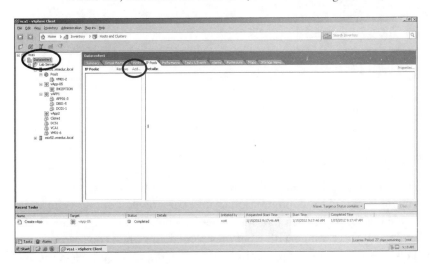

Figure 4-45   Adding an IP Pool

4. In the New IP Pool Properties dialog box, give your pool a name and open the IPv4 or the IPv6 tab, depending on which protocol you want to configure (in this case, IPv4).

5. Enter the IP subnet and gateway in their respective fields and (optionally) select **Enable IP Pool** to enter an IP address range, as shown in Figure 4-46. You can use a comma-separated list of a host ranges in the Ranges field. The ranges must be within the subnet, but must exclude the gateway address.

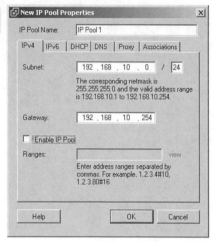

Figure 4-46   Configuring an IP Pool

6. Review your settings and click **OK**.

Suspending/Resuming a vApp

You can suspend a vApp and thereby pause all of its VMs until you resume the vApp. This might be useful for configuration changes or troubleshooting. The VMs will be suspended based on their stop order. When you resume the vApp, the order is reversed and the VMs continue with what they were doing when you suspended the vApp. To suspend/resume a vApp, simply right-click the vApp and select the appropriate option.

Determining When a Tiered Application Should Be Deployed as a vApp

The more you learn about vApps, the more curious you will likely become as to how they might help you in given situations. I can't really think of a scenario where a vApp is an absolute *requirement*; there are always other options. However, I can think of a few examples where a vApp could be very useful.

A disaster recovery situation comes to mind where everything has gone down and needs to be restarted (worst-case scenario). In a conventional environment (even in a virtual datacenter without vApps), you would have to make sure that the right servers were started first (DNS, domain controllers, DHCP servers) so that other servers didn't error out and maybe require more restarts or troubleshooting. However, if you were using vApps, you could just restart the vApps, and the start order would be followed automatically to ensure a smooth restart to full productivity.

Another example is one involving permissions. Suppose that you have a "night team" who doesn't have the training or expertise to be allowed specific permissions for VM servers, but you want to give them a "restart button" just in case, mainly so that you don't get that call while you are sleeping. Because vApps are an object in your vCenter, it's possible to give a person (junior administrator) the permissions to restart the vApp. Because the start order will take care of itself, the person doesn't have to have knowledge of what to start first and so on. This is a case when having a vApp within a vApp might give even greater granularity to permissions control.

My final example is one of portability. If you have an organization with multiple locations or departments, vApps might be advantageous to you. Suppose from your own experience you have come upon a great solution to offer an application to the end user, one that involves more than one VM and specific configuration between them. It works so well, that you wish that you could "bottle it" and use it in other parts of your organization. Well, you can, only it's not called a *bottle*, it's called an OVF. In other words, you can put all the elements of your solution into a vApp and then export the whole package to another part of your organization, or even to another organization. In fact, even if some of the resources that are eventually used will come from Cloud providers instead of your internal network, the OVF format will ensure that the resources are provided in the manner that you have found to be successful.

Those are just a few examples of determining when a tiered application should be deployed as a vApp. You probably have your own examples as well. The main point is that vApps can sometimes make it easier to work with multiple VMs, especially in situations where it takes multiple VMs to provide a high-quality application to the end user.

Managing Virtual Machine Clones and Templates

When you create your first VMs, you will likely use the wizard and create them "from scratch," what I call "the old-fashioned way." You could continue to create all of your VMs in this manner, but that would be what I call "the hard way." Instead, you could leverage the tools in the vSphere to create VMs faster and with more accuracy than with the wizard. Your vCenter Server and the ESXi hosts to which it is connected offer an array of tools and the power to build out your virtual datacenter.

In this section, I will first discuss the vCenter Server, ESXi hosts, and VM maximum configurations. That way, you will know how much you have to work with when you start using all of the tools. In addition, I will discuss faster and more efficient ways to create VMs using clones and templates. Specifically, I will discuss creating, deploying, and updating templates and clones in your vCenter. Finally, I will discuss using vCenter to deploy OVF templates of VMs and vApps. All of this will help you determine when it might be best to use one deployment methodology over another.

Identifying the vCenter Server, Managed ESXi Hosts, and Virtual Machine Maximums

It's a good idea to know the maximum configuration for a component, even if you don't plan on configuring it to the maximum. For example, if you said that you were a race car expert, I would expect you to know the maximum horsepower, torque, red-line, and so on for your car. That said, it's fair that VMware wants VMware Certified Professionals (VCPs) to know what their products are capable of handling, especially if it's a higher maximum than the previous version.

You can find all the configuration maximums for vSphere 5 in the *Configuration Maximums Guide* on the VMware site at http://www.vmware.com/pdf/vsphere5/r50/vsphere-50-configuration-maximums.pdf.

I suggest that you spend some time with this guide to gain familiarity with vSphere 5 configuration maximums of all kinds. You will find the information to be essential for the exam and useful for your own network. In this section, I will focus on configuration maximums for the vCenter Server, ESXi hosts, and VMs, and I will give you a table for each of these important maximums.

Table 4-3 lists the vCenter Server Maximums that you should know:

Table 4-3 vCenter Server Maximums

vCenter Component	Maximum Configuration / vCenter
Hosts/vCenter Server	1000
Powered-on VMs	10,000
Registered VMs	15,000
Linked vCenter Servers	10
Hosts in linked vCenter Servers	3000
Powered-on VMs in linked vCenter Servers	30,000
Registered VMs in linked vCenter Servers	50,000
Concurrent vSphere Clients	100
Hosts / Datacenter	500
MAC addresses / vCenter	65,536
USB devices connected at vSphere Client	20

The ESXi host maximums are divided into five categories: compute, memory, storage, networking, and cluster and resource pool. While it would be best that you know all the configuration maximums for all the categories, it might also lead to a "brain overload." For this reason, I am including in Table 4-4 the configuration maximums that I believe are best for you to know. I left out configuration maximums that are associated with a specific vendor or that apply in only certain conditions. Consult the specific vendor documentation for those.

Table 4-4   ESXi Host Maximums

Host Component	Maximum / Host
Logical CPUs	160
VMs	512
Virtual CPUs	2048
Virtual CPUs / Core	25
RAM	2TB
#Swap files	1 per VM
Swap file size	1TB
Virtual disks	2048
LUNs	256
Number of total storage paths	1024
Software iSCSI targets	256
NFS mounts	256
Number of FC paths per LUN	32
VMFS volumes	256
VMFS-3 RDM size (physical)	2TB – 512 B
VMFS-3 RDM size (virtual)	2TB – 512 B
VMFS-5 RDM size (physical)	64TB
VMFS-5 RDM size (virtual)	2TB – 512B
Volume size	64TB
Physical NICs	32
Network switchports	4096
Active ports	1016
Hosts / VDS	350
DVS / vCenter	32
Hosts / Cluster	32
VMs / Cluster	3000

As I discussed at the beginning of this chapter, VM maximums have grown steadily with each new version of vSphere. The VM maximums that I am listing in Table 4-5 are for Version 8 VMs. Where there is overlap with Table 4-2, I have listed the configuration maximums again for your convenience.

Table 4-5   Virtual Machine Configuration Maximums

VM Component	Maximum / VM
vCPUs	32
RAM	1TB
Swap file size	1TB
SCSI adapters	4
SCSI targets / adapter	15
Virtual disk size	2TB – 512 B
IDE controllers	1
Floppy controllers	2
vNICs	10
USB controllers	1
USB devices	20
Parallel ports	3
Serial ports	4
Video memory	128 MB

Identifying Cloning and Template Options

If you have a VM that you like and you want another one identical to it, you can clone the VM. The catch is that a clone is an exact copy and you might not want an exact copy. For example, it's unlikely that you want the same NetBIOS name, IP address, or SID, especially if you are planning on continuing to use the VM that you cloned. In these cases (with VMs using a Microsoft guest OS), you can use Sysprep to provide customization while you are creating the clone. Later in this section, I will briefly discuss this concept.

Suppose that you don't want just one copy of a VM that you currently have running. Assume instead that you are in charge of standardizing the OS and applications that will be used for a certain type of VM. In that case, you might want to create a template that will thereafter be used by anyone who creates that type of VM. A template is a VM that cannot be powered on but that can be used as master copy to create VMs that can be powered on. By enforcing the use of the template to create certain VMs, you will improve not only the speed at which VMs can be created but also the accuracy of their creation.

Cloning an Existing Virtual Machine

Let's take my first example a little further now. Suppose that you have a VM that you want to clone. Can you clone it with it powered on, or do you have to power it off first? The answer is "yes," you can clone it with it powered on, but you could also clone it with it powered off; it's your choice. The tradeoff is that cloning with the VM powered on might be more convenient because the users can continue to use it, but cloning with it powered off will definitely be a bit faster. To clone an existing VM, follow the steps outlined in Activity 4-7.

Activity 4-7 Cloning an Existing Virtual Machine

1. Log on to your vSphere Client.

2. Select **Home** and then **Hosts and Clusters**.

3. Right-click the VM that you want to clone and select **Clone**, as shown in Figure 4-47. (The VM can be powered off or on; in this case, the VM is powered on.)

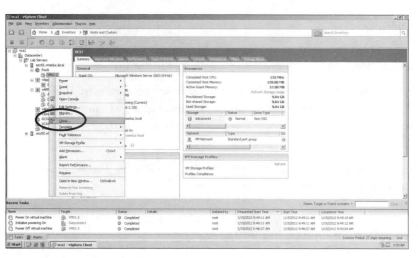

Figure 4-47   Cloning a VM

4. From Name and Location, give your new VM a name and select the inventory location, as shown in figure 4-48, and then click **Next**.

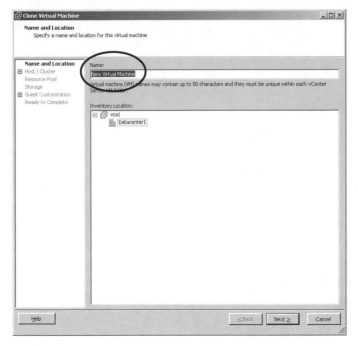

Figure 4-48 The Name and Location Page

5. In Host/Cluster, select the host for the new VM, and click **Next**.

6. In Resource Pool, select the Resource Pool or vApp for the new VM, and click **Next**.

7. In Storage, select the datastore that you will use for the VM, and click **Next**.

8. In Guest Customization, choose to customize based on a standard that you have created, or choose not to customize (in this case, we will not use customization) and click **Next**. (You can also choose to power on the VM after creation.)

9. Review your settings and click **Finish**. Monitor the Recent Tasks pane and your inventory to see your new VM.

Creating a Template from an Existing Virtual Machine

As I said before, you might use a template to create a new standard that you want everyone to use in the future. In that case, the VM that you are using for the template might not even be in your production environment. In that situation, the easiest and fastest way to create a template from the VM would be to convert the VM into the template. Of course, then you wouldn't have your VM anymore until you created a new VM from the template or converted it back. The upside of this method is that it happens almost instantaneously.

Another method of creating the template would be to clone the template from the running VM. As you can imagine, this takes longer to do; however, it allows the users to continue to use the VM while the template is being created, possibly with minor loss in performance. Either way, you end up with a template. However, cloning the template from the running VM results in ending up with a template and still retaining the VM from which you created the template.

To create a template from an existing VM, follow the steps outlined in Activity 4-8.

Activity 4-8 Creating a Template from an Existing VM

1. Log on to your vSphere Client.

2. Select **Home** and then **VMs and Templates**.

3. Right-click the VM from which you want to create the template and select **Template**, and then choose either **Convert to Template** or **Clone to Template** (in this case, Clone to Template), as shown in Figure 4-49. The VM can be powered off or on if you are cloning. If you are converting, the VM must be powered off. In this case, I am cloning the template with the VM powered on.

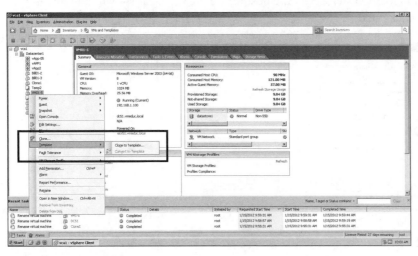

Figure 4-49   Creating a Template

4. From Name and Location, give your new VM a name and select the inventory location, as shown in Figure 4-50, and then click **Next**.

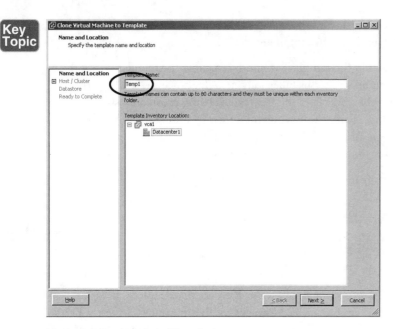

Figure 4-50   Naming a Template

> **5.** From Host/Cluster, select the host for the new VM, as shown in Figure 4-51, and click **Next**.

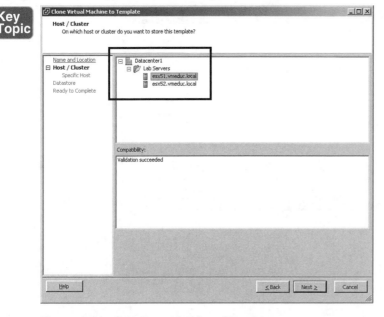

Figure 4-51   Selecting a Host for a Template

6. From Datastore, select the datastore that you will use for the VM and the VM disk format, and click **Next**.

7. Review your settings and click **Finish**. Monitor the Recent Tasks pane and your inventory to see your new template.

Deploying a Virtual Machine from a Template

Of course, the reason that you made the template is not just to have a template but to be able to deploy VMs more quickly and accurately by using the template. Once you have created the template, you can deploy VMs from it and create them anywhere in your vCenter. To deploy a VM from your template, follow the steps outlined in Activity 4-9.

Activity 4-9 Deploying a VM from a Template

1. Log on to your vSphere Client.

2. Select **Home** and then **VMs and Templates**.

3. Right-click the template from which you want deploy the VM and select **Deploy Virtual Machine from this Template**, as shown in Figure 4-52.

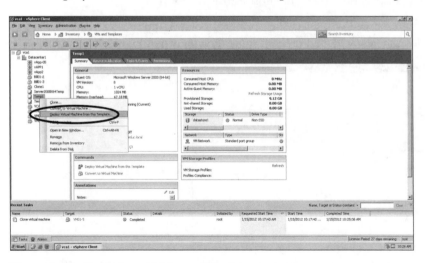

Figure 4-52   Deploying a VM from a Template

4. From Name and Location, give your new VM a name and select the inventory location, as shown in Figure 4-53, and then click **Next**. The location can even be a different datacenter in the same vCenter.

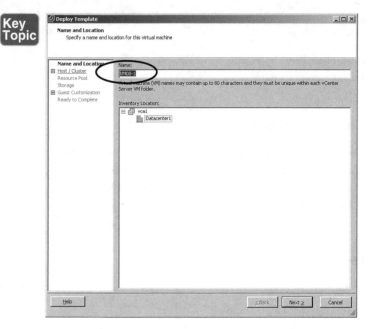

Figure 4-53 Naming a Template

5. From Host/Cluster, select the host for the new VM.

6. From Resource Pool, select the resource pool or vApp to which you want to deploy the new VM, and then click **Next**, as shown in Figure 4-54.

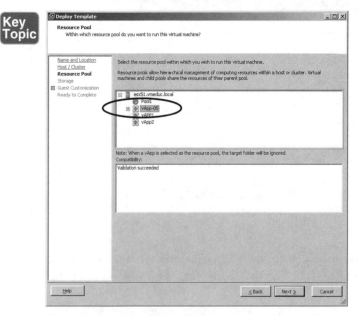

Figure 4-54 Selecting a Resource Pool or vApp

7. From Datastore, select the datastore that you will use for the VM and the VM disk format, and click **Next**.

8. From Guest Customization, select whether you want to use a custom group of settings that you have previously created (in this case, we will not use customization), and then click **Next**, as shown in Figure 4-55.

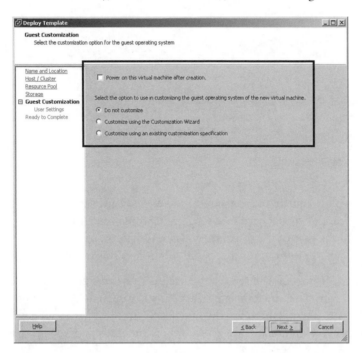

Figure 4-55   The Guest Customization Option

9. Review your settings and click **Finish**. Monitor the Recent Tasks pane and your inventory to see your new template.

Updating Existing Virtual Machine Templates

Not only is a template a VM that can't be powered on, but it's a VM on which you can't change settings, at least not as long as it's a VM. If you right-click a template, you will not see an option to edit its settings, as shown in Figure 4-56. This is actually good because it makes it unlikely that someone could change your template by accident.

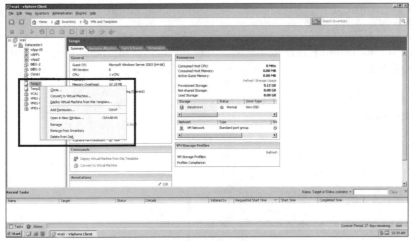

Figure 4-56 Templates Cannot Be Powered On

However, what if you need to update the software or the virtual hardware settings on the template? In the case of virtual hardware settings, it would seem that you don't have the option. In the case of the software, you certainly can't update software on a VM that you can't power on, so what is the solution to this problem?

If you look again at Figure 4-56, you will see that you can convert the template back to a VM. After you have converted the template to a VM, you can apply the updates and convert the VM back to a template to use the updates for future VMs created with the template. To convert a template into a VM, follow the steps outlined in Activity 4-10.

Activity 4-10 Converting a Template to a VM

1. Log on to your vSphere Client.

2. Select **Home** and then **VMs and Templates**, right-click the template that you want to convert to a VM, and select **Convert to Virtual Machine**, as shown in Figure 4-57.

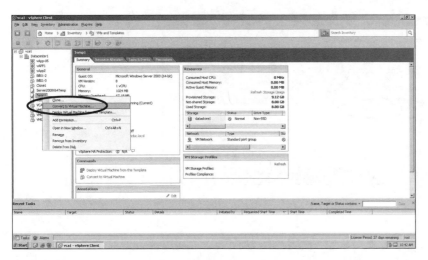

Figure 4-57   Converting a Template to a VM

3. From **Host/Cluster**, select the Host for the new VM, as shown in Figure 4-58, and click **Next**.

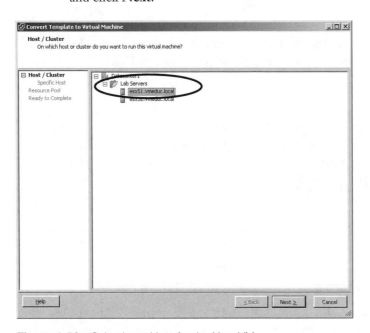

Figure 4-58   Selecting a Host for the New VM

4. From Resource Pool, select the resource pool or vApp to which you want to deploy the new VM, and then click **Next**, as shown in Figure 4-59.

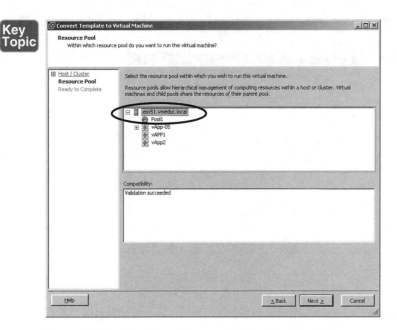

Figure 4-59   Selecting a Resource Pool for the New VM

5. From Ready to Complete, review your settings and click **Finish**. Monitor the
    Recent Tasks pane and your inventory for your converted VM.

NOTE   You should make sure that you don't bring up a VM that has server services
such as DNS or DHCP onto your production network unwittingly. To keep this
from happening, you should place the new VM in an isolated network or select to disconnect its vNIC from the network.

You can also use software, such as VMware Update Manager, to automate much of
this process.

Deploying Virtual Appliances and/or vApps from an OVF Template

For convenience, you can also deploy VMs and vApps from an OVF template that is
stored in a location outside of your vSphere. This could include local drives, shared
network drives, CD, DVD, USB, and so on. This increases portability and allows
you to add preconfigured VMs and vApps to your vCenter. To deploy a new VM or
vApp using an OVF, follow the steps outlined in Activity 4-11.

Activity 4-11 Deploying VMs and vApps from an OVF Template

1. Log on to your vSphere Client.

2. From the File menu at the top left, select **File**, and then **Deploy OVF Template**, as shown in Figure 4-60.

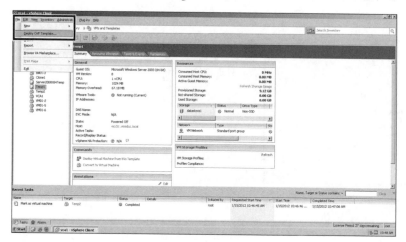

Figure 4-60   Deploying an OVF Template

3. From Source, choose to browse your file systems for the template, or enter the complete address within or connected to your network, as shown in Figure 4-61.

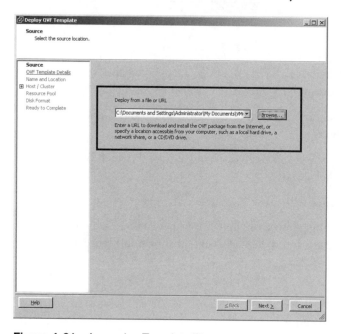

Figure 4-61   Accessing Template Files

4. From OVF Template Details, review the details of the OVF to which you are connected, (in this case, the vCenter Server Appliance), as shown in Figure 4-62, and then click **Next**.

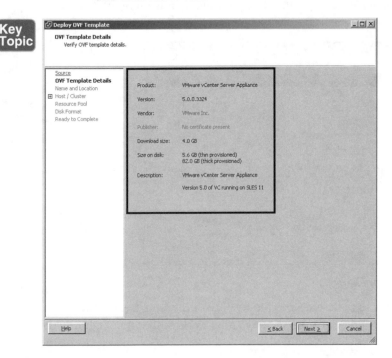

Figure 4-62   Reviewing OVF Details

5. From Name and Location, give your new VM a name and choose the location where it will first be created in your virtual datacenter, and click **Next**.

6. From Host/Cluster, choose the host or cluster in which the VM should be created, and click **Next**.

7. From Resource Pool, select the vApp or resource pool to which the VM will be added, and then click **Next**.

8. From Disk Format, choose the disk format, and then click **Next**.

9. From Network Mapping, choose the network or networks to which you want your new VM connected, and then click **Next**, as shown in Figure 4-63.

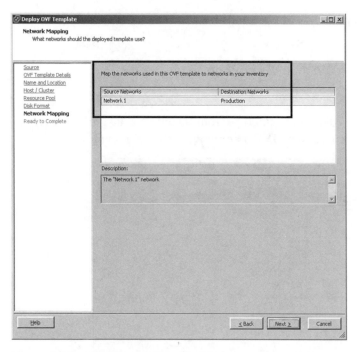

Figure 4-63   The Network Mapping Page

> **10.** On the Ready to Complete page, review your settings, and then click **Finish**.

Importing and /or Exporting an OVF Template

If you were paying attention before, you might have wondered how the OVF template became "stored in a location outside of your vSphere." Well, you can export the state of a VM or a vApp as an OVF, so that it can be imported at another location or division of your organization to be deployed as a VM.

When you export the state of a VM or vApp, you can choose from two different formats, as follows:

- **Folder of files (OVF):** This format is best if you plan to publish the OVF files to a web server or image library. It creates a set of three files (OVF, VMDK, and MF). These files can be used separately; for example, the package could be imported into a vSphere Client by publishing the URL to the OVF file.

- **Single file (OVA):** This format is best to use when you will need the template represented as a single file. This might be used for explicit download from a website or to transport the file using a USB drive or other removable software device.

To export the state of a VM or vApp as an OVF or and OVA, follow the steps outlined in Activity 4-12.

Activity 4-12 Exporting an OVF of a VM or vApp

1. Log on to your vSphere Client.

2. First select your VM or vApp, and then from the File menu at the top left, select **File > Export > Export OVF Template**, as shown in Figure 4-64.

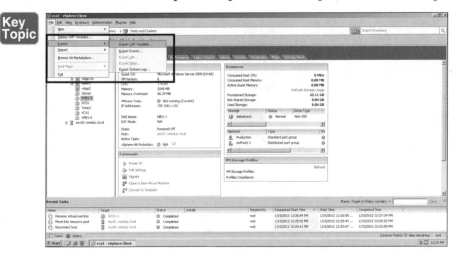

Figure 4-64   Exporting an OVF Template

3. In the Export OVF Template dialog box, type the name of the template, enter or
   browse for the directory that will contain the VM or vApp template, select **OVF** or
   OVA, and optionally enter a description for the template, as shown in Figure 4-65.

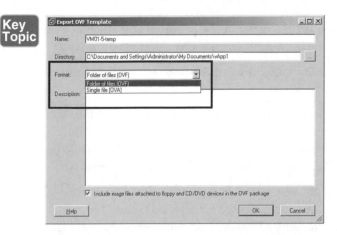

Figure 4-65   Selecting the Open Virtualization Format Type

4. Review all settings and click **OK** to export the VM or vApp. Monitor your recent tasks and the export dialog box until complete.

Of course, importing the OVF or OVA is just a matter of using the vSphere Client to find it and then selecting to deploy your new VM or vApp from it.

Determining the Appropriate Development Methodology for a Given Virtual Machine Application

To sum it up, I have discussed two main methods that can help you create VMs faster than the "old-fashioned" wizard does: clones and templates. You should understand which of these methods is best, given a set of circumstances. I will use this section to summarize what I've already said and clarify the difference between using clones and using templates.

If you just want one more VM like the one you have, there probably isn't any good reason to go through the process of creating a template just to turn around and deploy a VM from the template. In fact, that would be extra work and simply cloning the VM (whether powered on or powered off) would likely be faster. You could also choose to apply the customization as part of creating the clone. Most of the customization methodology is beyond the scope of the text.

However, if you want to create a standard that will be followed in your organization at your location and even in other locations, you should consider using templates. If it's all within your same vCenter, there may not be any need to create OVF templates, but if you want to increase the portability of the state of the VMs and vApps so that they can be imported into other vCenters, you should consider using OVF templates.

Administering Virtual Machines and vApps

The word *administering* covers a lot of ground and means a great many things. To effectively administer VMs and vApps, first you have to know what they are made up of and where to find their components. Also, you need to understand what is possible in their configuration and how you can configure power settings, boot options, storage policies, resources, and other advanced settings. Finally, you need to know how to troubleshoot them when there is a problem. In this section, I will focus on administering VMs and vApps.

Identifying Files Used by Virtual Machines

As I said earlier, a VM is a VM even without an OS or applications installed on it. A VM is a "box" that is made of software which we call virtual hardware. The virtual hardware is constructed using many files. Each file takes the place of what would otherwise be hardware or firmware on a physical machine. It's important that you understand the main files that make up each of your VMs and what they do on the VM. Table 4-6 shows the main files that make up a VM, their naming convention, and their purpose.

Table 4-6   Virtual Machine Files

File	Filename	Description
Configuration file	[VM_name].vmx	A text file that describes the VM and all of its configuration settings.
Swap file	[VM_name].vswp	A file that is created by the VMkernel when the VM is powered on and deleted when powered off. The size of this file is equal to the available (configured) memory minus any reservation. The file can be as large as available memory if there is no reservation.
BIOS file	[VM_name].nvram	A file that takes the place of BIOS (Basic Input Output System). This is important will full virtualization because the guest OS on the VM might need to address something that looks to it like BIOS.
Log files	vmware.log	Files that keep a record of events and tasks that have occurred on the VM, its OS, and its applications. These files might be useful for troubleshooting.
Disk descriptor files	[VM_name].vmdk	A small file for each virtual disk on a VM that describes the virtual disk, such as how large it is, thick or thin, and where it is located.
Disk data files	[VM_name]-flat.vmdk	Typically a rather large file for each virtual disk on a VM that represents the actual pre-allocated space that has been allowed on the datastore for this virtual disk.
Suspend state file	[VM_name]. vmss	A file that holds the state of a VM when the VM is suspended (only CPU activity).
Snapshot data file	[VM_name].vmsd	A centralized file for storing information and metadata about snapshots.
Snapshot state file	[VM_name].vmsn	A descriptor file for each snapshot capturing the state of the VM at a particular point in time.

File	Filename	Description
Snapshot disk file	[VM_name].00000x.vmdk This 6-digit number is based on the snapshot files that exist in the directory and does not consider the number of disks attached to the VM. It starts with 000001 is incremented by 1 when each additional snapshot is taken.	A file that contains a linear list of all changes to a VM after a snapshot is taken. This file is used along with the descriptor files to return a VM to a previous state.
Template file	[VM_name].vmtx	A text file describing a VM that has been converted or cloned to a template. The file cannot be used to power on a VM.
Raw device map file	[VM_name]-rdmp.vmdk if physical compatibility or -rdm.vmdk if virtual compatibility	A special pointer file that can allow a VM to see the raw LUN instead of using data from a VMFS or NFS datastore.

Identifying Locations for Virtual Machine Configuration Files and Virtual Disks

Of course, the locations for the VM files and the VM disks are "on the datastores," so what does this topic mean? Well, here's the question, "Should you store your VM swap file for a particular VM in the same location that you store the rest of its files?" The answer, of course, is "It depends."

As a best practice, you should store all the files for a VM in the same location whenever possible. This will make it easier for you to administer the VM and it will generally increase the speed of migrating the VM during vMotion.

However, a relatively new technology called solid state drives (SSD) is changing this practice. If you have SSDs on your host, you might very well want to consider placing the VSWP files for the VMs on the SSDs. This would ensure that the swap file could still give the best performance technologically available and allow for even more memory overcommitment. (I will discuss these resources in greater detail in Chapter 5.)

Now you might be wondering when you get this choice and how you can easily separate the VSWP file from the other VM files. Actually, there are multiple places in the virtual datacenter where you can configure this option. I will give you a brief description of each as well as illustration of where you can configure this setting.

You can configure the location for VM swap files in the cluster and then accept this setting as a default throughout the datacenter or you can configure this setting on each host as shown in Figure 4-66, and, of course, you can configure this setting on each VM as shown in Figure 4-67. In other words, you can take the easy way out and just configure the setting for all VM swap files at the cluster level and then accept the cluster settings everywhere else. However, if you have SSDs or some other reason that you want to use a different location (purchased storage and so on), you can choose a different location for any host or VM.

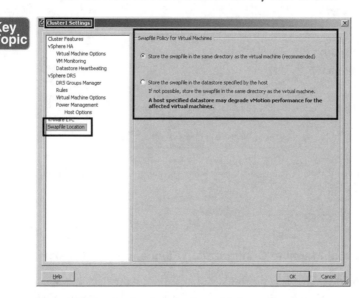

Figure 4-66 Configuring the Swap File Location at the Cluster Level

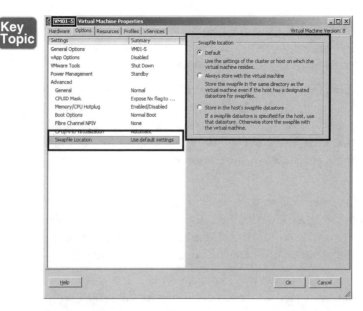

Figure 4-67 Configuring the Swap File Location on the VM Settings

To identify the datastores that a VM is using, you can examine the Storage Panel in the Summary tab. In addition, you can right-click the datastore and click **Browse Datastore** to see the actual files associated with the VM, as shown in Figure 4-68.

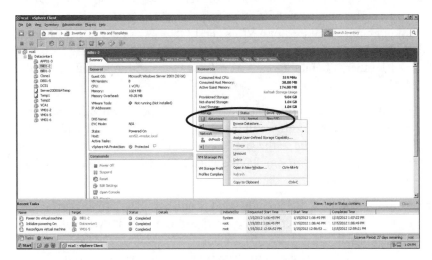

Figure 4-68   Browsing VM Files from the Storage Panel

You can also drill down to the VM files using the Storage Views tab, as shown in Figure 4-69.

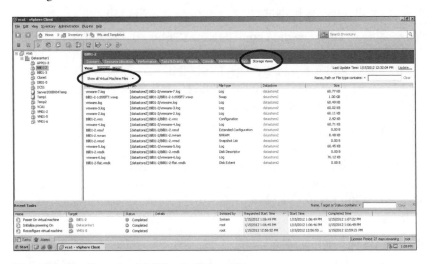

Figure 4-69   Browsing VM Files in Storage Views

Identifying Common Practices for Securing Virtual Machines

In general, a VM is inherently very secure. By its very design, each VM is isolated from all the other VMs, even if it's running on the same host. This isolation allows the VM to run securely, even though it is sharing physical hardware with other VMs. Permission granted to a user for a VM's guest OS does not allow that user to access any other VMs, even if it is administrative permission. Also, because VMs are isolated from each other, a failure in one VM will not cause a "domino effect" failure in other VMs.

That said, there are some precautions that VMware recommends when administering VMs. Some of these precautions are the same as if the machine were a physical machine, while others are specific to the virtual environment. The following is a list of general precautions that you should take when administering security for the VMs and a brief description of each one:

- **Use antivirus software:** It is generally good practice to have antivirus protection on all computers, whether they are virtual or physical. Remember, however, that installed antivirus software does take resources, and you should balance the need for security against the need for performance. This might mean that some systems that are only used in a lab environment and not used in production will not require antivirus software. Alternatively, you could use a VMware product called vShield Endpoint to offload the key antivirus and anti-malware functions to a security VM and improve the guest OS performance of your VMs by eliminating the antivirus footprint on each of them.

- **Limit exposure of sensitive data copied to the Clipboard:** Because it could be possible to copy data from a guest OS to the remote console, you should limit this by training administrators. By default, the ability to copy from a VMs guest OS to remote console is disabled. Although it is possible to enable this function, the best practice is to leave it disabled.

- **Remove unnecessary hardware devices:** Because users without administrative privileges can connect and disconnect hardware devices, such as CD-ROM drives and network cards, you should make sure that there is no virtual hardware on VMs that is not being used. Hardware that is "out of sight, out of mind" to the administrator makes a perfect tool for the experimentation of an attacker.

- **Limit guest OS writes to host memory:** The guest OS processes sometimes send informational messages to the host through VMware Tools. There is nothing wrong with a little of this, but an unrestricted amount could open the door for a denial-of-service attack. For this reason, the configuration file for these messages is limited to 1MB of storage. Although it's possible to change this parameter, it's not a recommended practice.

- **Configure logging levels for the guest OS:** VMs can write troubleshooting information into a log file stored on the VMFS. Over time, these log files can become very large and could cause problems in performance. To prevent this from happening, you can modify the parameters for the total size of the log files and for the total number of log files. VMware recommends saving 10 log files, each one limited to 100KB.

- **Secure your fault-tolerance logging traffic:** When you enable and configure fault tolerance (FT), VMware Lockstep captures inputs and events that occur on the Primary VM and sends them to the Secondary VM, which is running on a different host. This logging traffic is then sent from the Primary VM to the Secondary VM in an unencrypted format. Because the traffic could potentially include sensitive information, such as passwords in clear text, you should use methods such as IPsec to encrypt data sent between hosts. I will discuss FT in more detail in Chapter 5.

Hot Extending a Virtual Disk

It seems that you can never have enough disk space on your servers. Unforeseen events and changes can make it necessary to add space on regular basis. In the case of a VM, this can be a very easy process and it can be accomplished without having to power down the server and affect the productivity of the end users, referred to as a *hot extend*.

To hot extend a virtual disk on a server, you simply change the properties of the virtual disk and save your changes. Note that I said we are extending the size of the *disk*, not the *volume* that the guest OS sees. In other words, if you have a disk that has 2GB worth of space and you want to hot extend it to 20GB, you should simply increase the disk to 20GB and save your changes. The result will be a 20GB disk with a 2GB volume and 18GB of unallocated space. If that is what you really wanted, you are done. If you really wanted a 20GB volume, you can use a third-party tool such as Diskpart or Extpart to finish the job within the guest OS.

To hot extend a disk on your VM, follow the steps outlined in Activity 4-13.

Activity 4-13 Hot Extending a Virtual Disk

1. Log on to your vSphere Client.

2. Click **Home** and then **Host and Clusters**.

3. In the console pane, locate the VM that contains the disk that you want to hot extend. If the VM is not powered on, power it on now, as shown in Figure 4-70.

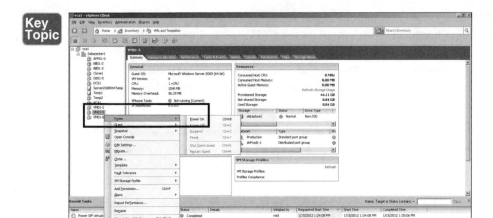

Figure 4-70   Powering On a VM

4. When the VM is powered on, right-click it and select **Edit Settings**, as shown in Figure 4-71.

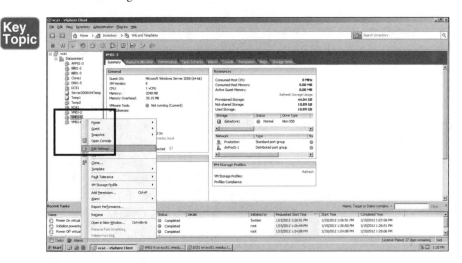

Figure 4-71   Editing VM Settings

5. On the Hardware tab, locate the virtual disk that you want to hot extend and change the provisioned size of the disk to the new setting (in this case, 20GB.) The maximum size will be indicated, as shown in Figure 4-72.

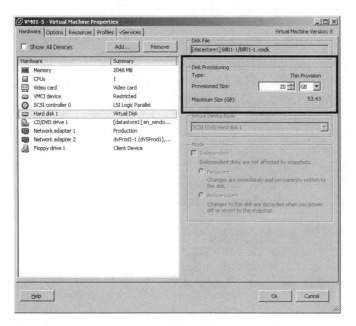

Figure 4-72   Hot Extending a Virtual Disk

    6. Click **OK** to save your changes and monitor the Recent Tasks pane for completion.

Configuring Virtual Machine Options

You might have noticed that when you right-click a VM and then click **Edit Settings** there are multiple tabs, each with its own set of configuration settings. One of these tabs is the Options tab, on which you can configure VM options. These options are organized into five categories:

- General

- vApp

- VMware Tools

- Power Management

- Advanced

In this section, I will give a brief overview of the settings in each of the categories.

General Options

There are many settings and areas of information on the General Options page, as shown in Figure 4-73. At the top-right corner, the version of the VM is indicated, in this case Version 8. Below that, the VM name is listed. This is the only parameter on this page that can be changed with the VM powered on. The VM name listed here is also referred to as the display name. It is the name that the VM will be represented by in your vCenter inventory. Still further down, the VM's configuration file and working location are listed. The names of these files will start with the display name. The last setting is that of the OS on the VM. Based on this setting, the system updates the VM with the latest drivers and VMware Tools. This setting should always match the actual OS that starts when you power on your VM.

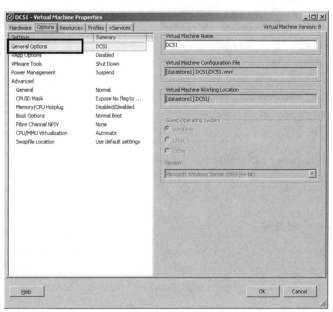

Figure 4-73 General Options

vApp Options

vApp Options is a rather simple setting that allows you to control whether certain options can be configured for vApps, as shown in Figure 4-74. Note that this setting does not configure the ability to create vApps. Instead, it configures the ability to create options on vApps that modify OVF properties, IP Allocation, and product information.

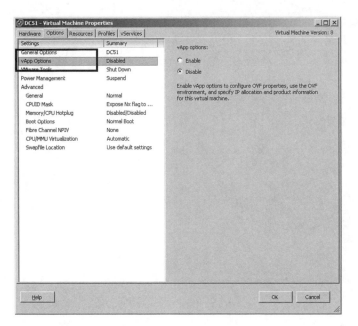

Figure 4-74   vApp Options

VMware Tools

The VMware Tools options are organized into three categories as shown in Figure 4-75:

- Power Controls
- Run VMware Tools and Scripts
- Advanced

The default setting of Power Controls provides for a graceful shutdown of the guest OS, a suspend, and restart guest. These default settings should be fine for most VMs. Below that, the Run VMware Tools Scripts controls when the scripts are run. These are optional scripts installed in a VM along with VMware Tools that do things like answer the annoying Windows Server 2008 "Why are you shutting down?" question. If the tools have changed, running the scripts takes a short period of time, but the tradeoff is that you have the latest options. You can decide whether you want that to happen when changing power states or before shutting down the guest OS. The VM represented in Figure 4-75 is powered on. As you can see, changing most of these settings requires powering down the VM, and therefore many of the settings are "grayed out" (dimmed).

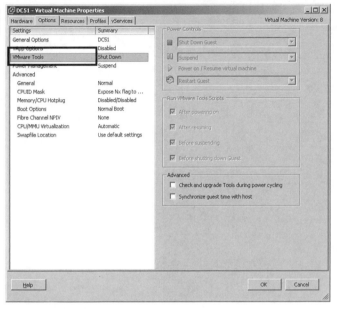

Figure 4-75 VMware Tools Options

Power Management

The Power Management setting determines how the VM will respond when the guest OS is placed into standby mode. It is by set by default to leave the VM powered on. Later, in the section, "Configuring Virtual Machine Power Settings," I will discuss configuration options for this setting.

Advanced

As you can see from Figure 4-76, the options included under the Advanced category can usually be left at their defaults. They are configurable for the unusual "one-off" situation when you might need to make a change. Later, in the section "Determining When an Advanced Virtual Machine Parameter is Required," I will discuss each of these Advanced options and how you can determine when you might want to use an advanced parameter.

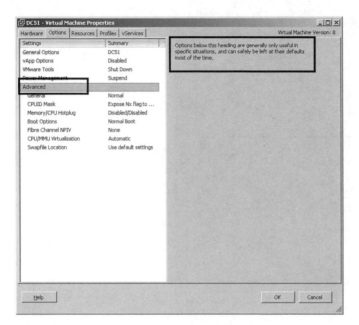

Figure 4-76   Advanced Options

Configuring Virtual Machine Power Settings

As I mentioned before, you can set the management options for a VM on the Options tab. The default setting is that the VM will remain powered on even when the OS is placed into Standby mode. For servers, this is usually the appropriate setting.

If you elect to suspend the VM, the VM will have to be resumed to be used when the guest OS comes out of Standby mode. Because Standby mode was originally created to save energy and reduce the amount of heat that a computer puts into a room, and because this does not apply to a VM, it might be best to let the VM's guest OS go into Standby mode but keep the VM powered on, as shown in Figure 4-77. Changing this setting requires first powering down the VM.

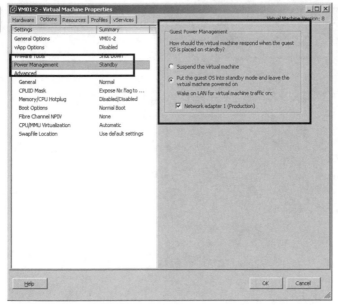

Figure 4-77   Power Settings

Configuring Virtual Machine Boot Options

You can configure VM boot options in four categories, as shown in Figure 4-78:

- **Firmware:** Allows you to specify the boot firmware for your VM, but changing to a setting that does not match your capabilities may render the VM unbootable. You should use this setting if your host supports EFI.

- **Power On Boot Delay:** Allows you to specify a number of milliseconds between the time that POST is finished and the OS begins to load. This can give you time to press the appropriate key (such as F2) to enter setup. This might be useful, for example, to change the boot sequence to recognize a CD-ROM drive, but it will delay the start of the VM every time you power it on.

- **Force BIOS Setup:** This is a run-once type of setting that will clear itself automatically after you use it.

- **Failed Boot Recovery:** Used to configure the action of the VM if it should fail to find a boot device. This could be especially helpful if you are attempting to boot and install an operating system through a network, which can cause a delay in the VMs sensing the boot device.

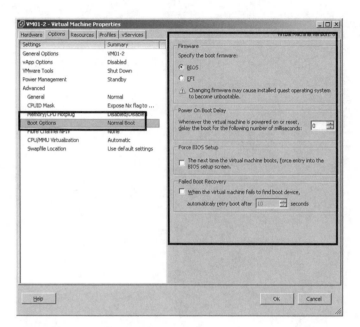

Figure 4-78   Advanced Boot Options

Configuring Virtual Machine Troubleshooting Options

Troubleshooting is a process of isolating an issue. To isolate an issue, what you need more than anything is information (in other words, *logs*). Normal logging of events and tasks associated with a VM is enabled by default. You can see this by logging on to your vSphere Client, choosing a VM, and examining the advanced options, as shown in Figure 4-79. You can disable logging on this setting as well, but that is not a recommended practice. In addition, if you are troubleshooting a VM and you want much more verbose debugging information or statistics, you can change this setting to force the system to record the information that you want. The information that is collected might also be useful to VMware technical support.

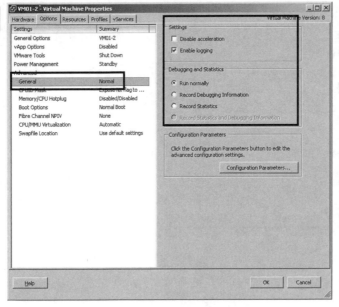

Figure 4-79   Advanced Troubleshooting Options

Assigning a Storage Policy to a VM

You might have noticed that there are a couple of tabs on the VM settings that were not there in previous VM versions. One of these tabs is labeled Profiles. Using this tab, you can assign a storage policy to a VM. This will be paired up with your Storage Profiles settings on your datastores. (I will discuss storage profiles in detail in Chapter 5. This activity assumes that storage profiles have been configured and enabled on the vCenter.) To assign a storage policy to your VM, follow the steps outlined in Activity 4-14.

Activity 4-14 Assigning a Storage Policy to a Virtual Machine

1. Log on to your vSphere Client.

2. Click **Home** and then **Host and Clusters**.

3. In the console pane, right-click the VM on which you want to assign the storage policy, click **VM Storage Profiles**, and then click **Manage Profiles**, as shown in Figure 4-80. (You can also choose the Profiles tab from Edit Settings.)

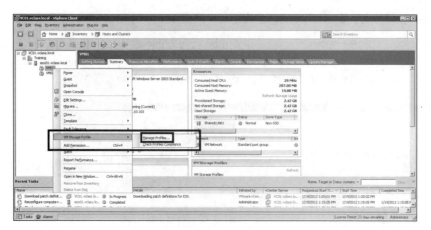

Figure 4-80   Assigning a Storage Policy to a VM

4. Select the VM storage profiles that can be used on this VM on each of its virtual disks, as shown in Figure 4-81.

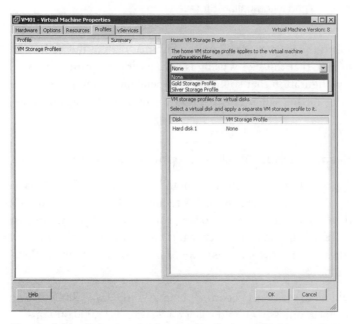

Figure 4-81   Selecting the Storage Profile for a VM Storage Policy

5. Click **OK** to save your changes and monitor the Recent Tasks pane for completion.

Verifying Storage Policy Compliance for Virtual Machines

Once you have a storage policy in place, it will be very obvious to anyone who considers moving the VM files to a datastore that does not meet the policy that they are violating the parameters of the policy, as shown in Figure 4-82.

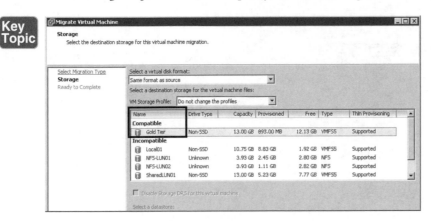

Figure 4-82   Identifying Compatible and Incompatible Storage

Also, you can simply look at the Storage Panel on the Summary tab of the VM to see whether all of the storage that the VM is using is in line with the profile. This helps prevent errors in configuration that could affect dependability and performance. (I will illustrate this further when I discuss how to configure storage profiles in Chapter 5.)

Determining When an Advanced Virtual Machine Parameter is Required

Actually, the name of this objective says it all. You should only use an advanced parameter when it is required. When is it required? It's required when the normal settings don't quite have the option that you need to set—for example, if you wanted to configure a specific CPUID mask (the feature set that is visible to the guest OS on a VM) to work with some software that you are using or if you wanted to make the VM see a thumb drive on boot.

One other example would be to set the keyboard.typematicMinDelay="2000000" so that characters won't repeat unless you hold a key for 2 seconds (2,000,000 microseconds). I could list many other "one-offs," but I think you've got the idea. You don't configure Advanced settings for the "heck of it," you only configure them when nothing else will do.

Adjusting Virtual Machine Resources (shares, limits and reservations) Based on Virtual Machine Workloads

On the Resources tab for each VM, you can configure settings to control how much access that VM gets to the physical resources versus the other VMs on the same host. These settings include shares, limits, and reservations for CPU, memory, and disk. Using these settings, you can establish higher-priority VMs (what I call big dogs) and lower-priority VMs (little dogs). Although it's possible to configure these settings on each VM, it's not the recommended place to do it, at least not initially. In Chapter 5, I will discuss how you can configure these settings for Resource Pools and thereby control many more machines at once. The VM settings can then be used to create a "biggest dog of the big dogs."

Summary

The main topics covered in this chapter are the following:

- I began this chapter discussing all aspects of the creation and deployment of VMs.

- I then covered the creation, configuration, and deployment of vApps.

- I continued by examining clones and templates and comparing and contrasting these two methods of creating additional VMs.

- Finally, you learned about the administration of VMs and vApps, including setting options, controlling power, and troubleshooting, storage polices, and resources.

Exam Preparation Tasks

Review All of the Key Topics

Review the most important topics from inside the chapter, noted with the Key Topic icon in the outer margin of the page. Table 4-7 lists these key topics and the page numbers where each is found. Know the main differences VMs and vApps and how to create, deploy, and administer each. Also, you should know when a vApp would be appropriate to use, rather than just a VM.

Table 4-7   Key Topics for Chapter 4

Key Topic Element	Description	Page Number
Table 4-2	Virtual Machine Hardware Versions	239
Bullet List	VMware Tools Device Drivers	240
Figure 4-1	Opening a VM Console	241
Figure 4-2	The VM Console Tab	241
Figure 4-3	Identifying Storage	242
Figure 4-4	Browsing a Datastore	242
Figure 4-5	Editing Settings During Creation of a VM	243
Figure 4-6	Adding the ISO	244
Figure 4-7	Windows Installer	244
Figure 4-8	Virtual Disk Provisioning	245
Bullet List	Disk Provisioning	246
Activity 4-1	Configuring Disk Shares on a VM	247
Figure 4-9	Editing VM Settings	248
Figure 4-10	Configuring Disk Resources	248
Figure 4-11	Configuring Disk Shares	249
Activity 4-2	Automatic Installation/Upgrade of VMware Tools	250
Figure 4-12	Install/Upgrade VMware Tools	250
Figure 4-13	Automatic Upgrade of VMware Tools	250
Figure 4-14	Version Checking for VMware Tools	251
Figure 4-15	Configuring Time Synchronization	252

Key Topic Element	Description	Page Number
Figure 4-64	Exporting an OVF Template	294
Figure 4-65	Selecting the Open Virtualization Format Type	294
Table 4-6	Virtual Machine Files	296
Figure 4-66	Configuring the Swap File Location at the Cluster Level	298
Figure 4-67	Configuring the Swap File Location on the VM Settings	298
Figure 4-68	Browsing VM Files from the Storage Panel	299
Figure 4-69	Browsing VM Files in Storage Views	299
Activity 4-13	Hot Extending a Virtual Disk	301
Figure 4-70	Powering on a VM	302
Figure 4-71	Editing VM Settings	302
Figure 4-72	Hot Extending a Virtual Disk	303
Figure 4-73	General Options	304
Figure 4-74	vApp Options	305
Figure 4-75	VMware Tools Options	306
Figure 4-76	Advanced Options	307
Figure 4-77	Power Settings	308
Figure 4-78	Advanced Boot Options	309
Figure 4-79	Advanced Troubleshooting Options	310
Activity 4-14	Assigning a Storage Policy to a Virtual Machine	310
Figure 4-80	Assigning a Storage Policy to a VM	311
Figure 4-81	Selecting a Storage Profile for a VM Storage Policy	311
Figure 4-82	Identifying Compatible and Incompatible Storage	312

Review Questions

The answers to these review questions are in Appendix A.

1. What is the maximum number of vCPUs supported by a Version 8 VM?

   a. 8

   b. 4

   c. 64

   d. 32

2. Which of the following is true with regard to Version 8 hardware? (Choose two.)

   a. Fully backward compatible to ESX/ESXi 3.5 and 4.x

   b. Can support up to 1TB available memory

   c. Can support up to 2TB available memory

   d. Can support hot plug CPU and hot add memory

3. Which of following is *not* an enhancement resulting from installation of VMware Tools?

   a. SVGA display

   b. Ability to hot plug vCPU

   c. Balloon driver mechanism for memory control

   d. VM Heartbeat

4. If disk shares were configured Normal for a VM, how many shares would it have?

   a. 100

   b. 10

   c. 1000

   d. 0

5. What is the maximum number of powered on VMs on a single unlinked vCenter?

   a. 10,000

   b. 15,000

   c. 20,000

   d. 25,000

6. On Version 8 virtual hardware, what is the maximum number of USB devices that can be simultaneously connected to a VM through the vSphere Client?

   a. 4

   b. 20

   c. 32

   d. 127

7. What is the maximum physical RDM size that can be connected to a VM through a VMFS-5 datastore?

   a. 2TB – 512B

   b. 64TB

   c. 2TB

   d. 64GB

8. When exporting a VM or vApp, which type of file format should you use if you are planning on exporting it to a thumb drive and therefore you want only one consolidated file?

   a. VMDK

   b. OVF

   c. OVA

   d. Snapshot

9. Which of following is the extension of a text file that describes a VM that is marked to never be powered on?

   a. .vmtx

   b. .vmx

   c. -flat.vmdk

   d. There is no such file.

10. Which of following is the extension of a special pointer file that allows the VM to see a LUN instead of using data from a VMFS or NFS?

   a. .vmx

   b. .vmdk

   c. -flat.vmdk

   d. -rdmp.vmdk

11. Which of the following is *not* a major category of virtual hardware?

    a. CPU

    b. Memory

    c. Disk

    d. Guest OS

12. Which of the following are enhancements to a VM that are provided by the installation of VMware Tools? (Choose two.)

    a. The ability to hot add memory

    b. Sync driver for quiescing I/O

    c. VGA display

    d. Improved mouse support

13. Which of the following is the maximum amount of memory supported by Version 8 VMs?

    a. 256GB

    b. 1TB

    c. 64GB

    d. 2TB

14. Which type of disk provisioning gives the greatest level of initial performance?

    a. Thin

    b. Thick - Lazy Zeroed

    c. Thick Eager Zeroed

    d. Initial performance is unaffected by disk provisioning.

15. What is the maximum number of registered VMs on a single unlinked vCenter?

    a. 15,000

    b. 10,000

    c. 20,000

    d. 25,000

16. What is the maximum number of VMs that can be on a single ESXi host?

    a. 32

    b. 512

    c. 256

    d. 120

17. Which of the following is the best definition of a template?

    a. A template is a list of all the characteristics of a VM.

    b. A template is a master copy of a VM that cannot be powered on but that can be used to create VMs that can be powered on.

    c. A template is an exact copy of a VM.

    d. A template is a file that captures the state of a VM.

18. Which of following must you do with regard to a template before you can edit its settings?

    a. Power the template off.

    b. Power the template on.

    c. Convert the template to a VM

    d. Take a snapshot of the template.

19. Which file extension is used on the file that takes the place of BIOS on VM?

    a. .nvram

    b. .vmx

    c. -flat.vmdk

    d. There is no such file.

20. After right-clicking a VM and selecting Edit Settings, which tab should you select to configure a storage policy for the VM?

    a. vServices

    b. Resources

    c. Options

    d. Profiles

This chapter covers the following subjects:

- Creating and Configuring VMware Clusters
- Planning and Implementing VMware Fault Tolerance
- Creating and Administering Resource Pools
- Migrating Virtual Machines
- Backing Up and Restoring Virtual Machines
- Patching and Updating ESXi and Virtual Machines

CHAPTER 5

Establishing and Maintaining Service Levels

The good news that goes with enterprise datacenter virtualization is that you can use many fewer physical machines because you can host many virtual servers on one physical machine. That's good news with regard to resource utilization, space utilization, power costs, and so on. However, it does mean that you have all, or at least a lot, of your "eggs in one basket." In other words, what would happen if your physical machine that is hosting many of your virtual servers should fail? You probably don't want to leave that up to chance. In this chapter, I will discuss creating and administering clusters of physical servers that can keep watch over each other and share the loads as well. In addition, I will discuss how you can migrate, back up and restore, patch, and update the hosts and virtual machines (VMs) within your clusters.

"Do I Know This Already?" Quiz

The "Do I Know This Already?" quiz allows you to assess whether you should read this entire chapter or simply jump to the "Exam Preparation Tasks" section for review. If you are in doubt, read the entire chapter. Table 5-1 outlines the major headings in this chapter and the corresponding "Do I Know This Already?" quiz questions. You can find the answers in Appendix A, "Answers to the 'Do I Know This Already?' Quizzes and Chapter Review Questions."

Table 5-1 "Do I Know This Already?" Section-to-Question Mapping

Foundations Topics Section	Questions Covered in This Section
Creating and Configuring VMware Clusters	1–3
Planning and Implementing VMware Fault Tolerance	4
Creating and Administering Resource Pools	5
Migrating Virtual Machines	6–8
Backing Up and Restoring Virtual Machines	9
Patching and Updating ESXi and Virtual Machines	10

1. What does it mean to "graft in" a host's resource settings when you create a cluster?

   a. You are adding a host that is not ESXi 5.0.

   b. You are using DRS but not HA.

   c. You are maintaining the hierarchy that was set by the host's Resource Pools.

   d. You will only add the host for a temporary project.

2. Which of the following is an optional parameter for Storage DRS configuration?

   a. Capacity

   b. I/O performance

   c. CPU

   d. Memory

3. Which of the following is not decided by DRS in Partially Automated mode, but is decided by DRS in Fully Automated mode?

   a. Initial placement

   b. Storage

   c. Network fault tolerance

   d. Load balancing

4. What is the maximum number of vCPUs that can be on a fault-tolerant (FT) virtual machine?

   a. 32

   b. 4

   c. 1

   d. 2

5. Which of the following cannot be placed into a Resource Pool? (Choose two.)

   a. Cluster

   b. VM

   c. Resource Pool

   d. Host

6. Which of the following is true about vMotion?

    a. You can vMotion VMs whether they are powered on or off.

    b. You cannot vMotion and Storage vMotion the same VM at the same time.

    c. vMotion involves moving a VM's files to a different datastore.

    d. Storage vMotion involves moving the state of VM from one host to another.

7. Which of the following is *not* a component of the state of a VM?

    a. Settings

    b. Disk

    c. Power

    d. Memory

8. Which of the following would prevent a VM from using vMotion?

    a. An internal switch on its host, to which the VM is not connected

    b. CPU affinity not configured

    c. A swap file that is local to a host

    d. An ISO mounted on the local host, to which the VM is connected

9. What is the maximum number of VMs that can be included in a single VDR backup job?

    a. 10

    b. 100

    c. 32

    d. 1000

10. Which of the following types of updates is no longer supported with VUM?

    a. Host

    b. Guest OS

    c. VM hardware

    d. Virtual appliance

Creating and Configuring VMware Clusters

When you decide to create a cluster by combining the resources of two or more hosts (physical servers), you are generally doing it primarily for one or both of two reasons: Distributed Resource Scheduler (DRS) and/or High Availability (HA). In this section, I will discuss many aspects of both of these vSphere features and how they can improve the reliability, performance, and survivability of your VMs. In particular, I will discuss DRS VM entitlement, creating and deleting DRS/HA clusters, and adding and removing VMs from a cluster. In addition, I will discuss a feature that is new to vSphere 5 and allows VM files to be migrated automatically when needed for space utilization and/or performance enhancement. Finally, I will discuss enabling and configuring the many aspects of DRS and HA so that you can take advantage of automatic restarts of VMs when needed and load balancing of VMs on an ongoing basis.

Describing DRS Virtual Machine Entitlement

All the VMs that are in the same cluster are using everything at their disposal to fight for the RAM (physical memory from the hosts) that they need to satisfy the expectations of their guest OS and applications. When a cluster is undercommitted (has plenty of physical memory), each VM's memory entitlement will be the same as its demand for memory. It will be allocated whatever it asks for, which will be capped by its configured limit if that is lower than its available memory setting.

Now, what happens if the cluster becomes overcommitted (less physical memory than demand)? Well, that's an important question to answer because when there isn't enough physical RAM to go around some VMs are going to have to use their swap file (at least in some portion), which means their performance will take a hit, because using memory from a disk is much slower than using physical RAM. So, how does the VMkernel decide which VMs take priority and which VMs will be forced to use their swap file?

When the cluster is overcommitted, DRS and the VMkernel work together to allocate resources based on the resource entitlement of each VM. This is based on a variety of factors and how they relate to each other. In a nutshell, it is based on configured shares, configured memory size, reservations, current demands on the VMs and the Resource Pools that contain them, and on the working set (active utilization of the VM at a particular point in time). In Chapter 6, "Performing Basic Troubleshooting," I will discuss much more about DRS and its capability to control and balance resources and provide you with troubleshooting information.

Creating/Deleting a DRS/HA Cluster

After you have connected to your vCenter Server with your vSphere Client, creating a cluster is simply a matter of adding the Cluster inventory object, dragging your ESXi hosts into it, and configuring the options that you need. You can independently configure options for DRS, HA, and other related settings. To create a DRS/HA cluster, follow the steps outlined in Activity 5-1.

Activity 5-1 Creating a DRS/HA Cluster

1. Log on to your vSphere Client.

2. Select **Home** and then **Hosts and Clusters**.

3. Right-click your datacenter and select **New Cluster**, as shown in Figure 5-1.

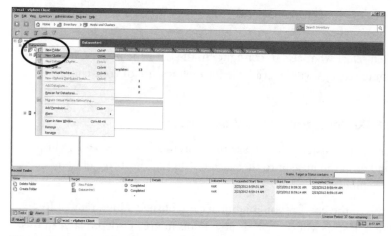

Figure 5-1   Creating a New Cluster

4. Enter a name for your new cluster and then select to **Turn On vSphere HA** and/or **Turn On vSphere DRS**, and then click **Next**, as shown in Figure 5-2.

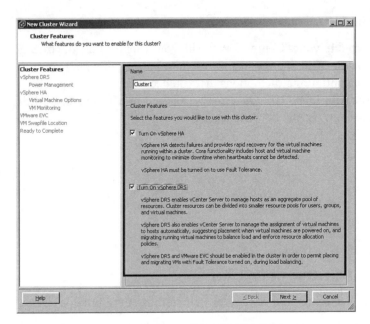

Figure 5-2 Naming a Cluster and Enabling HA/DRS

5. You can then select what else to configure in the left pane under Cluster Features. Separate settings will be available for each feature of your cluster.

Adding/Removing ESXi Hosts from a DRS/HA Cluster

After you have created a cluster, you can use the tools to add hosts to your cluster or simply drag and drop the hosts into the cluster. Adding a host to a cluster is like creating a "giant computer."

Before the host was in the cluster, you might have established a hierarchy of Resource Pools on the host. (I will cover Resource Pools in greater depth later in this chapter, in the section "Creating and Administering Resource Pools.") In this case, when you add the host to a cluster, the system will ask you if you want to "graft" that hierarchy into the cluster or just start a new hierarchy in the new cluster. This is an important decision and not just one regarding what the inventory will look like when you get done. If you have created Resource Pools on your host, and you want to retain that hierarchy, you will need to "graft" it in; otherwise, all the Resource Pools will be deleted when you add the host to the cluster. To add a host to an existing cluster, follow the steps outlined in Activity 5-2.

Activity 5-2 Adding a Host to a Cluster

1. Log on to your vSphere Client.

2. Select **Home** and then **Hosts and Clusters**.

3. Right-click your cluster and select **Add Host**, as shown in Figure 5-3.

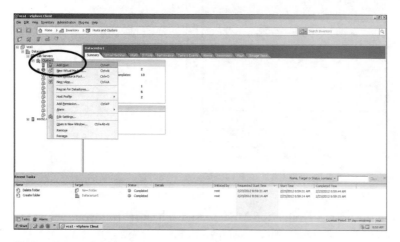

Figure 5-3   Adding a Host to a Cluster

4. Enter the fully qualified domain name (FQDN) of the host that you want to add as well as the credentials associated with the host as it is now, as shown in Figure 5-4. If the host is not current in your vCenter, this will likely be a root account or an account with root privileges. If the host is a member of your vCenter, the credentials are not required, and you could really just drag and drop the host into the cluster.

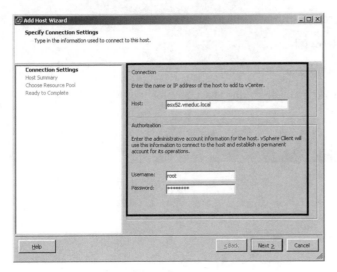

Figure 5-4   Providing Credentials to Add Host to a Cluster

> **5.** You can add the host in Evaluation Mode, assign a license from your vCenter, or assign a new key of your choice, as shown in Figure 5-5.

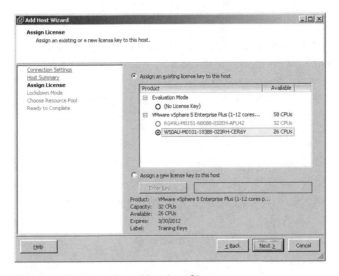

Figure 5-5   Licensing a Host in a Cluster

> **6.** You can enable Lockdown Mode so that the only users that will have access are local console and authenticated vCenter users (no other remote users), as shown in Figure 5-6.

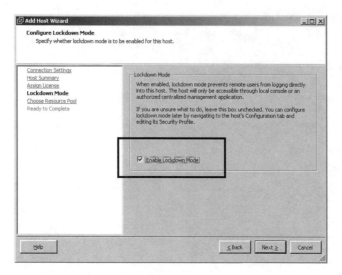

Figure 5-6   Enabling Lockdown Mode for a Host

7. In this case, we had Resource Pools on the host, and we will not be "grafting" them into the cluster Resource Settings, as shown in Figure 5-7.

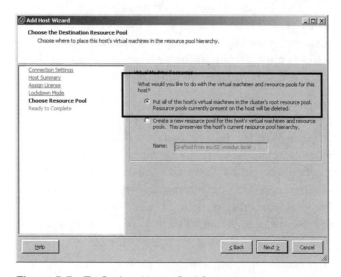

Figure 5-7   To Graft or Not to Graft?

8. On the Ready to Complete page, review your settings, and then click **Finish**, as shown in Figure 5-8.

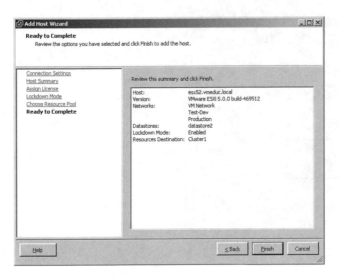

Figure 5-8 The Ready to Complete Page

9. View your inventory in Hosts and Clusters view to see the change.

You might think that removing a host from a cluster would be as simple as just reversing the process that I just covered, but that would not be wholly correct. If you have been using a host within a cluster for any time at all, you will likely have VMs on the host. You will first need to either migrate all the VMs off of the host or shut them down. You can begin this process by entering Maintenance Mode.

When you place a host in Maintenance Mode, you are in essence telling the rest of the hosts in the cluster that this host is "closed for new business" for now. When a host enters Maintenance Mode, no VMs will be migrated to that host, you cannot power on any new VMs, and you cannot make any configuration changes to existing VMs. With the proper configuration of DRS (which I will discuss later in this chapter), all of the VMs that can use vMotion to (automatically migrate) will immediately do so. You will then decide whether to shut the others down and move them to another host, or just leave them on the host that you are removing from the cluster.

After you have made these preparations, it is just a matter of reversing the steps that I covered earlier. In fact, the easiest way to remove a host from a cluster after the host is in Maintenance Mode is to drag the host object back to the datacenter. More specifically, to remove a host from an existing cluster, follow the steps outlined in Activity 5-3.

Activity 5-3 Removing a Host from a Cluster

1. Log on to your vSphere Client.

2. Select **Home** and then **Hosts and Clusters**.

3. Right-click the host that you want to remove and select **Enter Maintenance Mode**, as shown in Figure 5-9.

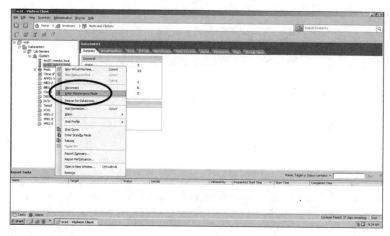

Figure 5-9   Enter Maintenance Mode

4. Confirm that you want to enter Maintenance Mode, and select whether you want to also move powered off and suspended VMs to other hosts in the cluster, and then click **Yes**, as shown in Figure 5-10. If you choose not to move the VMs, they will be "orphaned" while the host is in Maintenance Mode because they will logically remain on that host.

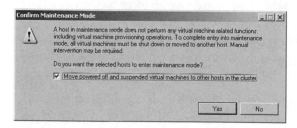

Figure 5-10   Maintenance Mode Confirmation

5. Click and hold the host that you want to remove from the cluster and drag the host to another inventory object, such as your datacenter or a folder that is higher in the hierarchy than the cluster. Figure 5-11 shows esx52.vmeduc.local in Maintenance Mode.

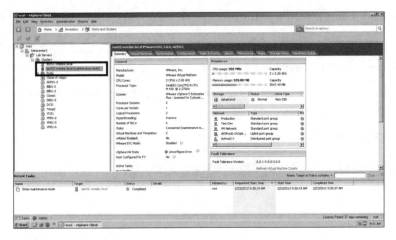

Figure 5-11 Maintenance Mode Icon

NOTE If you are have configured Fully Automated DRS, as I will discuss later in this chapter, the VMs that can vMotion will line up and "exit stage right" as soon as you put your host into Maintenance Mode.

Adding or Removing Virtual Machines from a DRS/HA Cluster

As I said earlier, once you have created a cluster, you in essence have a giant computer that combines the aggregate resources of the hosts in the cluster. Notice that I didn't say "super computer." You can't total up all the resources in a large cluster and assign them all to one VM and then play Jeopardy with it! In fact, a VM will always take all of its CPU and memory from one host or another, depending on where it is powered on and whether it has been migrated to another host. You will, however, have larger pools of resources from which you can create more VMs or larger VMs.

Adding or removing a VM with regard to the cluster is really no different than with a host. In other words, you can just drag and drop the VM to the appropriate place in your hierarchy, whether that place happens to be a host in a cluster or a host that is not in a cluster. To determine which of your VMs are in a specific cluster, you can click the cluster in the console pane and then on the Virtual Machines tab.

Configuring Storage DRS

One of the main reasons that you place your hosts into clusters is to use Distributed Resource Scheduler (DRS), which I will discuss in detail later in this chapter in the section "Adding/Removing ESXi Hosts from a DRS/HA Cluster." As your network grows, you need to use your resources in the most efficient manner, so having a tool that balances the loads of VMs across the hosts is very useful. If you've configured it properly, DRS does a wonderful job of balancing the loads of the VMs by using algorithms that take into account the *CPU* and the *memory* of the VMs on each host. This has the effect of strengthening two of the critical resources on each VM, namely "*CPU*" and "*memory*."

If CPU and memory were the only two resources on your VMs, I would be at the end of my story, but you also have to consider *network* and *storage*. Because I already discussed networking in Chapter 2, "Planning and Configuring vSphere Networking," let's focus here on storage. As you know, the weakest link in the chain will determine the strength of the chain. By the same logic, if you took great care to provide plenty of CPU and memory to your VMs, but you starved them with regard to storage, the end result might be poor-performing VMs.

Too bad you can't do something with storage that's similar to what DRS does with CPU and memory; but wait, you can! What if you organized datastores into *datastore clusters* made of multiple datastores with the same characteristics? Then, when you created a VM, you would place the VM into the datastore cluster and the appropriate datastore would be chosen by the system based on the available space on the logical unit numbers (LUNs) of each datastore and on the I/O performance (if you chose that, too). Better yet, in the interim, the datastore cluster would monitor itself and use Storage vMotion whenever necessary to provide balance across the datastore cluster and to increase the overall performance of all datastores in the datastore cluster.

This is what Storage DRS (SDRS) can do for your virtual datacenter. When you set it up, you choose whether to take I/O into consideration with regard to automated Storage vMotions, and it always takes the available storage into consideration. Once you have configured it, SDRS runs automatically and in a very conservative way (so as not to use Storage vMotion resources too often) maintains balance in the datastore clusters that you have configured. This results in an overall performance increase in "storage" for your VMs to go right along with the performance increases in *CPU* and *memory* that DRS has provided, a nice combination.

To configure SDRS, you will first create the Datastore Clusters. This configuration includes selecting the automation level and runtime rules for the cluster as well as selecting the datastores that you will include in the cluster. The datastores should have equal capabilities so that one is "as good as the other" to the SDRS system. To create an SDRS Datastore Cluster, follow the steps outlined in Activity 5-4.

Activity 5-4 Creating and Configuring an SDRS Cluster

1. Log on to your vSphere Client.

2. Select **Home** and then **Datastores and Datastore Clusters**, as shown in Figure 5-12.

Figure 5-12 Entering Datastores and Datastore Clusters View

3. Right-click the datacenter in which you want to create the Datastore Cluster and select **New Datastore Cluster**, as shown in Figure 5-13.

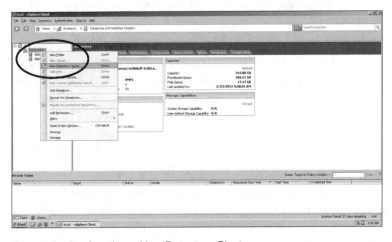

Figure 5-13 Creating a New Datastore Cluster

4. On the General page, enter a name for your datastore cluster and leave the check box selected to **Turn On Storage DRS**, as shown in Figure 5-14, and click **Next**. (If you are creating the datastore cluster for future use but not for immediate use, you can uncheck the **Turn On Storage DRS** box.)

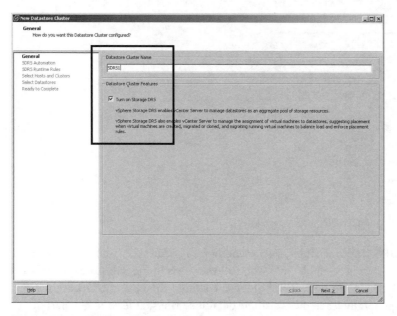

Figure 5-14   Enabling SDRS in a Datastore Cluster

5. From SDRS Automation, select the automation level for your datastore cluster and click **Next**, as shown in Figure 5-15. Selecting No Automation will only provide recommendations and will not cause the system to Storage vMotion your VM files without your intervention. The Fully Automated setting will use Storage vMotion to migrate VM files as needed based on the loads and on the rest of your configuration.

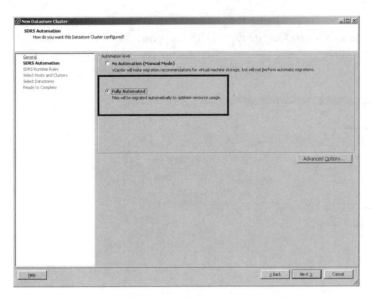

Figure 5-15 Selecting the SDRS Automation Level

6. From SDRS Runtime Rules, select whether you want to enable I/O Metric Inclusion. This is available only when all the hosts in the datastore cluster are ESXi 5.0. Select the DRS thresholds for **Utilized Space** and **I/O Latency**. You can generally leave these at their default settings, at least to get started. There is also an Advanced Options setting, as shown in Figure 5-16, that you can almost always leave at the default, but that you can tweak if needed. When you are finished with all these settings, click **Next** to continue.

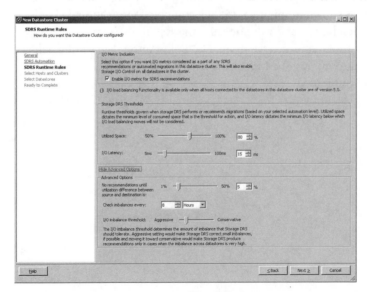

Figure 5-16 Configuring SDRS Runtime Rules

7. Select the Hosts and Clusters that you want to include in your Datastore Cluster and click **Next**, as shown in Figure 5-17.

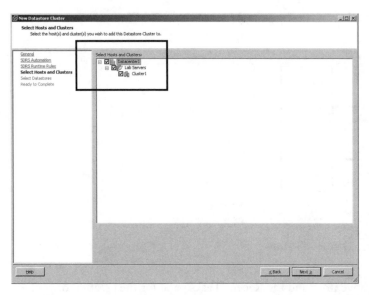

Figure 5-17   Selecting Hosts and Clusters for SDRS

8. Select the datastores that you want to include in your datastore cluster and click **Next**. The status of each datastore will be listed along with its capacity, free space, and so on. If the datastore does not have a connection to all the hosts you have chosen, it will be indicated in the Host Connection Status, as shown in Figure 5-18.

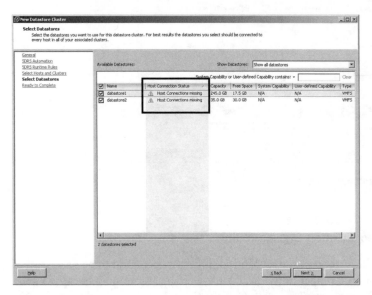

Figure 5-18   Selecting Datastores for SDRS Datastore Clusters

9. On the Ready to Complete page, you can review your selections, address any configuration issues, and then click **Finish**, as shown in Figure 5-19.

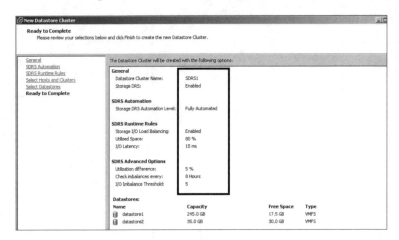

Figure 5-19   The Ready to Complete Page

10. Monitor your inventory and the Recent Tasks pane for the creation of your new datastore cluster, as shown in Figure 5-20.

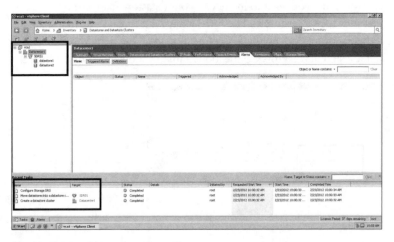

Figure 5-20   A New Datastore Cluster

Configuring Enhanced vMotion Compatibility

Considering that I have yet to discuss vMotion, it might seem odd to be discussing Enhanced vMotion Compatibility (EVC) at this point, but remember that I am following the blueprint "to the letter." Suffice it to say for now that the process of vMotion is sort of a sleight-of-hand trick performed by the VMkernel and his assistants. In this process, the guest OS on the VM, and therefore the end user, are unaware that anything has changed even though the user's server has been moved from one physical computer (host) to another.

If the guest OS can determine that anything has changed, then the "trick" is ruined and vMotion will not work. Although it's possible to set the guest OS on the VM to ignore any differences in the CPUID of the source host versus that of the target host, it's much easier to just make sure that both hosts' CPUID look the same. In fact, it would be best if all of the CPUIDs of hosts in the same cluster looked the same, so that wherever the guest OS of the VM goes... it's all the same.

This is what you do when you configure EVC on the cluster. You must first determine that all the hosts in the cluster will support EVC. Only the relatively newer AMD and Intel CPUs support it, as shown in Figure 5-21. Once you have determined that all of your hosts will support EVC, you will need to configure the EVC setting with a CPU baseline with which all hosts can comply. If your host's CPUs are different, this might mean choosing the "least common denominator" of the CPUs on your hosts so that you allow for more flexibility in adding new hosts or choosing the "highest common denominator" if you want to have the most capability across the hosts. After you have chosen a baseline, all hosts must meet that baseline in order to be in your cluster.

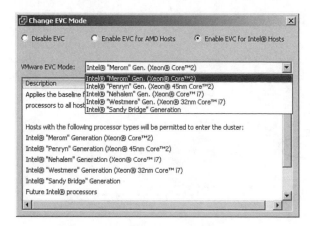

Figure 5-21   CPU Support for EVC

> **NOTE**   EVC can be used by legacy hosts with ESX 3.5 and Update 2, but the host must support the appropriate CPU hardware so as to meet the baseline. To allow for the most flexibility with regard to additional hosts for the cluster, you should select the lowest baseline that is common to all current hosts. It should also be noted the EVC requires hardware virtualization (Intel VT/AMD-V) and XD/NX enabled.

Monitoring a DRS/HA Cluster

In earlier versions of the software, VMware used to say in essence, "Just set the defaults and trust us," and then they didn't really give the administrator a lot of tools to check up on what was actually happening on the cluster. Well, that has changed dramatically in vSphere 5.0. You now have tools with which to monitor the cluster for DRS and HA and address any issues that you notice, as shown in Figure 5-22. (In Chapter 6, I will discuss the proper use of the tools for troubleshooting issues with HA and DRS.)

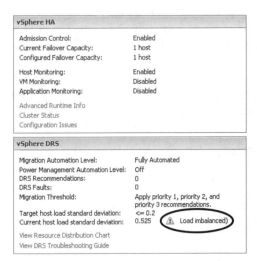

Figure 5-22   Tools to Monitor HA and DRS

Configuring Migration Thresholds for DRS and Virtual Machines

As I mentioned earlier, DRS uses algorithms to balance the loads of VMs based on the CPU and memory resources that they are using on a host. The main premise here is that by balancing the resources across the hosts you can improve the overall performance of all the VMs, especially when the physical resources of CPU and memory are much more heavily used on one host than on another. When this occurs, DRS can use vMotion to automatically move the state of one or more VMs on one host to another host. Moving the state of the VMs means moving them to another physical place (host). As an alternative, DRS can also just make recommendations to move the VMs, which you can then read and follow.

If you decide to let DRS in essence read its own recommendations and then automatically migrate the VMs (this is a called Fully Automated Mode, and I will discuss it next), the question then becomes, "How far off balance does the resource usage have to be to create a situation where a migration is actually performed?" The answer to this question can be configured in the Migration Threshold setting for DRS on the cluster, as shown in Figure 5-23. If you configure this setting too conservatively, you might not get the balance that you really desire, but if you configure it too aggressively, any imbalance might cause a system to use vMotion to migrate the VMs and thereby use resources needlessly.

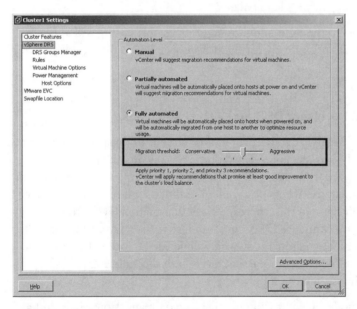

Figure 5-23   Configuration the DRS Migration Threshold

To help you make the right decision, the Migration Threshold slider control identifies five settings and the expected impact of that setting. You should read over each of the settings and make the choice that will work best for you. The settings on the Migration Threshold are as follows:

- **Setting 1:** This is the leftmost setting on the slider and also the most conservative. It will apply only the most important, Priority 1, recommendations. As indicated below the slider, these are recommendations that "must be taken to satisfy cluster constraints like affinity rules and host maintenance" (both of which I will discuss in more detail, later in this chapter in the section "Creating VM-Host and VM-VM Affinity Rules").

- **Setting 2:** One notch to the right from Setting 1, this will apply only Priority 1 and Priority 2 recommendations. These are deemed by the vCenter, based on its calculations, to "promise a significant improvement to the cluster's balance."

- **Setting 3:** One more over to the right, this will apply Priority 1, 2, and 3 recommendations. These "promise at least good improvement to the cluster's load balance."

- **Setting 4:** One more to the right, as you imagine, this one applies Priority 1, 2, 3, and 4 recommendations. These are expected to "promise even a moderate improvement to the cluster's load balance."

- **Setting 5:** Farthest to the right and most aggressive, this setting will apply recommendations that "promise even a slight improvement to the cluster's load balance."

Configuring Automation Levels for DRS and Virtual Machines

You might think that we really already covered this in the previous paragraphs, but that would not be totally correct. You see, in addition to making the recommendations and decisions with regard to balancing cluster loads, DRS is also involved with choosing the host to which the VM is powered on in the first place. This is referred to as *initial placement*. Because of this, there are three automation levels from which you can choose when you configure DRS for your cluster. Each level addresses who will decide initial placement and separately who will decide on load balancing, you or DRS? The three possible DRS automation levels, also shown in Figure 5-23, from which you can choose, are the following:

- **Manual:** In this mode, vCenter will only make recommendations about initial placement and load balancing. You can choose to accept the recommendation, accept some of them (if there are more than one at a time), or ignore them altogether. For example, if vCenter makes a recommendation to move a VM and you accept it, DRS will use vMotion to migrate the VM while it's powered on with no disruption in service.

- **Partially Automated:** In this mode, vCenter will automatically choose the right host for the initial placement of the VM. There will be no recommendations with regard to initial placement. In addition, vCenter will make recommendations with regard to load balance in the cluster, which you can choose to accept, partially accept, or ignore.

- **Fully Automated:** As you might expect, this setting allows vCenter to make all the decisions on your behalf. These will include initial placement and load balance. DRS will use algorithms to generate recommendations and then "follow its own advice" based on the Migration Threshold, as we discussed earlier. To be more specific, the Target Host Load Standard Deviation, as shown previously in Figure 5-22, is monitored by DRS. When the current exceeds the target, DRS will move VMs to balance the load. You will not see any recommendations.

Now you might be thinking that these cluster settings will be fine for most of your VMs, but that there are some VMs that are different, and you need a little more flexibility in their settings. For example, what if you have a VM that is connected to a serial security dongle on a single host, and that therefore will need to stay on that host? If you are in Manual Mode, will you have to constantly answer those recommendations? If you are in Fully Automated Mode, can it just ignore that one?

Thankfully, there are DRS settings for each of the VMs in your cluster. These Virtual Machine Options settings will default to the cluster setting unless you change them, as shown in Figure 5-24. For example, the setting that would be best for our security dongle scenario would be **Disabled**, which does not disable the VM, but rather disables DRS for the VM and therefore does not create recommendations.

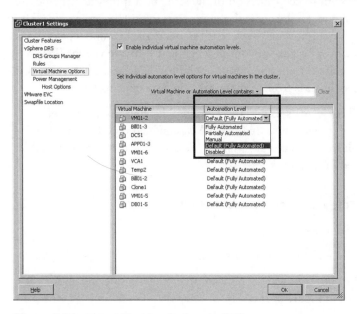

Figure 5-24   Virtual Machine Options in DRS

Creating VM-Host and VM-VM Affinity Rules

In my classes, when we begin to discuss affinity and anti-affinity rules we have often just finished with some labs in which we set processor affinity for the purpose of creating contention for the CPU resource. When the students see the word *affinity* again, they naturally think of processor, as you might also be thinking right now. Well, if you are, please wipe that idea out of your mind.

Affinity, in fact means "togetherness or likeness", and anti-affinity means "separate-ness or difference." So, what am I referring to as being together or separate in this discussion? I am referring the VMs themselves, not their CPUs.

VM affinity rules in DRS specify that certain VMs should or must stay on the same host. I say *should or must* because it depends on whether you configure them as strictly enforced or as softly enforced. Likewise, VM anti-affinity rules specify that certain VMs *should not* or *must not* be on the same host. You can configure the VM relationships and the host relationships in very flexible ways.

So, why would you want to keep two or more VMs together on the same host? Well, if the VMs work closely with each other, having them on the same host would be a way to maintain a robust and reliable connection between them, especially if they were on the same switch and in the same subnet. In that case, communication between them would be nothing more than an exchange of RAM, which is extremely fast and robust.

Conversely, you might want to keep VMs off of the same host if they all provide the same type of service and you don't want "all of your eggs in one basket" in case the host should fail. Also, you might want to prevent too many of the same type of VMs from being on the same host because of your independent software vendor (ISV) licenses that only allow for a certain number on each host. For the same reason, you might want to keep specific VMs from ever running on a specific host.

You can accomplish all these goals using DRS Groups Manager. As an example, suppose that you wanted to make sure that two VMs remained together and that they remained on one host unless that host failed. To accomplish this, you would follow the steps outlined in Activity 5-5.

Activity 5-5 Creating a Softly Enforced VM-VM-Host Rule

1. Log on to your vSphere Client.

2. Select **Home** and then **Hosts and Clusters**.

3. Right-click on the cluster in which you want to create the rule and click **Edit Settings**, as shown in Figure 5-25.

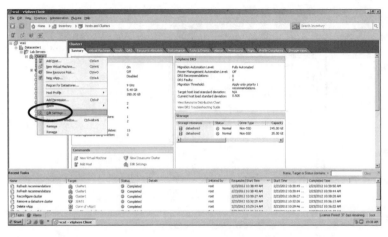

Figure 5-25   Editing Cluster Settings to Create a VM-VM-Host Rule

4. On Cluster Settings, select **DRS Groups Manager** and click **Add**, as shown in Figure 5-26.

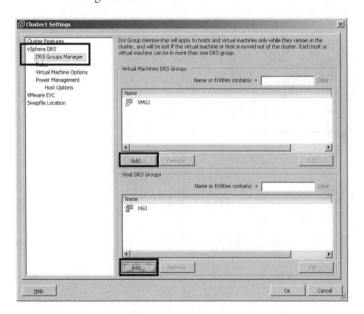

Figure 5-26   DRS Groups Manager

5. Under Virtual Machines DRS Groups, click **Add**. Type a name for the group or use the group name provide and click **Edit**, and then choose the VMs that you want to associate to this group, as shown in Figure 5-27.

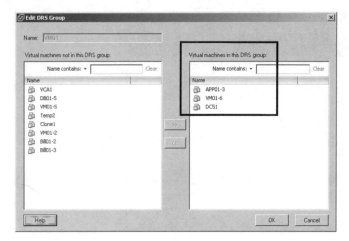

Figure 5-27 Creating DRS Group - Adding VMs

6. Under Host DRS Groups, click **Add**, type a name for the group or use the group name provided, and then choose the host(s) that you want to associate to this group, as shown in Figure 5-28.

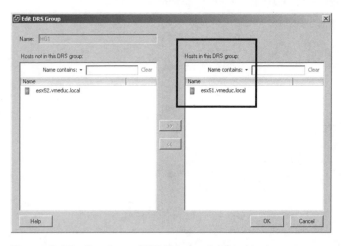

Figure 5-28 Creating a DRS Group - Adding Hosts

7. Select **Rules**, and then click **Add**, type a name for your rule, and then under Type select **Virtual Machines to Hosts**, and finally select **Should Run on Hosts in Group** and click **OK**, as shown in Figure 5-29.

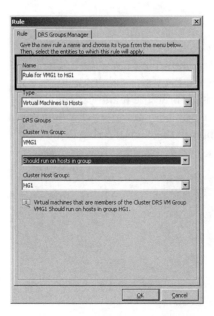

Figure 5-29   Creating a DRS Group - Adding Rules

8. View your new rule and click **OK** to close, as shown in Figure 5-30. (You can also click **Add** to create another rule.)

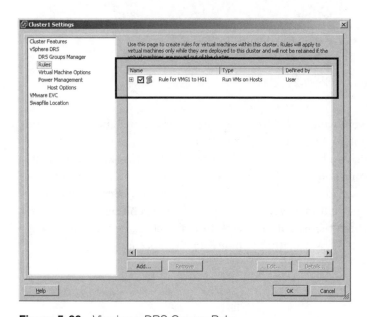

Figure 5-30   Viewing a DRS Groups Rule

Enabling/Disabling Host Monitoring

When you create a cluster and configure HA, a check box that is labeled **Enable Host Monitoring** is already checked by default, as shown in Figure 5-31. The reasoning behind this is that you wouldn't be configuring it if you didn't want to use it. That said, there might come a time that you don't want to use it and yet you don't want to completely remove the service and your entire configuration. (I will discuss the details of HA configuration later in this chapter in the "Configuring Admission Control for HA and Virtual Machines" section.)

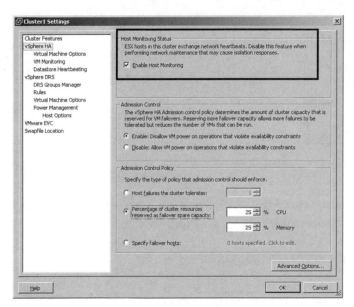

Figure 5-31 Enabling/Disabling Host Monitoring

Suppose that you are removing a host from the cluster for maintenance. If the host monitoring is still enabled, the system will expect a heartbeat from other hosts. Because it will not receive a heartbeat, it might conclude that it is isolated and continue with its isolation response. I will discuss isolation response in a later section, "Configuring Admission Control for HA and Virtual Machines." Because you know that HA can't really work until you get the host back up and running in the cluster, you might as well uncheck the **Enable Host Monitoring** check box. Doing so will ensure that an unexpected host isolation response does not occur.

Enabling/Configuring/Disabling Virtual Machine and Application Monitoring

Again, the order in which I discuss these topics is interesting. Suffice it to say that the original HA product that was released from VMware many years ago was specifically and exclusively used to restart VMs on another host when the host on which they were running had a physical failure or became disconnected from an important network. That part of product still exists, and I will discuss it in detail later in later in this chapter in the section "Determining Appropriate Failover Methodology and Required Resources for an HA Implementation," but that is not what I am discussing here.

With vSphere 5.0, VMware has broadened that offering substantially by offering the capability to restart VMs just because the OS has failed or even just because a monitored application has failed, even though the host is functioning normally. In this section, I will discuss how you can enable, configure, and disable VM Monitoring and Application Monitoring.

Enabling/Configuring/Disabling Virtual Machine Monitoring

VM Monitoring is actually quite simple and straightforward. When you are running a VM with VMware Tools installed on it, and its running on a host in an HA cluster, the VM sends frequent heartbeats (quick communications) to the host to indicate that the OS is still healthy. The principle idea here is that if the OS fails (such as an MS "blue screen of death") then the heartbeats will not be received. In some cases, a VM could still be running and heartbeats not be received. For this reason, HA also checks for disk/network connectivity over the past 120 seconds. If activity is discovered, the VM will not be restarted. This helps prevent unnecessary restarts.

If there is no heartbeat and no I/O activity, and VM Monitoring is enabled, the VM can be powered off and then restarted on the same host. To configure VM Monitoring, you select **VM Monitoring Only** in the cluster feature under vSphere HA and then configure the **Monitoring sensitivity** and custom settings. You can simply choose a high/medium/low setting on a slider or you can customize your configuration, as shown in Figure 5-32.

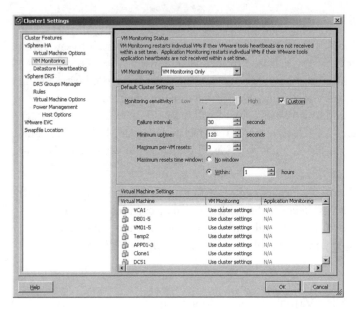

Figure 5-32   Configuring VM Monitoring

The following is a brief description of each setting that you can configure in VM Monitoring:

- **Failure Interval:** The period of time that the system waits without receiving a heartbeat before checking I/O requests for networking and storage.

- **Minimum Uptime:** The period of time that a VM must run after restart to count as having been restarted.

- **Maximum Per-VM Resets:** The maximum number of times that a VM can be restarted within the Maximum Resets Time Window.

- **Maximum Resets Time Window:** The period of time that must expire before the system resets and the VM can be restarted again based on the number configured in Maximum Per-VM Resets. You can also opt for no window.

Enabling/Configuring/Disabling Application Monitoring

Application Monitoring goes a step further than VM Monitoring to provide a graceful shutdown of the OS on a VM and a restart on the same host if a monitored application should fail. To enable this feature, you must first obtain a software development kit (SDK) or be using an application that supports the function. This will allow you to set up a custom heartbeat for the application. You can then configure the settings in the same way as for VM Monitoring and you can elect to include or exclude each VM in the cluster, as shown in Figure 5-33.

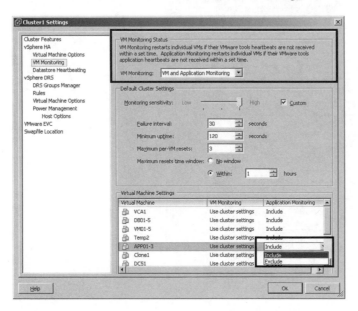

Figure 5-33   Configuring VM and Application Monitoring

Configuring Admission Control for HA and Virtual Machines

As I mentioned earlier, HA provides for the automatic restart of VMs on another host when the host on which they are running has failed or become disconnected from the cluster. If you think about, how could the other hosts help out in a "time of crisis" if they themselves had already given all of their resources to other VMs? The answer is, they couldn't! For this reason, Admission Control settings cause a host to "hold back" some of its resources by not allowing any more VMs to start on a host so that it can be of assistance if another host should fail. The amount of resources held back is up to you. In fact, this is central question that you are answering when you configure Admission Control.

In this section, I will discuss two topics: Admission Control and Admission Control Policy. As you can see in Figure 5-34, Admission Control has two possible settings: Enable or Disable. Admission Control Policy, however, is much more complex. I will first discuss Admission Control in general, and then I will discuss the finer points of configuring Admission Control Policy.

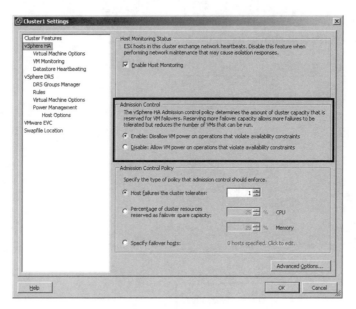

Figure 5-34   Admission Control Settings

Admission Control

The radio button for Admission Control is the "master switch" that turns on HA. In most cases, you want the master switch in the "on" position, in other words, you want HA enabled. In some unusual cases when you need to start a critical VM and the system won't let you, then you can use the Disable option to temporarily override the HA Admission Control and get the VM started. If you do this, you should address the real resource issue and enable Admission Control as soon as possible. It is not a best practice to leave Admission Control disabled.

Admission Control Policy

Once you have enabled Admission Control, you can choose between three options for Admission Control Policy. The central question is this: "If HA is supposed to make the hosts save enough resources so that VMs on a failed host can be restarted on the other hosts, then how does it know how much to save?" When you configure Admission Control Policy, you answer two questions. First, how many hosts will I "allow" to fail and still know that the VMs on the failed hosts can be restarted on the remaining hosts? Second, how will I tell HA how to calculate the amount of resources to "hold back" on each host?

The following is a brief description of each of the three Admission Control Policies:

- **Host Failures the Cluster Tolerates:** This setting is configurable from 1–31, although in most cases you probably wouldn't configure it any higher than 2. This policy is the oldest of the three and is sometimes used in organizations today, although it might no longer be considered the favorite. It relies on a "slot size," which is a calculation that it determines to be an estimate of CPU and memory needs for every VM in the cluster. A setting of 2 means that two hosts could fail at the same time in a cluster and all of the VMs that are on the failed hosts could be restarted on the remaining resources of the other hosts in the cluster. You can imagine the additional resources that would have to be "held back" to allow for this setting. In most cases, organizations use a setting of 1, unless they are configuring very large clusters.

- **Percentage of Cluster Resources Reserved as Failover Spare Capacity:** If you choose this method, you will then set the percentages that you need for your organization. In addition, you can set a different percentage for CPU than you do for memory. After you have chosen your settings, HA continually compares the total resource requirements for all VMs with the total failover capacity that it has derived from your settings. When you are attempting to power on a VM that would cause the first calculation to become higher than the second, HA will prevent the VM from being powered on. How you derive the percentages is beyond the scope of this book, but you should know that this option should be used when you have highly variable CPU and memory reservations.

- **Specify Failover Hosts:** If you choose this option, you will then choose a host that is in your cluster that will become a passive standby host. It should have the same amount of resources of any of the hosts in your cluster, or more. This option at first seems to violate all that HA stands for, because part of the goal is to provide fault tolerance without the need for passive standby hardware, but there is a reason that it's there, as you'll see very soon when I discuss determining the most appropriate methodology to use.

NOTE   Memory overhead is additional memory allocated to a running VM that is based on the number of vCPUs and the amount of memory reservation.

Finally, as with DRS, you have options with regard to each VM that can be different from what is set for the cluster, as shown in Figure 5-35. These options do not have anything to do with admission control, or at least not directly. That said, they do have an impact on what happens to each VM when HA is used. The list that follows provides a brief description of each of these two settings.

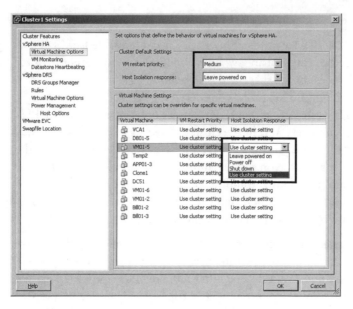

Figure 5-35   Virtual Machine Options for HA

- **VM Restart Priority:** The default configuration in the cluster is Medium. If you leave the default setting, all VMs will have the same priority on restart; in other words, no VMs will have any priority over any others. If there are some VMs that you want to have a greater priority (closer to the front of the line), you can change the restart priority on the specific VMs. Only by leaving the cluster setting at the default of Medium will you yourself the option to give each VM a priority that is lower or higher than the default setting. You can also change the default setting on the cluster, though it's not often needed.

- **Host Isolation Response:** This is the setting that determines what the host does with regard to VMs when the host is not receiving heartbeats on its management network. The options are to leave powered on, power off, or gracefully shut down the VMs. The default setting in the cluster is Leave Powered On, but this can be set specifically for each VM in the cluster. In most cases, you do not want to power off a server that has applications running on it because it can corrupt the applications and cause a very long restart time. For this reason, you should generally use either the default setting of Leave Powered On or a setting of Shut Down VMs to shut the servers down gracefully and not corrupt the applications that they are running.

Determining Appropriate Failover Methodology and Required Resources for an HA Implementation

Okay, before looking at appropriate failover methodology, I think I need to discuss how very different HA is now (in vSphere 5.0) than it was in previous versions of vSphere. In fact, it's been totally redesigned from the ground up. The previous version of HA was a carryover from Automated Availability Manager from EMC Legato (AAM). The new system, called Fault Domain Manager (FDM), offers many advantages over the older system. Because the test blueprint does not list that you should know these advantages or the "inner workings of FDM," I am not going to spend much time on them in this book. If you want to learn more about FDM, there are many books that you can read, including some from VMware Press. One that I've found particularly helpful is "VMware vSphere 5 Technical Deep Dive," by Duncan Epping and Frank Denneman.

That said, my main focus here will be to analyze the differences between the three Admission Control methods of which we've spoken. In addition, I will discuss the use of each method and when one would be more appropriate than another. You should understand your options with regard to configuring HA and the impact of each possible decision on your overall failover methodology.

Host Failures the Cluster Tolerates

By default, HA calculates the slot size for a VM in a very conservative manner. It uses the largest reservation for CPU of any VM on each host in a cluster and then largest reservation for memory plus the memory overhead. These numbers are used, in essence, to assume that every VM is that size, a value called *slot size*. This calculation is then used determine how many "slots" each host can support. The fact is that no VM may actually have both of those values so the calculation can result in a much larger slot size than actually needed. This is turn can result in less capacity for VMs in the cluster.

You can use advanced settings to change the slot size, but that will only be valid until you create a VM that is even larger. The actual calculations to make advanced settings changes are beyond the scope of this book, but you should know how the default slot size is determined. The only factor that might make this option appropriate and simple is if your VMs all have similar CPU and memory reservations and similar "memory overhead."

NOTE   You can obtain additional information about these calculations and settings in the vSphere Documentation Center at http://pubs.vmware.com/vsphere-50/index.jsp.

Percentage of Cluster Resources as Failover Spare Capacity

Unlike the previous option, this option works very well when you have VMs with highly variable CPU and memory reservations. In addition, you can now configure separate percentages for CPU and memory, making it even more flexible and saving your resources. How you derive the percentages is beyond the scope of this book, but you should know that this option should be used when you have highly variable CPU and memory reservations. This method is generally most preferred now because it uses resources in an efficient manner and does not require the manipulation of slot sizes.

> **NOTE**   You can obtain additional information about these calculations and settings in the vSphere Documentation Center at http://pubs.vmware.com/vsphere-50/index.jsp.

Specify Failover Hosts

If you think about it, part of the reason that you used HA rather than clustering was to avoid passive standby hosts, so why even offer this option? The main reason this is an option is that some organizational policies dictate that passive standby hosts must be available. To provide flexibility is these instances, VMware offers this option, but it should not be considered a best practice.

Planning and Implementing VMware Fault Tolerance

For some of your VMs, the option of restarting them when their host fails is not good enough. What you want is for them never to go down at all, even if their host fails. The only way that this could be possible is if the VM was actually running on two different hosts at the same time. In essence, this is what VMware Fault Tolerance (FT) does, as shown in Figure 5-36. In this section, I will discuss the requirements of FT including the network configuration requirements. In addition, I will discuss how you can enable, test, and disable FT for your critical VMs. Finally, I will assist you in determining a use case for enabling FT on a VM.

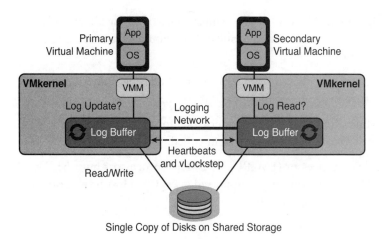

Figure 5-36   vSphere FT Architecture

Identifying VMware Fault Tolerance Requirements

Based on my description of FT, you might have already decided that you want all or at least most of your VMs to take advantage of FT. Well, there are two sides to every story, and you should hear the other side of this one before you make any decisions. You will find that FT works best for only those critical VMs that absolutely need it, and that is what it's designed for anyway.

The requirements and limitations with regard to FT are many. I tell my students that this stuff is truly "rocket surgery!" Most people consider the biggest limitation to be the fact that it doesn't allow for VMs with more than one vCPU. Because most of your VMs don't need more than one, this may not seem like much of a limitation, however many of your "critical" VMs (the kind on which you want to use FT) do perform better with more than one vCPU. For example, MS Exchange and Lotus Notes can be used with one vCPU, but might perform much better with more than one.

As I said, that is the main concern of most administrators when they look at FT, but it's not the only requirement of the system. There are many requirements with regard to networking, memory, and storage. The following is a list of requirements and limitations of FT:

- **vSphere configuration:** All host hardware must be certified for FT and all hosts must have certificate checking enabled. You should have a minimum of three hosts in a cluster.

- **Storage:** VMs must have shared storage. VMs must be provisioned with eager-zeroed thick virtual disks and cannot be on physical RDMs.

- **Networking:** Minimum of two 1Gbps vmnics, one for vMotion and one for FT Logging. Three or more vmnics are recommended.

- **Processor:** Only uniprocessor (1 vCPU) VMs. Host processors must be FT-compatible. VMs must be running a supported guest OS. Host processors must be compatible with one another.

NOTE   You can obtain additional information about host processor compatibility on the VMware Knowledge Base article at http://vmware.com/kb/1008027. It should also be noted that FT fully supports power saving features on processors such as Intel Speedstep and AMD PowerNow.

- **Host BIOS:** Host must have Hardware Virtualization enabled. Hosts must run same instruction set.

- **VM limitations/host:** You can have no more than four FT machines (primaries or secondaries) on any host.

NOTE   At the time of this writing, VM snapshots were not supported with vSphere 4.1 or vSphere 5.0 for backing up VMs covered by FT. You can obtain additional information about backing up VMs that are covered by FT from the VMware Knowledge Base article at http://vmware.com/kb/1016619.

Configuring VMware Fault Tolerance Networking

As I mentioned earlier, the networking requirements for FT are that you must have at least two vmnics, one for vMotion and at least one for FT Logging. This is because when you use FT, the VM in essence uses vMotion to copy of itself to another host and then begins the FT Logging process using vLockstep technology from then on. Actually, there is a little more to configuring an FT network than just two vmnics. Each configuration will have its own challenges. The following is a list of guidelines to follow with regard to FT networking:

- Distribute each vmnic team over two physical switches to eliminate a single point of failure at Layer 2.

- Use a deterministic teaming policy, such as originating port ID. This will ensure that specific traffic types stay on their own specific vmnics.

- When using active/standby policies, take into account the traffic types that would share a vmnic in the event of a failure.

- Configure all active adapters for a particular type of traffic (for example, FT Logging) to the same physical switch. The standby adapter should use the other switch.

Enabling/Disabling VMware Fault Tolerance on a Virtual Machine

Now let's discuss what really happens when you enable FT on a VM. What you are looking for is a way to run the VM in two different places at the same time. That way, a physical failure of a host won't mean that the server goes down, because it is running on another host as well. This means that the VM needs to make a copy of itself and place it on another host. This, in essence, is what happens when you enable FT on a VM. The VM on which you enabled FT becomes the Primary VM and uses vMotion to copy of itself to another host, with one important exception.

Whereas the Primary VM continues to operate normally, the new Secondary VM does not connect to the network normally but instead is connected to the Primary VM using the FT Logging connection and vLockstep technology. Everything that happens on the Primary VM is recorded and played back on the secondary VM, only milliseconds later. The Secondary VM is always "up to speed" so that if the host on which the Primary VM resides should fail, the system needs only to connect the Secondary VM to the main network. If that happens, the Secondary VM becomes the new Primary VM and it creates a new secondary VM on yet another (third) host.

To enable FT on a VM, after the hosts have been properly configured, follow the steps outlined in Activity 5-6.

Activity 5-6 Enabling Fault Tolerance on a Virtual Machine

1. Log on to your vSphere Client.

2. Select **Home** and then **Networking**.

3. Right-click the VM on which you would like to enable FT and select **Turn On Fault Tolerance**, as shown in Figure 5-37.

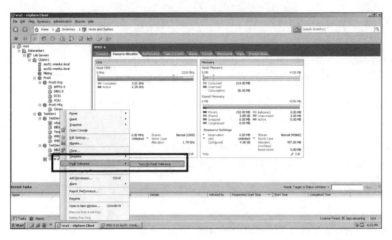

Figure 5-37 Enabling FT for a VM on a Configured Cluster

4. Monitor the Recent Tasks pane and your inventory to see the changes.

Testing an FT Configuration

Once FT is enabled for a VM, you can test to verify that it works if the host should fail. Now, shutting down the host on which the VM resides would definitely kick off a test, but you might not want to get that drastic. If you have other VMs on the same host and you want to perform as safe and noninvasive a test as possible, you can right-click the VM that is protected by FT and select **Test Fault Tolerance**.

Determining Use Case for Enabling VMware Fault Tolerance on a Virtual Machine

Now that you have seen the advantages and drawbacks of FT, it's up to you to decide where, or even whether, it fits into your virtual datacenter. If you have VMs that are critical to the point that lives or millions of dollars are on the line, you might consider using FT to provide for zero disruption in the event of a physical failure of a host. This assumes that the critical VM can function with only one vCPU. You will need to evaluate the need for FT in your own organization. In general, organizations use FT for the following reasons:

- Important applications that need to available at all times, even in the event of a hardware failure.

- Custom applications that are not cluster aware and therefore have no other way of being protected from a physical failure.

- Cases where clustering might be used but the complexity of configuring and maintaining it is beyond the capabilities of the Administrators.

- In cases where a critical transaction is happening such as the transfer of a large database or the creation of an important and time sensitive report. In this case, FT can be enabled "on demand" for the servers used in this event and can be disabled when the transaction is finished.

Creating and Administering Resource Pools

As you know, the four resources that you manage for all of your VMs are CPU, memory, disk, and network. You could manage each of these resources individually for every VM in your organization, but that would be doing it the hard way. Instead, you can combine VMs that share the same characteristics and resource needs into logical abstractions called Resource Pools and manage the aggregate total of the pools to satisfy the needs of the VMs that they contain. In addition, you can use Resource Pools to establish relative priorities between groups of VMs and give some VMs more priority to physical resources just because they reside in the appropriate Resource Pool.

In this section, I will discuss the Resource Pool hierarchy and its relationship to managing resources in your organization. In addition, I will define expandable reservations and discuss the advantages and disadvantages of configuring them. You will learn how to create, configure, and remove a Resource Pool. Also, you will learn how to add and remove VMs from and to a Resource Pool and how to clone a vApp that is part of a Resource Pool. I will also assist you in determining Resource Pool requirements for a given vSphere implementation. Finally, I will help you evaluate the appropriate shares, reservations, and limits for a Resource Pool based on VM workloads.

Describing the Resource Pool Hierarchy

The root of the Resource Pool hierarchy can be a standalone host or a DRS cluster. This "invisible" point of reference establishes the top of your Resource Pool hierarchy. When you create your first Resource Pool on a host or a DRS cluster, it extends the hierarchy and is called a *Parent pool*. You can create multiple Parent pools, as needed for your organization to identify departments or functions that you want to differentiate. In addition, you can create a Resource Pool within a Resource Pool, called a *Child pool*. If you create multiple Child pools within the same Parent pool, they are referred to as *siblings*, seriously! I know, I know. Figure 5-38 will help you make sense of all of this.

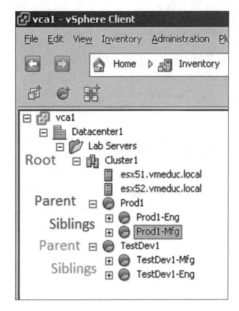

Figure 5-38 The Resource Pool Hierarchy

Establishing a hierarchy of Resource Pools allows you to manage your VMs in a much more organized fashion than without Resource Pools. If you plan this properly for your organization, you will be able to take full advantage of the benefits offered by Resource Pools. The specific benefits offered vary by organization, but in general these Resource Pool hierarchies allow the following:

- Flexible hierarchical organization.

- Isolation of resources between pools and sharing of resources within pools.

- Access control and delegation.

- Separation of resources from hardware.

- Management of sets of VMs running a multitier service. These VMs need each other and therefore need the same priorities to resources.

Defining the Expandable Reservation Parameter

The expandable reservation parameter will make a lot more sense toward the end of this section, when I have discussed shares, reservations, and limits for Resource Pools. Suffice it to say that an expandable reservation allows a pool to borrow resources from a pool that is higher in the hierarchy; for example, a Child pool can borrow from a Parent pool, and a Parent pool can borrow from the root pool. I will return to this topic briefly, after I have discussed shares, reservations, and limits for Resource Pools.

Creating/Removing a Resource Pool

I tell my students that you can create a Resource Pool by just "pretending like it exists already." In other words, since you are only creating a logical abstraction, you can just create the object in the inventory, name it, configure it, and immediately begin to use it. To create a Resource Pool, follow the steps outlined in Activity 5-7.

Activity 5-7 Creating a Resource Pool

1. Log on to your vSphere Client.

2. Select **Home** and then **Hosts and Clusters**.

3. Right-click the host or DRS cluster on which you would like to create the Resource Pool and select **New Resource Pool**. In this case, because the host is already a member of a cluster, the capability to create Resource Pools on the host itself has been removed (grayed out), as shown in Figure 5-39.

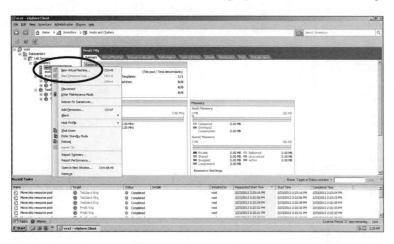

Figure 5-39 Resource Pool Creation on Clustered Hosts Is Disabled

Create a Resource Pool in the cluster by right-clicking the cluster and selecting **New Resource Pool**, as shown in Figure 5-40.

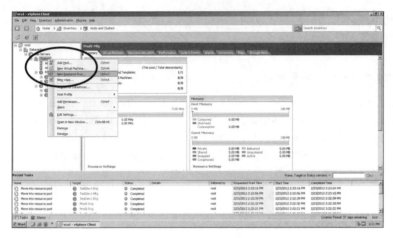

Figure 5-40   Creating a Resource Pool in a Cluster

4. Type a Name for your new Resource Pool and then set CPU Resources and Memory Resources if necessary. (I will discuss these settings in detail later in this chapter, in the section "Evaluating Appropriate Shares, Reservations and Limits for a Resource Pool Based on Virtual Machine Workloads."). Then click **OK**, as shown in Figure 5-41.

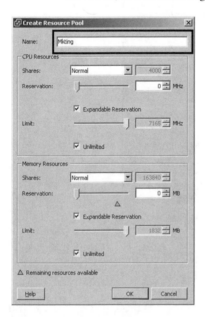

Figure 5-41   Naming a Resource Pool

5. Monitor your Recent Tasks pane and your vCenter inventory for the creation of your new Resource Pool.

Configuring Resource Pool Attributes

As I said earlier, Resource Pools allow you to manage the aggregate totals of resources allowed to the VMs in the pool. You can control the CPU Resources and the Memory Resources with regard to shares, reservation, limit, and expandability. You should understand the impact of each of these options on your Resource Pool. The following is a brief explanation of each of these Resource Pool attributes:

- **Shares:** These establish relative priority between sibling Resource Pools. They are both relative and proportional. They are relative in their settings of Low, Normal, High, or Custom. They are proportional in that how much of the physical resource they receive will depend on how many other sibling Resource Pools are competing for the same physical resource. (Later in this chapter, I will discuss each of the settings for shares, and their impact on the whole, in the section entitled "Evaluating Appropriate Shares, Reservations and Limits for a Resource Pool Based on Virtual Machine Workloads."

- **Reservation:** This is a guarantee that a fixed amount of certain resource is to be given to this Resource Pool. With this guarantee, the VMs in this pool do not have to compete with their shares for these resources. In essence, they are given a "head start" or advantage over the VMs in pools that do not have a reservation.

- **Limit:** This is a cap on the aggregate physical resources that can be consumed by the VMs in this Resource Pool. In might be useful if there are many large VMs that can "take turns" but you don't want all of them taking resources from the root at the same time. The limit "chokes" back the resources that the pool can use, even if the resources are not being consumed by other VMs in other pools. Because of this, you should be careful using limits. I will discuss this in more detail later in the section entitled "Evaluating Appropriate Shares, Reservations and Limits for a Resource Pool Based on Virtual Machine Workloads."

- **Expandable Reservation:** As I mentioned earlier, this refers to whether the Resource Pool can borrow the resources from its parent. I will discuss the impacts of this setting later in the section entilted "Evaluating Appropriate Shares, Reservations and Limits for a Resource Pool Based on Virtual Machine Workloads."

Adding/Removing Virtual Machines from a Resource Pool

Once you have created a Resource Pool, you can add VMs to it by simply dragging and dropping. Any VMs that are added to a Resource Pool will then share in the resources of the pool as configured in the Resource Pool's attributes. To remove a VM from a Resource Pool, simply drag it to another appropriate object (Resource Pool, host, cluster, or datacenter.) and drop it. In the case of an object higher in the hierarchy, you might have to answer the question as to which host.

Determining Resource Pool Requirements for a Given vSphere Implementation

Remember that the purpose of Resource Pools is to establish relative priorities within the same host or cluster of your vSphere. For most organizations this will be a real-world advantage. For example, the ability to give production VMs an edge when competing for physical resources with testing and development VMs could be assist you in managing your resources. Of course, you could also put the two types of VMs on entirely different clusters, but that would require that you use more hosts. I will discuss this in great depth in the next section.

Evaluating Appropriate Shares, Reservations, and Limits for Resource Pool Based on Virtual Machine Workloads

Each organization will define its own needs and uses for Resource Pools. By understanding what is possible, you will be able to see how you can use these configuration options to your advantage. For example, please evaluate the following scenario and then consider how you might use the same principles in your own organization. I'm going to use as few numbers and values as possible so that you can concentrate on the "philosophy" and not on the math.

Your cluster has multiple hosts and multiple VMs on each host. Your VMs can be divided into categories based on their function. Some of your VMs are servers that are used by end users for normal daily production. Others are servers used for testing and development, an important role, but not as urgent a function as the production servers.

To begin to control the resources given to your servers, you create two Resource Pools named Production and TestDev. You then drag each of your VMs into their respective Resource Pools. You configure the CPU and memory Shares on Production to High and the CPU and memory Shares on TestDev to Low. This gives Production an advantage for any resources for which it must compete with TestDev. Giving the Resource Pool an advantage will give all the VMs in the Resource Pool a potential advantage, as well, but it also depends on how many VMs are in the same pool and competing for resources.

In addition, so that Production has some CPU and memory guaranteed to it, for which it does not have to compete, you give Production a reservation in each category of CPU and memory. This reservation is a guarantee to the aggregate total of all VMs running in the Production Resource Pool.

Now, here's the really good thing. Even though Production is guaranteed those reservations, the resources are not "locked" to Production and only Production. In other words, if the VMs in Production are not using the resources, the VMs in TestDev can have them. This means that the resources won't be wasted, no matter what happens.

Your VMs that are in TestDev are powered on and off for testing purposes. Some of them are rather large and, if too many of them were to be powered on and run at the same time, they might have a negative effect on Production. Please don't misunderstand this concept. Production would still get its reservation and, due to its high shares, it would win the competition for the rest of resources more often than TestDev. However, TestDev might put up quite a fight for those resources. Because of this, you decide to throttle back the capability of TestDev by placing a limit on the amount of CPU and memory for which it's allowed to compete. You do this by setting a limit on CPU and memory in the settings of TestDev.

As you can see, the purpose in this scenario was to provide an appropriate balance of physical resources to VMs, not an equal one. Your organization might have the same needs (or totally different needs), so you should understand how you can use the Resource Pool configuration settings to your advantage. The math involved will be specific to the individual scenario, and it's all yours!

> **NOTE** Allowing an expandable reservation can add flexibility to your resource management. It's a great benefit as long as all the "good guys stay in charge." However, a rogue administrator or even a rogue application could create a VM that would consume all the remaining resources. If this happens, the only way to reclaim the resources would be to power down the offending VM. This might be made more complicated if the administrator or application configured restrictive permissions on the VM as well.

Cloning a vApp

As you might remember, we discussed vApps in Chapter 4, "Deploying and Administering Virtual Machine and vApps." In fact, we went into quite a bit of detail about them, including cloning them. The only reason that this topic has surfaced again is that I have vowed to follow the test blueprint to the letter. I don't see any difference in cloning a vApp that is part of a Resource Pool versus one that is not. That said, to clone a vApp, follow the steps outlined in Activity 5-8.

Activity 5-8 Cloning a vApp

1. Log on to your vSphere Client.

2. Select **Home** and then **Hosts and Clusters**.

3. Right-click the vApp that you want to clone and select **Clone**, as shown in Figure 5-42.

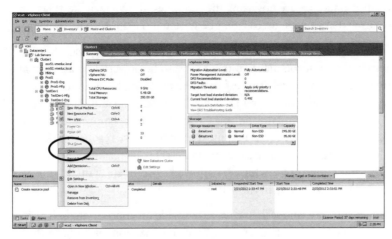

Figure 5-42 Cloning a vApp in a Resource Pool

4. Select the destination for your cloned vApp and click **Next**, and as shown in Figure 5-43.

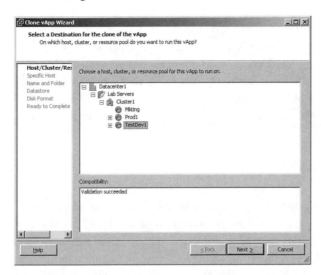

Figure 5-43 Selecting the Destination for a Cloned vApp

5. Type the name for your new vApp and select the datacenter, as shown Figure 5-44.

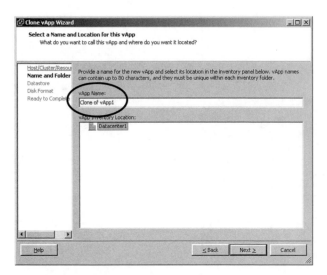

Figure 5-44   Naming a Cloned vApp

6. Choose the datastore or datastore cluster on which to place your cloned vApp and click **Next**, as shown in Figure 5-45.

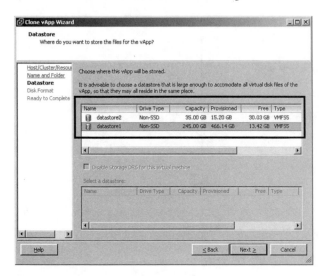

Figure 5-45   Choosing the Datastore or Datastore Cluster for the Cloned vApp

7. Choose the disk format for your cloned vApp, as shown in Figure 5-46, and then click **Next**.

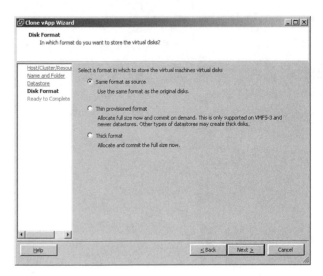

Figure 5-46   Choosing the Disk Format for the Cloned vApp

8. On the Ready to Complete page, review your settings and click **Finish**, as shown in Figure 5-47.

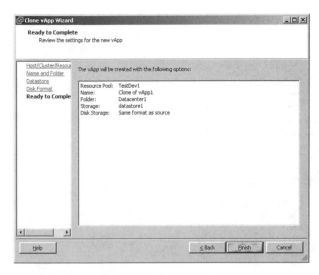

Figure 5-47   The Ready to Complete Page

9. Monitor your Recent Tasks pane and your vCenter inventory for the creation of your cloned vApp.

Migrating Virtual Machines

When you think about it, *migration* is not a technical term; birds migrate. To migrate means to move from one place to another. So, what is moving with regard to our studies? What is moving is either the state of the VMs, the files that the VMs use, or both. These moves can be done with the VMs powered off or powered on.

When the VMs are powered off, we refer the moving of their state and their files as *cold migration*. When they are powered on, we refer to the moving of their state as *vMotion* and the moving of their files as *Storage vMotion*. There are advantages and disadvantages to each option. To facilitate any option, you must have your vSphere configured properly.

I will first identify the ESXi host and VM requirements for vMotion and Storage vMotion. In addition, I will define and identify the requirements for Enhanced Storage vMotion. I will also discuss the new requirements (or actually lack of requirements) with regard to snapshots and vMotion/Storage vMotion. In addition, I will discuss how you can configure the VM swap file location. Finally, I will cover utilizing Storage vMotion techniques for other creative uses such as changing the disk type, changing the provisioning, and renaming the VM folders.

Identifying ESXi Host and Virtual Machine Requirements for vMotion and Storage vMotion

This is really too big a "bite to chew" all at once. I'm going to break this up into two discussions, one for vMotion and the other for Storage vMotion. Although some of the requirements are the same for both, not all of the requirements are the same.

ESXi and VM Requirements for vMotion

As you might remember, vMotion means moving the state of the VM from one host to another without disrupting the user. You may be wondering, "What exactly is the *state* of the VM?" The state of the VM consists of three components as follows:

- **Settings:** These are the settings that you will see on all the tabs if you right-click the VM and select **Edit Settings**. These are also the configuration settings as defined in the VMX file. These settings describe and all of its attributes and virtual hardware.

- **Disk:** These are all the VMDK files and virtual compatibility RDMs that make up the source volumes for the VM.

- **Memory:** This is the active memory on the VM at the time that you are performing the vMotion.

Each of these components of the state of the VM is handled in a very different manner. The settings state is very simple to move, or actually re-create, on another host. The disk state cannot be re-created in the short amount of time allowed, therefore we have to use shared storage. The memory state must be gradually copied over to the destination host so that when the guest OS on the VM is quiesced, the OS "wakes up" on the destination host with the same memory it had on the source host.

As I mentioned before, we are fooling the guest OS on the VM into thinking that it hasn't migrated at all. This means that all the components of the host and the VM must be configured properly to pull off the trick. The requirements for the host with regard to vMotion are as follows:

- Source and destination hosts must both have visibility to shared storage used by the VM on Fibre Channel, iSCSI, or NAS.

- All hosts must have access to at least a 1Gbps Ethernet network.

- Source and destination hosts must have access to the same physical network or the same VLAN.

- Source and destination hosts must have VMkernel ports configured on a vSS or a vDS that are enabled for vMotion and have a proper IP configuration.

- Host CPUs must be the same vendor and family (for example, Intel Xeon) and must share the same CPUID unless configured otherwise in Advanced settings or by using EVC. (I will discuss these options in the next section.)

Just as the hosts must be configured properly for vMotion, the VMs must also be configured properly. If you remember what you are trying to pull off here, you will see that you can't have anything that the VM can see on the source host that it won't be able to "see" when it gets to the destination host. With that in mind, the following are the VM requirements with regard to vMotion:

- VMs must not have a connection to an internal switch (zero uplink adapters).

- VMs must not have a connection to a virtual device with a local image mounted (locally mounted CD, floppy drive, or ISO).

- VMs must not have CPU affinity configured.

- If the VMs swap file is not accessible to the destination host, vMotion must be able to create a swap file accessible to the destination host before migration can begin. (This option can be advantageous when using SSD hard drives locally on a host.)

- If the VM uses an RDM, the RDM must be accessible to the destination host as well.

NOTE   These are considered the main requirements and the ones to know for the test. For a complete list of all vMotion requirements, see the *vSphere Datacenter Administration Guide* at http://www.vmware.com/support/pubs.

ESXi and VM Requirements for Storage vMotion

The main thing about Storage vMotion that I want you to understand very clearly is that the VM's state doesn't move at all! What moves (or rather are copied) are the files that the VM is using. In other words, when you use Storage vMotion, you have a running VM (in our case, a server) that continues to operate while the files that it requires to operate are moved to another physical location. When the migration happens, the OS on the running server is unaware that it has taken place at all. The advantages of this technology are the following:

- You can perform storage maintenance and reconfiguration, without VM downtime.

- You can redistribute storage loads, without VM downtime.

- You can evacuate physical storage about to be retired and perform storage tiering, without VM downtime.

Another really cool fact is that Storage vMotion is completely storage type independent. That means that you can move files that are on Fibre Channel SAN LUNs to NAS (for an extreme example) while the server is running without any disruption to the OS or the user. This is really just the beginning, and I will discuss some other creative things that you can do with Storage vMotion later in this section. The bottom line is that having to tell users that they won't be able to get onto the system because you have to do some hardware maintenance to the drives should now be a thing of the past.

NOTE   The inner workings of Storage vMotion are very different from those of previous versions of vSphere. Because their specifics are not listed on the test blueprint, I am not covering them in this book. To get more details about Storage vMotion for vSphere 5, you should see the *vSphere Datacenter Administration Guide* at http://www.vmware.com/support/pubs.

Identifying Enhanced vMotion Compatibility CPU Requirements

When you initiate the use of vMotion or a migration of a suspended machine (still running a CPU instruction set), the wizard checks the destination host for compatibility. The CPU feature set that was detected when the VM was powered on to the source host is checked against what will be available on the destination host. The CPU feature set includes all of the following:

- Host CPU vendor, family, and model

- Settings in the BIOS that might disable CPU features

- The ESX/ESXi version running on the host

- The VMs virtual hardware version (for example, 4, 7, or 8)

- The VM's guest OS

If the feature set is determined to be different on the destination host than on the source host, the system lets you know with a detailed error message if there are compatibility problems that will prevent the successful migration of the VM. You can hide some of the instruction set from the guest OS and satisfy the wizard by masking the CPUID in the advanced settings of each VM on the host, as shown in Figure 5-48.

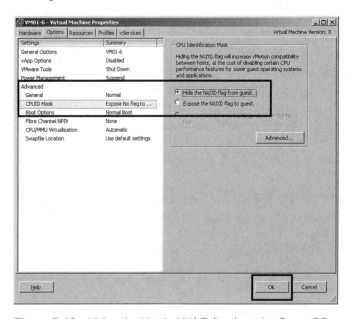

Figure 5-48   Hiding the Host's NX/XD flag from the Guest OS

An easier way to improve CPU compatibility between hosts of varying feature sets is to configure Enhanced vMotion Compatibility (EVC) on your cluster. EVC ensures that all hosts in your cluster present the same feature set to VMs, even if the actual CPUs on the host differ from each other. When you configure EVC, you are telling all host processors to present a feature set of the baseline processor. This feature set is referred to as the *EVC mode*. As you might remember from earlier in this chapter, you can configure EVC in your cluster, but only if certain compatibility requirements are met first. The following are the compatibility requirements for EVC:

- All VMs that are running on the cluster with a feature set greater than that of the EVC mode you intend to enable must be must be powered off or migrated out of the cluster before EVC is enabled.

- All hosts in the cluster must have CPUs from a single vendor, either AMD or Intel (not both).

- All hosts in the cluster must be running ESX/ESXi 3.5 Update 2 or later.

- All hosts in the cluster must be connected to the vCenter System.

- All hosts in the cluster must have advanced CPU features, such as hardware virtualization support (AMD-V or Intel VT) and AMD No eXecute (NX) or Intel eXecute Disable (XD), enabled in the BIOS if they are available.

- All hosts in the cluster should be configured for vMotion.

- All hosts in the cluster must have supported CPUs for the EVC mode you want to enable.

Any new host, added to the cluster after EVC is enabled, must also meet these requirements.

NOTE   Because all hosts and all future hosts must share the same baseline, you should choose the lowest EVC mode that is common to all hosts in the cluster, if your goal is to be as flexible as possible when adding new hosts. If your goal is to provide as many features as possible for each CPU, you should use the highest EVC mode that is common to all hosts in the cluster. It is a best practice to favor additional performance versus backward compatibility.

Identifying Snapshot Requirements for vMotion/Storage vMotion Migration

This is kind of a funny topic to discuss at this point, for two reasons. One, I haven't discussed VM snapshots yet, but I will later in this chapter in the section entitled

"Identifying Snapshot Requirements." Two, there aren't any snapshot requirements anymore with regard to vMotion or Storage vMotion. Let's address these issues briefly one at a time.

Basically, a *snapshot* is a capture of the state of a VM at a specific point in time. As you should remember, the state can include settings, disk, and memory. Until vSphere 5.0, it was important to know that you could use vMotion to migrate VMs that had VM snapshots but that you could not use Storage vMotion to move VM files. This was because the technologies that worked with VM snapshots and those that worked with Storage vMotion were "oil and water"; in other words, they didn't work well together. With vSphere 5.0, the technologies and methods used to Storage vMotion VM files have changed completely, so you can use Storage vMotion on VMs that have snapshots. If you think about it, this had to be done if Storage DRS was going to be used. Otherwise, how would the system automatically move VM files from one datastore to another on a datastore cluster if the administrator was using snapshots at the same time?

Migrating Virtual Machines Using vMotion/Storage vMotion

Again, I'm going to break this objective up into two objectives because I want to stress the fact that these are two very different features in vSphere. In fact, as you might remember from Chapter 1, "Planning, Installing, Configuring, and Upgrading vCenter Server and VMware ESXi," Storage vMotion is not even included with the Standard vSphere license, but vMotion is included. I will first discuss the process of migrating VMs using vMotion, and then I will cover the process of migrating VM files using Storage vMotion.

Migrating a VM Using vMotion

When I say that we are migrating the VM, I am saying that the state of the VM is moving from one host to another host. When I do this with the VM powered on, then by definition it's vMotion. I've heard some people use this term improperly by saying that "We vMotioned them but we powered them down first." You should understand clearly that what they did was a cold migration, not an actual vMotion.

That said, you know that DRS uses vMotion to balance loads automatically, but what if you want to initiate the process yourself? If your hosts, your VMs, and your network meet all the requirements for vMotion, the process is easy. For example to vMotion a VM from one host to another on the same cluster, follow the steps outlined in Activity 5-9.

Activity 5-9 Migrating a VM Using vMotion

1. Log on to your vSphere client.

2. Select **Home** and then **Hosts and Clusters**.

3. Right-click the powered-on VM that you want to vMotion and select **Migrate**, as shown in Figure 5-49.

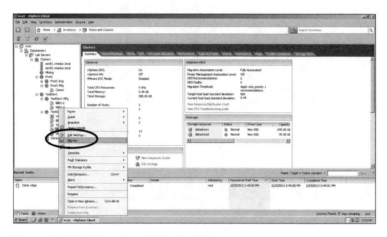

Figure 5-49   Migrating a VM with vMotion

4. On the Select Migration Type page, select the radio button for **Change Host**, and then click **Next**, as shown in Figure 5-50.

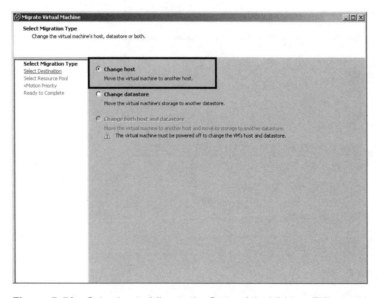

Figure 5-50   Selecting to Migrate the State of the VM to a Different Host

5. Select the destination host on your inventory and wait for the compatibility check to complete, as shown in Figure 5-51, and then click **Next**.

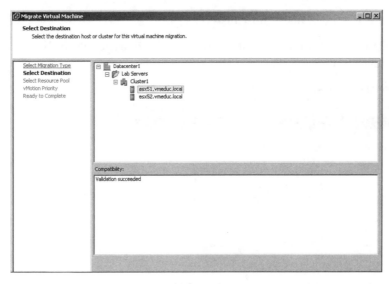

Figure 5-51   Destination Host and Compatibility Check

6. Choose any Resource Pool or vApp in which you would like to place the VM (or just leave it in the cluster), and then click **Next**, as shown in Figure 5-52.

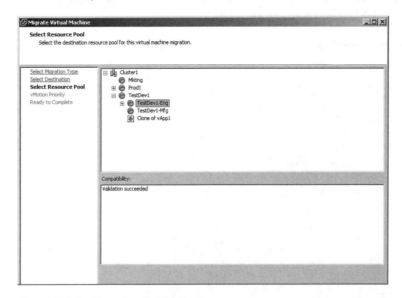

Figure 5-52   Choosing the Destination

7. Choose between High priority and Standard priority and click **Next**, as shown in Figure 5-53. High priority will reserve all the necessary resources are available on the destination before proceeding. Standard priority will proceed without verifying that the resources are available. High priority is the preferred method when you are using ESX/ESXi 4.1 or later.

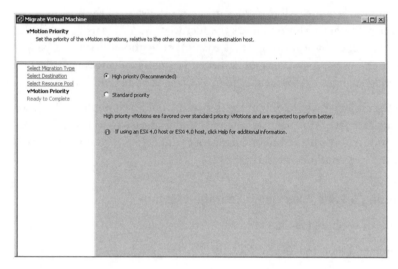

Figure 5-53   Choosing High Priority or Standard Priority vMotion

8. Review your settings and click **Next**, as shown in Figure 5-54.

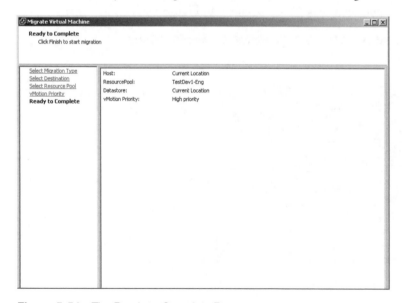

Figure 5-54   The Ready to Complete Page

9. Monitor your Recent Tasks pane and your inventory for the results of the vMotion.

Migrating a VM's Files Using Storage vMotion

As I mentioned before, Storage vMotion does not move the state of the VM from one host to another. Storage vMotion moves the files that the VM is using, while it's using them, from one physical storage area to another, without disrupting your VM's OS or your end users. As I discussed earlier, this greatly enhances your flexibility when making changes to storage due to growth, ages of disk, and so on.

It's such a cool technology that you might think that it would be complicated to use, but you would not be correct. In fact, Storage vMotion is as easy to use as vMotion. To Storage vMotion a VM's files from one datastore connected to your vSphere to another, follow the steps outlined in Activity 5-10.

Activity 5-10 Migrating a VM's Files Using Storage vMotion

1. Log on to your vSphere Client.

2. Select **Home** and then **Hosts and Clusters**.

3. Right-click the powered-on VM that you want to Storage vMotion and select **Migrate**.

4. On the Select Migration Type page, select the radio button for **Change Datastore,** and then click **Next**, as shown in Figure 5-55.

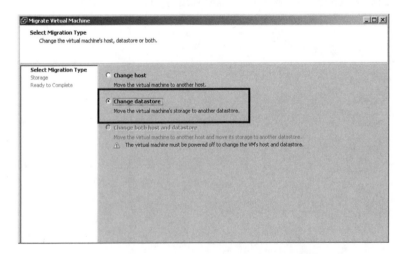

Figure 5-55   Selecting to Migrate the VM's Files to a Different Datastore

5. Select the destination datastore on your inventory and the disk format that you, wait for validation of compatibility, and click **Next**, as shown in Figure 5-56.

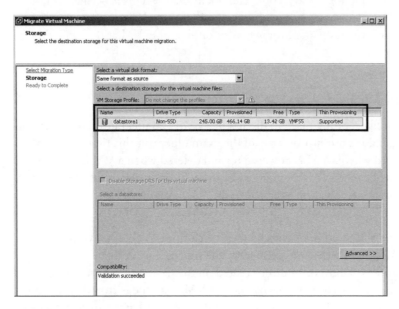

Figure 5-56   Selecting the Destination Datastore

6. Review your settings and click **Next**, as shown in Figure 5-57.

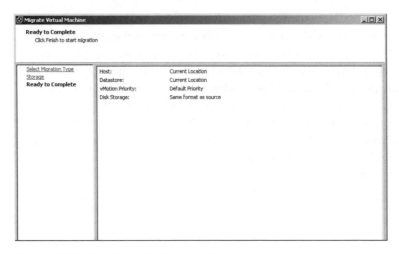

Figure 5-57   The Ready to Complete Page

7. Monitor your Recent Tasks pane and your inventory for the results of the Storage vMotion.

NOTE   You might have noticed that the capability to move the state of a VM and the datastore at the same time was "grayed out" and not available. This is because you cannot move the state of VM and its files concurrently if the VM is powered on. In other words, you can't vMotion and Storage vMotion the same VM at the same time.

Configuring Virtual Machine Swap File Location

This might seem like a funny place to discuss the VM swap file, but there is method to my madness, and it's not just because of the exam blueprint this time. The VM swap file is created when a VM is powered on and deleted when a VM is powered off. Its size is equal to the available memory of the VM (what the guest OS is told that is has) minus the reservation assigned to the VM. I discussed the VM swap file in Chapter 4, when I identified how it is used by VMs.

So, what does the VM swap file have to do with vMotion? Well, for vMotion to succeed, the VM swap file that was created by the source host must be visible to the destination host (shared) or must be created on the destination host before the migration can begin. This usually means that the VM swap file is stored in the same location with the other VM files. Now, you might think that having to create a new swap file would slow down migration significantly, and you would be right, unless you used the right kind of drives for the VM swap files. What is slower than RAM but still much faster than conventional disk? That's right, solid state drives (SSDs).

If you are using local SSDs, you might very well want to allow the host to provide the swap file locally. This could provide better performance in the event that the swap file is used when memory is in serious contention. If you are using conventional disk, you should make sure that the datastore containing the swap file is shared by the source and destination hosts; otherwise, your vMotion performance will be degraded. You can configure this option on the cluster as a default and then you can make changes further down in your hierarchy by configuring it on the host and even on the individual VM. Figures 5-58, 5-59, and 5-60 show the three places where you can configure your VM swap files.

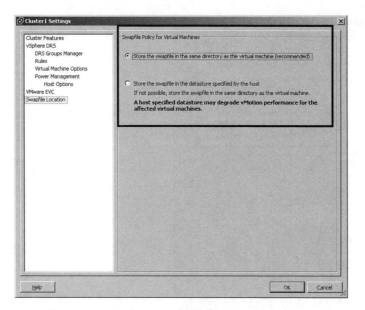

Figure 5-58   Configuring the VM Swap File Setting in the Cluster

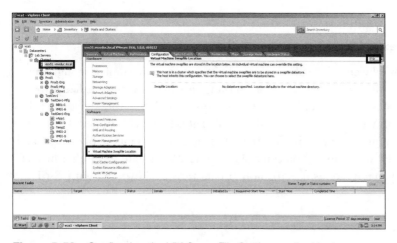

Figure 5-59   Configuring the VM Swap File Setting on the Host

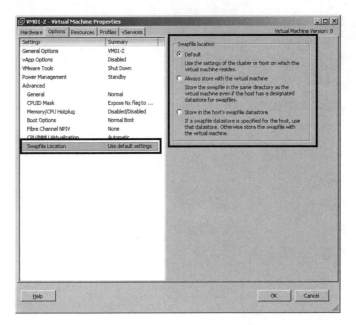

Figure 5-60 Configuring the VM Swap File Setting on the VM

Migrating a Powered-Off or Suspended Virtual Machine

Once more, this objective is really two objectives, but they are similar enough this time that I'll handle them as one. The main thing that I want you to realize is that a suspended VM is still running a CPU instruction set and therefore must meet the CPU compatibility requirements just like a VM that is being vMotioned. Other than that, migrating a VM that is powered off or suspended is incredibly simple and there are very few limitations. You can even migrate a VMs state to another host at the same time you migrate its files to another datastore, as shown in Figure 5-61.

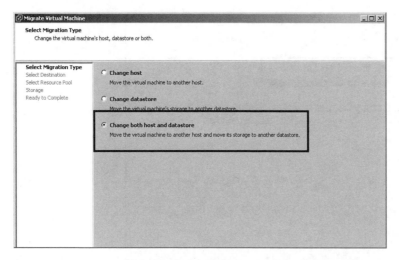

Figure 5-61   Cold Migrating the VM Host and Datastore Simultaneously

Utilizing Storage vMotion Techniques

I have already discussed the main reason that Storage vMotion was created: to make it easier to move the VMs files from one datastore to another while the VM was powered on. This is likely the main reason that you will use Storage vMotion in your vCenter. However, you might find that some of the options that are given to you when you Storage vMotion can come in handy if you just need to make a change, but really don't need to move the VMs files at all. In addition, one of the side effects might interest you as well.

As you might have noticed when we did the Storage vMotion exercise earlier in this chapter, you were given the choice of virtual disk format on the Storage page of the wizard, as shown in Figure 5-62. What if you just want to change the virtual disk on a VM from thick-provisioned eager zeroed to thin-provisioned (for example)? Could you move the VM files to another location just to make that change? Yes you could; in fact, any change in disk provisioning is possible. Then, if you want them back where they were, you can simply Storage vMotion again. Remember that you are not disrupting the user, at least not directly.

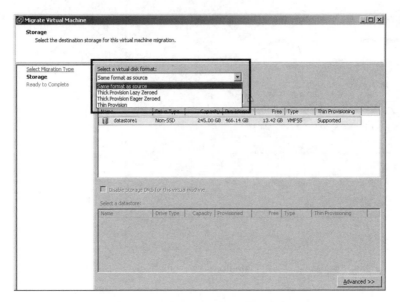

Figure 5-62   Changing Disk Format During Storage vMotion

Here's another example of using Storage vMotion creatively by taking advantage of a side effect of moving the VM files. Suppose that you have decided to change the display name of a VM so that it shows up differently in your inventory. You should know that just changing the display name does not change the VM filenames that are in the datastore. If you Storage vMotion the VM files to another datastore, the VM's folder name is changed to match that of the new display name that you've given the VM. That could be a convenience to keep you from being confused later on, but the files within the folder (at the time of this writing) are not changed. Also, the NetBIOS name and hostname are not changed, and you are on your own there. In fact, that's a good reason to seriously consider your options before you change a display name on a VM.

NOTE   Before you use Storage vMotion, you should verify that you have the available resources with regard to your storage network and CPU. Also, it's not a best practice to perform Storage vMotions during peak times.

Backing Up and Restoring Virtual Machines

Here's a question for you. What percentage of your VMs are software? Hopefully you answered 100%. Because 100% of your VMs are software, and because they are the type of software that you really don't want to take a chance on losing, you should perform regular backups on your VM files. In this section, I will discuss many different aspects regarding backing up and restoring VMs.

I will begin by identifying snapshot requirements as they relate to backing up and restoring VMs. You will learn how to create, delete, and consolidate VM snapshots. In addition, I will discuss VMware Data Recovery (VDR), which is a backup appliance designed primarily for small to medium-sized companies. You will learn how to install and configure VDR as well as how to create a backup job using the VDR appliance and an add-on named File Level Restore (FLR). Finally, I will examine your options with regard to backups and assist you in determining the most appropriate backup solution for your vSphere implementation.

Identifying Snapshot Requirements

First, you should understand that even though we are discussing snapshots in a section regarding backups, *snapshots* should never be regarded as *backups*. That said, taking a snapshot is often used by backup software as part of the process of creating a backup. This is because backing up the snapshot is efficient and allows for a static image of the VM. In addition, vSphere can provide an incremental backup mechanism called *changed block tracking*, which saves backup time and disk storage space. Typically, after a backup is performed from the snapshot, the snapshot is deleted.

Creating/Deleting/Consolidating Virtual Machine Snapshots

If you wanted to perform all the backup steps yourself, rather than use third-party backup software, you could. You would first have to understand how to create snapshots. Once you created them, you could copy the snapshots for the backup and finally delete them. In this section, I will cover the process of creating, deleting, and consolidating snapshots. You can use what you learn here for snapshots used for backups or just to create snapshots when testing software.

When you create a snapshot, you create a static capture of the VM at a specific point in time. The -flat.vmdk file on your VM is in essence "frozen," and a delta.vmdk file begins to record changes. Every time you take another snapshot, a descriptor is used to note the amount of the delta.vmdk file that should be used in addition to the -flat.vmdk file to revert to a specific point.. The -flat.vmdk file and a portion of the delta.vmdk file can then be used to revert to any point in time as defined by the descriptor file with an extension of .vmsd. If you have chosen to include VM memory in your snapshot, another file with an extension of .vmsn is also created. Including memory with a snapshot takes longer but you can then revert the VM to a previous state without it having to be powered off and restarted. If you don't have memory included in a snapshot, when you revert to a previous state, the VM will restart and "make its own memories."

Now that you have a brief understanding of what happens when you take a snapshot, let's look at the process of taking one. You can use this same process to take snapshots for backups or for any other use. To create a snapshot of your VM, follow the steps outlined in Activity 5-11.

Activity 5-11 Creating a VM Snapshot

1. Log on to your vSphere Client.

2. Select **Home** and then **Hosts and Clusters**.

3. Right-click the VM that you want to snapshot and select **Snapshot**, and then **Take Snapshot**, as shown in Figure 5-63.

Figure 5-63   Taking a VM Snapshot

4. Type a name and description for your snapshot (usually defined by its purpose), and then choose whether to snapshot the VM memory and whether to quiesce (quiet or pause) the guest file system. It's best to quiesce the guest file system if the snapshot will be used as part of a backup because it will allow you to get a static image of the VM. Finally, click **OK**, as shown in Figure 5-64.

Figure 5-64   Naming a Snapshot and Selecting Options

5. Monitor the progress of your snapshot in the Recent Tasks pane, as shown in Figure 5-65. Snapshots with memory will take longer to complete, but you can revert to them without restarting the VM.

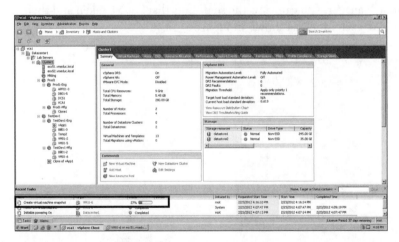

Figure 5-65   Monitoring Snapshot Progress

6. When the snapshot is complete, right-click the same VM and select **Snapshot**, and then **Snapshot Manager**, as shown in Figure 5-66.

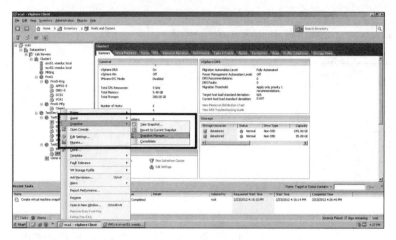

Figure 5-66   Entering Snapshot Manager

7. In Snapshot Manager, you can view the snapshots that you've taken and their
relationship to each other, as shown in Figure 5-67.

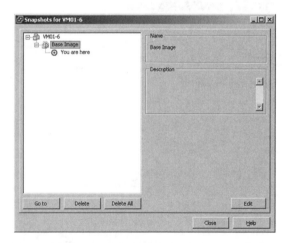

Figure 5-67   Snapshot Manager

Now that you know how to create snapshots, it's important that you know how to
delete them as well. Leaving snapshots on a VM for long periods of time can consume the rest of your disk, because the delta.vmdk file will continue to grow with
every activity that happens on the disk and can take up all of the allocated space on
the drive. Because of this, it's important that you know how to delete snapshots and
how to consolidate them when necessary.

You might think that deleting a snapshot would be as simple as just selecting it and selecting **Delete**, and you would be half right. You should understand that what really happens to the effect of the snapshot will depend on where the You Are Here indicator is when you delete the snapshot. The You Are Here indicator is the current state of the VM and its position relative to the snapshot makes all the difference. To illustrate this point, I will use a series of snapshots that you can see in Figure 5-68.

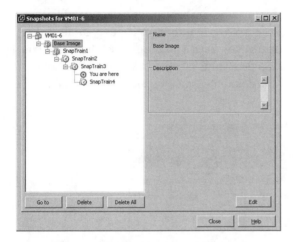

Figure 5-68   A Series of Snapshots

As you can see, I took four snapshots of VM01-6 in addition to my Base Image snapshot, SnapTrain1–SnapTrain4. I made subtle changes to the configuration before I took each snapshot in succession. The specific changes that I made are not important, just the fact that I made some changes. (If you were doing this, maybe you added some software or changed a setting.) For contrast, both the Base Image and SnapTrain1 included the memory, as indicated by the green arrow. SnapTrain2, through SnapTrain4 did not include the memory. After I took SnapTrain4, I reverted back to SnapTrain3 by selecting it and clicking **Go to** and then restarting VM01-6.

If I were to position my mouse pointer on SnapTrain4 and select **Delete**, what would happen? You may have guessed that SnapTrain4 would simply be deleted. Because it is after the You Are Here indicator, you would be right. SnapTrain4 would be gone and forgotten. Any configuration that it and only it contained would be lost.

Now, if I were to position my mouse pointer on any of the snapshots before the You Are Here indicator and select **Delete**, what would happen with them? The answer is, the snapshots would be gone but their effect would be committed to the current state of the VM. In fact, if I were to select **Delete All**, no matter where my mouse pointer happened to be, all the snapshots would be deleted, but the ones after the You Are Here indicator would be deleted and forgotten while the ones before the You Are Here indicator would be deleted but "remembered." In other words, any configuration changes that they included would have already been rolled in to the current state of the VM. Just deleting the snapshot would not change that fact.

I hope this simple scenario has helped you to see the true nature of VM snapshots and helped you realize that they are not meant to be kept around like a template. In fact, because of a known issue that causes a VM's snapshots to fail to commit and therefore do away with the delta.vmdk file, you have a new tool in vSphere that you can use to consolidate the snapshots. To determine whether a VM has snapshots that need consolidating, you can add the column to your Virtual Machines tab, as shown in Figure 5-69.

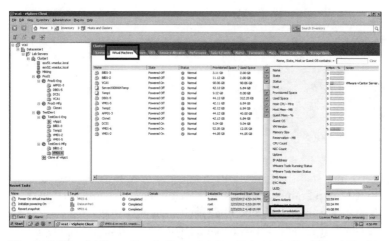

Figure 5-69 Adding a Needs Consolidation Column to the Virtual Machines Tab

A simple Yes or No will indicate whether the VM needs consolidation. To consolidate snapshots on the VM, you should right-click and select **Consolidate**, as shown in Figure 5-70.

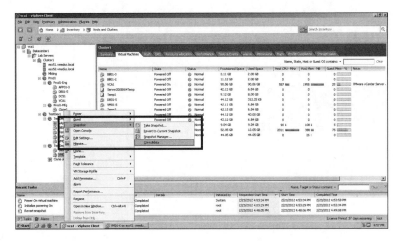

Figure 5-70   Consolidating the VMs Snapshots

Installing and Configuring VMware Data Recovery

VMware Data Recovery (VDR) is a backup appliance built on the VMware vStorage API for data protection. You can use it to create backups of VMs without interrupting their use. It also supports deduplication to remove redundant data and make more efficient use of disk space. It is integrated with vCenter Server, allowing you to centralize the scheduling of backup jobs. The deduplication datatstores can be VMDKs, RDMs, or CIFS shares. You can have a maximum of two deduplication datastores per appliance. If they are VMDKs or RDMs, they can each be up to 1TB in size. If they are CIFS shares, they are limited to 500GB in size.

It is primarily designed for small to medium-sized organizations; because each backup job can contain a maximum of 100 VMs, you can backup only 8 VMs simultaneously. In addition, each vCenter can manage up to 10 VDR appliances, each with 100 VMs. The installation of VDR can be described in three major steps as follows:

1. Install the VDR client plug-in on your vSphere Client.

2. Install the VDR backup appliance on an ESX/ESXi 3.5 Update 2 or later host.

3. Add a hard disk to the backup appliance. You can download an ISO file from http://www.vmware.com and burn a CD with all the files that you need, as shown in Figure 5-71.

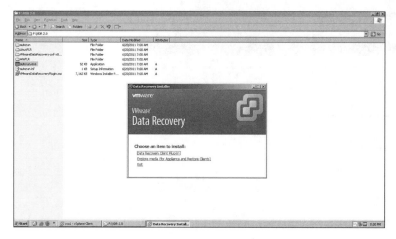

Figure 5-71　Files for Installing VDR

Creating a Backup Job with VMware Data Recovery

Once you have completed the installation and configuration of VDR, you are ready to create a backup job. You should find VDR under Solutions and Applications in your Home panel. From there, it's just a matter of connecting to the virtual appliance and selecting the VMs to backup. When you have properly installed the VDR appliance and then connected to it with your vSphere Client and the enabled plug-in, you can simply choose VMs on the network to backup, just as you would any other files, as shown in Figure 5-72.

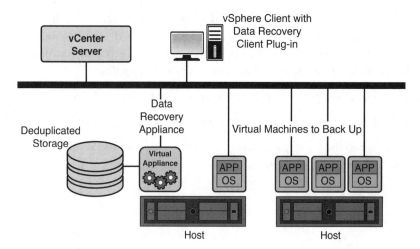

Figure 5-72　VDR at a Glance

Performing a Test and Live Full/File-Level Restore with VMware Data Recovery

As you may have noticed in Figure 5-71, the installation files for VDR include a WindowsFLR folder and a LinuxFLR folder. These are additional tools that are not required for the proper functioning of VDR. They do, however, provide some nice additional features such as the ability to restore individual files from a backed up VM instead of the entire VM.

To use the FLR in Windows, follow the steps outlined in Activity 5-12.

Activity 5-12 Using FLR in Windows

1. Insert the Data Recovery installation CD.

2. Click **Explore Media**.

3. Copy the FLR client executable from the installation CD at *Drive Letter*:\
   WinFLR\VMwareRestoreClient.exe to the Windows virtual machine that will use the FLR client.

The FLR client is now ready to use on the VM.

To use FLR in Linux, follow the steps outlined in Activity 5-13.

Activity 5-13 Using FLR in Linux

1. Insert the Data Recovery installation CD.

2. Install FUSE 2.5 and LVM, add them to your PATH, then copy the FLR client archive Linux/FLR/VMwareRestoreClient.tgz on the installation CD to the virtual machine that will use the FLR client.

3. Extract the archive using **tar xzvf VMwareRestoreClient.tgz**.

4. Navigate to the VMwareRestoreClient directory and invoke by executing **./
   VdrFileRestore**. (Ensure that you use VdrFileRestore rather than vdrFileRe-store; these are two separate executables.)

Determining Appropriate Backup Solution for a Given vSphere Implementation

If your organization has more than 100 server VMs, the chances are good that you are using some type of third-party backup solution. There are a good number of them and they usually offer some nice features such a data deduplication, sometimes even at the source. VMware is more than happy to offer the application programming interfaces (APIs) so that you can use all the latest backup software that is designed for VMs. However, if you have a small organization with fewer than 100 server VMs, VDR might be just the tool for you to provide a relatively inexpensive backup solution that includes deduplication of data at the destination.

Patching and Updating ESXi and Virtual Machines

Someone once said that the only constant is change. This certainly applies to anything in today's IT world, including your virtual datacenter. In this section, I will discuss the two primary tools that you can use to keep up with changes with regard to your ESXi hosts and your VMs: VMware Update Manager and Host Profiles. I will discuss many specific aspects of each tool and how you can use each of them assist in managing your vSphere.

More specifically, I will identify patching requirements for ESXi hosts and VMs. I will then discuss creating, editing, and removing a host profile from an ESXi host. In addition, I will discuss attaching and applying a host profile to an ESXi host or cluster. This will include using a host profile to perform compliance scanning and remediation of an ESXi host.

I will then turn my attention to VMware Update Manager (VUM). I will discuss installing and configuring VUM, including configuring patch download options. In addition, I will discuss creating, editing, and deleting an Update Manager baseline to an ESXi host or cluster. Finally, I will cover scanning and remediating ESXi hosts and VMs using VUM, as well as staging ESXi host updates to run at a predetermined time in the future.

Identifying Patching Requirements for ESXi Hosts and Virtual Machine Hardware/Tools

It's important to keep your ESXi hosts up to date with the latest patches. This will give you the most capability and it will also enhance the security of your systems. In addition, it's important to keep VMs up to date. In our context, most (if not all) of your VMs are servers, so keeping them up to date will enhance the user experience for many users. With this in mind, you should upgrade your VMware Tools with any host upgrade and you should upgrade your virtual machine hardware if there is an option or feature on the newer hardware that is not supported on your current hardware.

Creating/Editing/Removing a Host Profile from an ESXi Host

Installing the software for an ESXi host is the easy part, which I already discussed in Chapter 1. After you have installed the host, the configuration steps that are required can be time-consuming and complicated. They might include configuration settings that relate to CPU, memory, storage, networking, licensing, DNS and routing, firewall settings, and so on. Because you really want your ESXi hosts to be consistent, especially if they are in the same clusters, wouldn't it be nice to be able to configure a "reference host" and then use that as a baseline to configure the other hosts? This is exactly what you can do with Host Profiles in vSphere, if you have an Enterprise Plus license. In addition, any fields that are specific to one host can be completed by prompting the user for input. Once the user has supplied the information, an answer file is created and stored in the Auto Deploy cache and the vCenter Server host object.

After you have configured and tested your reference host, follow the steps outlined in Activity 5-14.

Activity 5-14 Creating a Host Profile

1. Log on to your vSphere Client.

2. Select **Home** and then, under Management, select **Host Profiles**, as shown in Figure 5-73. You must have an Enterprise Plus license to use host profiles.

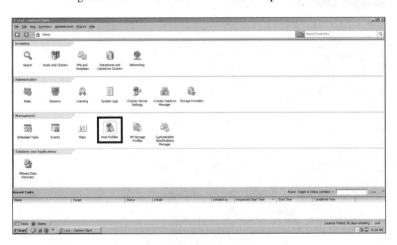

Figure 5-73 Using Host Profiles

3. Click the **Create Profile** link in the upper-left corner, as shown in Figure 5-74.

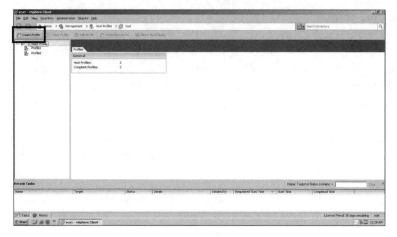

Figure 5-74 Creating a New Host Profile

4. From the Create Profile Wizard, select the option to **Create Profile from Existing Host** and click **Next**, as shown in Figure 5-75.

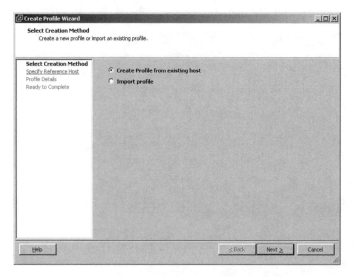

Figure 5-75 Creating a Profile from an Existing Host

5. Expand the inventory and select the host you want to designate as the reference host, and then click **Next**, as shown Figure 5-76.

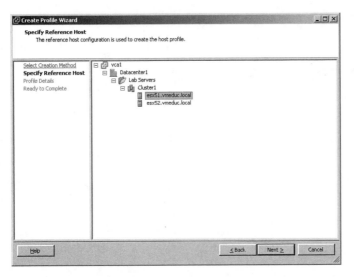

Figure 5-76   Selecting the Reference Host

6. Type the name of your new profile and (optionally) a description, as shown in Figure 5-77.

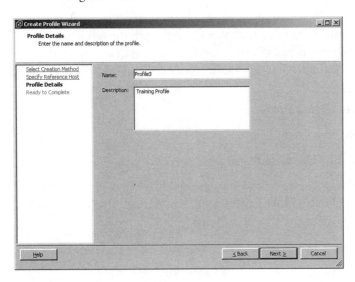

Figure 5-77   Naming Your Profile

7. Review the summary information and click **Finish**, as shown in Figure 5-78. Your new profile will appear on the list under Host Profiles.

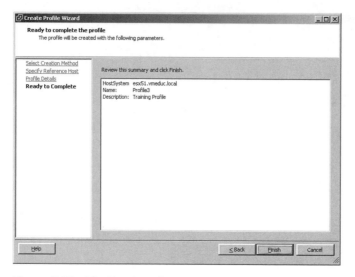

Figure 5-78   The Ready to Complete Page

Attach/Apply a Host Profile to an ESXi Host or Cluster

Just creating a profile doesn't change anything; you have to attach it to a host or cluster and apply it for it to change the host. You should attach the profile to the host or cluster by opening Hosts and Cluster view first. To attach and apply your profile to a host or cluster, follow the steps outlined in Activity 5-15.

Activity 5-15 Attach/Apply a Host Profile

1. Log on to your vSphere Client.

2. Select **Home** and then **Hosts and Clusters**.

3. Right-click the host or cluster to which you would like to attach the profile (in this case, esx52), and select **Host Profile** and then **Manage Profile,** as shown in Figure 5-79.

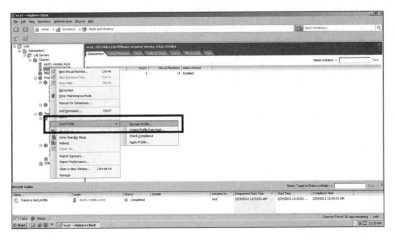

Figure 5-79   Managing Host Profiles

4. In the Attach Profile dialog box, select the profile to attach and click **OK**, as shown in Figure 5-80.

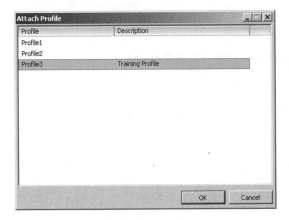

Figure 5-80   Attaching Profile to a Host

5. Right-click the host and select **Enter Maintenance Mode**. You will either vMotion, cold migrate, or shut down all the VMs on the host while you are applying the profile. This will be required to enter Maintenance Mode.

6. To apply the attached profile, select **Home > Management > Host Profiles**.

7. Select the profile that you want to apply to the host, and then open the Hosts and Clusters tab. A list of hosts and clusters with that profile attached to them will appear, click the host or cluster to which you will apply to profile and click **Apply Profile**, as shown in Figure 5-81.

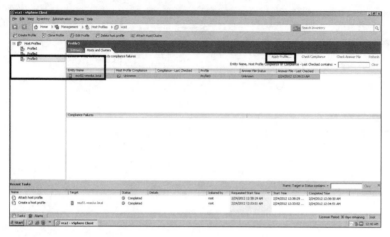

Figure 5-81 Applying a Profile to a Host

8. Follow the wizard and answer any questions that it asks with regard to the profile, as shown in Figure 5-82, click **Next** repeatedly (if necessary), and finally click **Finish**. You can take the host out of Maintenance Mode once the process is finished.

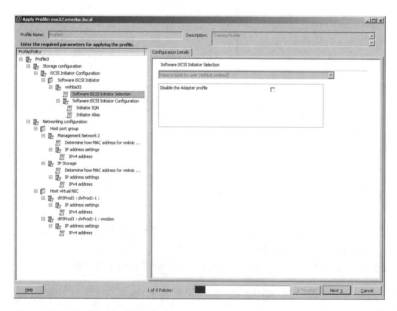

Figure 5-82 The Profile Wizard

Performing Compliance Scanning and Remediation of an ESXi Host Using Host Profiles

Even if Host Profiles could only be used for initial configuration of hosts, it would still be quite handy to have around, but you can also use it assure that hosts stay in ongoing compliance with a reference host or baseline. This means that errant configurations in your hosts can be quickly and easily remediated, even if the specific configurations are not discovered until after you run your Host Profile's compliance check.

To check whether a host is still in compliance with the profile to which it is attached, follow the steps outlined in Activity 5-16.

Activity 5-16 Checking Host Compliance to an Attached Host Profile

1. Log on to your vSphere Client.

2. Select **Home** and then **Hosts and Clusters**.

3. Right-click the host on which you would like to check compliance and select **Host Profile** and then **Check Compliance**, as shown in Figure 5-83.

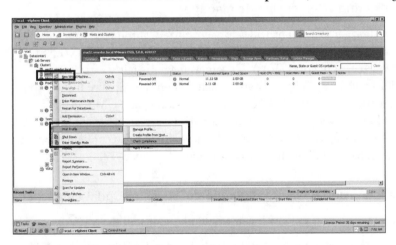

Figure 5-83   Checking a Host for Profile Compliance

4. Monitor the Recent Tasks pane for compliance status. The status will also be displayed in the Summary tab when the check is complete.

5. Click **Profile Compliance** to see details of compliance issues to be addressed, a shown in Figure 5-84. (I made this one messy so that you could see some detail.)

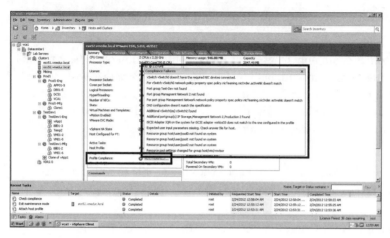

Figure 5-84   Profile Compliance Details

> **6.** If necessary, you can reapply the attached profile to remediate the host.

Installing and Configuring vCenter Update Manager

vCenter Update Manager (VUM) provides for centralized, automated patch and version management for your vSphere. It offers support for VMware ESX/ESXi hosts, VMs, and virtual appliances (VAs). Update Manager is fairly easy to install and configure for your needs. The software is included on the vSphere Installation Manager and can also be downloaded from VMware's website. VUM must be installed on a Windows Server and connected to a SQL or Oracle database. IBM DB2 is not supported as a VUM database. To install and perform basic configuration on vCenter Update Manager, follow the steps outlined in Activity 5-17.

Activity 5-17 Installation and Basic Configuration of vSphere Update Manager

> **1.** Log on to the computer on which you would like to install the VUM.
>
> **2.** Using the VIM Setup software and the vSphere Installer Package, click **VMware vSphere Update Manager** and click **Install**, as shown in Figure 5-85. If you do not have the prerequisites of Microsoft.NET 3.5 SP1 and Windows Installer 4.1, you can install them at this time as well, straight from the VIM Setup software.

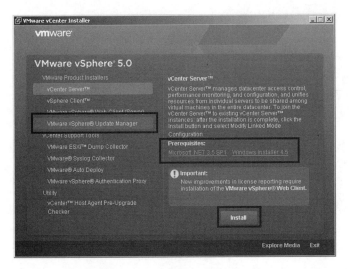

Figure 5-85 The vSphere Installer Package

3. Choose your installation language and click **OK**.

4. Click **Next** and accept to the terms to begin the installation.

5. The default configuration option is to download updates immediately after installation, as shown in Figure 5-86. The updates that are downloaded are just descriptions of the patches. The actual patch binary is never downloaded until you remediate an object that needs that patch.

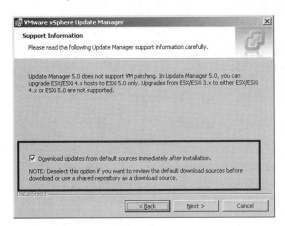

Figure 5-86 Default Installation Downloads Patches

6. Enter your vCenter address and credentials and click **Next**, as shown in Figure 5-87.

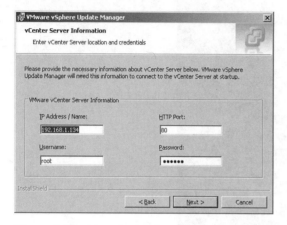

Figure 5-87 The vCenter Connection to VUM

7. Configure for DSN of your connected database or use the SQL Server 2008 R2 Express (for small deployments, demo, and testing) and click **Next**, as shown in Figure 5-88.

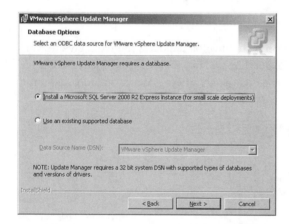

Figure 5-88 Connecting the Database or Using SQL Express

8. Most of the time, you can accept the default ports as shown in Figure 5-89, unless your network requires special considerations with regard to ports.

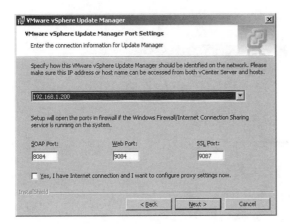

Figure 5-89 Default Ports Will Usually Suffice

9. Most of the time, you can accept the default locations for the installation packages, as shown in Figure 5-90, and click **Next**.

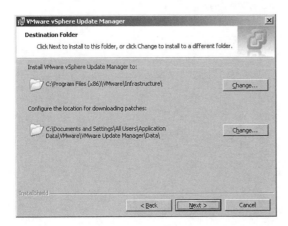

Figure 5-90 Default Installation Folders Will Usually Suffice

10. Click **Install** to begin the installation. The software installation will begin by
    extracting many files and then will continue into a graphical installation.

11. After the installation finishes, log on to your vSphere Client and go to **Plug-**
    Ins > Manage Plug-ins to download and install the Update Manager plug-in,
    as shown in Figure 5-91.

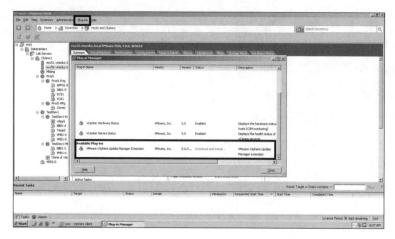

Figure 5-91   The VDR Plug-in

12. After the plug-in is downloaded and installed, the link will appear in the Home
screen under Solutions and Utilities, as shown in Figure 5-92.

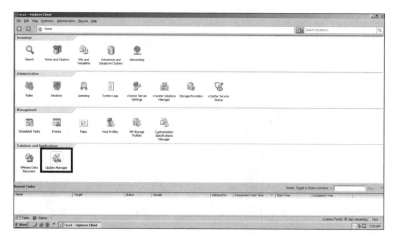

Figure 5-92   The VUM Link in Solutions and Utilities

Configuring Patch Download Options

After you have the software installed, you can add to the patch download options that are already configured by default by connecting the Internet or to and optional server, as shown in Figure 5-93.

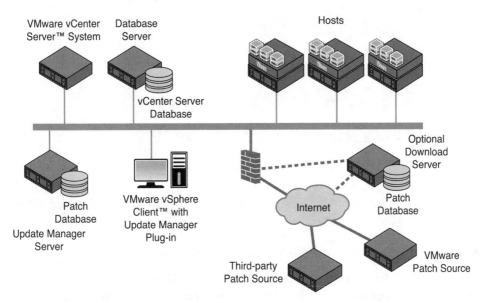

Figure 5-93   Options for vCenter Update Manager

You should note that additional patch downloads are intended as enhancements to the host and to networking, storage, and so on. The VUM is no longer supported for patching guest OSs. To configure additional download options after you have installed VUM, follow the steps outlined in Activity 5-18.

Activity 5-18 Configuring Patch Download Options

1. Login on to your vSphere Client.

2. Go to **Home > Solutions and Applications** and click **Update Manager**.

3. Click the **Configuration** tab at the top of the screen and then on **Add Download Source**, as shown in Figure 5-94.

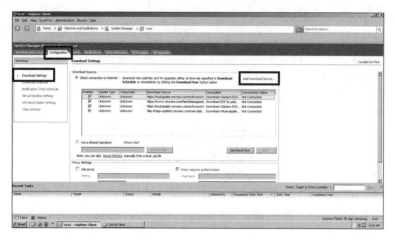

Figure 5-94   Adding Download Sources to VUM

4. You can then specify the Source URL and click **OK** to contact the third-party source for your patches.

Creating/Editing/Deleting an Update Manager Baseline

After you have downloaded your patches, you can combine them to form groups of patches called *baselines*. To create a baseline, you first choose the type of baseline that you want to create, and then, based on your first choice, you choose the patches that will be part of the baseline. You can create five different types of baselines. The following is a brief description of each type of baseline.

- **Host patch:** VMware patches that can be applied to a host or a set of hosts

- **Host extension:** Plug-ins and other software from VMware or third-parties that extend the capabilities of the host

- **Host upgrade:** Patches that are specifically for the purpose of upgrading the ESX/ESXi host to the next level

- **VA upgrade:** Updates that the virtual appliance vendors provide for upgrade of the VA

- **VM Upgrade:** Upgrades the VMware Tools and virtual hardware on VMs and templates

To create a baseline in VUM, follow the steps outlined in Activity 5-19.

Activity 5-19 Creating a Baseline in VUM

1. Login on to your vSphere Client.

2. Go to **Home > Solutions and Applications** and click **Update Manager**.

3. Open the Baseline and Groups tab, choose between **Hosts** and **VMs/VAs**, and click the **Create** link next to Baselines, as shown in Figure 5-95.

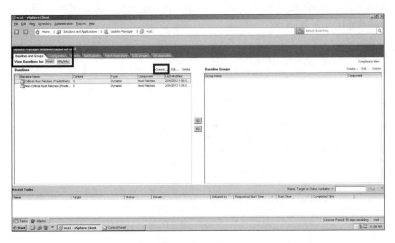

Figure 5-95   Creating a Baseline

4. On the Baseline Name and Type screen, type a name for your baseline and optionally a description, and then choose the applicable baseline type, as shown in Figure 5-96.

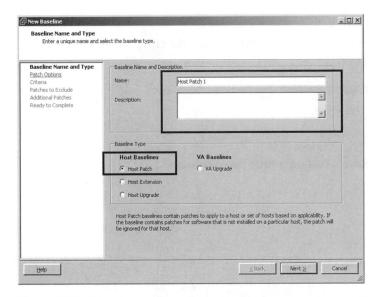

Figure 5-96   Naming and Describing a Baseline

5. Choose whether the patches in this baseline will be the same every time it's applied (Fixed) or whether new patches that meet the criteria will be automatically added to enhance or replace the old patches (Dynamic), as shown in Figure 5-97, and then click **Next**.

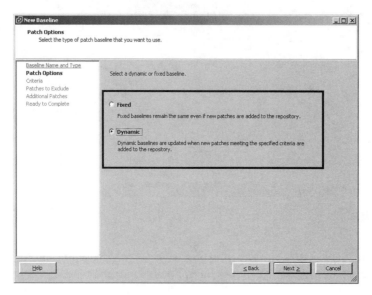

Figure 5-97   Choosing Patch Options

6. If you chose to create a dynamic baseline, enter the criteria to be considered, as shown in Figure 5-98.

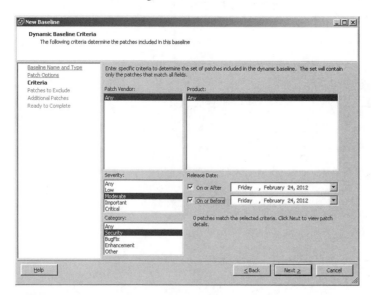

Figure 5-98   Dynamic Baseline Criteria

7. List any patches that you want to exclude (if applicable), as shown in Figure 5-99. Then click **Next** and list any additional patches to be included (if you chose Dynamic).

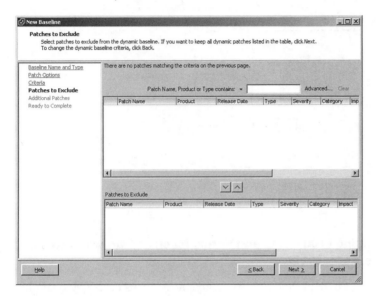

Figure 5-99   Patch Inclusion/Exclusion

8. On the Ready to Complete page, review your settings and click **Finish**.

Attaching an Update Manager Baseline to an ESXi Host or Cluster

Just creating a baseline for a host or cluster does not change the host in any way; you have to attach the baseline to the host or cluster and then apply it to change the host or cluster. Attaching the baseline gives you a standard to which the host must measure up or be considered out of compliance. To attach your newly created baseline to a host, return to Hosts and Clusters view, click the host on which you would like to attach the baseline, click **Attach**, select your baseline, and confirm by clicking **Attach** in the dialog box, all shown on Figure 5-100.

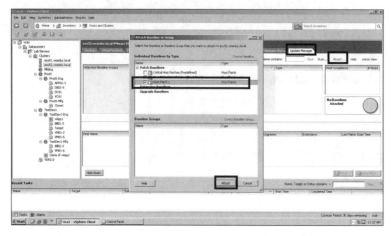

Figure 5-100   Attaching a Baseline to an ESXi Host

Scanning and Remediating ESXi Hosts and Virtual Machine Hardware/Tools Using Update Manager

Once you have created a baseline and attached it to a host, a cluster, a VM, or multiple VMs, you can scan the objects for compliance to the standard set by the baseline. If the objects that you scan are found to be noncompliant, they can then be remediated (fixed) to match the standard set by the baseline and its patches and settings. You can also elect to stage the patches for a later time when there is not as much demand on the resources, all shown in Figure 5-101.

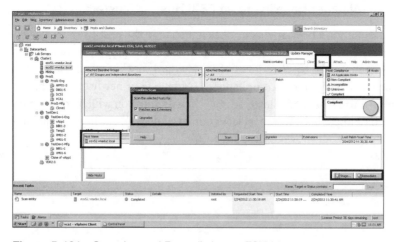

Figure 5-101   Scanning and Remediating an ESXi Host

Summary

The main topics covered in this chapter are the following:

- I began this chapter by discussing and examining the concept of a cluster. I discussed creating, configuring, adding/removing hosts, and adding and removing VMs. Then we became more specific and examined the two features that are prevalent in a cluster, HA and DRS. We discussed configuring the basics of each technology as well as some of the finer points of each type of configuration as they relate to real world issues as well as to the exam.

- I then focused my attention on VMware fault tolerance (FT) and the advantages that it can offer your most critical VMs at the most critical times. We discussed the necessary network configuration for FT as well as enabling/disabling FT on a VM. I also covered the proper way to test FT without actually failing a host. Finally, we determined use cases for enabling FT on a VM.

- My next topic of discussion was administering Resource Pools. I described the Resource Pool hierarchy in general terms. We then becoming more specific with our discussion of the Expandable Reservation parameter, creating and removing Resource Pools, configuring Resource Pool attributes, and adding and removing VMs. I discussed shares, reservations, and limits for Resource Pools and how you can strategically use each of these. Finally, we discussed cloning a vApp in a Resource Pool.

- Our next topic of discussion was migrating VMs. I identified the requirements for vMotion and Storage vMotion. In addition, I discussed EVC, snapshots, and swap files as they relate to vMotion. Finally, I examined the capabilities of Storage vMotion with regard to changing virtual disk type and renaming VMs.

- Then we turned our attention to backing up and restoring VMs. I identified snapshot requirements and discussed creating, deleting and consolidating VM snapshots. I also discussed using third-party backup tools with VMware APIs versus using VDR.

- Finally, we discussed patching and updating ESXi and VMs. This centered around two primary tools: host profiles and VUM. We covered the steps required to create host profiles, attach them to a host, and then apply them. I also discussed how to scan the hosts for compliance at a later date. Last, but not least, we discussed the installation, configuration, and operation and VUM, and how you can use it to scan and remediate your hosts as well as your VMs and VAs.

Exam Preparation Tasks

Review All the Key Topics

Review the most important topics from inside the chapter, noted with the Key Topic icon in the outer margin of the page. Table 5-2 lists these key topics and the page numbers where each is found.

Table 5-2   Key Topics for Chapter 5

Key Topic Element	Description	Page Number
Activity 5-1	Creating a DRS/HA Cluster	327
Activity 5-2	Adding a Host to a Cluster	329
Activity 5-3	Removing a Host from a Cluster	333
Activity 5-4	Creating and Configuring an SDRS Cluster	336
Bullet List	Migration Threshold Settings	344
Bullet List	DRS Automation Levels	344
Activity 5-5	Creating a Softly Enforced VM-VM-Host Rule	346
Bullet List	VM Monitoring Configuration Settings	352
Bullet List	Admission Control Policies	355
Bullet List	HA Configuration Settings	356
Bullet List	Requirements and Limitations of FT	360
Bullet List	Guidelines to Follow for FT Networking	361
Activity 5-6	Enabling Fault Tolerance on a Virtual Machine	361
Bullet List	Reasons to Use FT	362
Bullet List	Benefits of Using Resource Pools	364
Activity 5-7	Creating a Resource Pool	365
Bullet List	Resource Pool Attributes	367
Bullet List	The State of a VM	373
Bullet List	Host Requirements for vMotion	374
Bullet List	VM Requirement for vMotion	374
Bullet List	Advantages of Storage vMotion	375
Bullet List	Components of a CPU Feature Set	376
Bullet List	Compatibility Requirements for EVC	377

Key Topic Element	Description	Page Number
Activity 5-9	Migrating a VM Using vMotion	379
Activity 5-10	Migrating a VM's Files Using Storage vMotion	382
Activity 5-11	Creating a VM Snapshot	390
Numbered List	Steps to Install VDR	395
Activity 5-12	Using FLR in Windows	397
Activity 5-13	Using FLR in Linux	397
Activity 5-14	Creating a Host Profile	399
Activity 5-15	Attach/Apply a Host Profile	402
Activity 5-16	Checking Host Compliance to an Attached Host Profile	405
Activity 5-17	Installation and Basic Configuration of vSphere Update Manager	406
Activity 5-18	Configuring Patch Download Options	411
Bullet List	Types of Baselines in VUM	412
Activity 5-19	Creating a Baseline in VUM	412

Review Questions

The answers to these review questions are in Appendix A.

1. Which of the following should you use on a cluster to address differences in CPUIDs on the hosts?

    a. DRS

    b. HA

    c. FT

    d. EVC

2. Which of the following can only be used on a host that is part of a cluster? (Choose two.)

    a. vMotion

    b. DRS

    c. Resource Pools

    d. HA

3. Which Admission Control method would be best for an organization that has many VMs with highly variable reservations?

   a. Specify failover hosts

   b. Percentage of cluster resources reserved as failover space capacity

   c. Host failures that the cluster tolerates

   d. Any of these methods would work fine

4. What is the maximum number of FT VMs on any single host?

   a. 32

   b. 10

   c. 4

   d. 256

5. Which of the following is *not* a benefit of using Resource Pools?

   a. Fault-tolerant design for VMs

   b. Isolation of resources between pools

   c. Management of multitier services

   d. Access control and delegation

6. What is the minimum network bandwidth for vMotion of one VM?

   a. 100Mbps

   b. 1Gbps

   c. 10Gbps

   d. There is no minimum.

7. Which of the following is *not* examined by EVC?

   a. Settings in the BIOS that might differ from host to host

   b. Connected local CDs and ISOs

   c. The ESX/ESXi version running on the host

   d. The guest OS of the VM

8. If you want to allow for more flexibility in adding hosts to your clusters, you should use an EVC mode that is which of the following?

   a. An EVC mode that works with both Intel and AMD hosts

   b. An EVC mode that is the highest and best that all of your hosts share

   c. An EVC mode that is the lowest common denominator to all the hosts in your cluster

   d. A different EVC mode for each host in your cluster

9. Which of the following snapshot files will continue to grow and consume the remainder of your disk if you do not delete/consolidate snapshots properly?

   a. delta.vmdk

   b. -flat.vmdk

   c. .vmx

   d. .vmsd

10. If you delete a snapshot that is before the You Are Here indicator, which of the following is true?

   a. The snapshot will be deleted and will not be merged with the current configuration of the VM.

   b. The snapshot will not actually be deleted.

   c. The You Are Here indicator will be deleted as well.

   d. The snapshot will be deleted, but its attributes will be merged with the current configuration of the VM.

This chapter covers the following subjects:

- Performing Basic Troubleshooting for ESXi Hosts

- Performing Basic vSphere Network Troubleshooting

- Performing Basic vSphere Storage Troubleshooting

- Performing Basic Troubleshooting for HA/DRS Clusters and vMotion/ Storage vMotion

Troubleshooting is a process of isolating the components of a system from each other to systematically determine what works. That's right, I said "what works" and not "what doesn't work." If you can determine what does work in a system and how "far" it does work, then you can determine the point at which it begins to not work.

Just as with any other product or service, there are many things that can go wrong with vSphere if they are not configured properly or if something unexpected and unaccounted for should happen. As a vSphere administrator, part of your job is to minimize the chance of these unexpected issues and to minimize their impact to your organization when they occur. The other part of your job is to understand how to work your way out of an issue so as to provide a solution for yourself and your servers with the least disruption possible to your users.

In this chapter, I will discuss performing basic troubleshooting on your ESXi hosts, virtual networks, and storage. In addition, I will discuss basic troubleshooting for the features that put all of these resources to work in an organized manner that makes the vSphere and the virtual datacenter possible. This chapter is to assist you in truly understanding more about your vSphere and not just "having head knowledge" of its components. This understanding will help you troubleshoot your own systems and is essential to successfully navigate the troubleshooting questions on the exam.

CHAPTER 6

Performing Basic Troubleshooting

"Do I Know This Already?" Quiz

The "Do I Know This Already?" quiz allows you to assess whether you should read this entire chapter or simply jump to the "Exam Preparation Tasks" section for review. If you are in doubt, read the entire chapter. Table 6-1 outlines the major headings in this chapter and the corresponding "Do I Know This Already?" quiz questions. You can find the answers in Appendix A, "Answers to the 'Do I Know This Already?' Quizzes and Chapter Review Questions."

Table 6-1 "Do I Know This Already?" Section-to-Question Mapping

Foundations Topics Section	Questions Covered in This Section
Performing Basic Troubleshooting for ESXi Hosts	1–3
Performing Basic vSphere Network Troubleshooting	4, 5
Performing Basic vSphere Storage Troubleshooting	6–8
Performing Basic Troubleshooting for HA/DRS Clusters and vMotion/Storage vMotion	9, 10

1. Which of following is provided by VMware as a last resort to troubleshoot issues that cannot be resolved through more normal means?

    a. vCLI

    b. vSphere Client

    c. TSM

    d. PowerCLI

2. Which of the following should you select in the DCUI to review the system logs?

    a. View Support Information

    b. View System Logs

    c. Troubleshooting Options

    d. System Customization

3. If you are logged directly on to a host, which of the following tabs should you select to monitor the system health status of the host?

    a. Health Status

    b. Hardware Status

    c. Summary

    d. Configuration

4. Which of the following is true about the speed of a network connection in vSphere?

    a. The speed of the connection is configurable on the settings for the vNIC.

    b. The speed of the connection is based on the underlying network and is not configurable.

    c. The speed of the connection is configurable on the settings for the vmnic.

    d. The speed of the network connection must be hard-coded and cannot be autonegotiated.

5. Which of the following is true with regard to vSS switch settings and port group settings?

    a. Conflicting port group settings will override switch settings.

    b. Conflicting switch settings will override port group settings.

    c. Port group and switch settings are different, so there is no possibility of a conflict.

    d. If settings conflict, an error will result and the administrator will have to address the issue.

6. Which of the following is *not* a native VMware path-selection type?

    a. Round-Robin

    b. Load based

    c. Most recently used

    d. Fixed

7. Which of the following is the maximum number of powered-on VMs per VMFS-5 datastore?

    a. 32

    b. 10,000

    c. 2048

    d. 256

8. Which of the following is true about active-active arrays?

    a. Active-Active arrays will often cause path thrashing.

    b. Active-active arrays should never be used with vSphere.

    c. Active-active arrays should always be used with vSphere.

    d. Active-active arrays do not cause path thrashing.

9. Which of the following is the minimum network speed required for vMotion?

    a. 100 Mbps

    b. 1Gbps

    c. 10Gbps

    d. vMotion can work at any speed.

10. Which of the following is *not* a requirement of HA?

    a. Hosts must be in the same cluster.

    b. Hosts must share the same CPU vendor and family.

    c. Hosts must have shared datastores.

    d. Hosts must have access to the same physical networks.

Foundation Topics

Performing Basic Troubleshooting for ESXi Hosts

Your ESXi hosts are the most important physical resources in your virtual data-center. They provide the platform upon which all the VMs are supported and from which they obtain their resources. When there is a problem with an ESXi host, that problem will likely affect many VMs as well.

In this section, I will begin by identifying general troubleshooting guidelines for ESXi hosts. Then, I will discuss troubleshooting common installation issues and how you should avoid them. I will continue by discussing the ongoing monitoring of the health of your ESXi host. Finally, I will discuss how you can export diagnostic information to examine for yourself and especially to send to the VMware Technical Support Team.

Identifying General ESXi Host Troubleshooting Guidelines

Your vSphere is unique, just as everyone's vSphere is unique, but there are some guidelines that you can follow to effectively troubleshoot your ESXi hosts. You can use these general guidelines to determine more specific steps for your own organization. The following sections document some basic troubleshooting guidelines for ESXi.

Learn How to Access Support Mode

Tech Support Mode (TSM) consists of a command-line interface that you can use to troubleshoot abnormalities on ESXi Hosts. You can access it by logging in to the Direct Console User Interface (DCUI) or by logging in remotely using Secure Shell (SSH). It is provided by VMware specifically for the purpose of troubleshooting issues that cannot be resolved through the use of more normal means such as the vSphere Client, vCLI, or PowerCLI. It is generally used with the assistance of the VMware Technical Support Team.

To enable TSM from the DCUI, follow the steps in Activity 6-1.

Activity 6-1 Enabling TSM from the DCUI

1. Access the DCUI of your ESXi host.

2. Press **F2** and enter your username and password, and then press **F2** again to proceed, as shown in Figure 6-1.

Figure 6-1   Logging On to the DCUI

> 3. Scroll to Troubleshooting Options, as shown in Figure 6-2, and press **Enter**.

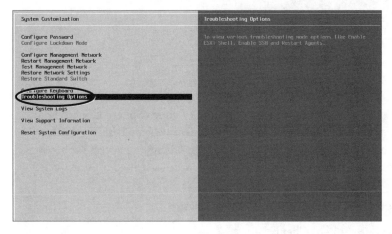

Figure 6-2   Selecting Troubleshooting Options

> 4. Select **Enable ESXi Shell** and press **Enter**. The panel on the right should
>   now show that ESXi Shell Is Enabled, as shown in Figure 6-3.

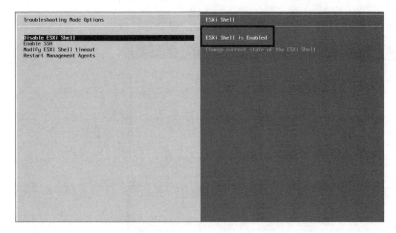

Figure 6-3   Enabling ESXi Shell

5. Select **Enable SSH** and press **Enter** to also enable remote TSM through SSH, and then press **Enter** and view the panel on the right to confirm the change.

6. Optionally, you can configure a timeout to enhance security if the logged in user should walk away. To enable a timeout, select **Modify ESXi Shell Timeout**, press **Enter**, and configure your desired timeout value, as shown in Figure 6-4.

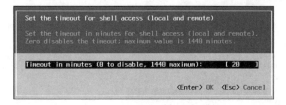

Figure 6-4   Modifying ESXi Shell Timeout

7. Press **Esc** three times to return to the main DCUI screen.

You can also enable TSM from the security profile of your vSphere Client. To illustrate how these are tied together, I am going to demonstrate that TSM is now enabled and then we will disable it from the vSphere Client. To access the settings of the security profile of your ESXi host, follow the steps outlined in Activity 6-2.

Activity 6-2 Configuring TSM from the vSphere Client

1. Log on to your vSphere Client.

2. Select the host on which you want to configure TSM, and (if necessary) open the Summary tab. Note the warnings that SSH and the ESXi Shell are enabled, as shown in Figure 6-5.

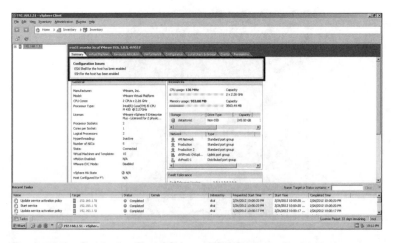

Figure 6-5   Confirming That SSH and ESXi Shell Are Enabled

3. Open the Configuration tab, and then under Software select **Security Pro-file**. Click the **Properties** link in the upper right and note that the services of SSH and ESXi Shell are enabled. Select **ESXi Shell**, click **Options** and then **Stop the Service**, as shown in Figure 6-6. (You should also change the startup policy to **Start and Stop Manually**.)

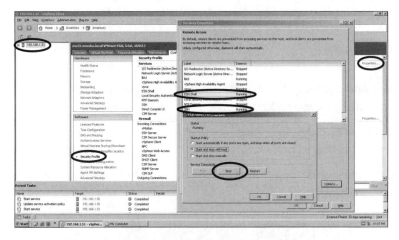

Figure 6-6   Configuring the ESXi Shell and SSH Services

4. Select **SSH**, click **Options** and **Stop the Service**, and then Click **OK**.

5. Open the **Summary** tab and note that the warnings are no longer there.

Know How to Retrieve Logs

One thing that computers and networking components are very good at is keeping up with has happened to them, who or what made it happen, and when it happened. This information is stored in logs. Although there is generally no need for you to understand all the verbose information that is in every log, it is important that you know where to find logs and how to export them when needed. In this section, I will explore three different locations where you can access logs for your most essential vSphere components.

There are two locations on your ESXi hosts from which you can access logs: your DCUI and your vSphere Client. As I said before, it's not essential that you understand all the information on the log, but what's important is your ability to access it when working with a VMware Support person. I will briefly describe how to access logs in each of these locations.

To access the logs from your DCUI, you should access your host's DCUI and then select **View System Logs**. From this screen, you can select from six different logs, as shown in Figure 6-7.

- **Syslog:** Logs messages from the VMkernel and other system components to local files or to the remote host

- **VMkernel:** Used to determine uptime and availability statistics

- **Config:** Potentially useful in the case of a host hang, crash, or authentication issue

- **Management Agent (hostd):** Logs specific to the host services that connect your vSphere Client to you ESXi host

- **Virtualcenter Agent (vpxa):** Additional logs that appear when your ESXi host connected to and managed by a vCenter

- **VMware ESXi Observation Log (vobd):** Logs changes to the configuration of your host and their result.

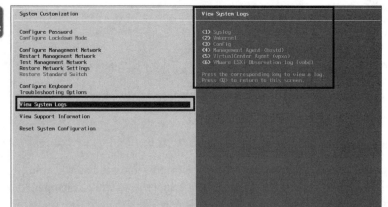

Figure 6-7   Viewing Logs on the DCUI

You can view each of these logs by simply pressing the number associated with it. For example, you can view the vmkernel log by pressing **2**. Figure 6-8 is an example of a VMkernel log. When you are finished viewing the log, you can press **Q** to return to the previous screen.

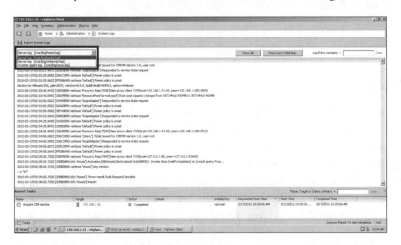

Figure 6-8 Viewing the VMkernel Log

To access your host's logs using your vSphere Client, log on to your host (not your vCenter). You can log on to your host using its hostname or IP address. After you log on to your vSphere Client, click **Home > Administration > System Logs**, where you can view hostd, VMkernel, and vCenter logs, as shown in Figure 6-9.

Figure 6-9 Viewing Logs on a Single Host

Troubleshooting Common Installation Issues

For your hosts to function well in your vCenter, you must first install them properly. As discussed in Chapter 1, "Planning, Installing, Configuring, and Upgrading vCenter Server and VMware ESXi," there are many different ways to install the software for an ESXi host, including interactive installation, USB key, scripted, or even loaded directly into the memory of the host. That makes this objective a very broad one indeed. With that in mind, I'm going to list three of the most common installation issues and how you should address them.

Troubleshooting Boot Order

If you are installing ESXi, you might need to reconfigure BIOS settings. The boot configuration in BIOS is likely to be set to CD-ROM and then ordered by the list of drives available in your computer. You can change this setting by reconfiguring the boot order in BIOS or by selecting a boot device for the selection menu. If you change this in the BIOS, it will affect all subsequent boots. If you change it in the boot selection menu, it will affect only the current boot.

> **NOTE**   Some servers do not offer a boot device selection menu. Also, if you using ESXi embedded, the BIOS boot configuration determines whether your server boots into the ESXi boot device or another boot device. Generally, the USB flash device is not listed first and requires additional steps (based on the specific vendor) to allow the system to boot from it. Also, other BIOS settings such as NX/XD, VT, SpeedStep, and so on should be considered.

Troubleshooting License Assignment

Suppose you have a vSphere key with the vRAM capacity for 16 processors. Now, suppose that you attempt to install that key on a host that has 32 processors. You might assume that the key would install, but only enable the host to use the processors covered by the key. In fact, you will not be able to install the key on that host. In addition, you will not be able to install license keys that do not cover all the features that you have enabled for a host (for example, DRS, Host Profile, Fault Tolerance, and so on). To address the issue, you should do one of the following:

- Obtain and assign the appropriate key with a larger capacity.

- Upgrade your license edition to cover the features that you are using on your host.

- Disable the features that are not covered by the key that you are attempting to assign.

Troubleshooting Plug-Ins

As you might know, plug-ins are used in the vCenter so it might seem unusual to discuss them under this heading. However, if you think about it, the services to the VMs are actually provided by the hosts and are only controlled by the vCenter. In addition, plug-ins that fail to enable can be very frustrating, so I think troubleshooting them warrants discussion here.

In cases where plug-ins are not working, you have several troubleshooting options. You should first understand that plug-ins that run on the Tomcat server have extension.xml files that contain the URL of the application that can be accessed by the plug-in. These files are located in C:\Program Files\VMware\Infrastructure\ VirtualCenter Server\extensions. If your vCenter Server and your vSphere Client are not on the same domain, or if the hostname of the plug-in server is changed, the clients will not be able to access the URL, and then the plug-in will not enable. You can address this issue by replacing the hostname in the extension file with the IP address of the plug-in server.

Monitoring ESXi System Health

You can use your vSphere Client to monitor the state of your host hardware components. The host health monitoring tool allows you to monitor the health of many hardware components including CPU, memory, fans, temperature, voltage, power, network, battery, storage, cable/interconnect, software, watchdog, and so on. Actually, the specific information that you will obtain will vary somewhat by the sensors available in your server hardware.

The host health monitoring tool will gather and present data using Systems Management Architecture for Server Hardware (SMASH) profiles. SMASH (isn't that a fun acronym!) is an industry standard specification. You can obtain more information about SMASH at http://www.dmtf.org/standards/smash. You can monitor the host health status by connecting your vSphere Client directly to your host and selecting **Configuration > Health Status**, as shown in Figure 6-10. As you might imagine, you are looking for a green check mark here. The status will turn yellow or red if the component violates a performance threshold or is not performing properly. Generally speaking, a yellow indicator signifies degraded performance, and a red indicator signifies that the component has either stopped or has tripped the highest (worst) threshold possible.

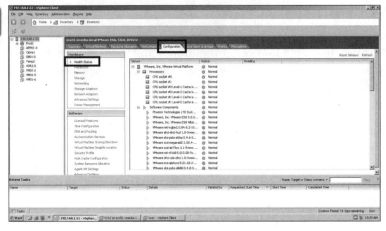

Figure 6-10   Viewing Health Status on a Specific Host

You can also monitor your host's health by logging on to your vCenter, selecting the host, and then opening its Hardware Status tab, as shown in Figure 6-11.

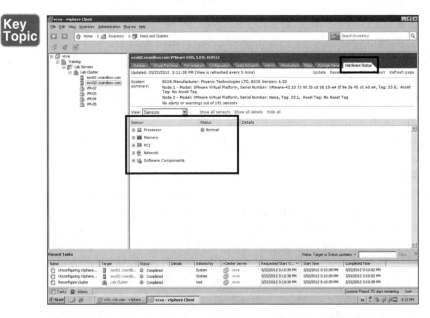

Figure 6-11   Viewing Hardware Status on a Host Through vCenter

Exporting Diagnostic Information

If you have an issue that warrants contacting VMware technical support, they might ask you to send them a log or two. If they want to see multiple logs, the easy way to send them "everything you've got" is to generate a diagnostic bundle. That sounds like more work for you, doesn't it? Actually, it's a very simple task that you can perform on your vCenter through your vSphere Client. I will discuss this briefly here and then I will discuss it in more detail in Chapter 7, "Monitoring vSphere Implementation and Managing vCenter Alarms."

To export a diagnostic data bundle, you use either a host logon, as detailed in Activity 6-3, or use a vCenter logon, as detailed in Activity 6-4.

Activity 6-3 Exporting Diagnostic Information from a Host Log-In

1. Log on to your host with your vSphere Client.

2. Click your ESXi host in the console pane, and then select **File > Export > Export System Logs**, as shown in Figure 6-12.

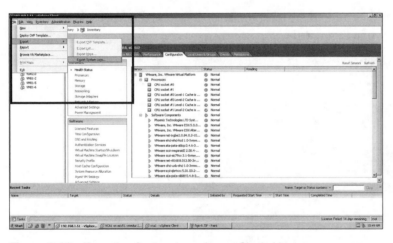

Figure 6-12   Exporting System Logs from a Single Host

3. Specify the system logs that you want to be exported, likely as directed by the VMware Support Team, and click **Next**, as shown in Figure 6-13.

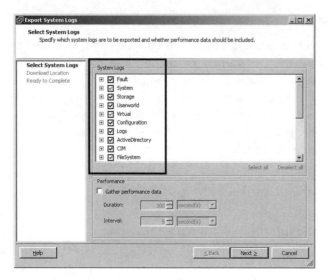

Figure 6-13 Selecting Logs to Export

4. Enter or Browse to find the location to which you would like to download the file, as shown in Figure 6-14.

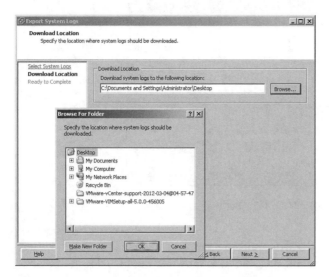

Figure 6-14 Selecting the Location for Exported Logs

5. You can view the progress of your System Log Bundle as it is downloaded to the destination, as shown in Figure 6-15.

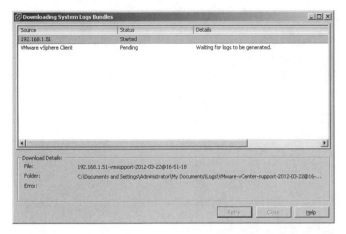

Figure 6-15   Viewing the Progress of a System Log Bundle on a Single Host

Activity 6-4 Exporting Diagnostic Information from a vCenter Log-In

1. Log on to your vCenter with your vSphere Client.

2. Click your root object and then select **Administration > Export System Logs**, as shown in Figure 6-16 (you can also select **File > Export > Export System Logs**).

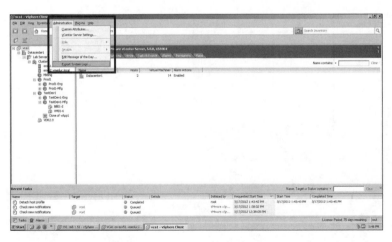

Figure 6-16   Exporting System Logs from vCenter

3. Specify the roots (if you are using Linked Mode), datacenters, folders, clusters, and finally hosts for which you want to create logs, as shown in Figure 6-17, and click **Next**. These decisions will likely be directed by the VMware Support Team.

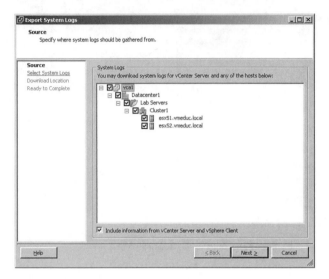

Figure 6-17   Specifying Objects for Log Creation

> **4.** Choose the logs that you would like to download from the list, as directed by
> the VMware Support Team, as shown in Figure 6-18.

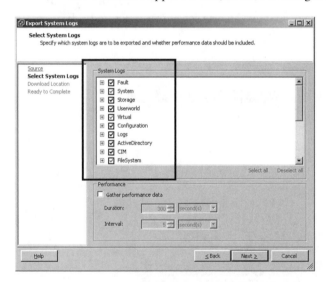

Figure 6-18   Selecting the Logs to Create from a vCenter Log-On

> **5.** Enter or Browse to find the location to which you would like to download the
> file, as shown in Figure 6-19.

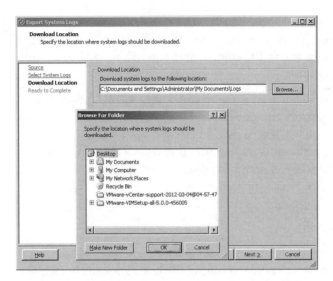

Figure 6-19   Selecting the Location for Exported Logs

6. You can view the progress of your System Log Bundle as it is downloaded to the destination, as shown in Figure 6-20.

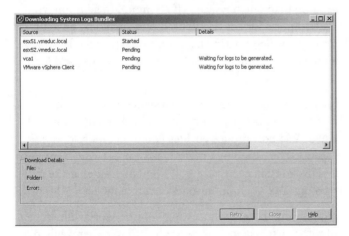

Figure 6-20   Viewing the Progress of a System Log Bundle on a vCenter

Performing Basic vSphere Network Troubleshooting

Your vSphere network should connect your VMs to each other and also allow your VMs to connect to physical resources outside of your vSphere. In addition, your network should provide a management port (or multiple management ports) that allow you to control your hosts and VMs. Finally, your network might very well be involved with your storage, if you are using IP storage options such as Internet Small Computer System Interface (iSCSI), storage-area networking (SAN), or Network File System (NFS) datastores.

Because your vSphere network is such an integral part or your virtual datacenter, you should understand the network components and their correct configuration so that you can troubleshoot them when necessary. In this section, I will discuss verifying and troubleshooting network configuration including your VMs, port groups, and physical network adapters. In addition, I will discuss identifying the root cause of a network issue based on troubleshooting information.

Verifying Network Configuration

At the very least, your network configuration should include a VMkernel port for management; otherwise, you won't be able to control the host remotely. In fact, one is provided for you with the default installation of an ESXi host. If you are using vSSs, you will need at least one VMkernel management port on each host. If you are using a vDS, you will need at least one VMkernel management port on the vDS. Of course, it is possible to configure more than one management port, and that is certainly recommended on a vDS. Another option is to configure one VMkernel port, but then configure it to use more than one physical NIC (vmnic). In addition, you might have additional VMkernel ports for a myriad of reasons, including an additional heartbeat network for high availability (HA), an additional port for IP storage (iSCSI or NFS), fault tolerance (FT) logging for vSphere fault tolerance, and for vMotion.

Other than the VMkernel ports, the rest of the ports on a switch will be used for uplinks to the physical world or for VM port groups, most will likely be used for VM port groups. The correct use of VM port groups enables you to get more options out of a single switch (vSS or vDS) by assigning different attributes to different port groups. As you know, with vDSs you can even assign different attributes at the individual port level. VM port groups give you options on which to connect a VM.

Verifying your network configuration consists of viewing your network with an understanding of how all of these virtual components are linked together. Only by understanding how it should be connected will you be able to troubleshoot any configuration issues. Figure 6-21 shows a typical network configuration and the general IP addressing information and attribute information for a port group. In this case, the port group is labeled IP Storage.

Figure 6-21   A Typical Configuration on a vSS

Verifying a Given Virtual Machine Is Configured with the Correct Network Resources

As I said earlier, port groups give you options on which to connect a VM. In my opinion, you can really see this much more clearly from the VM's standpoint. In Figure 6-22, I have right-clicked a VM and then selected **Edit Settings**. As you can see, I have a list of port groups from which to choose for the virtual network interface card (vNIC) on this VM. These port groups are all VM port groups on this switch or on the vDS to which this host is connected. Also note the Device Status check boxes at the top right of the screen. These should be selected on an active connection. When the VM is connected to the appropriate port group, it can be configured with the correct network resources. If it is not on the correct port group, a great number of issues could result including having the wrong security, traffic shaping, NIC teaming options, or even having a total lack of connectivity.

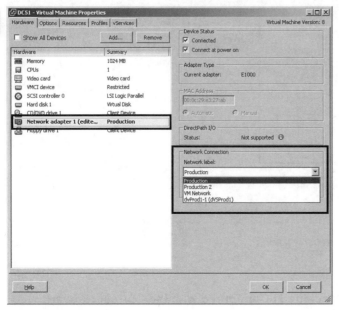

Figure 6-22   Viewing a VM's Network Configuration

Troubleshooting Virtual Switch and Port Group Configuration Issues

Just connecting the VM to a port group does not guarantee that you get the desired configuration. What if the port group itself is not configured properly? You should understand that any configuration options on a vSS will be overridden by conflicting options on a port group of the same switch. In addition, any options on a port group of a vDS will be overridden by conflicting options on a specific port. I covered these options in detail in Chapter 2, "Planning and Configuring vSphere Networking," so I will not go into great detail about security, traffic shaping, NIC teaming, and so on, but Figure 6-23 shows the general area in which you can find them on a vDS. The main point here is to verify that you have set the properties appropriately for the VMs that are connected to the port group.

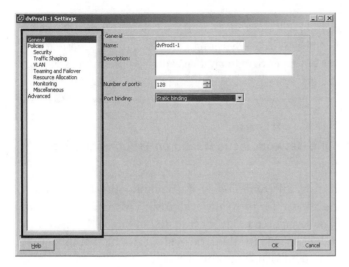

Figure 6-23   Port Group Settings on a vDS

Troubleshooting Physical Network Adapter Configuration Issues

It can't all be virtual! At some point, you have to connect your vSphere to the physical world. The point at which the data moves out of the host and into the physical world can be referred to as a physical network adapter, a vmnic, or an uplink. Because the configuration of this point of reference is for a piece of physical equipment, the available settings are what you might expect for any other physical adapter, namely speed and duplex, as shown in Figure 6-24.

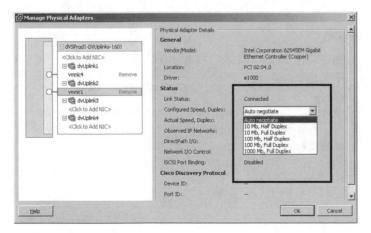

Figure 6-24   Settings for a Physical Adapter

NOTE   If the autonegotiate setting will work in your organization, you should use it for convenience. You should check it carefully though, because, in my experience, two different vendors will often autonegotiate to an unacceptable option, such as 100Mbps half-duplex.

Identifying the Root Cause of a Network Issue Based on Troubleshooting Information

I've seen and written about many different models of troubleshooting that look great on paper but might be overkill for the real world. Also, VMware doesn't subscribe to a certain five-step or seven-step model of troubleshooting with regard to the exam. That said, you should be able to "think through" a troubleshooting question based on what you know about virtual networking.

In general, a VM's network performance is dependent on two things: its application workload, and your network configuration. Dropped network packets indicate a bottleneck in the network. Slow network performance could be a sign of load-balancing issues, or the lack of load balancing altogether.

You'll know if you have high latency and slow network performance; there is no hiding that! How will you know if you have dropped packets? You can use esxtop, resxtop, or the Advanced performance charts to examine dropped transmit (droppedTx) and dropped receive (droppedRx) packets. These should be zero (or very close to it) if you don't have bottleneck I will discuss resxtop in our next chapter entitled "Monitoring vSphere Implementation and Managing vCenter Alarms."

If these utilities indicate that there is an issue, you can verify or adjust each of the following to address the issue:

- Verify that each of the VMs has VMware Tools installed.

- Verify that vmxnet3 vNIC drivers are being used wherever possible.

- If possible, place VMs that communicate to each other frequently onto the same host on the same switch in the same subnet so they can communicate without using the external network at all.

- Verify that the speed and duplex settings on your physical NICs are what you expected.

- Use separate physical NICs to handle different types of traffic, such as VM, iSCSI, VMotion, and so on.

- If you are using 1Gbps NICs, consider upgrading to 10Gbps NICs.

- Use vNIC drivers that are TSO-capable (as I discussed in Chapter 2).

Of course, this is not an exhaustive list, but it's a good start toward better virtual network performance. You should apply each of these potential solutions "one at a time" and retest. In this way, you can determine the root cause of your network issue, even as you are fixing it.

Performing Basic vSphere Storage Troubleshooting

As you know, it's possible for a VM to be given visibility to its actual physical storage locations, as with a physical compatibility Raw Device Mapping (RDM). That said, it should not be the norm in your virtual datacenter. In most cases, you will use either a Virtual Machine File System (VMFS) datastore or an NFS datastore, either of which hides the specifics of the actual physical storage from the VM.

Regardless of what type of storage you use, you will need to configure it properly in order to get your desired result. In this section, I will discuss verifying storage configuration. I will also cover troubleshooting many aspects of storage, including storage contention issues, overcommitment issues, and iSCSI software initiator issues. In addition, I will discuss storage reports and storage maps that you can use for troubleshooting. Finally, you will learn how to identify the root cause of a storage issue based on troubleshooting information.

Verifying Storage Configuration

Your vCenter includes two tools that will assist you in verifying your storage configuration: the Storage link and the Storage Views tab. Each of these tools lists information about your storage and there is some overlap with regard to what these tools list. Actually, the Storage Views tab is a new enhancement that came with vSphere 4.0 and was not included in what is now legacy Virtual Center 2.5.

You can find the Storage link in vCenter by first selecting a host and then opening the Configuration tab, as shown in Figure 6-25.

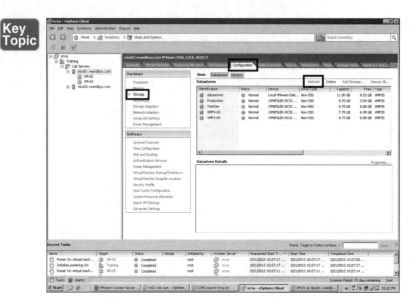

Figure 6-25 The Storage Link on the Configuration Tab

You should click **Refresh** to make sure that you are seeing the latest information. You can use the Storage link to quickly identify the datastores that are accessible to that host. In addition, you can view the status, type, capacity, free space, and so on, for each datastore. You can even customize what you show by right-clicking at the top of a column and selecting only your own choices, as shown in Figure 6-26.

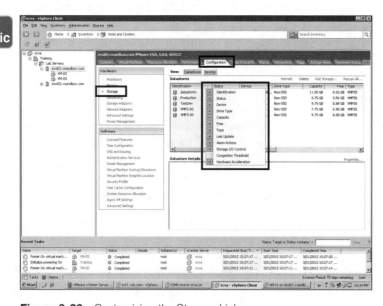

Figure 6-26 Customizing the Storage Link

The Storage Views tab allows you to view some of the same information as the Storage link, but also much, much more. You can access the Storage Views tab by clicking one of your hosts (in Hosts and Clusters view) or one of your datastores (in Datastores and Datastore Clusters view). You should click the **Update** link to make sure that you are seeing the latest information. Figure 6-27 shows the Storage Views tab with a datastore selected in the console pane. As you can see, you can also show many more options. In addition, as shown in Figure 6-28, you can customize the columns in your Storage Views tab.

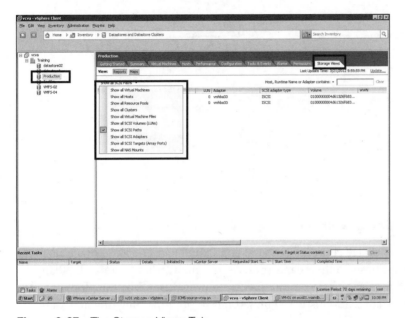

Figure 6-27   The Storage Views Tab

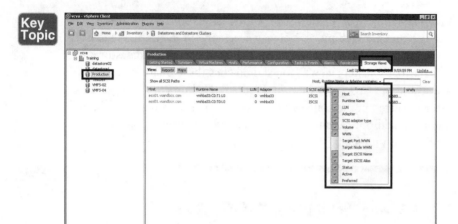

Figure 6-28 Customizing the Storage Views Tab

Troubleshooting Storage Contention Issues

To troubleshoot storage contention issues, you should focus on the storage adapters that connect your hosts to their datastores. As you know, from Chapter 3, "Planning and Configuring vSphere Storage," you can provide multipathing for your storage to relieve contention issues. The settings for multipathing of your storage are located under your Storage link on the Manage Paths button. Once you have clicked the Manage Paths button, you can select your path-selection policy from the drop-down next to Path Selection, as shown in Figure 6-29. You can also view these settings on the Storage Views tab by selecting **Show All Datastores**, as shown in Figure 6-30, but you cannot modify the settings using your Storage Views tab.

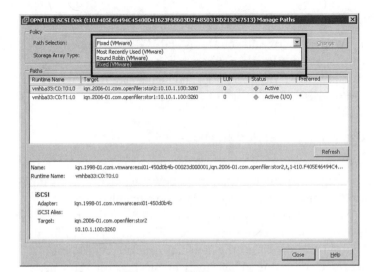

Figure 6-29   Settings for Multipathing of Storage

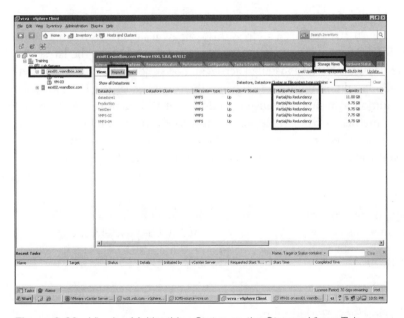

Figure 6-30   Viewing Multipathing Status on the Storage Views Tab

Troubleshooting Storage Over-Commitment Issues

As you continue to grow your vSphere, and your hosts and VMs are competing for the same resources, many factors can begin to affect storage performance. These include excessive SCSI reservations, path thrashing, and inadequate LUN queue depth. In this section, I will briefly discuss each of these issues.

Excessive Reservations Cause Slow Host Performance

Some operations require the system to get a file lock or a metadata lock in VMFS. These might include creating or expanding a datastore, powering on a VM, creating of deleting a file, creating a template, deploying a VM from a template, creating a new VM, migrating a VM with vMotion, changing a vmdk file from thin to thick, and so on. These types of operations create a short-lived SCSI reservation, which temporarily locks the entire LUN or at least the metadata database. As you can imagine, excessive SCSI reservations caused by activity on one host can cause performance degradation on other servers that are accessing the same VMFS. Actually, ESXi 5.0 does a much better job of handling this issue since only the metadata is locked and not the entire LUN.

If you have older hosts and you need address this issue, you should ensure that you have the latest BIOS updates installed on your hosts and that you have the latest host bus adapter (HBA) firmware installed across all hosts. You should also consider using more small logical unit numbers (LUNs) rather than less large LUNs for your datastores. In addition, you should reduce the number of VM snapshots, because they can cause numerous SCSI reservations. Finally, follow the Configuration Maximums document and reduce the number of VMs per LUN to the recommended maximum, even if you have seen that you can actually add more than that figure.

NOTE   According to the Configuration Maximums document at the time of this writing, the maximum number of powered-on VMs per VMFS-5 is 2048, http://www.vmware.com/pdf/vsphere5/r50/vsphere-50-configuration-maximums.pdf.

Path Thrashing Causes Slow Performance

Path thrashing is most likely to occur on active-passive arrays. It's caused by two hosts attempting access the same LUN through different storage processors. The result is that the LUN is often seen as not available to both hosts. The default setting for the Patch Selection Policy (PSP) of Most Recently Used will generally keep this from occurring. In addition, you should ensure that all hosts that share the same set of LUNs on the active-passive arrays use the same storage processor as well. Properly configured active-active arrays do not cause path thrashing.

Troubleshooting iSCSI Software Initiator Configuration Issues

If your ESXi host generates more commands to a LUN than it can possibly handle, the excess commands are queued by the VMkernel. This situation causes increased latency, which can affect the performance of your VMs. It is generally caused by an improper setting of LUN queue depth, the setting of which varies by the type of storage. You should determine the proper LUN queue depth for your storage from your vendor documentation and then adjust your Disk.SchedNumReqOutstanding parameter accordingly.

Troubleshooting Storage Reports and Storage Maps

As you have no doubt already noticed, you can use a great number of reports and tools for troubleshooting vSphere. In addition, you can use the maps view to see a graphical representation of the relationships between the objects in your vSphere. In fact, you can view storage reports for every object in your datacenters except for the networking objects, which have their own reports and maps. In this section, I will briefly discuss the use of these storage reports and maps.

Storage Reports

Using your Storage Views tab, you can display storage reports to view storage information for any object except networking. For example, you can view datastores and LUNs used by a VM, the adapters that are used to access the LUN, and even the status of the paths to the LUNs. To access storage reports from the Storage Views tab, follow the steps outlined in Activity 6-5.

Activity 6-5 Viewing Storage Reports

1. Log on to your vCenter with your vSphere Client.

2. In the console pane, select the object on which you want to view connected storage (in this case, VM-02), and then open the Storage Views tabs and click the **Reports** button, as shown in Figure 6-31.

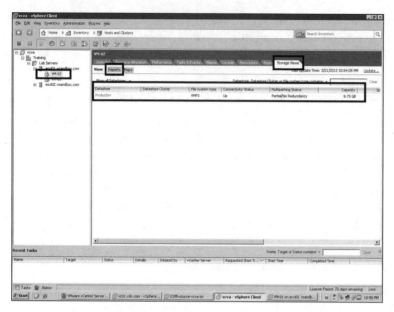

Figure 6-31 The Storage Views Tab and Reports Button

3. Select **View > Filtering** to display the Show All [*Category of Items*] or click the amazingly small drop-down arrow, as shown in Figure 6-32.

Figure 6-32 Choosing the Display on the Storage Views Tab

4. Move the cursor over the column heading to the description of each attribute, as shown in Figure 6-33.

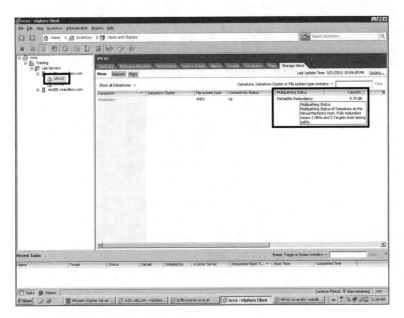

Figure 6-33   Viewing Column Descriptions

Storage Maps

As you can see, Storage Reports can give you a lot of information about your datastores, but all the information is in the form of text. The problem is that we (people) don't think in text; we think in pictures. We can generally understand a situation better if someone will take the time to "draw us a picture."

In essence, that's just what VMware has done with the Maps view of the Storage Views tab. You can use the view to display a graphical representation of every object that relates to your storage. For example, you can tell whether a specific VM has access to a host that has access to a storage processor that has access to a LUN, and whether or not there is a datastore on the LUN. To use your Maps view on your Storage Views tab, follow the steps outlined in Activity 6-6.

Activity 6-6 Viewing Storage Maps

1. Log on to your vCenter with your vSphere Client.

2. In the console pane, select the object on which you want to view connected storage objects (in this case VM-03), and then open the Storage Views tab and click the **Maps** button, as shown in Figure 6-34.

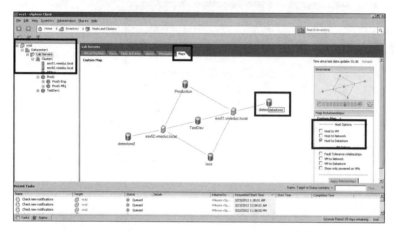

Figure 6-34   Viewing Maps in Storage Views

3. You can choose the objects that you would like to display on your map.

4. You can also hover your mouse over an object for a few seconds to see the "callout" that gives a detailed description of that object.

Identifying the Root Cause of a Storage Issue Based on Troubleshooting Information

After you have obtained information from the reports and maps provided by your vCenter, you can use your knowledge of your systems to compare what you are viewing to what should be occurring. One "catch 22" on this is that the time that you are most likely to need the information is also the time at which it is most likely to be unavailable. For this reason, you should consider printing a copy of your storage maps when everything is running smoothly to be kept on hand for a time when you need to troubleshoot. Then, if you have access to the current maps you can compare what you are seeing with what you have in print. However, if you can no longer use the tools, you have the printed map to use as an initial guide until you can access the current configuration.

Performing Basic Troubleshooting for HA/DRS Clusters and vMotion/Storage vMotion

If you think about it, the technologies that are engaged when we use vMotion, Storage vMotion, HA, and DRS are quite amazing! These are reliable technologies and services as long as they are configured properly with all that is required and as long as that configuration stays in place. Troubleshooting them is therefore just a matter of knowing what is required in order for them to operate properly and then verifying that the correct configurations still exist in your vSphere. In this section, I will discuss the steps involved in verifying the configurations of vMotion, Storage vMotion, HA, and DRS. In addition, I will discuss how to troubleshoot the most common issues associated with these services and how to identify the root cause of the issue so as to make only the appropriate changes.

Identifying HA/DRS and vMotion Requirements

This might seem at first to be too many topics to discuss all at once, but the reason that I can cover them all "rather simultaneously" is that the requirements are very much the same for each of these features. At least the host requirements are very much the same, but the VM requirements vary some from feature to feature. I will first discuss the requirements that are the same and then I will discuss some requirements that only apply to one or two of these features, but not all three.

The requirements for all of HA, DRS, and vMotion are the following:

- All hosts must have at minimum 1Gbps NICs.

- All hosts must share the same datastores or data space. These can be VMFS, NFS, or even RDMs.

- All hosts must have access to the same physical networks.

Additional requirements that apply to vMotion and DRS, but not to HA are as follows:

- All hosts must have compatible CPUs.

- The VMs on the hosts must not have any locally attached CD-ROMs or ISOs that are loaded.

- The VMs cannot have a connection to an internal switch with no uplinks.

- The VMs swap file must either be shared by the hosts or must be created before migration can begin. Solid state drives (SSDs) are now being used for the swap files.

- If the VM uses an RDM, it must be accessible to the source and destination hosts.

None of this should really seem any different than what I discussed previously in Chapter 5, "Establishing and Maintaining Service Levels," but the main point here is that the second bulleted list does not apply to HA. I want to make this very clear, HA does not use vMotion in any way shape or form! HA provides for the automatic restart of VMs when the host that they were on has failed. At that point, the VMs can be restarted on another host as long as the host meets the requirements in the first set of bullet points. It doesn't matter at that point whether the CPUs of the host are compatible or whether the VM had connections to ISOs or an internal switch (and so on). All that matters is that the VMs are protected and that the hosts are in the same HA cluster with a shared datastore and 1Gbps or higher links.

That leaves us with Storage vMotion. You should clearly understand that when you Storage vMotion a VM's files, the VM's state is not moved from one host to another. Therefore, to have a list of requirements for "all hosts" is not needed, because only one host is involved.

For Storage vMotion to be successful, the following requirements must be met:

- The host must have access to both the source and the destination datastores.

- A minimum of one 1Gbps link is required.

- The VM's disks must be in persistent mode or be RDMs.

Verifying vMotion/Storage vMotion Configuration

Now that I have identified what you must have configured in order for vMotion to be successful versus what you must have configured in order for Storage vMotion to be successful, I'll examine where you would look to verify that the proper configuration exists. Because these are two very different types of migration, I will continue to treat them independently of each other. I will first discuss verifying vMotion configuration and then I will discuss verifying Storage vMotion configuration.

Verifying vMotion Configuration

As you might remember, to succeed with vMotion you will need to have a VMkernel port on a switch that is associated to each of the hosts that are involved in the vMotion. In addition, the VMkernel port will need to be enabled for vMotion and the IP addresses of the hosts should be in the same subnet. (point-to-point is best). In addition, consistency is a key factor so unless you are using a vDS (which guarantees consistency of port group naming) you should ensure that your port group names are identical, including correct spelling and case sensitivity.

In addition to the networking requirement, your hosts must have shared datastores. You can verify whether two hosts share the same datastore by looking at the Datastores for each host associated with the VM that you want to vMotion, as shown in Figure 6-35.

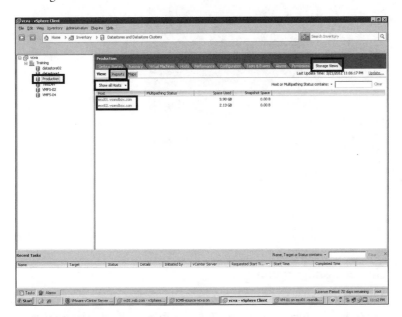

Figure 6-35   Verifying Whether Hosts Share the Same Datastores

Verifying HA Network Configuration

To verify the requirements for HA to function, you should start with the cluster settings. Because the purpose of the cluster is to provide for HA, DRS, or both, it would seem logical that you should check those settings first. However, because I'm following the exam blueprint "to the letter," I will discuss that in our next topic.

What else should you verify then to assure that HA should be able to function? You should look at the vmnics used on the hosts and assure that they are 1Gbps or better. As you should remember from Chapter 2, "Planning and Configuring vSphere Networking," you can modify the properties of the switch by opening its Properties tab on the Networking link of the Configuration tab. After you have done this, you can open the Network Adapters tab, as shown in Figure 6-36. You will need at least 1Gbps vmnics to have an effective HA cluster. You should also verify that the hosts share a datastore, as you did with vMotion requirements.

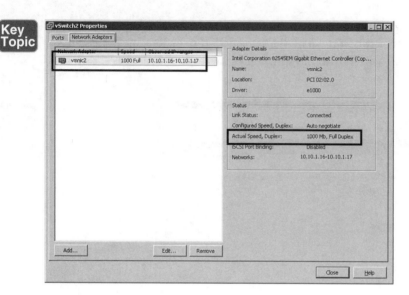

Figure 6-36   Verifying the Speed of the Underlying Network

Verifying HA/DRS Cluster Configuration

Speaking of the cluster configuration, the most general verification that you can make is whether HA/DRS are turned on in the cluster settings. To do this, you should right-click your cluster and then click **Edit Settings**. This will allow you to view the current settings of your cluster, as shown in Figure 6-37. In addition, even if HA is turned on, you should check to make sure that HA monitoring is enabled, as it's possible to turn it off for a maintenance event. Finally, you should ensure that the policies that are configured for HA/DRS are what you configured and that you have followed the guidelines of which I spoke in Chapter 5. For example, check admission control polices for HA and VM affinity rules for DRS.

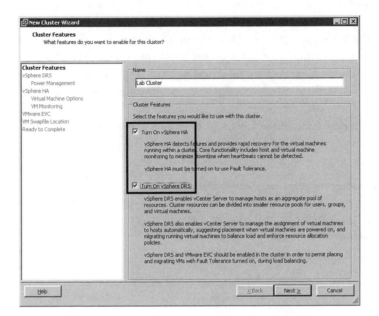

Figure 6-37   Verifying Cluster Settings for HA and DRS

Troubleshooting HA Capacity Issues

This is kind of a "funny" title because I took it straight from the blueprint. What it should say is "Troubleshooting Cluster Capacity Issues that are Due to HA." As you know, admission control policy in HA causes each host to reserve enough resources to recover VMs in the case of a host's failure. This means that if you set your admission control policy too conservatively then you might not be able to start as many VMs as you may have thought possible. For example, changing from a policy that allows for only one host failure to one that allows two host failures can have a dramatic affect on the VM capacity of your cluster, especially in a small cluster. Therefore, without rehashing all of what I discussed in Chapter 5, you should just verify that the settings that you expect to see are still there.

Troubleshooting HA Redundancy Issues

As you know, HA stands for *high availability*. This high availability is maintained by the heartbeats that are exchanged between hosts in an HA cluster. When the cluster determines that a host is isolated or has failed, it will follow the isolation response that you have configured. The default isolation response in vSphere 5.0 is Leave Powered On, which will leave the VMs powered on with the assumption that they still have the resources that they need. Other options are power off or shut down. If you have a separate management network or a separate heartbeat network, you can give the host another tool with which to make a more accurate decision with regard to whether to leave powered on or to shut down. If you are troubleshooting the configuration of this network, you should examine your network settings to ensure that the network is in place. If you have not configured redundancy for management, the host will let you know about it when you open its Summary tab, as shown in Figure 6-38.

Figure 6-38   The No Management Network Redundancy Warning

Interpreting the DRS Resource Distributing Graph and Target/Current Host Load Deviation

VMware used to just say, "Set DRS at Fully Automated, set the Migration Threshold in the center, and trust us." Then they really didn't give you native tools to check how well they were doing for you. Now, you have tool called the Resource Distribution Chart that allows you to see a graphical representation of the current resources being used by each VM on each host, as shown in Figure 6-39.

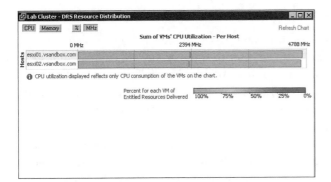

Figure 6-39   Viewing the Resource Distribution Chart

You can also view general information in the DRS panel on the Summary tab for the host by clicking the **View Resource Distribution Chart** link in the vSphere DRS panel, as shown in Figure 6-40. In general, if the standard deviation is within an acceptable level for the balance of the VMs across the hosts in the cluster, it will be indicated by a green checkmark and a statement that says "Load balanced." An imbalance will be indicated by a yellow warning and a statement of "Load imbalance."

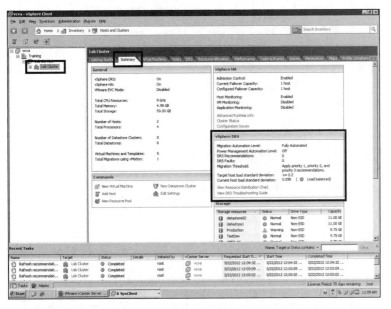

Figure 6-40   Viewing the DRS Panel on the Summary Tab for a Cluster

Troubleshooting DRS Load Imbalance Issues

If you notice a load imbalance, you will want to determine why the imbalance was allowed to happen. It could be that the cluster or some of the VMs in it are not set to Fully Automated. It could also be that it was "intentionally" allowed by the system based on your Migration Threshold or VM-VM-Host affinity configuration. In addition, you should check to make sure that there are no VMs that are using a large amount of resources and that cannot be vMotioned, as that will stop DRS from being effective. Finally, you might want to check to see if there is one huge VM that must be on one host or another and seems to throw off the balance no matter where DRS places it. You can view the resources of VMs and compare on the Virtual Machines tab of your cluster. You can also sort them in host order by clicking the column label, so that you can easily determine which VMs are on which host, as shown in Figure 6-41

Figure 6-41   Viewing the Resources of VMs in a Cluster

Troubleshooting vMotion/Storage vMotion Migration Issues

If your vSphere and your VMs meet all the requirements for vMotion, you should be able to vMotion. If you can vMotion, you should also be able to Storage vMotion (given that you have an Enterprise or Enterprise+ license), because vMotion has all of the configuration requirements of Storage vMotion, and more. If you cannot vMotion or Storage vMotion, go back through the list of requirements to see what you are missing. You can refresh your memory by looking again at the "Migrating Virtual Machines" section of Chapter 5.

Interpreting vMotion Resource Maps

As I said earlier, we don't really think in text, so wouldn't it be great to have a tool that will show you in an easy to read picture format whether your vSphere meets all of the requirements to vMotion a VM from one host to another. That's what the vMotion Resource Map does. You can access a vMotion Resource Map for a VM by simply selecting the VM on the console pane and then opening the **Maps** tab, as shown in Figure 6-42. The vMotion Resources Map will show you what resources are currently connected to the VM and whether those resources would be available if the VM were to be vMotioned to another host. If you can "read between the lines," you will see what is missing and why the VM might not be able to vMotion to another host. In this case, VM-02 is connected to a local ISO image on datastore1 of esxi01 and would not have a connection to the same ISO from esxi02.

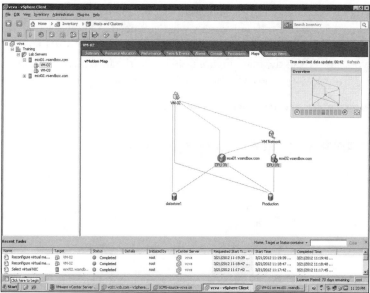

Figure 6-42   A vMotion Map with an Error

Identifying the Root Cause for a DRS/HA Cluster or Migration Issue Based on Troubleshooting Information

If you know all of the configuration pieces that are supposed to be there, you can just start checking them off one by one to determine whether they are present. The nice thing about Storage vMotion and especially about vMotion is that the wizard will validate most of the configuration for you and give you a list of changes that you must make to perform the migration, as shown in Figure 6-43.

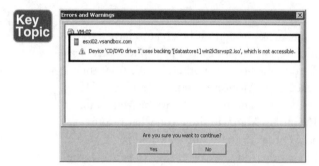

Figure 6-43   An Easy-to-Interpret Error Message

By carefully reading the information under Compatibility, you can determine the root cause of the issue that is keeping you from being able to vMotion or Storage vMotion. This is a very intuitive wizard that tells you exactly what you need to know, as long as you understand enough about your vSphere to interpret what it's telling you. Once you fix the issue, you can refresh the map. Figure 6-44 shows the map after the ISO file was unmounted from VM-02; the vMotion should succeed now.

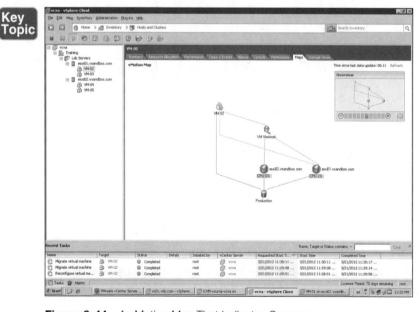

Figure 6-44   A vMotion Map That Indicates Success

Summary

The main topics covered in this chapter are the following:

- I began this chapter by discussing basic troubleshooting techniques for ESXi hosts. In particular, I discussed how you can enable the tools that you can use along with the VMware Support Team as a last resort when more conventional tools are not working. In addition, I discussed how you can monitor an ESXi host's health on the host itself as well as through your vCenter. Finally, I discussed how you easily export a diagnostic bundle to assist the VMware Support Team in assisting you.

- I then discussed basic vSphere network troubleshooting tools and techniques. In particular, I discussed how to verify your network configuration and the configuration of the VMs on your network. In addition, I discussed troubleshooting port group issues and issues with physical network cards. Finally, I covered how to identify the root cause of a network issue based on troubleshooting information.

- I then turned my attention toward troubleshooting vSphere storage. I discussed the tools and techniques that you can use to verify your vSphere storage. In addition, I discussed troubleshooting storage contention issues, over-commitment issues, and iSCSI software initiator configuration issues. I also discussed the proper use of storage reports and storage maps. Finally, I discussed how to identify the root cause of a storage issue based on troubleshooting information.

- I ended this chapter with a discussion of basic troubleshooting for HA/DRS clusters and vMotion/Storage vMotion. In particular, I identified the requirements for each of these features and compared and contrasted them. In addition, I discussed how you can verify the configuration of each of these requirements using the tools provided by your vCenter. Finally, I discussed troubleshooting issues with regard to HA and DRS by using the reports and maps provided by your vCenter.

Exam Preparation Tasks

Review All the Key Topics

Review the most important topics from inside the chapter, noted with the Key Topic icon in the outer margin of the page. Table 6-2 lists these key topics and the page numbers where each is found. Know how to perform basic troubleshooting on ESXi hosts, vSphere networks, vSphere storage, and HA/DRS clusters.

Table 6-2 Key Topics for Chapter 6

Key Topic Element	Description	Page Number
Activity 6-1	Enabling TSM from the DCUI	426
Activity 6-2	Configuring TSM from the vSphere Client	428
Figure 6-7	Viewing Logs on the DCUI	430
Figure 6-8	Viewing the VMkernel Log	431
Figure 6-9	Viewing Logs on a Single Host	431
Bullet List	Troubleshooting License Issues	432
Figure 6-10	Viewing Health Status on a Specific Host	434
Figure 6-11	Viewing Hardware Status on a Host Through vCenter	434
Activity 6-3	Exporting Diagnostic Information from a Host Log-In	435
Activity 6-4	Exporting Diagnostic Information from a vCenter Log-In	437
Figure 6-21	A Typical Configuration on a vSS	441
Figure 6-22	Viewing a VM's Network Configuration	442
Figure 6-23	Port Group Settings on a vDS	443
Figure 6-24	Settings for a Physical Adapter	443
Bullet List	Troubleshooting Virtual Networking Issues	444
Figure 6-25	The Storage Link on the Configuration Tab	446
Figure 6-26	Customizing the Storage Link	446
Figure 6-27	The Storage Views Tab	447
Figure 6-28	Customizing the Storage Views Tab	448
Figure 6-29	Settings for Multipathing of Storage	449
Figure 6-30	Viewing Multipathing Status on the Storage Views Tab	449

Key Topic Element	Description	Page Number
Note	Configuration Maximum of VMs per VMFS-5 Datastore	450
Activity 6-5	Viewing Storage Reports	451
Activity 6-6	Viewing Storage Maps	453
Bullet List	Requirements Common to HA, DRS, and vMotion	455
Bullet List	Requirements That Apply to vMotion and DRS, but Not to HA	455
Bullet List	Requirements for Storage vMotion	456
Figure 6-35	Verifying Whether Hosts Share the Same Datastores	457
Figure 6-36	Verifying the Speed of the Underlying Network	458
Figure 6-37	Verifying Cluster Settings for HA and DRS	459
Figure 6-38	The No Management Redundancy Warning	460
Figure 6-39	Viewing the Resource Distribution Chart	461
Figure 6-40	Viewing the DRS Panel on the Summary Tab for a Cluster	461
Figure 6-41	Viewing the Resources of VMs in a Cluster	462
Figure 6-42	A vMotion Map with an Error	463
Figure 6-43	An Easy-to-Interpret Error Message	464
Figure 6-44	A vMotion Map That Indicates Success	464

Review Questions

The answers to these review questions are in Appendix A.

1. Which of the following is designed by VMware to be used as a last resort?

  a. vSphere Client

  b. PowerCLI

  c. vCLI

  d. TSM

2. In which of the following locations can you enable ESXi Shell? (Choose two.)

   a. The Administration tab

   b. DCUI

   c. The firewall properties of a host

   d. Security profile

3. Which of the following logs cannot be retrieved from a DCUI?

   a. Syslog

   b. vCenter

   c. VMkernel

   d. Config

4. Which of the following is an absolute network requirement to manage an ESXi host remotely?

   a. A VMkernel port configured for vMotion

   b. A separate vSS or vDS for Management

   c. A VMkernel port configured for Management

   d. A VM port group configured for Management

5. Which type of vNIC driver is a best practice to use whenever possible?

   a. vmxnet3

   b. e1000

   c. vmxnet1

   d. You should never use a vnic driver.

6. Which of the following is *not* a possible view of the Storage Views tab?

   a. Show All Virtual Machines

   b. Show All VMkernel Ports

   c. Show All Clusters

   d. Show All SCSI Adapters

7. Which of the following path selection policies cannot cause path thrashing?

    a. MRU on an active-passive array

    b. Fixed on an active-active array

    c. All path selection policies can cause path thrashing.

    d. Path thrashing in no longer a concern with any path selection policy.

8. Which of the following is a requirement for DRS, but not a requirement for HA?

    a. All hosts must have shared datastores.

    b. All hosts must be in the same cluster.

    c. All hosts must share the same processor vendor and family.

    d. All hosts must have access to the same physical networks.

9. Which of the following is *not* a requirement for Storage vMotion?

    a. VMs must have compatible CPUs.

    b. The host must have access to both the source and destination datastores.

    c. A minimum of 1Gbps link.

    d. VMs must be in persistent mode or be RDMs.

10. What tool should you use to get detailed information about the CPU and memory in use on your DRS clusters?

    a. Admission Control

    b. Tasks and Events

    c. The DRS Panel

    d. The Resource Distribution Chart

This chapter covers the following subjects:

- Monitoring ESXi, vCenter, and Virtual Machines
- Creating and Administering vCenter Server Alarms

CHAPTER 7

Monitoring vSphere Implementation and Managing vCenter Alarms

As you know, there are four core resources in any computer system; CPU, memory, disk, and network. Which one is most important? The one that is giving you a problem; that's the one that is most important at any given time! Seriously, to get the most out of your vSphere implementation, you have to know which tools to use, what to look for, and what you expect to see. Then, by comparing what you see to what you should be seeing, you can make critical decisions and changes.

In this chapter, I will discuss two main topics: monitoring tools, and alarms. To understand your options with each of these, you should first understand the metrics and measurements and then you should know which tools are appropriate to monitor each metric. In addition, you should know how to build specific bundles of logs to send to VMware Support. You should also be familiar with the process of stopping and starting critical services and configuring timeout settings for vCenter Server. Finally, you should know how to use tools to determine performance data and how to set alarms to alert you when your preset thresholds are reached.

"Do I Know This Already?" Quiz

The "Do I Know This Already?" quiz allows you to assess whether you should read this entire chapter or simply jump to the "Exam Preparation Tasks" section for review. If you are in doubt, read the entire chapter. Table 7-1 outlines the major headings in this chapter and the corresponding "Do I Know This Already?" quiz questions. You can find the answers in Appendix A, "Answers to the 'Do I Know This Already?' Quizzes and Chapter Review Questions."

Table 7-1 "Do I Know This Already?" Section-to-Question Mapping

Foundations Topics Section	Questions Covered in This Section
Monitoring ESXi, vCenter, and Virtual Machines	1–8
Creating and Administering vCenter Server Alarms	9–10

1. Which of the following is *not* viewable on your vSphere Client when you are logged on directly to a host?

   a. The Events tab

   b. Recent Tasks

   c. The Tasks and Events tab

   d. The Performance tab

2. Which of the following memory technologies is most closely associated with ballooning technique?

   a. TPS

   b. vmmemctl

   c. Memory compression

   d. Swap

3. Which of the following memory conservation techniques is used by default, even when memory is *not* in contention?

   a. Ballooning

   b. Memory compression

   c. Swap file

   d. TPS

4. Which of following are true about CPU Ready value on VMs? (Choose two.)

   a. The lower the CPU Ready value, the better.

   b. A CPU Ready value of 5% is considered high.

   c. A CPU Ready value of 5% is considered acceptable.

   d. The higher the CPU Ready value, the better.

5. Which of the following would be considered a storage issue that needs to be addressed? (Choose two.)

   a. VMkernel command latency of 5ms

   b. VMkernel command latency of 1ms

   c. Physical device command latency of 30ms

   d. Physical device command latency of 10ms

6. Which of the following can your vCenter be configured as in your SNMP network?

   a. A Management Information Base (MIB)

   b. An agent

   c. A trap

   d. A community

7. Which of the following vCenter log settings are only recommended for troubleshooting? (Choose two.)

   a. Error

   b. Information

   c. Verbose

   d. Trivia

8. In which of the following tools can you restart management agents?

   a. vSphere Client

   b. Hosts and Clusters view

   c. VMs and Templates view

   d. DCUI

9. Which of the following is *not* a default utilization alarm in vCenter?

   a. Host CPU Usage

   b. Cluster Network Usage

   c. Virtual Machine CPU Usage

   d. Datastore Usage on Disk

10. Which of the following is *not* a possible action for VM alarms without the use of a script?

   a. Send a notification email

   b. Increase memory of VM

   c. Migrate VM

   d. Shut down guest on VM

Monitoring ESXi, vCenter Server, and Virtual Machines

In this section, I will focus on four tools and the data that you can gather using them:

- Tasks and Events

- Performance Charts

- Resxtop

- Perfmon

I will discuss how to use each of these tools to monitor your hosts, vCenters, and VMs. Finally, given the performance data gathered, I will discuss how you can identify the affected vSphere resource.

Describing How Tasks and Events are Viewed in vCenter Server

Tasks and Events in vCenter is a very flexible tool. You can view tasks and events that are associated with a single object, or all objects in your vSphere inventory. So, what is the difference between a task and an event? Well, basically an event is an indication of an occurrence in vCenter that was part of running vCenter. In contrast, a task is an indication that an administrator has performed an action that has yet to complete. In essence, you could say that a task is an event that an administrator caused to happen. Because there are many tasks and events that you can monitor, it is useful to know how to filter your view so that you focus on what is most important to you.

Note that the title of this section relates to viewing tasks and events in vCenter. This is the best practice method because when your vSphere Client is connected directly to an ESXi host, the Tasks and Events option will not be offered. In fact, it is replaced by an Events tab. You can still view Recent Tasks pane at the bottom of your vSphere Client, as shown in Figure 7-1.

Figure 7-1   The Events Tab and Recent Tasks Status Bar on a Host Login

In contrast, your vCenter not only shows you Recent Tasks but also includes a Tasks and Events tab that you can use to gather information about either or both types of occurrences. In addition, you can filter the information in three different ways. I will briefly discuss each of the ways by which you can filter the information shown in your vCenter Tasks and Events tab.

Viewing by Object Selected in Console Pane

The first choice that you make with regard to Tasks and Events is which object to select in the console pane, on the left. By default, the tasks list for an object includes that object and all of its child objects in your inventory. This can give you a good overall view at any level of the inventory hierarchy that you desire. As you can see in Figure 7-2, I have selected Cluster1 in the console pane, but I can view information about child objects, such as hosts and VMs, in my output as well. This is because I still have the default of **Show All Entries** selected.

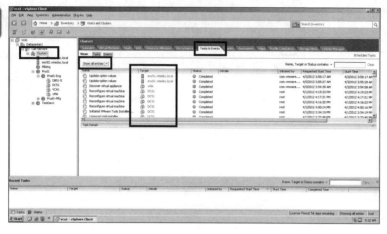

Figure 7-2   Viewing All Entries Within an Object

Showing Only Object Entries

After you have chosen the object in your console pane, you can change the default behavior so that you can view only tasks and events that are directly associated with that object, not its child objects. This might allow you to focus your attention on something specific to that object, especially if the object has many child objects. You can do this by simply clicking the drop-down next to Show All Entries and selecting the other option, as shown in Figure 7-3.

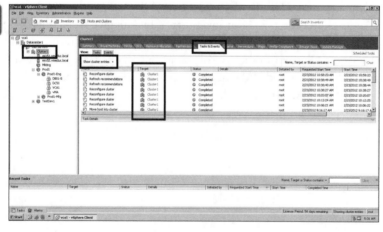

Figure 7-3   Showing Only Object Entries

Filtering by Keyword

You can also filter tasks and events based on any attribute, including name, target, status, initiator, change history, and time. These can be associated to any keyword of your choice. In essence, you are asking vCenter, "What tasks or events do you know about that have 'this' in them?" You can choose one of these attributes or multiples of them, as shown in Figure 7-4. This can be an effective tool to quickly drill down to the information that that you need to obtain.

Figure 7-4   Filtering by Keyword

NOTE   If the Show All Entries and Keyword Filtering selections do not appear, they have been disabled. You should click **View** in the File menu at the top of vCenter and then select **Filtering** to reenable them.

Identifying Critical Performance Metrics

To reiterate what I said at the beginning of this chapter, you have four core resources to monitor and manage: memory, CPU, network, and storage. A weakness in any of these core four will most certainly be felt by your VMs and therefore by your end users. I will first briefly touch on the most common suspects in each of your core four, and then I will explain more about how you can monitor each one and what you should expect to see:

- **Memory:** You should keep your attention on whether you are seeing any "ballooning," which indicates use of virtual machine memory control (vmmemctl). Ballooning indicates that memory is becoming scarce and therefore the VMkernel has instructed the VM to create a shared memory area from which each VM will draw a portion of its memory. As I will explain later in this section, a little ballooning is not bad, but a lot of ballooning is not good.

- **CPU:** You should pay close attention to the CPU Ready values on your VMs. A higher-than-normal CPU ready value is an indicator that the VM is starved for CPU resources. I know that sounds backward, but I will discuss it in greater detail later in this section.

- **Network:** You can do a number of things to improve network performance, such as installing the latest VMware Tools, using traffic shaping, using faster physical network interface cards (NICs), load balancing, and so on. You should also consider placing VMs that frequently communicate to each other on the same host, same switch, same subnet, so they can communicate internally without using your LAN and free up that bandwidth on your LAN. To monitor network traffic, you are really just measuring the effective bandwidth between the VM and its peer and looking for dropped transmit packets and dropped receive packets. I will discuss this all in greater detail later in this section.

- **Storage:** The main factors here are with regard to the datastores that you've chosen and the speed of the logical unit numbers (LUNs) to which they are connected. You can enhance performance somewhat by using a multipathing method such as round-robin. You can also enhance availability using a multipathing method such as fixed or most recently used (MRU). To measure the effectiveness of storage, you can compare your statistics to known standards, but it's much better to have your own baselines to use for comparison. I will discuss this in greater detail later in this section.

Explaining Common Memory Metrics

You should understand that many of the components in your vSphere are playing a "shell game" with regard to memory. As shown in Figure 7-5, the only true physical memory is the memory that is installed in your physical ESXi hosts. The guest operating system in each of your VMs "believes" that it has a specific amount of a physical memory available to it, expressed as its available memory. This is the memory that was assigned to the VM when it was created. In reality, the VMkernel could elect to supply that memory using a swap file, which would hamper the VM's performance. In addition, the guest operating is telling the applications that are using its memory that it is physical as well, when it "knows" that some of the memory that it provides the applications is actually from its own virtual memory area on its connected disks. For example, pagefile.sys is used by Microsoft's client and server guest OSs.

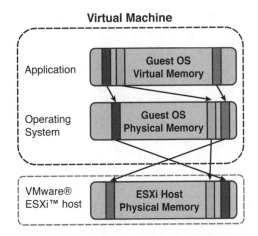

Figure 7-5   The Memory "Shell Game"

Because of this elaborate shell game with memory, it's possible to provide the VMs with the memory that they need when they need it. However, because we don't want to hamper the VM's performance, we use some very cool and patented technologies and processes that allow us to get the most out of the physical RAM provided by the host and use the swap file only as a last resort. To know what you are monitoring, you really need to understand these technologies and processes first. I will briefly describe each of these processes and how the VMkernel uses them to enhance the memory usage of the VMs on your hosts:

- **Transparent page sharing (TPS):** The best way that I can describe this is that it's like memory de-dupe. You may be familiar with data deduplication when running a backup so that redundant components only have to be stored once. Well, this is like that, but with memory pages. As shown in Figure 7-6, if several VMs on a host are running the same guest OS and the same applications, this technology can be very effective because it will require that only one copy of each page be stored in physical RAM on the host. This memory sharing will ensure that the host uses far less physical memory than it otherwise would have and allow for significant overcommitment of memory resources without performance degradation. TPS is a built-in component of ESX/ESXi and is enabled by default. It is used whether there is contention for memory or not.

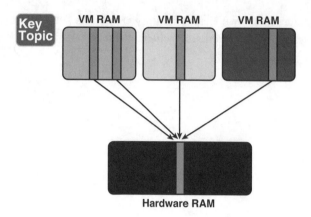

Figure 7-6   Transparent Page Sharing

- **Balloon driver mechanism (vmmemctl):** This system works along with the guest OS on the server to reclaim pages that are considered least valuable to the guest operating system. The balloon driver is installed when you install VMware Tools on a VM. It uses a proprietary technique that creates a shared memory area from the reclaimed pages and allows the VMs to use the shared (ballooned) memory without a significant performance hit. When the VMkernel has determined that memory is scarce and therefore in contention, this technique increases pressure on the guest OS and forces it to use more of its native swap file (pagefile.sys in Microsoft servers). The genius of this system is that the guest OS is the one that determines when pages are "old" and can come out of physical RAM (as it knows best) and the VMkernel just takes advantage of the opportunity to reclaim the unused memory space for its own use. If you notice that a VM is using its swap file but has not used any ballooning, you should suspect that VMware Tools are not installed on the VM and verify their proper installation. Figure 7-7 illustrates the balloon driver mechanism.

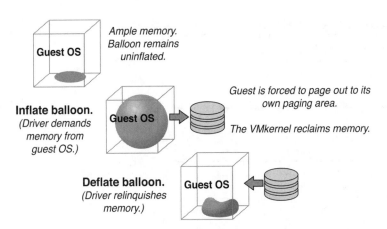

Figure 7-7   The Balloon Driver Mechanism

■ **Memory compression:** When there is contention for memory, large pages are broken down so that each individual memory page is 4KB in size. With 100% memory compression, the VMkernel can compress each page to 2KB in size, thereby allowing many more pages of memory to be stored in the same physical memory space. This patented memory compression technique is used only when the VMkernel has determined that memory is scarce. You might ask, "Why don't you just compress them all the time?" Well, compressed memory has to be decompressed before being used, causing a performance hit. However, the idea behind this technology is that the decompression performance hit is not as significant as the performance hit of running memory off of disk. Therefore, your ESXi host will attempt to compress the page first, if the memory compression cache allows and if it can compress the page to 2KB, before sending it to disk. You can set the maximum size of the memory compression cache as a percentage of memory in the Advanced Settings for memory within the Configuration tab and the Software section, as shown in Figure 7-8. The default setting is 10% of memory.

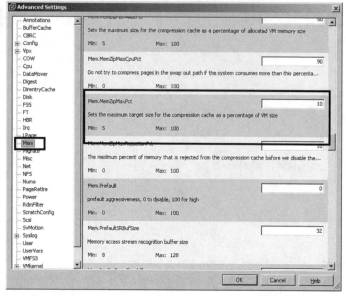

Figure 7-8   The Memory Compression Cache Setting

■ **Swap file:** A swap file named *VMname*.vwsp is created by the VMkernel when-ever a VM is powered on and deleted when it is powered off. Its size is equal to the available memory of the VM (the amount the guest OS is told that it has) minus its reservation (a guarantee of physical RAM). Even though it is created when the VM is powered on, we don't really want to use it. Why, then, do we create it? Well, basically, just in case.

If you were to push the system past its limits without a swap file, the VMs would each freeze up and the users, and ultimately you, would be negatively affected. With a swap file configured, you can determine by monitoring that it is being used and make the necessary changes, which might include adding more memory or maybe just redistributing VM loads. Any use of the swap file should be considered an issue to be resolved.

NOTE   The size of the swap file will increase on-the-fly if the reservation is reduced, but it will not decrease until you a restart the VM.

When you examine the Memory Panel on the Resource Allocation tab of a VM, as shown in Figure 7-9, you will notice many different types of memory that bear mentioning here so that you have a better understanding of the big picture with regard to memory use.

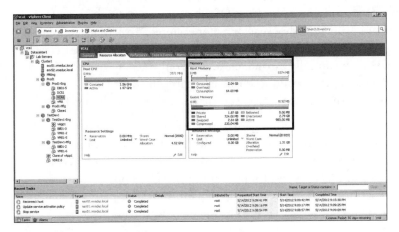

Figure 7-9   The Memory Panel of a VM

The following are memory terms with which you should be familiar:

- **Host memory:** The amount of memory with which you provisioned your VM (in other words, the amount that you told the guest OS it could use).

- **Overhead:** The amount of memory that the VMkernel thinks it will use to run the virtualized workload.

- **Consumed:** The amount of physical memory (RAM) that has been allocated to the VM. On the Resource Allocation tab, overhead memory is included, but on the Performance tab it is not included.

- **Private:** The amount of memory that is currently being provided from the physical memory (RAM) of the host.

- **Shared:** The total amount of memory that is currently being shared by Transparent Page Sharing (TPS).

- **Swapped:** The amount of memory that is currently being reclaimed by VM-kernel swapping.

- **Compressed:** The amount of memory that is currently stored in the VM's compression cache.

- **Ballooned:** The amount of memory reclaimed by the balloon driver. It's best if this is a value of zero.

- **Unaccessed:** The amount of memory that has never been accessed by this guest.

- **Active:** The total amount of memory that is actively used, an estimate done by statistical sampling.

Explaining Common CPU Metrics

First, you should understand that you can't necessarily believe everything that you see on the tools that are built in to the guest OS, since the guest OS is being fooled into "thinking" that it's on a physical machine. For example, Task Manager might report high usage of CPU for a VM because it doesn't "realize" that the CPU resource for that VM is dynamically expandable and it's only "seeing" part of the resource. That said, you can trust your performance charts on your vCenter, and you can trust VMware performance tools such as Resxtop, which I will discuss later.

What should you be looking for with regard to memory metrics? As I mentioned earlier, the most common memory metric is called CPU Ready value. It's a crazy name for this metric because it seems all backward, at least it does to me. What CPU Ready value really means is "wait time" for the vCPU. In other words, the vCPU is ready to perform, and has been asked to perform by the guest OS, but it is waiting for a logical CPU to provide it the processing power that it needs. (A logical CPU is a physical core on a non-hyperthreaded system or half of a physical core on a hyperthreaded system.)

Typically, a CPU Ready value that is higher than 1 for a sustained period of time should be investigated. A CPU Ready value of 2 or higher is considered very bad. Where do these numbers originate? The performance charts are taking a sample of vCPU activity every 20 seconds. If during that 20 seconds, a vCPU spends greater than 2 seconds waiting on a physical core, that is a CPU Ready value of 2, which is certainly considered to be an issue that should be addressed. To further complicate this value, it is actually expressed on the performance charts as 2000ms but on esxtop/resxtop as 10% (2 seconds/20 seconds). Later in this chapter, in the section entitled "Determining Host Performance Using Resxtop and Guest Perfmon," I will discuss these metrics as seen on each of these tools.

Explaining Common Network Metrics

As I discussed in our previous chapter on troubleshooting, your network performance is dependent on your application workload and on your network configuration. Dropped network packets indicate a bottleneck in the network. Slow network performance can also be a sign of load-balancing issues.

Make sure you have installed VMware Tools on each machine and that the machine is using the proper vnic driver. Whenever possible, use vmxnet3 vNIC drivers. You can then determine whether packets are being dropped by using esxtop, resxtop, or the Advanced performance charts to examine droppedTx and droppedRx counter values. Later in this chapter, in the section "Determining Host Performance Using Resxtop and Guest Perfmon," I will discuss how you can use the tools to examine your network metrics.

Explaining Common Storage Metrics

As I mentioned earlier, it's important to have a baseline of your core four resources, when everything is performing well, to use as a comparison when things begin to slow down. This is most important in the area of storage metrics. One of the reasons for this fact is that there are many variables to consider with regard to storage.

First, there is the storage as the host sees it and uses it for its datastores. The performance of the datastores is based on the speed of the underlying LUNs and the speed and efficiency of your access method to the LUNs. Your access method could be through Fibre Channel connectors and switches, through your IP network, or even local to the host. In addition, you could be using Fibre Channel, Fibre Channel over Ethernet (FCoE), Internet Small Computer System Interface (iSCSI), or network-attached storage (NAS). Second, although the VM sees all of its storage as "local SCSI," the underlying storage will still affect its performance.

You should be most concerned with two factors: the VMkernel command latency, and the physical device command latency. If the average time spent in the VMkernel per SCSI command is higher than 2ms to 3ms, the array or the host may be overworked. Likewise, if the average time that the physical device takes to complete a SCSI command is greater than 15ms to 20ms, you have a slow and likely overworked or underdesigned array. As you can see, these standards have some flexibility in them, which is why it's important to know your own baseline.

Comparing and Contrasting Overview and Advanced Charts

Your vCenter makes available a variety of tools to help you monitor and manage your vSphere. Included in these tools are performance charts for CPU, memory, storage, and networking. In this section, I will discuss two forms of these charts: Overview and Advanced.

You can easily create a view that gives you a little information about each of the core four resources by using the Overview performance charts. Overview charts give you a lot of general information in one place, and therefore might be a good place to start if you know your own baselines and could quickly spot a metric that was significantly different from normal. Included in your Overview charts is information about the object that you selected in the console pane before you selected the Performance tab. You can filter the information to show only the object or to show charts for child objects as well. In addition, you can filter the time range of the data that you are viewing so that you can spot a trend. There are also tools for refreshing the data and for help if you need more information about a specific chart or metric, all shown in Figure 7-10.

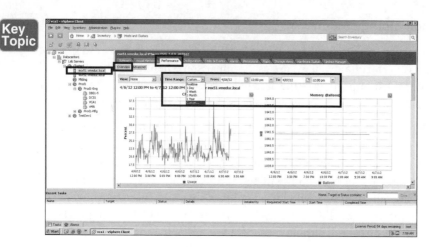

Figure 7-10   Overview Performance Charts

In contrast, the Advanced performance charts view allows you to drill down on a specific resource or metric and get more detailed information and even make comparisons to other objects. You can easily choose the objects that you want to monitor and the counters for those objects. In addition to viewing all of your selected objects, you can easily drill down on a specific counter to get the detailed information that you need, as shown in Figure 7-11. You can even save your chart settings to use them over and over as the data changes.

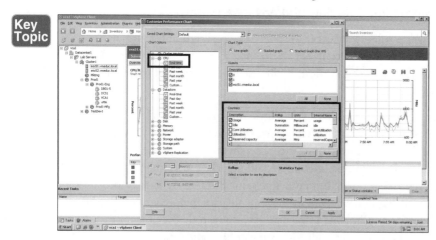

Figure 7-11   Choosing Performance Objects and Counters

In addition, you can specify the time period for the counters or examine them in real time. The default setting is for Overview charts when you open the Performance tab. You can change this default behavior in **Administration > vCenter Server**

Settings of your vSphere Client, as shown in Figure 7-12. Later in this chapter, in the section "Creating an Advanced Chart," I will discuss creating an Advanced performance chart to examine these counters.

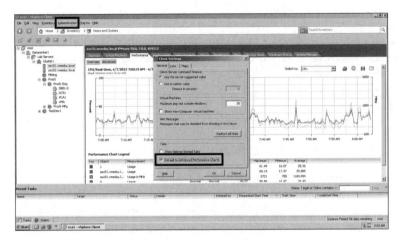

Figure 7-12   Changing Default View to Advanced Performance Charts

Configuring SNMP for vCenter Server

Simple Network Management Protocol (SNMP) is a lightweight protocol that has been around for many years and allows administrators to collect information about the devices in their network. The network collection area is referred to as a community. Within a community are a Management Information Base (MIB) and usually many agents. The agents can initiate and send a trap to the MIB in their community. In addition, agents can receive GET requests that might contain a configuration command for the agent.

Each of your ESXi hosts includes an SNMP agent that is embedded into hostd. It can send traps as well as receive GET requests, but it is disabled by default. To enable it, you must configure it using the vSphere command-line interface (CLI) command vicfg-snmp. Through the CLI, you must first configure the SNMP community to match that of your MIB. You can then configure the vCenter as an agent that will send traps regarding the hosts and the VMs in your vSphere. You can also configure the hosts to receive hardware events from Intelligent Platform Management Interface (IPMI) or Common Information Model (CIM) indicators and send that information to the MIB, filtering the output for just what you need. After you have configured the hosts to send the traps, you should configure your vSphere Client to receive and interpret them. The precise configuration of each of these steps is command line based and therefore not on the exam and beyond the scope of this text. You can find more information on the vSphere Documentation Center at http://pubs.vmware.com/vsphere-50/index.jsp

Configuring Active Directory and SMTP Settings for vCenter Server

This might seem at first like two topics that shouldn't go together. After all, configuring Active Directory settings is very different from configuring SMTP settings. The only reason that I can imagine for them being in the same blueprint objective is that they are right next to each other in the dialog box where the configuration is done. Even so, I will discuss each of the settings separate of each other.

Configuring Active Directory Settings for vCenter

It should be noted here that I am not discussing the configuration of vSphere for Active Directory authentication, because I discussed that previously in Chapter 1, "Planning, Installing, Configuring, and Upgrading vCenter Server and VMware ESXi." What I am discussing here are settings that affect the way that your vCenter interacts with Active Directory. The defaults for the settings, shown in Figure 7-13, are usually sufficient, but you can change them if needed.

Figure 7-13   Active Directory Settings for vCenter

The settings that you can configure and their general purpose are as follows:

- **Active Directory Timeout:** This is the timeout interval in seconds for connecting to your Active Directory server. The default is 60 seconds, which is generally ample time to make the connection. You can increase or decrease as needed for your own Active Directory servers. You might need to increase this setting if authentication is slower than normal in your Active Directory.

- **Enable Query Limit:** Without the box selected, all users and groups will appear in the Add Permissions dialog box. This prepopulation of the AD might take some time. To improve the speed at which you get the choices that you need, you can limit the number of users and groups that will be prepopulated. A setting of 0 here, after selecting to Enable Query Limit, will actually prepopulate all users and groups.

- **Enable Validation:** This is the "master switch" to have the vCenter periodically check its known AD users against the AD server in your domain. The default is to enable the validation.

- **Validation Period:** This is the number of minutes to wait before performing a synchronization and validation of vCenter known users and groups against your AD server. The default setting is 1440 minutes. (24 hours). You should leave this setting enabled. In addition, you should leave it at the default setting except in extremely dynamic environments where many users are continually being added/deleted.

Configuring SMTP Settings for a vCenter Server

You can use the Simple Mail Transfer Protocol (SMTP) agent included in vCenter to send email notifications when configured alarms are triggered. (Later in this chapter, in the section, "Creating and Administering vCenter Server Alarms," I will discuss the types of alarms that you can configure and how to configure them.) To configure the SMTP setting, follow the steps outlined in Activity 7-1.

Activity 7-1 Configuring SMTP Settings for a vCenter Server

1. Log on to your vCenter with your vSphere Client.

2. From the File menu at the top right, select **Administration** and then **vCenter Server Settings**, as shown in Figure 7-14.

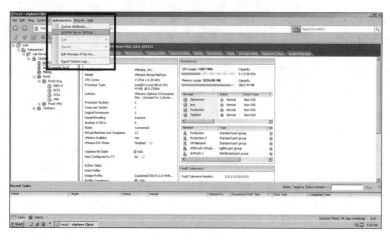

Figure 7-14   vCenter Settings

3. In the dialog box on the left column, select **Mail**.

4. Configure the address for your SMTP server in the form of an IP address or hostname, as shown in Figure 7-15.

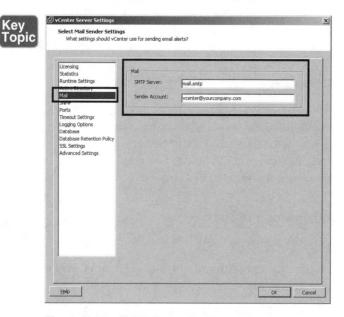

Figure 7-15   SMTP Server Settings

5. Configure the sender account that the vCenter will use to send information. This should be a valid email address in your network, also shown in Figure 7-15.

6. Click **OK** to save the changes.

Configuring vCenter Server Logging Options

You can easily configure the amount of detail that your vCenter will collect in log files. You can select the best option for you in **vCenter Server Settings > Logging Options**. You have six choices, as shown in Figure 7-16. Each selection down from the top to the bottom of the list gets you more information on your log. The default is at midpoint and is called Information (Normal Logging). Because more logging is not always better, and can cause performance degradation, you should leave the default selected unless you are specifically looking for information that would not appear in the Information logging, such as when troubleshooting.

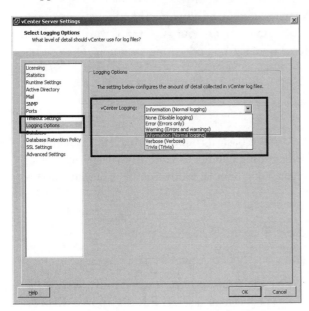

Figure 7-16   vCenter Server Logging Options

Your six choices, in order of increasing log information, are as follows:

- **None (Disable Logging):** This one speaks for itself. It is not a best practice to disable logging and is not recommended.

- **Error:** Displays only error log entries.

- **Warning (Errors and Warnings):** Displays information about errors and warnings. This setting might be useful as a filter, but the logs can be filtered when viewing as well.

- **Information (Normal Logging):** Displays information, error, and warning logs without verbose detail. This is the default and the recommended setting.

- **Verbose:** This setting displays information, error and warning logs with verbose detail. It can be useful for obtaining additional information for troubleshooting purposes.

- **Trivia:** This setting displays information, error and warning, and trivia logs with verbose detail. Trivia logs give the most detailed information and should be enabled only for advanced troubleshooting scenarios.

NOTE   You should enable verbose and/or trivia logging only for the purposes of short-term troubleshooting. Enabling verbose / trivia logging for a longer duration might cause significant performance degradation on your vCenter Server. You should revert back to normal logging as soon as your troubleshooting is complete.

Creating a Log Bundle

As I discussed in Chapter 6, "Performing Basic Troubleshooting," you can quickly create a log bundle, also called a diagnostic bundle, to send to VMware Support or for your own information. To create a log bundle, follow the steps outlined in Activity 7-2.

Activity 7-2 Creating a Log Bundle

1. Log on to your vCenter with your vSphere Client.

2. Click your root object and then select **Administration > Export System Logs**, as shown in Figure 7-17. (You can also select **File > Export > Export System Logs**.)

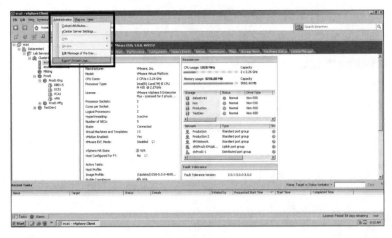

Figure 7-17   Preparing a Log Bundle

3. From Source, select the clusters and hosts from which you want to collect data, and then click **Next**, as shown in Figure 7-18.

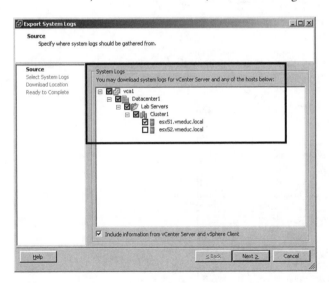

Figure 7-18   Choosing the vCenter Objects for Your Bundle

4. Select the specific logs to include in your bundle and then select whether you want to record performance data as well. You can be very specific by clicking the + signs of each category and selecting only the logs that you need. If you select to record performance data, then configure the duration and interval of the logging information, and then click **Next**, as shown in Figure 7-19. The

default is to not record performance data. The default when selected is to record data for 5 minutes at a 5-second interval.

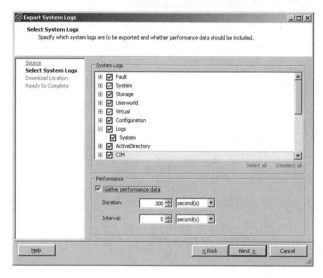

Figure 7-19 Choosing Specific Logs for Your Bundle

5. Browse for or type the location to which you will download your new bundle, as shown in Figure 7-20, and click **Next**.

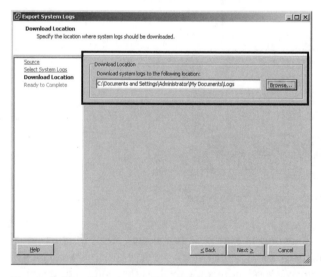

Figure 7-20 Choosing the Destination for Your Bundle

6. Review the Ready to Complete page to ensure that you have selected the proper logs and that your performance data selections are what you expect, and then click **Finish**.

Creating/Editing/Deleting a Scheduled Task

In general, a task is an action that is performed by the administrator. Most tasks are performed in real time by the administrator, but many tasks can also be configured to run at a later time or on a set schedule set by the administrator. These scheduled tasks can be for actions on hosts, VMs, resource pools, and even cluster resources. The tasks that you can schedule are listed and described in Table 7-2.

Table 7-2 Scheduled Tasks in vCenter

Scheduled Task	Description
Add a host	Adds a host to a specified datacenter or cluster.
Change power state of a VM	Powers on, powers off, or resets the state of a VM.
Change cluster power settings	Enable or disable Distributed Power Management (DPM) for hosts in a cluster.
Change resource settings of a resource pool or VM	Changes any of the following resource settings: CPU (shares, reservation, and limit) Memory (shares, reservation, and limit)
Check compliance of a profile	Checks that a host's configuration matches the configuration specified in an attached profile.
Clone a VM	Makes a clone of a VM and places it on a specified host and datastore.
Create a VM	Creates a new VM and places it on a specified host and datastore.
Deploy a VM	Creates a new VM from a specified template and places it on a specified host and datastore.
Export a VM	Exports VMs that vCenter Manages in a format that is specified by the administrator, such as OVF. Available only when vCenter Converter is installed.
Import a VM	Imports a physical machine, virtual machine, or system image into a new VM that vCenter manages. Available only when vCenter Converter is installed.
Migrate a VM	Moves a VM from one host to another or move its files from one datastore to another. This can be done with cold migration or with vMotion/Storage vMotion if properly configured.

Scheduled Task	Description
Make a snapshot of a VM	Captures the state of the VM at the specific point in time.
Scan for Updates	Scans templates, VMs, and hosts for available updates. Available only when vSphere Update Manager (VUM) is installed.
Remediate	Downloads any new patches discovered during the scan operation and applies the newly configured settings. Available only when VUM is installed.

You can create scheduled tasks using the Scheduled Task Wizard. For some scheduled tasks, the wizard opens another wizard to help you complete the task. For example, if your task is to migrate a VM, the Scheduled Task Wizard will open the Migrate VM Wizard in which you can configure the details.

Finally, you cannot create a single task to run on multiple objects. For example, you cannot create a task that powers on a host and all of the VMs on that host. You would need to create separate tasks for the host and each VM. As an example, to create a task that powers on a VM at a predetermined date and time, follow the steps outlined in Activity 7-3.

Activity 7-3 Creating a Scheduled Task to Power On a VM

1. Log on to your vCenter with your vSphere Client.

2. Click **Home**, and then under Management click **Scheduled Tasks**, as shown in Figure 7-21.

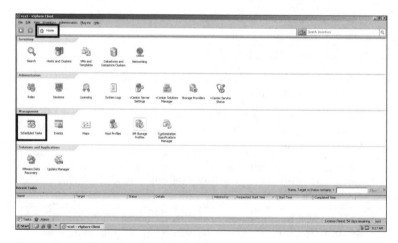

Figure 7-21   The Scheduled Tasks Icon

3. In the upper-left corner, click **New**, as shown in Figure 7-22. (You can also right-click in the white space below the other tasks, and then select **New Scheduled Task**.)

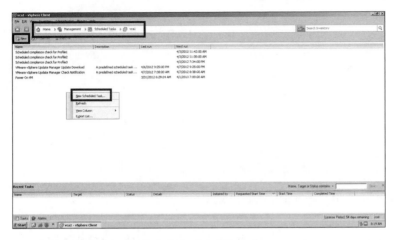

Figure 7-22 Creating a New Scheduled Task

4. From the Schedule Task dialog box, click the drop-down and select your task (in this case, **Change the VM Power State**), as shown in Figure 7-23, and click **OK**.

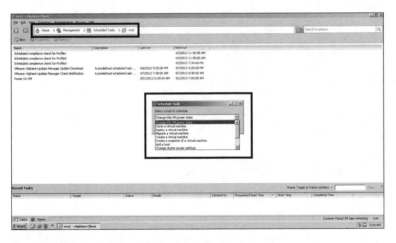

Figure 7-23 Choosing a Scheduled Task

5. Drill down into your inventory and select the VM to which this task will apply, and then click **Next**, as shown in Figure 7-24.

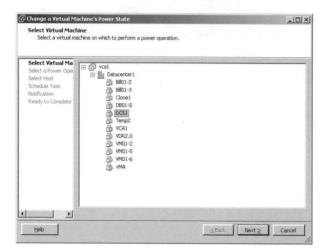

Figure 7-24   Choosing the Object for a Scheduled Task

6. Select the power operation of your choice (in this case, **Power On**), as shown in Figure 7-25, and then click **Next**.

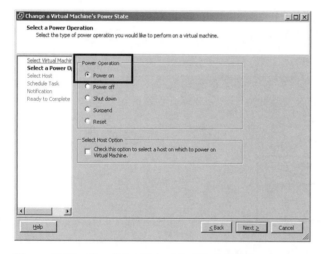

Figure 7-25   Specifying Scheduled Task Details

7. Assign the task a name and (optionally) a description and choose the frequency to run the task,\ and when to run it first. In this case, the task will be run Once at 7:00am on 4/1/13. April Fools.

8. From Notification, select to send an email when the task is complete, or leave blank if no email is required, as shown in Figure 7-26, and click **Next**.

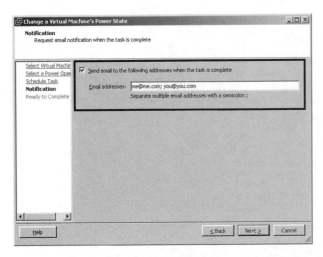

Figure 7-26   Setting Email Notification for a Scheduled Task

9. On the Summary page, review your settings and click **Finish**.

After you have configured your scheduled task, it will appear on the list of scheduled tasks. You can easily view the task, its description, the last time it was run, and the next time it is scheduled to run, as shown in Figure 7-27. To make changes to any of the properties of your scheduled task, you can click the **Properties** link and make the appropriate changes. The Properties link is at the top-left corner of the screen and also is available by right-clicking the task.

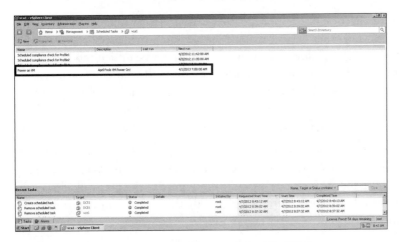

Figure 7-27   Viewing Information About a Scheduled Task

You can also elect to run the task immediately by right-clicking the task and selecting **Run**, as shown in Figure 7-28.

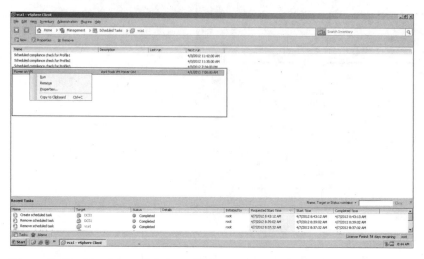

Figure 7-28 Running or Deleting a Task

Finally, to delete a schedule task that you no longer need, you click the task and select **Remove** or right-click the task and select **Remove**. In either case, you will need to confirm your selection.

Configuring/Viewing/Printing/Exporting Resource Maps

Your vSphere is a collection of components that work together to create a network of servers, switches, and other devices that can be used to provide applications and services to your end users. Unfortunately, it can sometimes be difficult to "get your head around" the big picture, especially considering many of your components are invisible! Resource maps in vCenter enable you to view relationships among hosts, clusters, networks, VMs, and so on. You can view a resource map for an entire vCenter System or for a specific object, based on how you configure your map.

Selecting what to view on your resource map is as easy as 1-2-3. You can simply select an object in the console in Hosts and Clusters view, open the Maps tab, and then choose the host and VM options, as shown in Figure 7-29. This will allow you to create a map with the vCenter hierarchy including the component that you suggested and downward in your vCenter hierarchy.

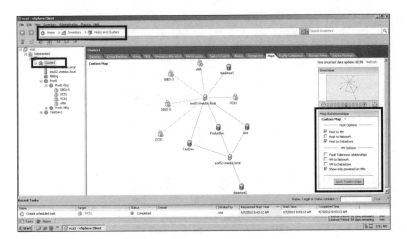

Figure 7-29   Creating a Resource Map from Hosts and Clusters View

You can also click **Home** and then click **Maps** under Management, as shown in Figure 7-30. This will allow you to quickly select the portions of your inventory that you want to include in a custom map of your choice, as shown in Figure 7-31. When you change the host and VM options and then select **Apply Relationships**, you will dramatically change your map. In this way, you can focus on the relationships that you want to examine and understand further.

Figure 7-30   The Maps Icon

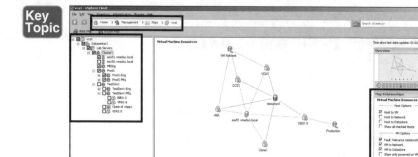

Figure 7-31   Creating a Custom Resource Map

One of the best times to have a copy of these maps is when something has gone wrong and there is an issue with your vSphere. As you might have guessed, this also might be a time at which obtaining a resource map would be impossible. To make sure that you have the maps that you need when you need them, you can print/export maps that you have created. To print a map that you are viewing, you should click **File** from the File menu at the top of vCenter and then click **Print Maps > Print** (you will also be able to select **Print Preview**), as shown in Figure 7-32. To export a map, click **File** on the File menu and then select **Export > Export Maps**. Then simply enter or browse for destination to which you will send the map, as shown in Figure 7-33.

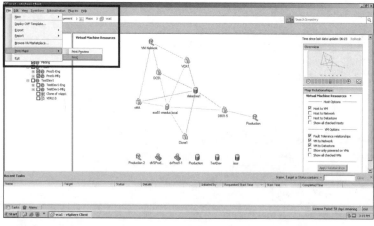

Figure 7-32   Printing Resource Maps

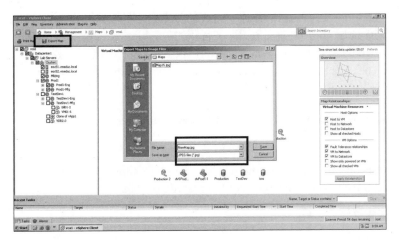

Figure 7-33   Exporting Resource Maps

Starting/Stopping/Verifying vCenter Service Status

When you install vCenter as a Windows machine, many services are started and run in the background. You can view these services by accessing Windows services and going "straight to the V's." Just about everything VMware related starts with "V", so it's easy to verify all of the services that are running, as shown in Figure 7-34.

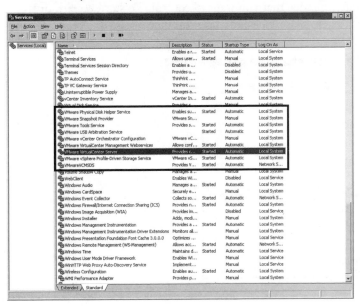

Figure 7-34   vCenter Services in Windows

One of the most important services is VMware VirtualCenter Server.. If this service is not started, you will not be able to log in to the vCenter. From time to time, you might find it beneficial in troubleshooting to restart the VirtualCenter Server.. For example, if a plug-in fails to enable, a restart of the services may very well fix the issue. To start, restart, and stop the VirtualCenter Server, follow the steps outlined in Activity 7-4.

Activity 7-4 Starting, Restarting, and Stopping the vCenter Server Services

1. Access your vCenter desktop (do not open a vSphere Client).

2. Click the **Start** and then **Run**. In the resulting window, shown in Figure 7-35, type **services.msc** to open the Services Microsoft Console.

Figure 7-35 Accessing Windows Services

3. Scroll to the V's or click any service and type **v** to get into the right area faster.

4. Locate the vCenter Service that you want to control. To start, restart, or stop the service, right-click the service and make the appropriate choice, as shown in Figure 7-36.

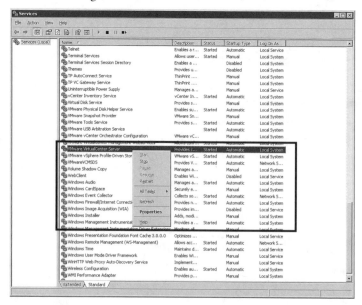

Figure 7-36 Starting, Restarting, or Stopping the vCenter Service

Starting/Stopping/Verifying ESXi Host Agent Status

The host agents on your hosts synchronize with vCenter and allow you to access the ESXi hosts directly with the vSphere Client or to access them through a vSphere Client logged on to a vCenter Server. If remote access is interrupted, you might need to restart the host agents on your ESXi hosts.

The best way to control the host agent status is through management agents in the Troubleshooting Options section of your Direct Console User Interface (DCUI) on your host. This will actually restart the host agent (hostd) as well as all of the other services involved. To start or stop and host agent status and verify that you have done so, follow the steps outlined in Activity 7-5.

Activity 7-5 Starting, Stopping, and Verifying Host Agent Status

1. From your DCUI, select **Troubleshooting Options**, as shown in Figure 7-37. You will likely need to provide credentials to log on to your DCUI.

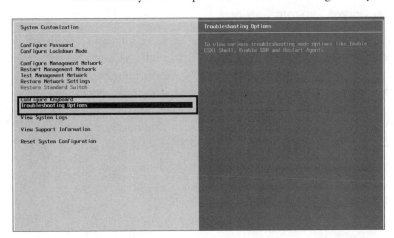

Figure 7-37   Troubleshooting Options in the DCUI

2. Using your arrow keys, select **Restart Management Agents**, and then press **Enter**, as shown in Figure 7-38.

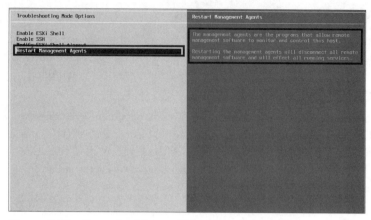

Figure 7-38   Restarting Management Agents

3. Press **F11** to confirm the restart.

Configuring vCenter Server Timeout Settings

In most cases, the default setting for vCenter Server timeout will be sufficient. If you need to change these settings, you can find them under **Administration > vCenter Server Settings**, as shown in Figure 7-39. The default settings are 30 seconds for normal operations and 120 seconds for long operations. These settings can be configured higher to allow an operation to complete. For example, if you experience an "operation timed out" error when trying to add a host to a vCenter, you can resolve the issue by changing the normal operations timeout from 30 seconds to 60 seconds. You should never set these to 0.

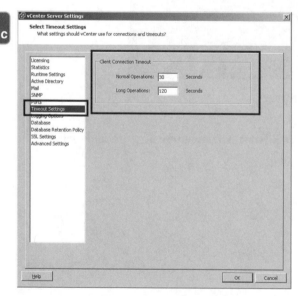

Figure 7-39   vCenter Server Timeout Settings

Monitoring/Administering vCenter Server Connections

You can view the connections to your vCenter by clicking **Home** and then **Sessions**, as shown in Figure 7-40. The Sessions tool shows the current number of Active and Idle sessions along with the username, full name, online time, and status of each session.

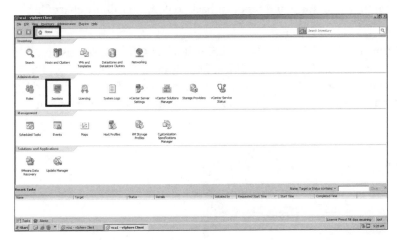

Figure 7-40   The vCenter Sessions Tool

You can terminate a session by clicking it and selecting **Terminate Session** from the upper-right corner, or by right-clicking it and selecting **Terminate Session**, as shown in Figure 7-41. As you might have noticed, you can also configure a Message of the Day that will be delivered whenever anyone logs on to your vCenter Server.

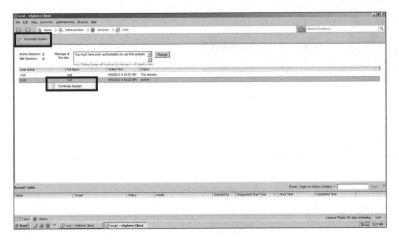

Figure 7-41   Terminating a vCenter Session

Creating an Advanced Chart

I discussed Advanced performance charts earlier in this section, but it wasn't time to create one just yet. Now I am going to create an Advanced performance chart that will gather data about one of the most important counters for a VM: CPU Ready value. The VM that I will use is my DC51. Because you don't have time to wait, I'll just collect real time data for it and report it back to you. I'll call my chart CPU Warning Sign.

To collect real-time data for CPU Ready value, I will select **Chart Options** and then click **Real-Time** under CPU. For vCPUs, I will leave the default of 0 and DC51. (Since it only has one vCPU, the 0 instance is the one vCPU.) Finally, under Counters, I will click **None** and then select only the **Ready** counter, as shown in Figure 7-42.

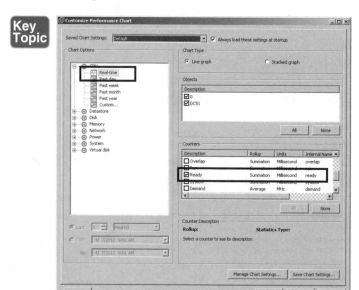

Figure 7-42   Choosing the Data to Gather on an Advanced Chart

When I click **OK**, the result is a real-time chart of CPU Ready value for DC51, as shown in Figure 7-43. As you can see, it is well within the acceptable range below 2000ms.

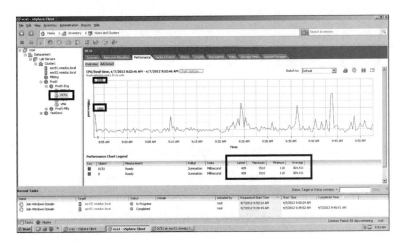

Figure 7-43   An Advanced Performance Chart for CPU Ready Value

To save these settings, I will click **Chart Options** again and then click **Save Chart Settings**, as shown in Figure 7-44. I will enter the name **CPU Warning Sign** for these settings, and that will become a quickly available option for use on this VM only, as shown in Figure 7-45. I could then click the icon to tear that chart off, with it still live, and create a new chart for a new metric while saving the process used to create it. As you can see, creating the charts is rather easy and as you learn more about your own system you'll know more of the counters that you want to see on your own charts.

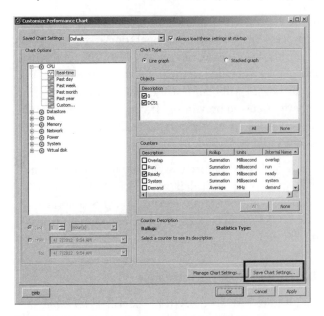

Figure 7-44   Saving Performance Chart Settings

Figure 7-45   Naming a Saved Performance Chart

Determining Host Performance Using Resxtop and Guest Perfmon

This is another one of those categories that is really more than one subject. Although resxtop and Perfmon are both performance tools, they could not be more different from each other. Resxtop is a command-line-based tool that gives you strictly digital output (numbers and letters). Perfmon, however, can paint colorful graphs with similar information. In this section, I will cover the use of each of these tools to determine host performance statistics.

Determining Host Performance Using Resxtop

The resxtop utility is a vSphere CLI utility that can provide a detailed look at how your ESXi uses its resources in real time. It lets you monitor the core four resources of CPU, memory, disk, and network. It consists of different screens with configurable information for each type of resource. Some statistics are reported as computed rates that are represented as a %, such as %USED for CPU.

Resxtop uses worlds and groups to express CPU statistics. A *world* is a VMkernel schedulable entity, similar to a process or thread in other operating systems. A *group* can therefore contain multiple worlds. In our case, our powered-on VM represents a group. As you can see, this can get very detailed to the point that entire books are written about resxtop. For our purposes, I will demonstrate how to examine the same types of statistics that we have discussed previously. If you would like to learn much more about resxtop, I suggest you start with the vSphere Documentation Center at http://pubs.vmware.com/vsphere-50/index.jsp

In vSphere 5.0, resxtop works only on Linux. Before you can use it, you must either install a vSphere CLI package on a Linux client or deploy a special Linux virtual appliance called the vSphere Management Assistant (vMA) to your ESXi host or vCenter System. Once you have a vCLI based on a Linux system, you use it from the command line by following the steps outlined in Activity 7-6.

Activity 7-6 Using Resxtop to Determine Host Performance

1. On your vCLI on vMA or a Linux VM, type **resxtop—server** *servername*, where *servername* is the name or IP address of the host that you want to moni-

tor, as shown in Figure 7-46 When prompted, enter the credentials for the server that to which you are connecting.

Figure 7-46   Connecting Resxtop to a Server

2. View the physical CPU used by the host (PCPU USED%), as shown in Figure 7-47. This shows an average of each CPU in real time. If these are close to 100%, you are overcommitting your physical CPU. PCPU UTIL% takes into account that some of the totals will include "idle" time and takes out the "idle" world before calculating the total. When these differ, it's usually due to hyperthreading, but can also be due to power management technologies.

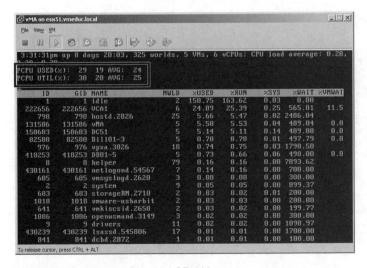

Figure 7-47   Viewing Physical CPU Usage

While you are on any screen, you can press the **f** key (lower case) to view available fields and then follow the instructions to add or delete them, thereby customizing your view, as shown in Figure 7-48.

Figure 7-48   Customizing Your View in Resxtop

3. To move to memory statistics, press the **m** key (lowercase). Note the totals of physical memory (PMEM) as well as balloon (MEMCTL), ZIP, and SWAP. In this case, I have memory in contention on this host. Because of this, I have some activity with regard to ballooning, compression, and even swap, as shown on Figure 7-49.

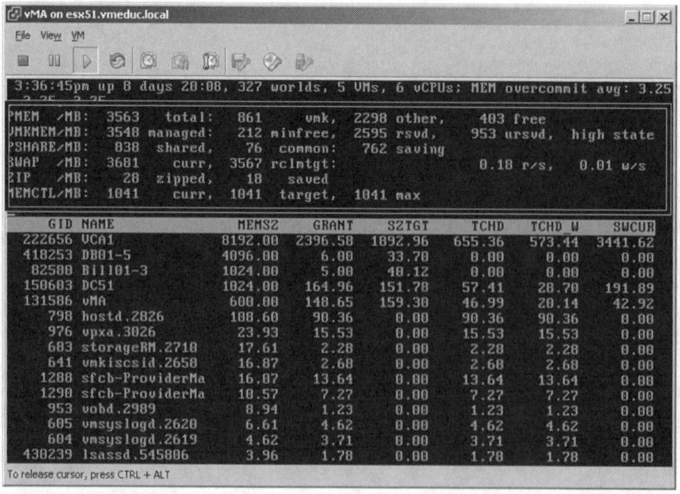

Figure 7-49   Viewing Memory in Resxtop

4. To move to virtual disk, press the **v** key (lowercase). I have filtered this report to read and write latency. Note that these are both well within normal levels, as shown in Figure 7-50.

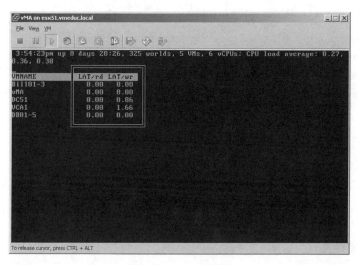

Figure 7-50   Viewing Virtual Disk in Resxtop

5. To move to networking, press the **n** key (lowercase). I have filtered the report to show primarily which packets are being dropped and where. As you can see, in Figure 7-51, I have an issue to address with regard to dropped receive packets on the network to which my vMA is connected.

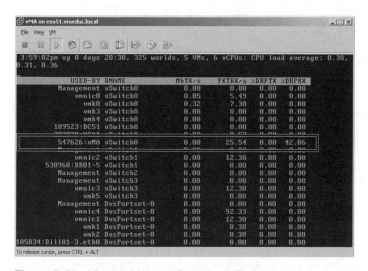

Figure 7-51   Viewing Network Statistics in Resxtop

By first asking the right questions and then determining and verifying the answers with resxtop, you will be able to monitor the system properly and troubleshoot any issues that occur.

Determining Host Performance Using Guest Perfmon

In general, you should not implicitly trust all of the data that you receive from performance tools that are built in to the OS such as Perfmon and Task Manager. This is because resources, such as CPU and memory, are being dynamically allocated by the VMkernel, a process that is entirely hidden from the guest OS. In other words, the guest OS doesn't really understand the "big picture" of what is occurring with regard to resources.

To give you accurate information, VMware provides performance counters that attach to the Microsoft Windows Perfmon utility when you install VMware Tools on a VM with a Microsoft OS. You can view performance data specific to VM performance on these special counters. To use these special counters, you simply select the objects that represent the counters in the Windows Perfmon utility, as shown in Figure 7-52.

Figure 7-52 VM Performance Counters in Perfmon

By determining what is really occurring with regard to VM resources, you open a window into realizing what is happening with host resources as well. You can examine the same types of counters that you do with resxtop, but you can create graphs and charts to see the information more clearly. Then, by comparing this information to your performance charts in vCenter, and ultimately to your own baseline, you can make accurate decisions about your vSphere. This will allow you to determine host performance and make the necessary corrections for improvement.

Given Performance Data, Identifying the Affected vSphere Resource

As you can see, there are many ways to collect performance data from your vSphere systems and the VMs that it contains. You can choose from a variety of tools to obtain information. Equally important to the tools that you use is how you interpret the data that you gather. You should always take into account that a weakness in one resource may be affecting another resource as well. In other words, all of the resources work together, not separate from each other. Knowing the standards, and especially your baseline, you should determine the weakest resource and make a change, then "rinse and repeat." By making one change at time and monitoring the results of that change, you will be able to continually strengthen your vSphere.

Creating and Administering vCenter Server Alarms

Another way to monitor your vSphere system is with alarms. The biggest advantage to using alarms as a monitoring tool is that an alarm is something that you can "set and forget" and it will still alert you when a threshold is met. The initial alert consists of a yellow Warning icon or a red Alert icon, depending on your settings and on the severity of the event. This is referred to as going from *green status* (normal) to *yellow status* or *red status*. Watching for these icons might allow you to stay ahead of the point at which the users will be affected.

In fact, that's not even the whole story about alarms because many alarms are already set for you on the default installation of vCenter Server. You can find all of these alarms by selecting the root object of your vCenter and then opening the Alarms tab, as shown in Figure 7-53. Because these alarms are set at root of the vCenter, they can be applied to all objects in the vCenter, based on the type of alarm that is set. In addition, alarm actions can include more than just alerting you; they can also run a script that could make your system somewhat "self-healing."

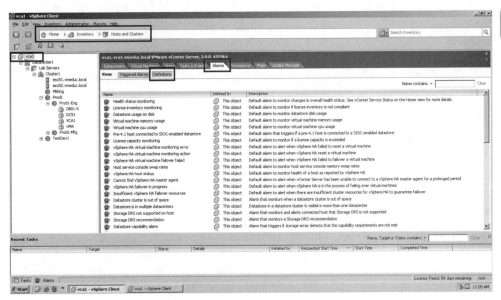

Figure 7-53   The Alarms Tab in vCenter

In this section, I will focus on the default utilization and connectivity alarms in vCenter and the actions that can be configured for these types of alarms. In addition, I will discuss how you can create your own utilization and connectivity alarms. Finally, I will discuss alarm triggers, alarm actions, and identifying the source of an alarm in your vSphere implementation.

Listing vCenter Default Utilization Alarms

Properly configured utilization alarms can assist in fixing a problem before it gets critical enough to have a negative effect on users. In fact, it's so important to have at least some properly configured utilization alarms that VMware has decided to provide you some right out of the box. By understanding your own network and keeping an eye out for your default utilization alarms, you can address developing problems and keep them from becoming more critical. Table 7-3 lists the default utilization alarms included with your vCenter as well as their general purpose and default threshold.

Table 7-3 Default Utilization Alarms in vCenter

Alarm	Purpose	Default Threshold
Host CPU usage	Monitors host CPU usage	75% for 5 min - Warning
		90% for 5 min - Alert
Host Memory usage	Monitors host physical memory usage	90% for 5 min - Warning
		95% for 5 min - Alert
Virtual Machine CPU usage	Monitors the use of the vCPU on each VM	75% for 5 min - Warning
		90% for 5 min - Alert
Virtual Machine memory usage	Monitors the use of available memory on each VM	85% for 10 min - Warning
		95% for 10 min - Alert
Datastore usage on disk	Monitors disk usage on all configured datastores on each host	75% - Warning
		85% - Alert

Listing vCenter Default Connectivity Alarms

Whereas utilization alarms can keep you ahead of potential issues, connectivity alarms will generally just give you the fastest start possible toward fixing an issue that has already developed. When a default connectivity alarm is triggered, there is a good chance that many users are affected. For this reason, you should be able to recognize the default connectivity alarms in vCenter. Table 7-4 lists the default connectivity alarms and their general purpose.

Table 7-4   Default Connectivity Alarms in vCenter

Alarm	Purpose
Cannot connect to storage	Monitors host connectivity to the storage devices to which each host is configured
Host connection failure	Monitors connections to network to which each host is configured
Network connectivity lost	Monitors network connectivity of a virtual switch to the hosts to which it is configured
Network uplink redundancy lost	Monitors the network redundancy configured on a virtual switch

Listing Possible Actions for Utilization and Connectivity Alarms

If the only action that utilization and connectivity alarms could perform was to make "pretty colors" next to your vCenter objects, you might very well miss a critical alarm. Because of this, in addition to showing yellow Warnings and red Alerts, the alarms can also cause other actions to be performed when they are triggered. Table 7-5 lists possible actions for utilization and connectivity alarms on hosts, VMs, virtual switches, and datastores. Later in this section, I will discuss how you can configure alarm actions.

Table 7-5   Possible Actions for Utilization and Connectivity Alarms

Alarm Type	Possible Actions
Host	Send a notification email
	Send a notification trap
	Run a command
	Enter Maintenance Mode
	Exit Maintenance Mode
	Enter standby
	Exit standby
	Reboot host
	Shutdown host

Alarm Type	Possible Actions
Virtual Machine	Send a notification email
	Send a notification trap
	Run a command
	Power on VM
	Power off VM
	Suspend VM
	Reset VM
	Migrate VM
	Reboot guest on VM
	Shutdown guest on VM
Virtual Switch	Send a notification email
	Send a notification trap
	Run a command
Datastore	Send a notification email
	Send a notification trap
	Run a command

Creating a vCenter Utilization Alarm

If you need a utilization alarm that is different from the default alarms, you should create a new utilization alarm rather than changing the default alarm. In other words, it is a best practice to leave the default alarms in place and add your own custom alarms to them. That way, if your alarms do not function properly or are removed or disabled at some point in the future, the default alarms will still be there backing you up regardless of any other configuration. For example, if you wanted to create a new utilization alarm that monitored for VM CPU Ready Time for all the VMs on all the hosts in Cluster1, you would follow the steps outlined in Activity 7-7.

Activity 7-7 Creating a vCenter Utilization Alarm

1. Log on to your vCenter using your vSphere Client.

2. Right-click an object in your inventory that includes the hosts and VMs on which you want to set the alarm, (in this case, I am right-clicking my cluster named **Cluster1**) select **Alarm > Add Alarm**, as shown in Figure 7-54.

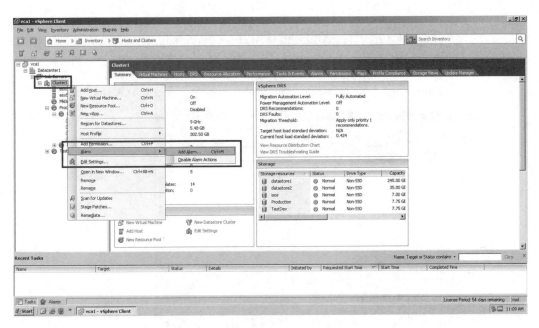

Figure 7-54   Adding a Custom Alarm to a Cluster

3. Type a name for your new alarm (in this case, **CPU Ready Time**; same as CPU Ready value). You can also type a description to help you remember what the alarm is monitoring. Set the alarm type (in this case, **Virtual Machines**). Choose whether to monitor specific conditions or state or to monitor specific events. (Later in this section, I will discuss how this affects your trigger options.) In this case, I am monitoring specific conditions. Finally, leave the **Enable This Alarm** check box checked, all shown in Figure 7-55.

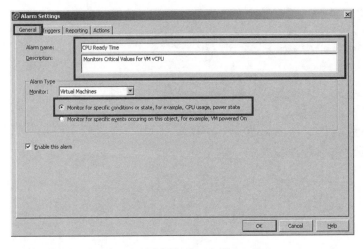

Figure 7-55   Creating a VM CPU Ready Time Alarm

4. Change to the Triggers tab by clicking **Triggers** at the top of the page (do not click **OK** yet). Click **Add**, and then choose your trigger type from the drop-down box, as shown in Figure 7-56. (It's a little tricky to see that there is actually a drop-down there at first.) In this case, I'm choosing **VM CPU Ready Time** since I discussed this important counter earlier in this chapter.

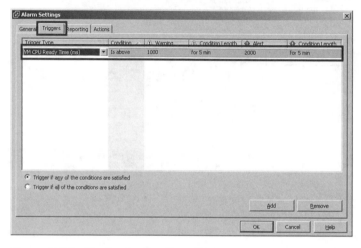

Figure 7-56 Configuring the Alarm Trigger

5. I will set the condition to **Is Above** and the warning to **1000 for 5 Min** as well as the alert to **2000 for 5 Min**. I will leave the setting of **Trigger If Any of the Conditions Are Satisfied**.

6. Next I will open the Reporting tab just to make sure that the default 0s are in place, but I will not be making any changes at this time, as shown in Figure 7-57. (This can be configured to avoid unnecessary re-alarms.)

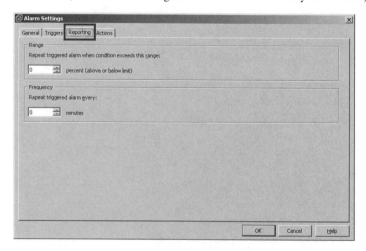

Figure 7-57 Verifying Default Reporting Options

7. Finally, I will open the Actions tab and click **Add**. I'm going to add an action that sends me (me@me.com) an email once when the status goes from green (Normal) to yellow (Warning). In addition, I am setting an action that will repeatedly send me an email every 15 minutes if it goes from yellow (Warning) to red (Alert), as shown in Figure 7-58. I don't need the action of an email sent to indicate that it's getting better, because I will be involved in fixing it.

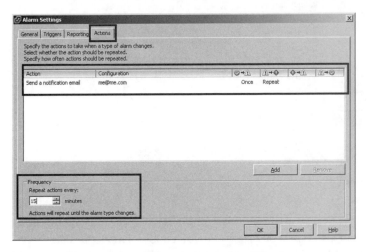

Figure 7-58   Configuring Alarm Action to Send Email

8. You can review your tabs and ensure that you have what you need, add additional triggers, and so on. When you are satisfied with your settings, click **OK** to create and enable the new alarm.

Creating a vCenter Connectivity Alarm

The best practice mentioned above with regard to utilization alarms applies equally to connectivity alarms. You will find that there are many connectivity alarms that you can configure in addition to the defaults, but you should leave the default alarms in place and intact. That said, to create a new alarm that monitors a specific VM's connection to its current port group, follow the steps outlined in Activity 7-8.

Activity 7-8 Creating a vCenter Connectivity Alarm

1. Log on to your vCenter using your vSphere Client.

2. Locate and right-click the specific VM that you want to monitor, and then select **Alarm > Add Alarm**, as shown in Figure 7-59 (You could also specify

a higher inventory object such as a host or cluster and monitor the same connectivity for all VMs associated.)

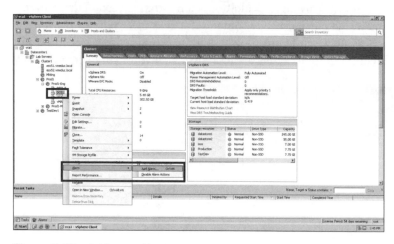

Figure 7-59 Adding an Alarm

3. Type a name for your new alarm; in this case I'm naming mine **Disconnect Warning**. You can also type a description if you choose. Leave the alarm type set to **Virtual Machine**. Change the setting below Alarm Type to **Monitor for Specific Events**, and leave the **Enable This Alarm** check box checked, all shown in Figure 7-60.

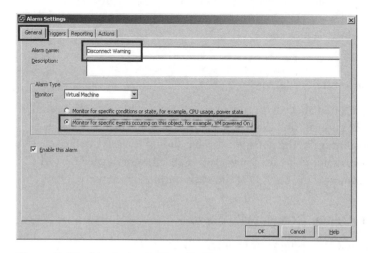

Figure 7-60 Monitoring for Specific Events

4. Move to the Triggers tab and click **Add**, and then choose VM disconnected from the drop-down box, as shown in Figure 7-61. Leave the status at **Alert** and do not set any advanced conditions.

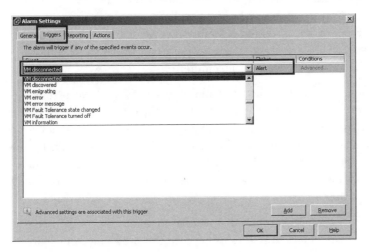

Figure 7-61 Choosing Your Alarm Trigger

5. Next, move to the Actions tab and click **Add**. Configure that an email will be sent to me@me.com when the alarm is triggered, as shown in Figure 7-62.

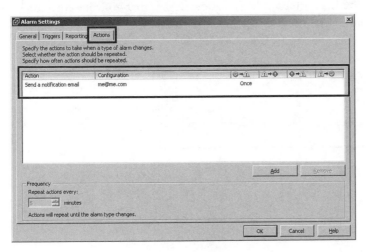

Figure 7-62 Configuring an Action for Email

6. Finally, review your setting, and when satisfied click **OK** to create and enable your new alarm.

Configuring Alarm Triggers

As you can see from my examples, a trigger is a threshold that once reached will activate the alarm. As I mentioned earlier, when you choose the alarm type you are also choosing the types of triggers from which you will choose on the Triggers tab. There are two main types of alarm triggers: Condition or State and Event. At first, the lines might seem a little blurry, to say the least. For example, why is "Cannot connect host" considered an event and not a condition?

Upon closer inspection, you will find that the Condition alarms can have a "timer" as part of the condition, as in my first example alarm. On the other hand, State and Event alarms do not have timers. If you can accomplish the same result with a Condition alarm and also have a time condition that reduces false positives, that is the way to go. However, you will also find that there are many more Event alarms than there are Condition alarms, so you may have more flexibility with Event alarms as long as you don't need the timers.

Finally, as shown in Figure 7-63, you should remember that you can configure triggers that activate the alarm when status goes from green to yellow and from yellow to red, as it gets worse. You can also configure triggers that activate the alarm when status goes from red to yellow and yellow to green, as it gets better.

NOTE You should realize that you cannot configure triggers that go from green to red or red to green because that would be "skipping" a status.

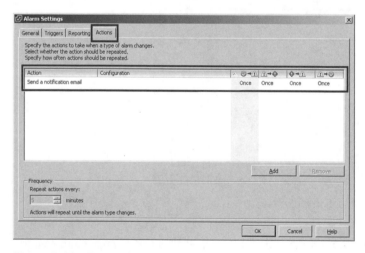

Figure 7-63 Trigger Options

Configuring Alarm Actions

As I mentioned before, alarm actions can go much further than just making "pretty colors" on your vCenter inventory. As you observed from my examples, you can also have the alarms send an email to you or to another email address that you designate. In addition, you can have the alarm send a trap to your SNMP MIB. Even that is just scratching the surface as to what the alarm actions can do.

As you saw previously from Table 7-5, you have great flexibility with regard to alarm actions and there are certain actions that are only available for certain types of objects. Configuring the actions is simple and you can configure whether you want them done just once or repeated, as you observed in my first example alarm. As you get to know your vCenter and its components better, you should familiarize yourself with all of your alarm options and see if there are some obvious combinations that might make life easier for you, such as my CPU Ready Time alarm with the send email action.

For a Given Alarm, Identifying the Affected Resource in a vSphere Implementation

Unlike monitoring tools such as resxtop or Perfmon, on which you have to consider a number of factors to identify the affected resource, alarms announce much about the affected resource as soon as they are activated. Based on the name and description of the alarm triggered, the trigger type and trigger specifics, and the object in your inventory that is suddenly boasting a new yellow "yield sign" or a red "diamond," you should be able to sleuth this one out!

Once you have determined which alarm was triggered, you should be well on your way to knowing why, especially if you set the alarm yourself. If you did not set the alarm, you may need to speak to the administrator who did set it. You might also determine that it was one of your default alarms, which is another reason that you should know your default alarms. You can also choose to acknowledge or clear an alarm, all shown in Figure 7-64.

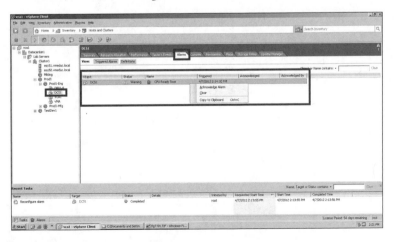

Figure 7-64   Identifying the Affected Resource

Summary

The main topics covered in this chapter are as follows:

- I began this chapter by discussing how to monitor ESXi, vCenter Server, and VMs. I identified critical performance metrics that are important to know for the real world as well as for the exam. I then compared and contrasted the various tools that are provided by vCenter, such as Overview and Advanced charts. In addition, I discussed configuring other methods of monitoring such as SNMP, Active Directory, and SMTP settings.

- I then discussed ways that you can preserve what you have monitored, such as creating log bundles and printing and exporting maps. I also covered starting and stopping critical services, such as your vCenter service and the host agent status. In addition, I discussed creating an Advanced performance chart and determining host performance using tools such as resxtop and guest Perfmon. To round out the monitoring section, you learned how to identify the affected resource with the performance data that you have collected.

- The other major section of this chapter was on alarms. I discussed creating and administering vCenter server alarms. This included listing the default utilization and connectivity alarms that can be found at the root of your vCenter. In addition, I discussed creating new utilization and connectivity alarms where needed without altering or deleting the default alarms. I then focused on alarm triggers and alarm actions that you can use for your alarms. Finally, I covered how to identify the affected resource when an alarm is activated.

Exam Preparation Tasks

Review All the Key Topics

Review the most important topics from inside the chapter, noted with the Key Topic icon in the outer margin of the page. Table 7-6 lists these key topics and the page numbers where each is found. Know the various tools that you can use to monitor your vSphere, and especially which ones you can trust. Understand how to use your default utilization and connectivity alarms and how to create custom alarms when needed.

Table 7-6   Key Topics for Chapter 7

Key Topic Element	Description	Page Number
Figure 7-1	The Events Tab and Recent Tasks Status Bar on a Host Login	475
Figure 7-2	Viewing All Entries Within an Object	476
Figure 7-3	Showing Only Object Entries	476
Figure 7-4	Filtering by Keyword	477
Bullet List	Identifying Critical Performance Metrics	478
Figure 7-5	The Memory "Shell Game"	479
Bullet List	Memory Technologies and Processes	479
Figure 7-6	Transparent Page Sharing	480
Figure 7-7	The Balloon Driver Mechanism	481
Figure 7-8	The Memory Compression Cache Setting	482
Figure 7-9	Overview Performance Charts	483
Figure 7-10	Choosing Performance Objects and Counters	486
Figure 7-11	Changing Default View to Advanced Performance Charts	486
Figure 7-12	Active Directory Settings for vCenter	487
Bullet List	Active Directory Settings for vCenter - Explained	489
Activity 7-1	Configuring SMTP Settings for vCenter Server	489
Figure 7-15	vCenter Logging Options	490
Bullet List	vCenter Logging Options - Explained	491

Key Topic Element	Description	Page Number
Activity 7-2	Creating a Log Bundle	492
Table 7-2	Scheduled Tasks in vCenter	495
Activity 7-3	Creating a Scheduled Task to Power On a VM	496
Figure 7-29	Creating a Resource Map from Hosts and Clusters View	501
Figure 7-30	The Maps Icon	501
Figure 7-31	Creating a Custom Resource Map	502
Figure 7-32	Printing Resource Maps	502
Figure 7-33	Exporting Resource Maps	503
Figure 7-34	vCenter Service in Windows	503
Activity 7-4	Starting, Restarting, and Stopping vCenter Services	504
Activity 7-5	Starting, Stopping, and Verifying Host Agent Status	505
Figure 7-39	vCenter Server Timeout Settings	506
Figure 7-40	The vCenter Sessions Tool	507
Figure 7-41	Terminating a vCenter Session	507
Figure 7-42	Choosing the Data to Gather on an Advanced Chart	508
Figure 7-43	An Advanced Performance Chart for CPU Ready Value	509
Figure 7-44	Saving Performance Chart Settings	509
Figure 7-45	Naming a Saved Performance Chart	510
Activity 7-6	Using Resxtop to Determine Host Performance	510
Figure 7-52	VM Performance Counters in Perfmon	514
Figure 7-53	The Alarms Tab in VCenter	515
Table 7-3	Default Utilization Alarms in vCenter	416
Table 7-4	Default Connectivity Alarms in vCenter	417
Table 7-5	Possible Actions for Utilization and Connectivity Alarms	417
Activity 7-7	Creating a vCenter Utilization Alarm	418
Activity 7-8	Creating a vCenter Connectivity Alarm	421
Figure 7-64	Identifying the Affected Resource	425

Review Questions

The answers to these review questions are in Appendix A.

1. Which of the following is not a valid view for Tasks and Events?

   a. Show Only Object Entries

   b. Filter by Keyword

   c. Show Object and Child Object Entries

   d. Show Object and Parent Object Entries

2. Which of the following are types of memory conservation techniques? (Choose two.)

   a. MRU

   b. Ballooning

   c. Ready value

   d. Compression

3. Which of the following memory techniques runs all the time by default, even when there is no contention for memory?

   a. Ballooning

   b. Transparent page sharing

   c. Compression

   d. Swap file

4. By default, how often does vCenter validate its list of known users against the Active Directory?

   a. Every 60 minutes

   b. vCenter does not validate its list of known users against Active Directory.

   c. Every 24 hours

   d. Every 7 days

5. Which type of vCenter logging gathers the most information?

   a. Trivia

   b. Information

   c. Verbose

   d. Error

6. Which of the following cannot be a scheduled task in vCenter?

   a. Add a host

   b. Add available memory to a VM

   c. Change resource settings on a resource pool

   d. Clone a VM

7. Which of the following cannot be added to a resource map in vCenter?

   a. VMs

   b. A physical switch

   c. Hosts

   d. Port groups

8. Which of the following is *not* a possible alarm action for a VM alarm?

   a. Send a notification email

   b. Reset VM

   c. Add a vNIC to VM

   d. Migrate VM

9. Which of the following is *not* a possible alarm action for a datastore alarm?

   a. Automatically expand datastore

   b. Run a command

   c. Send a notification email

   d. Send a notification trap

10. Which of the following type of alarm trigger allows for a "timer" to be set?

   a. State

   b. Event

   c. All alarm triggers can have timers.

   d. Condition

This chapter covers the following subjects:

- Scheduling the Test
- Comparing Your Knowledge to the VCP510 Exam Blueprint Objectives
- Studying the Questions at the End of Each Chapter and on the Bonus Material
- Taking the Mock Exam on the VMware Website
- The Day of the Test
- Sending Me an Email When You Pass

CHAPTER 8

What Do I Do Now?

Congratulations. You have finished reading this training material, and you are now on the path toward becoming a VCP5. Have you scheduled the test yet? If not, I highly recommend that you go ahead and schedule it now. You might be saying that you are not ready to take it yet. That's fine, but in my experience, if I go ahead a schedule it first, I study better and make it more of a priority.

In this relatively short chapter, I focus on what you should do to get prepared to take and pass the VCP510 test. In particular, I will discuss scheduling the test, comparing your knowledge to the VCP510 Exam Blueprint objectives, studying the questions at the end of each chapter and on the supplementary material, taking the Mock Exam on the VMware website, the day of the test, and sending me an email when you pass the test.

Foundation Topics

Scheduling the Test

I have taught hundreds of classes and thousands of students, and I can honestly say that not one student has ever passed a certification test for which they were not scheduled. Seriously, if part of your reason for reading this book was to prepare to take and pass the VCP510 test, do yourself a favor and schedule it now. You will find a link to schedule the test at http://www.vmware.com/certfication, under VCP5, as shown in Figure 8-1. You can use the link to connect to Pearson Virtual University Enterprises (Pearson VUE) sites where you can schedule to take the test. Pearson VUE sites are all over the world, so there is likely one near you. The cost of this exam at the time of this writing is $225, as stated in the Introduction to this book, but you get a free license for Workstation 8 when you pass, which has a value of $225.

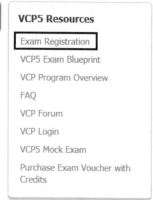

Figure 8-1   Scheduling the Test

Comparing Your Knowledge to the VCP510 Exam Blueprint Objectives

As I might have mentioned a few times, I wrote this book directly to the VCP510 Exam Blueprint. Therefore, if you have just read the whole book cover to cover, we have walked through the blueprint together. Each chapter of this book is a section of the blueprint with all of its objectives in the same order as the blueprint.

However, you might have chosen not to read the book from cover to cover and in-stead leveraged the "Do I Know This Already" feature to focus your attention on what you personally needed to learn. In that case, I strongly suggest that you review the Exam Blueprint line by line and make sure that you feel good about each of the topics listed. If you think that you might not know enough about a specific topic, you can refer back to the chapter and section in the book that applies to that topic. You can obtain a copy of the blueprint at http://www.vmware.com/certification, in the same location where you schedule the test, as shown in Figure 8-2. You must provide your MyLearn credentials or create a MyLearn account. Another great on-going reference is the VCP forum at http://communities.vmware.com/community/vmtn/certedu/certification/vcp.

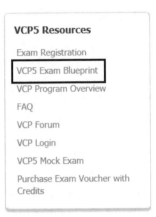

Figure 8-2 The VCP510 Blueprint Link

Studying the Questions at the End of Each Chapter and on the Bonus Material

At first glance, it might look easy. After all, it's just a multiple choice test on which you only need to complete 85 questions in 90 minutes and get a "low D" (300 out of 500) to pass. Well, don't be lulled into a sense of false security; this is not an easy exam to pass. In my opinion, the main factor that makes this test difficult is the "somewhat diabolical psychology" used by the people who write the test questions. Because there are no simulations or "drag and drop" questions, the test makers have to devise another way to determine whether you really understand the key concepts and don't just have rote knowledge of the facts.

To test your understanding, they build questions that are really "a question twisted within another question"; and they are very good at it. Because of this, your success in passing the test relies on very carefully reading what they are really asking you and then understanding the key concepts well enough to "untwist the question" in your mind and obtain the correct response. Their assumption is that, if you can do this, you have a true working knowledge of VMware vSphere 5.0 key concepts.

When you are studying the questions at the end of each chapter and on the other material, you should keep this "twisting/untwisting" concept in mind. You are not just memorizing content, but instead you should be seeking to truly understand the reason that the right answers are right and the wrong answers are wrong. What if I were to change one word or even one number. Would that make difference in your response, and why? There is difference between knowing something and understanding it. For example, a 16 year old might "know" how to drive a car, but probably doesn't "understand" how to drive the car yet. You need to understand these concepts, not just know them.

Taking the Mock Exam on the VMware Website

On the same VMware site as the blueprint and the Pearson VUE registration link, there is a Mock Exam that you can take to test your knowledge, as shown in Figure 8-3. You only get 25 to 30 questions per exam that are drawn from a pool of hundreds of questions. The questions on the Mock Exam are very much like the ones on the actual exam. In fact, they are written by the same people, and some of them were on the actual exam and have just been "retired."

You can take the Mock Exam as many times as you like with your MyLearn login ID associated with your email address, until you get a perfect score. My recommendation is this: "Don't get a perfect score, at least not until you have taken the Mock Exam a few dozen times." Instead, you should intentionally miss a question to which you really know the right answer. That way, you will see many more of the questions drawn from the question pool. They "kind of" tell you this on the page, but some people miss it and end up scoring too well for their own good.

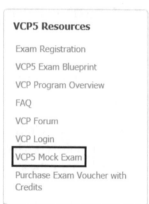

VCP5 Resources

Exam Registration

VCP5 Exam Blueprint

VCP Program Overview

FAQ

VCP Forum

VCP Login

VCP5 Mock Exam

Purchase Exam Voucher with Credits

Figure 8-3 The Mock Exam Link

The Day of the Test

Don't worry, I'm not going to tell you to get plenty of rest on the night before and eat a good breakfast on the day of the test, although those are good practices. My preparation tip is more of a psychological one. These tests tend to "beat up your brain" a little, so I want to make sure that you don't assist in the process.

In that regard, I suggest that you get to the test center early so that you don't have to feel rushed. You should make sure to bring two forms of identification, one with your picture on it. Review before the test, if you want to, but don't cram. Let your mind relax; it's not "life and death" after all.

There will be some survey questions at the very beginning of the test. These are strictly for survey purposes, so don't let them throw you. They might ask you how familiar you are with storage or with networking and so on. Answer these questions and move on because they have nothing to do with your specific test. Your test and all of its content will have already been delivered to the test center and will not be changed based on your responses to the survey questions.

When you read the test questions, read all the questions and all the possible responses first, and then reason it out. Do not turn one question into four questions. You should have plenty of time, but do not lose track of it. You can mark a question and go back on this test. If you choose this option, be very careful about changing a first response unless you really feel that you just learned something new from the test. Your brain will not be quite a sharp at the end of the test as it was when you began, so trust your first instincts unless you are absolutely sure that you should make a change.

Sending Me an Email When You Pass

Actually, despite the title of this section, I would love for you to send me an email whether you pass or not. I'm just being positive in assuming that you will pass, as you should. If you do not pass, then you should schedule the test again before you leave the testing center. You won't be allowed to take it again right away (you will have to wait wait 7 calendar days), but you will be allowed to schedule it again. If you keep at it, you can pass on the next try.

When you pass the test, please send me an email at billferguson@charter.net. Even if you are struggling to pass, send me an email and I'll give you whatever wisdom I can muster at the time. In fact, that leads me to my last recommendation with regard to instructor wisdom.

Since you will have to take a certified class with a VMware Certified Instructor for vSphere 5.0 (VCI5), I highly recommend that you use him or her for a resource. Pick that instructor's brain (especially if your instructor is me) while you are in class. You will be glad that you did when you take the test. Now, go take and *pass* the VCP510 test. I know you can do it!

Answers to the "Do I Know This Already?" Quizzes and Chapter Review Questions

"Do I Know This Already?" Answers

Chapter 1

1. B and C
2. B and D
3. C and D
4. B
5. A
6. A
7. C
8. D
9. B
10. B

Chapter 2

1. C
2. B
3. D
4. C
5. A
6. B
7. C
8. D
9. B
10. B

Chapter 3

1. C
2. D
3. D
4. C
5. A
6. B
7. B and D
8. D
9. D
10. C

Chapter 4

1. C
2. A and B
3. D
4. C
5. A
6. B
7. C
8. D
9. B
10. B

Chapter 5

1. C
2. B
3. D
4. C
5. A and D
6. B
7. C
8. D
9. B
10. B

Chapter 6

1. C
2. B
3. D
4. C
5. A
6. B
7. C
8. D
9. B
10. B

Chapter 7

1. C
2. B
3. D
4. A and C
5. A and C
6. B
7. C and D
8. D
9. B
10. B

Chapter Review Answers

Chapter 1

1. A and B
2. D
3. B
4. D
5. B
6. B
7. A and D
8. A and D
9. B
10. B

Chapter 2

1. D
2. B and D
3. B
4. C
5. A
6. B
7. B
8. C
9. A
10. D
11. D
12. B and D
13. B
14. C
15. A
16. B
17. B
18. C
19. A
20. D

Chapter 3

1. D
2. B and D
3. B
4. C
5. A
6. B
7. B
8. C
9. A
10. D
11. D
12. D
13. B
14. C
15. A
16. B
17. A
18. C
19. A
20. D

Chapter 4

1. D
2. B and D
3. B
4. C
5. A
6. B
7. B
8. C
9. A
10. D
11. D

12. B and D
13. B
14. C
15. A
16. B
17. B
18. C
19. A
20. D

Chapter 5

1. D
2. B and D
3. B
4. C
5. A
6. B
7. B
8. C
9. A
10. D

Chapter 6

1. D
2. B and D
3. B
4. C
5. A
6. B
7. B
8. C
9. A
10. D

Chapter 7

1. D
2. B and D
3. B
4. C
5. A
6. B
7. B
8. C
9. A
10. D

Index

M